Sepp Dietrich, as his soldiers will remember him, although to many he had a darker side.

Hitler's Gladiator

The Life and Times of Oberstgruppenführer and
Panzergeneral-Oberst der Waffen-SS Sepp Dietrich

Hitler's Gladiator

The Life and Times of Oberstgruppenführer and
Panzergeneral-Oberst der Waffen-SS Sepp Dietrich

by

CHARLES MESSENGER

BRASSEY'S DEFENCE PUBLISHERS
(A member of the Pergamon Group)

LONDON · OXFORD · WASHINGTON · NEW YORK · BEIJING
FRANKFURT · SAO PAULO · SYDNEY · TOKYO · TORONTO

First edition 1988
ISBN 0-08-031207-1
Printed in the USA

Acknowledgements

Photographs reproduced by kind permission of: Wolf-Dieter Dietrich (14,35,36); Strasheim collection, original taken by Theodor Larsen (4); Dipl.-Ing Franz Kosar (1,2); Munin Verlag (frontispiece, 18); The Trustees of the Imperial War Museum, London (3,5,11,12,19,30,32); U.S. National Archives (24,33,34); Historical Research Unit (10,13,15,16,17,20,21,22,23,25,26,27,28,29,31,37); Author's collection (6,7,8); Bruce Quarrie (9).

Contents

List of Maps

List of Plates

List of Plates

Introduction

The biographer who undertakes the portrayal of an important character from the Nazi era faces a problem which requires some self-examination. The enormities of the events, which the Third Reich brought upon the world, strain not only moral sensibilities, but also the intellectual objectivity that is the historian's duty to bring to his subject.

Recent events, such as the Waldheim controversy, the Barbie trial and the death of Rudolf Hess, show how long is the Nazi shadow, and dispel the temptation to imagine that, after more than forty years of peace in Europe, enough time has passed for passions to cool and for dispassionate analysis to prevail. I certainly make no such supposition, but believe that the reader who embarks on the study of this period will, as his knowledge of it grows, experience these strains of moral outrage versus cool appraisal just as vividly, regardless of whether he belongs to tomorrow's generation or yesterday's. Given then that the Nazi spectre will continue to haunt for many years to come, it is better to marshal the evidence while it is still comparatively fresh, than to wait for wounds to heal while it partially evaporates.

Besides, it is not the historian's duty to temper his tale to the sensibility of his reader, but to tell the truth, however unpalatable it may be. And truth, in the portrayal of Sepp Dietrich, a controversial character who ranked high in the Nazi hierarchy, requires both a strict avoidance of 'whitewashing' and 'black-washing' alike, and an exclusive attention to provable facts. Certainly it would have been much easier to portray Dietrich as the 'loud-mouth' and bully which popular opinion reckons him to have been, than to paint him according to the evidence.

And here Dietrich poses a special difficulty. Most biographers begin with the advantage that their subject has felt obliged to favour posterity with an autobiography, diaries, speeches or papers. With one or two very minor exceptions, Dietrich left none. He himself died over twenty years ago, and his second wife, Ursula, who could probably have thrown much light on her husband, died in 1983. His sons were too young, and saw too little of their father during the crucial years, to know much about him, and the memories of those who served with him have obviously dimmed with the passage of time. Much that has been written about him is inaccurate, and he was himself guilty of untruths over parts of his early life, something which has misled many historians. Furthermore, there are gaps in his life which it has proved very difficult, if not impossible, to fill.

The root question to be addressed is whether Dietrich was at base a wicked man. By virtue of the fact that he was for so long counted among Hitler's inner circle, it is easy to come to the conclusion that he was a wholehearted supporter of the Nazi ethic and all that it stood for. Lack of internal record means that the historian is seldom privy to Dietrich's innermost thoughts and can only observe his actions and what information exists as to what he confided to others. The resultant picture is grey, rather than pure black or white, which history seldom is. One can therefore make only tentative conclusions as to the degree to which he was motivated by National Socialism alone. What is clear, though, is that his rise to prominence was caused primarily by his personal qualities as a military leader and a major part of the book is devoted to the examination of these and his military weaknesses.

Here one finds oneself in another sensitive area. For much of the war Dietrich was held up by the Nazi hierarchy as the personification of all that was superior in the National Socialist soldier, the Waffen SS. To many, especially those who fought against them during the war, the character of the Waffen SS was stamped with a brutality which set it apart from other fighting formations. This is especially so over atrocities and Dietrich and his men stand or have stood accused of a goodly number, in Poland, France, Russia, Italy, the Ardennes and, in the last days of the war, Vienna. This is also not to forget his own involvement in the Night of the Long Knives. In only two cases – Long Knives and Ardennes – was Dietrich actually arraigned, and in the case of the latter, as the reader will see, serious questions were raised over the conduct of the trial. In some incidents the evidence, when carefully examined, is found to be conflicting. In these questions, the reader should bear in mind that, unlike most courts of law, history is not compelled to find for the accused on account of defects in the evidence, nor, for that matter, adopt the principle of 'guilty until proved innocent'. Instead it may leave the case on the file, non-proven.

While I have found it necessary to examine my duties to the reader in writing this history, it is important not to seem to apologize for that which needs no apology, namely the historical interest of its subject.

Indeed, with patient probing it has been possible to find out a surprising amount about Sepp Dietrich, and his contribution to the Nazi phenomenon, in spite of the problems described above. Furthermore, his life does provide a remarkably good vehicle for a history of 20th-century Germany, socially, politically and militarily. Indeed, it is surprising that no one has ever tried to write his life before now, although some Germans to whom I have talked have expressed surprise that I should do this, but without giving satisfactory reasons as to why they should think that a biography of him is not merited. This, to me, is difficult to understand. Indeed, my researches have taken me into a number of relatively uncharted areas of German history. This has been personally of deep interest and most rewarding, and I hope that the reader will agree. Whatever faults can be laid at Dietrich's door, there is no doubt that he was a colourful character and, in many ways, larger than life. His career encompassed many dramatic events and developments, from the storm troops and German tanks of 1914-18, through the turbulence of Germany in the immediate post-war area, in which he took a small but active part, to the rise of Hitler and the formation of what became the Waffen-SS, in which he played a leading role. He fought on every front in 1939-45 except North Africa, was a key figure in what was probably the most controversial war crimes trial in Europe and finally became a victim of the guilt which wracked the West German nation in the 1950s. In truth, the menu is rich and varied.

This book could have never been written without the help given to me by a number of institutions and individuals. In Germany I would very much like to give my thanks to Daniel P. Simon, Director, Berlin Document Center, for providing me with a copy of Dietrich's SS Personal File. Dr Heyl, *Archivdirektor Bayerisches Hauptstaatsarchiv, Kriegarchiv* patiently answered a number of questions which I put to him by letter. Herr Kirchhoff (*Deutsche Dienstelle*, Berlin), Herr Scholl (*Bundesarchiv Militärarchiv*, Freiburg im Breisgau) and Herr Baldes (*Bundesarchiv Zentralweisstelle*, Aachen) likewise gave me useful information. Marianne Loenitz of the *Bundesarchiv*, Koblenz was also most helpful in researching and sending copies of documents held there. I am grateful, too, to Herr Thöle of *Munin Verlag* for his help. Rainer Strasheim threw much light on Dietrich's experience of tanks in the First World War and Hans Weber, formerly of the *Freikorps Oberland*, was invaluable in giving me information on Dietrich's service with it. I owe a special debt of gratitude to Dipl.-Ing. (FH) Anton Joachimsthaler who was kind enough to share with me information which he has gleaned from his researches into Sepp Dietrich. Dr Bernd Wegner of the *Militärgeschichtliches Forschungsamt*, Freiburg im Breisgau, also shared his views on Dietrich and the Waffen-SS with me. There are, too, Sepp Dietrich's former comrades in the Waffen-SS who gave of their memories and impressions of Dietrich to me, or my research assistant Lothar Schäfer. Much gratitude goes to Otto Kumm, Georg Maier, Hubert Meyer, through whom I would also like to thank Paul Zimmermann for giving me copies of documents in Dietrich's estate, Richard Schulze-Kossens, Otto Weidinger and Max Wünsche and I sincerely hope that they will feel that their efforts on my behalf will have been worth it. Finally, my most sincere thanks go to Wolf-Dieter Dietrich, Sepp's eldest son. He was good enough to entertain Lothar Schäfer and I at his Munich apartment and, in the course of four hours of questions, to throw much new light on his father. He also very kindly copied and sent to me photographs from his album.

Dipl.-Ing. Franz Kosar of Vienna gave me something of his extensive knowledge of First World War German artillery and loaned me photographs, and I am also grateful to Ian Hogg for introducing me to him. Professor J.M. Feldbrugge of the University of Leiden in Holland, with whom I was put in contact by the Soviet Studies Research Centre, Royal Military Academy, Sandhurst, gave me information on Soviet war crimes trials and investigations. In the USA, my thanks go to Dr R. Raiber MD of Hockessin, Delaware, Denison Beach of the Widener Library, Harvard University and to John Toland, who was good enough to write to me on his personal impressions of meeting Sepp Dietrich. There are also a number of individuals in the US National Archives, Washington DC, who together provided me with a wealth of relevant material. They are George Wagner of the Military Reference Branch, Military Archives Division, Richard L. Boylan and Amy Schmidt of the Military Field Branch and G. Bryant and Paul White of the Still Pictures Branch, Special Archives Division.

In England there are a number of members of staff of the Imperial War Museum, London, who deserve my thanks. They are J.W. Pavey of the Department of Photographs, Philip Reed, Department of Documents and T.C. Charman and D.B. Nash of the Department of Printed Books. The last-named was especially helpful with his knowledge of the German Army of 1914. Others who answered some of my many questions were James Lucas, Bruce Quarrie, Max Hundleby and Denis Jenkinson of *Motor Sport*. Lieutenant Colonel Sir George Kennard Bt, in the course of a most entertaining session at the Guards and Cavalry Club, London, told me of his experiences of being captured by the *Leibstandarte* in Greece, and Lieutenant Colonel George Forty and David Fletcher of the Tank Museum, Bovington, Dorset, provided information and photographs on the German use of tanks in 1918. Colonel Paul Adair LVO assisted with introductions to former Waffen-SS officers and Jonathan Prickett of The History Bookshop, Friern Barnet, London gave me a number of useful leads. Thank you, too, to Ian Sayer for allowing me to ferret around his monumental Second World War library and archive. Further thanks go to the staffs of the Institute of Contemporary History and Wiener Library, the London Library, Ministry of Defence Old War Office Library and the Reference Library, West Hill, London Borough of Wandsworth, all of whom were tireless in their efforts to produce books, many obscure. Andrew Mollo also gave his time to me, and I am most grateful to his Historical Research Unit for providing many of the photographs. Further, I would like to thank Simon King for his helpful advice.

To Brian Bond of the Department of War Studies, King's College, London, my thanks for putting me in touch with Lothar Schäfer. As for Lothar himself, I owe him a greater debt than anyone. He was my research assistant throughout and, although in the midst of studies both at King's College, London and the University of Konstanz, gave me much of his time. His high intelligence and growing enthusiasm for the subject have been invaluable and he has been my strong right hand. Last, but not least, thank you to my publisher, General Tony Trythall, for inviting me to write this book and for giving me what has turned out to be a fascinating eighteen months of research, and to Brigadier Bryan Matthews for his sympathetic editing.

London, September 1987   CHARLES MESSENGER

CHAPTER 1

The Early Years
1892-1918

On 28 May 1892 there was born to Palagius and Kreszentia (*née* Dietrich) Dietrich in the village of Hawangen near Memmingen in Swabia a son, Josef. From his birth, Josef would always be known by the Bavarian diminutive 'Sepp', and as such he was to play what, in many ways, was a unique, although some will say notorious part in the history of 20th-century Germany. All this, however, lay many years in the future and would, given the humble origins of his parents, have filled them with disbelief if the course of Sepp's life had been revealed to them at his birth.

Swabia at the time was a province of the Kingdom of Bavaria. The Empire of Germany, which had been created by Bismarck and came into being on 1 January 1871, consisted of a confederation of German states, of which Prussia was the most powerful, followed by Bavaria. Although the Empire was ruled from Berlin and the Emperor came from the Prussian Royal House, the Hohenzollerns, the various states enjoyed a certain amount of autonomy, dependent on their size. For Bavaria, as the second largest, this meant her own parliament and army, although the latter was subordinated to that of Prussia in time of war, as were the other two semi-independent state armies, those of Saxony and Württemberg. Prussia also was the final arbiter in the matters of organisation, training and equipment. Nevertheless, Bavarians have traditionally regarded themselves as a people apart from the remainder of the German states. They speak a particular type of German, and tend to regard north Germans with a certain suspicion.

The Memmingen region is still to this day an area of great natural beauty and in the 1890s hops were its main produce. Some writers have inferred that Sepp Dietrich was illegitimate.[1] There are, however, no factual grounds for believing this and, although Sepp was the eldest, there were also two other sons, both of whom were killed in the First World War, and three girls.[2] Indeed, his parents were good Roman Catholics, the denomination followed by most Bavarians. Palagius himself was a *Packermeister* (Master Packer), but whether he was employed in this trade in the hops industry or not, history does not relate. In 1900, however, when Sepp was eight years old, the family moved to the town of Kempten, the capital of the Allgau region, which by the mid 1890s had a population of over 15000 compared to the 9000 inhabitants of

1

Memmingen, and was described at the time by Baedeker as 'picturesquely situated on the Iller'.[3] Sepp himself completed eight years of schooling and then became an agricultural driver. In 1907, at the age of fifteen, he succumbed to the *Wanderlust*, which has traditionally affected young Germans. He travelled to Austria and Italy, where he learnt some Italian, which would later prove useful to him, and finally to Zurich in Switzerland where he began an apprenticeship in the hotel trade.[4]

In 1911 Dietrich returned home since he was now due to be conscripted into the Royal Bavarian Army. He himself for many years liked to have it believed that he became a cavalryman and that he joined the 1st Bavarian Uhlan Regiment.[5] This may have been his ambition, but in fact he joined the 4th Field Artillery Regiment '*König*' at Augsburg and was posted to the 2nd Battery for his recruit training. Again, Dietrich claimed that he was a regular soldier from 1911 until the outbreak of war.[6] Indeed, in a record of his service which he drew up on June 1951, while a prisoner in Landsberg, he stated that he became a professional *Unteroffizier* (Non-Commissioned Officer) in 1912 and during 1913-14 was a training NCO for mounted troops.[7] The truth was less glamorous. Dietrich joined his regiment on 18 October 1911, but a month later, on 17 November, he was invalided out of the Bavarian Army after a fall from a horse.[8]

His enforced return to civilian life was clearly a disappointment to him. Many accounts state that he now entered the butchery trade, which, of course, fitted in well with his later image as a Nazi 'tough guy', and these appear to stem from what he told his US interrogators in 1945. The truth was a little more mundane. He returned to Kempten and became a baker's errand boy.[9]

By 1914 Dietrich had grown into a stocky man, five feet six inches tall, with blue eyes and brown hair. He wore a moustache and had a strong, square jaw. He spoke with a strong accent, which he never lost, and, indeed, as Baldur von Shirach later wrote, 'he was the original Bavarian'.[10] He had a well developed sense of humour and, like any good Bavarian, enjoyed his drink.

With the outbreak of war in 1914, Sepp, like all the youth of Europe, quickly became caught up in the patriotic fever of the time. On 6 August, he enlisted in the 7th Bavarian Field Artillery Regiment. Again, during the 1930s at least, Dietrich seemed to be ashamed of the fact that he had been an artilleryman. His SS Personal File, for instance, states that he went to war with the 1st Uhlans and then transferred to the 4th Infantry Regiment.[11] One source[12] claims he spent the war as a paymaster sergeant! In October 1914, he arrived on the Western Front with the 6th Bavarian Reserve Artillery Regiment, which was part of the 6th Bavarian Reserve Division. This came under the Crown Prince Rupprecht of Bavaria's Sixth Army and was in action almost the moment that it arrived in Flanders.

By mid-October, after the repulse of von Moltke's armies on the Marne and their withdrawal to the River Aisne, both sides had become engaged in what became known as 'the Race to the Sea', with the Germans trying to take advantage of the relative vacuum in Flanders in order to outflank the Allied forces. The remnants of the Belgian Army became anchored on the Yser Canal and the British Expeditionary Force (BEF) began to arrive from the Aisne from 10 October in order to cover the sector from Ypres to La Bassée. The line south of this was the responsibility of the French. As far as the Germans were concerned, 20 October marked the first day of what was to become the First Battle of Ypres and it was characterised by simultaneous attacks by the German Fourth and Sixth Armies respectively north and south of Ypres. 6th Bavarian Reserve Division constituted part of XIV Reserve Corps, which was engaged in attacking the French XXI Corps in the area of Lens. Dietrich himself was probably serving as a gun number in one of the six six-gun batteries in the Regiment, the gun being the 77 mm field gun. For the next ten days, the Sixth Army attempted to break through the Allied line, but without success. By the 27th, the Germans had decided to concentrate their efforts around Ypres itself and the Crown Prince Rupprecht was ordered to quieten things down on his front and told that his heavy artillery would be switched northwards.

The new German plan called for an attack on the St Yves-Gheluvelt sector. This was at this time held by four cavalry corps and the idea was to form an additional force of six divisions, called Gruppe von Fabeck, after its commander, behind them in order to give an overwhelming superiority in front of Ypres. 6th Bavarian Reserve Division was one of those earmarked for this group and moved northwards on 26 October. The division was given orders to attack Gheluvelt, together with I Cavalry Corps and XXVII Reserve Corps, on the 29th, in order to cover the deployment of the remainder of *Gruppe* von Fabeck. 6th Bavarian Reserve Division had a fierce tussle with the British 1st Guards Brigade and managed to capture some trenches, but suffered heavy casualties in the process. At the end of the day, the Division was placed in reserve in the Menin area while the remainder of von Fabeck's divisions continued throughout the next two days to struggle forward, inflicting heavy casualties on the enemy, but also suffering grievously themselves. Eventually, at about noon on the 31st, the village of Gheluvelt was finally captured, only to be lost a few hours later to a brilliant counter attack by the Worcesters which was to have a profound effect upon the security of the BEF and to make its place in history as a classic.

In view of the heavy casualties which they were suffering, the Germans decided to switch to night attacks and 6th Bavarian Reserve Division, now south of Ypres, began an attack on Wytschaete shortly after midnight on 1 November. The village was held by 400 men of the Composite Household Cavalry Regiment and sheer weight of numbers drove them out. Fruitless efforts were made during the remaining hours of darkness to counter-attack. At about 0800 hours, help for the hard pressed British came in the shape of the French 32nd Division, part of XVI French Corps which was being deployed to strengthen the Allied line. The French drove the Bavarians out of the village

MAP 1 Sepp Dietrich's southern Germany.

but, later in the day, the Bavarians managed to get into Wytschaete again before being driven out. The next day, the 2nd, the Bavarians attacked once more, this time reinforced by elements of neighbouring divisions, and finally secured Wytschaete but could not get any further forward. There was now a further pause while the Germans brought up more reinforcements, but attacks continued all along the front in order to prevent the Allies from improving their positions. The main weight of the German effort was now transferred to the nose of the Ypres Salient and 6th Bavarian Reserve Division, while remaining in the line, did enjoy a comparative lull. By 20 November, however, both sides were exhausted. The Germans had failed to break through and trench warfare had arrived on the Western Front and would dominate it for the next three years.

Foiled in the West, the German High Command now turned its eyes eastward. By the end of November, four corps, together with all the cavalry on the Ypres front, were on their way to face the Russians. This included 6th Bavarian Reserve Division, but Dietrich was no longer with it. At some stage during the fighting of the past month he had been wounded, having received shrapnel in the lower right leg and, somewhat surprisingly, since the days of mounted cavalry action were over by the time Sepp arrived on the Ypres front, a lance thrust above the left eye.[13] He was to bear the scars of these wounds for the rest of his life. Nevertheless, he had clearly shown promise as a soldier during the short time that he had been in action since, once he had recovered from his wounds, he was sent to the Bavarian artillery school at Sonthofen, by the border with Austria, in order to learn how to become a non-commissioned officer (NCO). At the same time he was put back on the books of the 7th Bavarian Field Artillery Regiment.

Probably in the summer of 1915, Dietrich was back in action, but it is virtually impossible to establish his movements during the next eighteen months. If he remained with the 7th Bavarian Artillery Regiment, he would have found himself in 1st Bavarian Division. Either later in 1915 or early in 1916, Dietrich was wounded again when he was buried alive in a shell explosion, also receiving a shell splinter in the right side of his head. This was when on the Somme.[14] Dietrich also claimed to have fought on the Italian front and to have been awarded the Austrian Medal for Bravery (*Ostereichische Tapferkeitsmedaille*),[15] although no record exists of when and where he won it. If he did serve on the Italian front it would have probably been during the Trentino offensive mounted by General Franz Conrad von Hötzendorff in May 1916, and the subsequent Italian counter-offensive on both the Trentino and Isonzo during that summer. In this case he would have probably been in 11th Bavarian Division.

In November 1916 Dietrich left the world of conventional field artillery to join *Infanterie-Geschütz-Batterie* (Infantry Gun Battery) 10 and became directly involved with storm troops. The *Sturmtruppen* concept had its origins in an experimental combat engineer unit formed by Major Calsow as *Sturmabteilung Calsow* in May 1915. This was designed to assist in the attack of strongpoints, and consisted of two engineer companies and a battery equipped with the newly introduced Krupp 37 mm cannon. In August 1915, the unit was taken over by Captain Willi Rohr and, in conjunction with Major Hermann Reddemann, who was commanding the 3rd Guard Pioneer Regiment (the German Army's flamethrower unit) developed a combined arms organisation for the *Sturmabteilungen* or *Stosstruppen* (assault troops), to use the term coined by Reddemann. They added a machine gun platoon (six machine guns), a trench mortar troop (four light mortars) and a flamethrower troop (six flame-throwers). After a number of successful experiments during the autumn of 1915, Rohr's unit was ordered to become a training cadre for the formation of divisional storm companies within the German Fifth Army under the Crown

Prince Wilhelm, about to begin preparations for the assault on Verdun. When the attack began in February 1916, Rohr, as well as continuing to carry out his training role, was also used for carrying out especially difficult attacks. By May 1916, the German High Command was so impressed with Rohr's *Sturmabteilung* that Ludendorff directed that he should enlarge his training brief to cover the remainder of the German armies. To this end, his *abteilung* set up a permanent training camp at Beuville near Montmédy, close to the border with Luxembourg. Shortly after this, it was decided to form Infantry Gun Batteries using a weapon that could 'pack more punch' than the 37 mm.

The weapon selected for these batteries was a modified version of the Russian 7.62cm Putilov fortress gun, a number of which had been captured by the Germans early in the war. Its original purpose was to provide enfilade fire along the ditch in front of a fortress wall. As such, it had a short carriage and low wheels, to enable it to be manhandled by its crew. The Germans, in order to make it easier to manhandle across trenches, now cut down the barrel by almost half and it was designated the 7.62mm Infantry Gun L/16.5 Krupp. [16] It fired a high explosive shell, using both contact and delay fuzes and had a maximum range of 1800 yards. Each battery had six such guns and a strength of three officers and 76 other ranks, but no horses, since the guns would be drawn by their crews. This meant that they had to be physically very fit. The infantry guns had two tasks. Before the stormtroops attacked the gunners put down rapid fire on the points of penetration in order to keep the enemy's heads down. They then advanced with the stormtroops and, once the objective had been seized, they were there to break up any counter-attacks which developed.

By the end of 1916, plans had been set in motion to organise a storm battalion for each army or equivalent formation. During the course of late 1916 and 1917, no less than seventeen such battalions were formed. In general terms, they took the number of the army which they supported. Thus Rohr's battalion became *Sturmbataillon* 5 because it supported the Fifth Army when it was not carrying out its training role. The only exception to this rule was that the unit numbers of the battalions supporting the Second and Third Armies were transposed. The reason for this was that the storm unit with Second Army was formed from the 3rd Jaeger Battalion, which had been converted to this role earlier in 1916, and this became *Sturmbataillon* 3. Each storm battalion consisted of from one to five storm companies, one or two machine gun companies, a flamethrower section, a *Minenwerfer* (trench mortar) company and an infantry gun battery. Additional infantry gun batteries were also formed and these would be used to reinforce a *sturmbataillon*. Dietrich, with Infantry Gun Battery 10, became part of *Sturmbataillon* 2 with the Third Army in the Champagne. [17]

The character of the storm troops was very different to that of the remainder of the German Army. For a start, they considered themselves to be an elite, which they undoubtedly were. Discipline in the formal sense was much more relaxed, with much less of the wide gulf which separated officers from men in more conventional units. They received better rations, were excused much of the general tedium of trench warfare and had more opportunity for rest. On the other hand, the demands on them when actually in combat were much greater. Indeed, it was their ability to infiltrate the enemy lines, which they developed during 1916-17, on which Ludendorff was to pin his hopes for the German offensives of 1918. This bred in them a toughness and ruthlessness aptly described by Ernst Junger, who became, post-war, their troubador:

'The turmoil of our feelings was called forth by rage, alcohol and the thirst for blood. As we advanced with difficulty but irresistibly towards the enemy lines, I was boiling over with a fury which gripped me – it gripped us all – in an inexplicable way. The overpowering desire to kill gave me wings. Rage squeezed bitter tears from my eyes . . . Only the spell of primaeval instinct remained.'[18]

It is no small wonder that many of them joined the Freikorps in the turmoil that was Germany in the immediate post-war years.

The spring of 1917 in the Champagne was marked by the Nivelle offensive. General Robert Nivelle, who had succeeded Joffre as the French Commander-in-Chief at the end of 1916, was, in spite of the British failure to break through on the Somme, convinced that he could get through the German lines in just 48 hours and secure a decisive victory as long as he had sufficient artillery to support him. His persuasive manner convinced both the French and British politicians and his plan was accepted. It called for attacks by the British north of the Somme and the French to the south in order to draw off the German reserves, followed by the main blow to be struck by the French north of the Aisne and centred on Craonne. The German withdrawal to the Hindenburg Line in March 1917, done in order to shorten their line, largely negated much of the plan, but Nivelle, in spite of growing misgivings on the part of the British and many French generals and politicians, was determined to press on. The only feasible diversionary attack left was that by the British at Arras, which was launched on 9 April. A week later, the main attack was mounted, primarily on the German Seventh Army in the Chemin des Dames sector, but also against First Army on its left and, still further to the left, on the right flank of Third Army. The result was a disaster. In driving wind and rain, the French suffered over 100,000 casualties on the first day alone and nine days later had nowhere advanced more than five miles. Morale cracked and the troops in many French divisions refused to attack any more. Nivelle was sacked and Pétain brought in to repair the damage. For the remainder of 1917, it was the British who had to take the maintenance of the offensive on their shoulders while the bulk of the French armies adopted a posture of passive defence. This meant that, from May onwards, Dietrich and his comrades enjoyed a relatively peaceful time, broken only by the odd raid. It was probably for his performance in one of these that Dietrich was awarded the Iron Cross 2nd Class on 14 November 1917. He was also supposed at sometime during 1914-18, to have won the Iron Cross 1st Class as well, but no record of the date and gazetting of this award can be found.[19]

On 19 February 1918, Dietrich received a new posting. He reported to Berlin-Schöneburg to join *Bayerische Sturmpanzerkampfwagen Abteilung* (Bavarian Storm Tank Detachment) 13. While the Germans had shown much interest in armoured cars prior to 1914 and had been using them to a limited extent during the war, they did not pursue the tank idea until after 15 September 1916. This was the day when the tank made its debut in action, in the Flers-Courcelette area of the Somme. Of the 49 tanks which took part in the fighting that day, the majority broke down before they reached the German lines, but one or two achieved significant successes. The Germans, who had had no previous inkling of them, were taken by surprise. The Chief of Staff of the German Third Army Group wrote: 'The enemy . . . have employed new engines of war, as cruel as effective. No doubt they will adopt on an extensive scale these monstrous engines, and it is urgent to take whatever methods are possible to counteract them.' Apart from spurring them to develop anti-tank weapons, the appearance of the tank on the battlefield also resolved the Germans to build their own.

Within a few days of the action at Flers, the German War Ministry had given its first order to build an experimental tank. Like the British, the Germans took the Holt caterpillar tractor as their starting point, having found one in Austria. On 16 January 1917 a prototype, with wooden body, of what became known as the A7V was first demonstrated, and four days later the War Ministry placed an order for one hundred tracked vehicles, based on the A7V chassis, but of these only ten were tanks *per se*, the remainder being transport vehicles with open tops. The first proper chassis was available for driving tests on 5 April 1917, but it would be a further six months before the first A7V was completed. The reasons for this were two-fold. For a start, the tank had to compete with many other weapons systems for the limited materials available. There was also dissipation in effort in that other designs were being investigated in parallel with the development of the A7V. Nevertheless, on 29 September came the order for the raising of *Abteilungen* 1 and 2. During the next few weeks their tanks began to arrive and the crews began their training.

The A7V, which stood for *Allgemeine Kriegsdepartement 7 Abteilung Verkehrswesen* (General War Department 7 Transport Branch, after the branch in the War Ministry department made responsible for tanks), was very much larger than its British counterparts and had a crew of eighteen. Initially it was planned to produce the majority as 'female' tanks, mounting just machine guns, one each fore and aft and two on each side, but this was altered in November 1917 and it was decreed that all tanks should be males, with a captured Nordenfeldt 57mm gun mounted in the front, two machine guns on each side and two in the rear. Unlike the British system, where the track passed over the top of the hull, the A7V track was much smaller in length and did not extend above the floor of the crew compartment. The total weight was 33 tons, compared to 31 tons for the British Mark IV male. Before the order to build male tanks only was put out, one female tank was delivered to *Abteilung* 1, but the remainder of the twenty A7Vs which were eventually built were all males.

Each *Abteilung* was equipped with five A7Vs and had a strength of five officers and 108 NCOs and men. They were controlled by the *Feldkraftvahr-Chef* (Chief of Motor Transport). On 1 December 1917 the order was given for Abteilung 3 to be raised and on 12 January 1918 Abteilungen 1 and 2 were ordered to the front. It was shortage of raw materials which brought about the restricted order for twenty tanks, although at one time it had been as high as 38 tanks. The situation was eased, however, as a result of the Battle of Cambrai in November 1917. On the 20th, the British Tank Corps came into its own when some four hundred tanks punched their way through the heavily fortified Hindenburg Line, but there was a failure to exploit this initial success and, at the end of the month, the Germans counter-attacked, driving the British virtually back to their start line. During this operation a number of Mark IV tanks were captured and it was decided to use these to supplement the limited number of A7Vs. Eventually, in addition to the three A7V *Abeitlungen*, six *Beutepanzerkampfwagen* ('booty' tank) *Abeitlungen* were formed, each of two male and three female Mark IVs. These were numbered 11-16, and *Abeitlungen* 13 and 16 were Bavarian.

It would seem that the manpower for the German tanks was found partly by calling for volunteers and partly by compulsory transfer. The Germans wanted to integrate the tanks into their 'storm' tactics, which they had, as we have seen, been developing from 1916 onwards and now intended to use as the cornerstone of their big spring 1918 offensive on the Western Front. In which category Dietrich fitted is not clear, but, having served with storm troops and being an artilleryman, he had the right type of experience, and indeed became a 6-pounder gunner in one of *Abteilung* 13's two male Mark IVs.

During their two months at Berlin-Schöneberg the members of *Abteilung* 13 did not see any Mark IVs because it was not considered worth shipping any back from France and the idea was that tanks and crews should marry up only when they arrived there. Consequently, the training was 'dry'. In the meantime, *Abteilungen* 1 and 2, together with the first Mark IV detachment, *Abteilung* 11, arrived in France and were sent to Beuville near Montmédy, where Captain Rohr, father of the stormtroops, was based with his *Sturmbataillon* 5. Here they were to carry out combined training in order to learn how to operate with the storm troops. On 27 February, *Abteilung* 1 and *Sturmbataillon* 5 gave a demonstration before the Kaiser. Three weeks later, German tanks found themselves in action for the first time.

Four tanks of *Abteilung* 1 were made available to XVII German Corps and the five 'booty' tanks of *Abteilung* 11 to XIX Corps, both of whom were attacking in the St Quentin area. The idea was that they should be used to mop up strongpoints which had been bypassed by the leading stormtroops. The fog on the morning of 21 March, the opening day of the first of the German drives, *Michael*, covered the move up of the tanks, but, of the A7Vs, two then broke down and only two were considered to have carried out their mission. In *Abteilung* 11, two tanks were damaged by artillery fire and two broke down, leaving just one to come to grips with the enemy. Not a very auspicious beginning, especially since their use was largely unnoticed by the British, with those who did see them being killed or captured before they could report back on them.

Both *Abteilungen* were now withdrawn to Charleroi, which had become the German tank base, with seven out of the nine tanks which had been used requiring extensive repairs.

The next occasion on which German tanks were used was historic in that it marked the first tank versus tank action. By early April, *Michael* had run out of steam and Ludendorff decided to launch a fresh offensive in Flanders, *Georgette*. Nevertheless, pressure was still maintained on the Somme front and, on 24 April, von der Marwitz's Second Army launched a local attack to capture high ground in the Villers Bretonneux-Cachy area, just to the east of Amiens. For this all three A7V *Abteilungen* were to be used, although only fourteen out of fifteen tanks actually took part since one from *Abteilung* 2 broke down before entraining at Charleroi. One group of three tanks from *Abteilung* 1 was highly successful in supporting 228th Infantry Division's attack on Villers-Bretonneux. The second group, of two tanks from *Abteilung* 1 and *Abteilung* 3 complete, was to attack the southern outskirts of Villers-Bretonneux and a wood to the east of the town in conjunction with 4th Guards Division. One tank broke down early on; another, having done some good work, became stuck in a shell hole and had to be abandoned. This tank, *Mephisto*, was salvaged by the Australians and is today the only surviving A7V and is to be found in the Queensland Museum, Brisbane, Australia. The remainder also performed creditably, although one broke down 30 metres from the British front line, but was recovered by its crew. The third group consisted of the four tanks of *Abteilung* 2 and had the village of Cachy as its objective. One of these, nicknamed '*Nixe*', was engaged by a section of three British Mark IVs, a male and two females, of A Company 1st Tank Battalion. *Nixe* succeeding in hitting and forcing the two females to retire, but was hit by the male, three crew members being killed and three slightly wounded. However, its commander, Lieutenant Bilz, succeeded in withdrawing it some two kilometres, where its engines gave up. It was successfully salvaged that night. Honours were therefore about even. Shortly afterwards, seven Whippet light tanks from the British 3rd Tank Battalion attacked German infantry advancing on Cachy, scattering them and causing heavy casualties. They were, however, driven off, thanks to the efforts of another A7V and a 77 mm field battery, with one being destroyed and three damaged. Of the other two tanks, one was progressing well when it slipped into a small quarry and overturned. After the commander had been killed in a British attempt to recover it, the remainder of the crew abandoned the tank, and the other did not really come to grips with the enemy. Thus, for a loss of two tanks, with two others damaged, six killed, twenty-eight wounded and one prisoner, the German tanks had performed in an encouraging fashion.[21]

On the very day that the attack on Villers-Bretonneux was being carried out, *Abteilung* 13 entrained in Berlin and arrived at Pierrepont, near Montmédy three days later. From where it marched, still without any tanks, to Beuville. Like other *Abteilungen*, it was to carry out training with Rohr's stormtroops for three or four weeks. This was quickly changed, however, and on 3 May the tank drivers left for Charleroi in order to begin taking over their tanks. Six days later, the gunners followed and, on 12 May, Abteilung 13 was declared operational[22] – very surprising in view of the very short time in which the crews had had their tanks – with an establishment of seven officers, an assistant paymaster, one sergeant major (*Feldwebel*), one staff sergeant (*Vizefeldwebel*), twenty lance-sergeants (*Unteroffizier*) and 112 men.

Dietrich's first male Mark IV was named *Moritz* and was commanded by Lt Heinz Kubierschky. Within two weeks of becoming operational, *Abteilungen* 11-14 were deployed to Seventh Army in order to support Ludendorff's third German drive, which was in the Chemin des Dames sector. The attack began on 27 May, but *Moritz* played little part since her commander was seriously wounded while holding a conference outside the tank. Consequently, the crew did not take part in the opening and very successful day, which saw the Germans cross the Aisne and advance twelve miles. Kubierschky's successor was Lt Fuchsbauer and it was under his command that *Moritz* was truly blooded five days later.

By 30 May the German advance had reached the Marne and it was decided that the salient must be widened. Consequently, First Army, which was operating on the left flank of the main thrust by Seventh Army, was tasked with capturing Reims. For this it was decided to employ tanks, both to the north and south of the town. *Abteilungen* 1 and 2 had now arrived in the area and the plan was for *Abteilung* 2 to take part in the attack north of Reims, while *Abteilungen* 1, 13 and 14 were to support the southern attack. These three were to operate under 238th Infantry Division and the main obstacle was seen as Fort La Pompelle. The attack was scheduled for the morning of 1 June.

The first task was for the detachment reconnaissance officers to go forward in motor vehicles to explore the ground. They noted that the going was likely to be difficult, with engineer assistance needed to get the tanks over the German trenches. The French trenches, on the other hand, were considered just narrow enough for the tanks to cross them under their own steam. In terms of tanks, *Abteilung* 1 had its full establishment available, but the 'booty' tank detachments already had some off the road because of the wear and tear of the past few days. *Abteilung* 13 had three tanks fit, including *Moritz* and was made up to strength with one tank from *Abteilung* 11 and one from *Abteilung* 12. *Abteilung* 14 had four of its own tanks. *Abteilung* 2, which was operating north of Reims with 242nd Infantry Division, had all five A7Vs available.

Shortly before 2000 hours on 31 May, while it was still light, the tanks left their leaguer areas, Bazancourt for *Abteilung* 2 and Witry for the remainder. Near Berru, after a 3km march, which took them about 30 minutes, *Abteilungen*

1, 13 and 14 halted to camouflage the tanks. They then proceeded a little further and halted once more to await the onset of darkness, since there was now a danger that they might be seen by the enemy. Eventually, at 0200 hours, they reached their jump off positions and here they refuelled. To their likely annoyance, they discovered that no engineers had been made available to bridge the trenches and hence they had to do this themselves. It is therefore unlikely that anyone got any sleep that night, not that much of it was left by the time they arrived.

The dawn broke, as it had often done during these 1918 German drives, with a thick fog and *Abteilungen* 1, 13 and 14 began their advance at 0400 hours. *Abteilung* 1 did not enjoy much success. Two tanks failed to cross the start line because of mechanical problems and two others fell into a tank trap in front of the enemy's trenches. One, under heavy artillery fire, managed to get out and return to the start line, but the other suffered a breakdown on the way back and had to be abandoned. The fifth broke down not far from the start line. By the time the problem had been righted, it met the other survivor coming back and returned to the start line with it. *Abteilung* 14 fared better. Advancing ahead of the infantry, its tanks penetrated three lines of trenches and inflicted a number of casualties. Unfortunately, though, only one of four tanks eventually arrived back at the start line, the others having been respectively ditched and been demolished, ditched and destroyed by artillery fire, and broken down and destroyed by artillery fire.

Like *Abteilung* 1, *Abteilung* 13 also suffered casualties on the way to the start line, with one tank falling into a ditch and another breaking a differential gear. Both therefore had to be abandoned. The tank from *Abteilung* 11 was initially held up in trying to extricate the ditched tank, but eventually got into the enemy trenches at 0530 hours, albeit under heavy artillery fire. Its foot brakes then jammed and burnt out, but this did not stop it helping the infantry by attacking several machine gun nests which were holding them up. It then got ahead of the infantry, which so often happened, but managed to break up the beginnings of a counter-attack. By this time Fort Pompelle had been captured, but this tank now received a call for assistance from infantry on the Aisne-Marne canal. On its way there, it was put out of action by shellfire. *Abteilung* 12's representative came close to Fort Pompelle before it came under fire of artillery directed by an aeroplane. The crew were forced to evacuate it temporarily, but then it continued forward. At the request of the accompanying infantry, the commander dismounted three of his machine guns to help repel a counter-attack. However, in the end, the enemy pressure grew too strong and the infantry were forced to retire, the tank crew going with them and abandoning their tank.

This left *Moritz*. This got into the French front line with no problem, using both its 6-pounder and machine guns to good effect. It then fell into a shell hole and the engine became overheated in the effort to get it out again. By the time the engine had sufficiently cooled down, the infantry had been driven back and

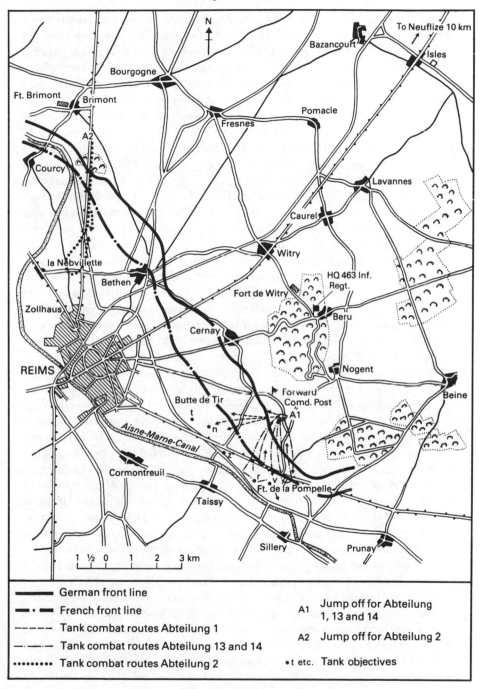

N

To Neuflize 10 km

Bazancourt
Isles
Bourgogne
Ft. Brimont   Brimont
Pomacle
Fresnes
A2
Courcy
Lavannes
Caurel
la Nebvilette
Witry
Bethen
HQ 463 Inf. Regt.
Fort de Witry
Zollhaus
Beru
Cernay
Nogent
REIMS
Butte de Tir
t
Forward Comd. Post
A1
Beine
n
Aisne-Marne-Canal
Cormontreuil
Ft. de la Pompelle
Taissy
1 ½ 0   1   2   3 km
Sillery
Prunay

▬▬▬▬	German front line	
▬·▬·▬	French front line	
‒‒‒‒	Tank combat routes Abteilung 1	
‒·‒·‒	Tank combat routes Abteilung 13 and 14	
••••••••	Tank combat routes Abteilung 2	

A1   Jump off for Abteilung 1, 13 and 14

A2   Jump off for Abteilung 2

•t etc.   Tank objectives

MAP 2 Tank action at Reims.

Moritz found itself in No. Man's Land. Lt Fuchsbauer therefore decided that the tank must be demolished. The demolition party consisted of Sergeant Leinauer, who was subsequently killed, Dietrich and the first driver, Maier, who afterwards became an SS *Standartenführer* in Munich, probably due, at least in part, to Sepp's wish to reward a fellow tank crewman. It was Maier who finally blew the tank up, but Sepp won everlasting renown within *Abteilung* 13 for his insistence on rescuing a bottle of Schnapps from *Moritz* under heavy fire before she was reduced to mere scrap iron. Whether it was for his sense of priorities or his coolness under fire, Unteroffizier Dietrich's performance on that day was recognised five weeks later when on 5 July 1918 he was awarded the Bavarian Military Merit Cross (*Bayerische Militär-Verdienstkreuz*) 3rd Class. [23] The attack north of Reims was similarly rebuffed, although it did not go in until the evening of 1 June. Two tanks failed to cross the start line and two others were lost, one from a direct hit and the other because the crew were being overcome by the effects of shellfire.

After the abortive battle of Reims and the eventual halting of the third German drive, the 'booty' tank detachments were withdrawn to Charleroi. The A7Vs stayed on to take part in the fourth German offensive, which was launched between Montdidier and Royon on 9 June. Both *Abteilungen* 1 and 3 did some good work and, in spite of mechanical troubles, did not lose any tanks. For *Abteilung* 13, the next action was to be on 15 July, the opening day of Ludendorff's final drive, the so called *Friedensturm* (Peace Offensive) which took place south-east of Soissons. When Sepp Dietrich revisited this area during the fighting in France in June 1940 he is supposed to have recalled that in July 1918 he fought against Allied tanks and achieved hits on them. [24] However, this is most unlikely. Abteilung 13's two male tanks at this time were *Bob*, on which Dietrich is sitting in the photograph at plate 4, and *Wolf*. Lt Ludwig commanded *Bob*, which was lost on 15 July, having been hit in the track and then in the front. It is more likely that, in spite of the impression given by the photograph, he was in *Wolf*, which was commanded by Lt Fuchsbauer of *Moritz* fame, and who would have almost certainly wished to take his old crew with him. If this is the case, then Dietrich would have seen little fighting that day because *Wolf* was disabled by a shell prior to the attack. Whichever tank he was in, the attack on this day made little progress and almost all the tanks involved were knocked out by artillery fire. Admittedly, the French did employ their Renault light tanks in counter-attacks during the period 15-18 July, but there is no evidence to suggest that they actually became involved in tank-versus-tank actions.

With the failure of *Friedensturm* and the taking to the offensive by the Allies, there was a lull in tank operations. Towards the end of September, however, the commander of the German tanks, Major Pornschlegel, was informed by High Command that the intention was to concentrate all available tanks in one place in order to use them for a counter-attack. Accordingly, all *Abteilungen* were to be brought together under the Crown Prince Wilhelm's Army Group. In the event, this proved impossible to achieve because of the number of tanks under repair and transport problems. It was therefore decided to use just *Abteilungen* 1, 15 and 16, then at Charleroi and 11 and 13, who were training with Seventeenth Army. First to be employed were *Abteilungen* 11, 15 and 16, who were subordinated to XIV Reserve Corps on 29 September in order to help stem the British advance north and south of Cambrai. For a week they lay in assembly areas waiting for the British attack to begin and, during this time, lost four tanks destroyed by artillery fire. When the attack did begin, south of Cambrai on the morning of 8 October, the *Abteilungen* found themselves being used in counter-attacks against tanks of 12th Battalion Tank Corps. In the ensuing actions two British tanks were damaged, as well as six out of the eleven 'booty' tanks which were present. The remainder all broke down. Some could not be recovered in the face of the British advance and so the surviving crews returned to Charleroi without a single battleworthy tank.

In the meantime, *Abteilungen* 1 and 13 had also been deployed to the north of Cambrai. On 9 October, both Abteilungen were placed under command of 371st Infantry Regiment in order to carry out a counter-attack north of the town. The five A7Vs performed well, driving the enemy back and getting in behind the British lines. *Abteilung* 13 did not enjoy such success. The wear and tear of the previous weeks' training and recent long marches was beginning to tell and only three tanks were available for the counter-attack, with *Wolf* being one of those off the road. Two tanks were set on fire and the third experienced clutch and gearbox problems and had to be abandoned. Both *Abteilungen* now returned once more to Charleroi.

Abteilung 13's last action, and indeed probably the last appearance of German tanks during the war, was on 1 November 1918. In order to try and forestall the Canadian and British capture of Valenciennes, four 'booty' tanks belonging to *Abteilungen* 12, 13 and 14 supported 28th Reserve Division in an attack in the Curgies area on the south-eastern outskirts of the town. The brunt hit the British 4th Division and drove it and parts of 49th and 61st Divisions on its flanks back a certain distance, although two tanks were knocked out by artillery fire in the course of the action. This, however, did no more than slightly delay the inevitable and the advance was resumed on the next day. During the course of that day, 61st Division captured two tanks, which were presumably the two survivors of the previous day's action. There is no record of what, if any, part Dietrich took in this last action. [25]

Presumably having no tanks left, *Abteilung* 13 was withdrawn to Germany. Here it became affected by the Soldiers' Councils which were springing up among the troops in the rear areas. These had been triggered off by a mutiny in the High Seas Fleet at Kiel. The Fleet had remained 'beleaguered' there since the Battle of Jutland in May 1916 and it was inevitable that, given the enforced idleness and worsening war situation, that discontent would breed among the lower decks. In July 1917 there had been a protest aboard the battleship *Prinzregent Luitpold*, when several sailors had complained about the poor quality of rations and had walked off the ship to carry out a protest march ashore. They then returned and were subsequently court-martialled. Some were sentenced to long terms of imprisonment, but two of the ring-leaders were shot. Discontent grew further over the next fifteen months, and was not helped by insensitive officers. During the last days of October 1918, rumours began that the Fleet was about to put to sea in order to challenge the British Grand Fleet and, if necessary, go down fighting. On 28 October, these rumours appeared to be confirmed when the Fleet was ordered to make steam and come together in the Schillig Roads. This it did, but, once there, the stokers in several ships warned that they would extinguish the boilers if the Fleet weighed anchor. Whatever their officers felt, the sailors thought that there was no point in sacrificing their lives in a war that was already lost. The Fleet returned to port after some 600 sailors on the two worst afflicted ships had been arrested. On 3 November, there were protest demonstrations by sailors in Kiel, with eight being shot. On the next day, the dock workers joined in, with sailors' and workers' councils being set up. The government sent Gustav Noske, the Majority Socialist defence expert, to Kiel and he succeeded in calming the situation by promising that there would be no 'suicide' attack on the British Fleet and that all prisoners would be released. The sailors even made him governor of Kiel, but it was too late. The revolutionary fervour had already swept much of the country and even *Abteilung* 13 set up its *Soldatenrat* on 9 November. Elected as Chairman was Sepp Dietrich,[26] which is indicative of the trust and standing in which he was held by his brother tankmen. He did not, however, have long in which to enjoy the fruits of his office. By 16 November, *Abteilung* 13 was in Munich. With the Armistice having come into effect on 11 November, it was speedily disbanded. On the 20th, Sepp was returned to the books of the 7th Bavarian Field Artillery Regiment and on 26 March 1919 he was discharged from the Bavarian Army as a *Vize-Wachtmeister* to his birthplace, Hawangen.

CHAPTER 2

Policeman and Oberlander
1919-27

The Bavaria to which Sepp Dietrich returned in November 1918 was seething with unrest. On the 8th, the day before Sepp had been elected Chairman of the *Abteilung* 13 *Soldatenrat*, Kurt Eisner, leader of the minority Independent Socialists in the Bavarian parliament, had declared a Bavarian Socialist and Democratic Republic. What had encouraged him to do this were the fears of the Bavarian peasantry that the collapse of Austro-Hungary might bring about an invasion of Bavaria unless peace was made, and general discontent with the Berlin government, which seemed to be dragging its feet over peace and on which the Bavarian people laid the blame for the hardships they were suffering. Eisner was immediately joined by the Independent Socialists and they set up a radical, but democratic government. The next day, in Berlin, after Hindenburg and Groener, Ludendorff's successor as Quartermaster General, had told Prince Max, the Imperial Chancellor, that the troops would no longer follow the Kaiser and that he must abdicate, Prince Max handed over the seals of office to Friedrich Ebert, leader of the Majority Socialists. He also announced the abdication of the Kaiser and the latter left for exile in Holland. As in Bavaria, the Independents joined the Majority Socialists in forming a government, but Ebert also had to reckon with the Soldiers' and Workers' Councils, who were considerably more to the left than he was. It was they, through an agreement made with the government on 22 November, who held the real power in what was now called the German Socialist Republic. While the Independents generally supported this structure, seeing it as the best way to consolidate the gains of the 'revolution', Ebert and the Majority Socialists saw it as a threat to democratic government as demonstrated by the Councils' attitude to the constituent assembly which Ebert intended to call.

In the meantime, Ebert established a strong link with General Groener, who feared that the revolution would cause civil war, especially if, as it seemed was happening, the traditional power vested in the officer corps was removed. Groener stated that the Army would support Ebert and ensure that the forces in France would cross over the Rhine by 12 December, the date demanded by the Allies and agreed in the armistice terms. In return, Ebert was to uphold officers' powers. This was easier said than done, especially after the All-German Congress of Workers' and Soldiers' Councils met in December and demanded that all military ranks be abolished, that henceforth all officers should be elected and the standing army be replaced by a peoples' militia. All Ebert could do was to execute a delicate balancing act, reassuring Groener and Hindenburg on one hand, and delaying the implementation of the Councils' demands on the other. Now, calling together the Councils once more and representatives of the German states, he managed to get agreement that elections for the constituent assembly be held in mid-January.

The more extreme of the Independents and the Spartacists were, however, becoming increasingly disillusioned with the course that the revolution was taking. The Spartacists themselves had been founded by a small group of left wing intellectuals and admirers of Lenin, led by Karl Liebknecht and Rosa Luxemburg, during the winter 1917-18 and assumed the mantle of the German Communist Party. The name of the movement came from Spartacus, the Thracian gladiator who led a revolt against the Romans in 73 B.C. The Spartacist demonstrations in Berlin were becoming ever more strident, and in early December matters came to a head when some soldiers fired on a crowd of Spartacists and killed several. Next day the Spartacists organised a protest demonstration and the prospect of civil war came closer. In order to try and reassert his grip on the situation, Ebert had announced the formation of a fourteen-battalion Republican Soldiers' Army under Otto Wels, governor of Berlin, to keep the peace. However, the force was totally ineffectual and riddled with left wing extremists. There now came trouble when the sailors from the Baltic ports, who had come to Berlin under the guise of the People's Naval Division, announced that they would join this force, but refused to take orders from Wels. Further confusion was created by two other paramilitary formations, the *Sicherheitswehr* (Security Force) created by left wing police commissioner Emil Eichhorn, and the Majority Socialist counter to this, the *Republikanische Schütztruppe*.

Matters came to a head when the government, in order to try and curtail the power of the People's Naval Division, bribed them to move out of their quarters in the former Imperial palace and to reduce their strength from 3000 to the 600 men of the other Republican Soldiers' Army battalions. Accepting this, the sailors then demanded a Christmas bonus and kidnapped Wels. Ebert now appealed to the Army and some 1800 troops, all that could be trusted, were sent to Berlin from garrisons just outside. They surrounded the palace and assaulted it on the morning of Christmas Eve. A truce was now called, but meanwhile the Spartacists had been busy and had gathered a large crowd of civilians, telling them that an Imperialist counter-coup was taking place. Before the soldiers could react, they were engulfed by the crowd and melted away. Deserted by the Independent Socialists and the Army, Ebert and his moderate Majority Socialists now seemed entirely isolated.

On 29 December 1918, the Spartacists held a conference in Berlin. Present were Karl Radek, Lenin's personal representative, and four other Bolshevik delegates. Radek saw that the moment for a full-blooded revolution was ripe and persuaded the delegates, in spite of fierce opposition from Rosa Luxemburg, to boycott the forthcoming constituent assembly elections and the Spartacists now became officially known as the German Communist Party. A week later, on 6 January, they formed a revolutionary committee, which announced the end of the Ebert government; armed Communists occupied public buildings in Berlin and a general strike was called.

That the central government in Berlin did not fall to Communism was due to two factors. The first was Ebert's appointment of Noske, who had so successfully restored order in Kiel, as defence minister, and he quickly showed more determination than his Majority Socialist compatriots, most of whom were not prepared to countenance any form of violence. The second factor was the tool which Noske was about to use to put down what had now become an armed insurrection.

On 12 December 1918, General Georg von Maercker, commanding 214th Infantry Division, which, like the remainder of the troops who had fought in France and Flanders, was now dissolving, asked permission of his corps commander to form a Corps of Volunteer Riflemen. The gathering momentum of events in Berlin and the anarchy biting deep into the Army, convinced him that, if Germany was to survive the rigours of defeat, a disciplined force was required to uphold Ebert's government until such time as the constituent assembly became fact. His superior, General von Morgen, agreed, and von Maercker set about obtaining volunteers from among his troops. In a matter of days he had found enough men to form three companies and an artillery battery, their base being a secluded monastery at Solzkotlen in Westphalia. The motivation of those who joined was mixed. Some were the true *Frontsoldaten*, those who had become inured to the hardships of war and feared to leave the 'security' of military life for the bleakness of the world outside. As Manfred von Killinger, later Hitler's Minister President of Saxony, wrote:

'The pure *Landsknechte* [mercenaries] didn't care why or for whom they fought. The main thing for them was that they were fighting. . . . War had become their career. They had no desire to look for another. . . . War made them happy – what more can you ask?'[1]

Others, usually the younger soldiers with a student background, did so in the genuine belief that Germany must be saved from Bolshevism, while another popular motive was the belief that the Army had not been defeated on the field of battle, but let down by the politicians and workers, the so called 'stab in the back'.

The companies operated on stormtroop lines, disciplined, but without the Prussian flavour, with their own integral mortars and transport. Yet, while the Supreme Command was happy enough to pay the volunteers, who were on thirty day contracts, they could not provide equipment. Von Maercker was hard-pressed, since the depots were either controlled by Soldiers' Councils, who refused to supply his needs, or the depots themselves had been wrecked.

Eventually, though, he did manage to find what he wanted. By the end of December, his force, the first of the *Freikorps*, had risen to 3000 men, thanks to additional recruiting efforts by three generals deputed to this task by the Supreme Command. Other *Freikorps* were also raised, including a number of naval brigades, most notable of which was the Freikorps Ehrhardt, and the Guard Rifle Cavalry Division formed from elements of the old Imperial Guard divisions.

On 28 December 1918, as a result of the disaster which had befallen the troops in their attempts to drive the sailors out of the palace in Berlin on Christmas Eve, von Maercker's Volunteer Rifles were ordered to move to Zossen, just to the south of Berlin. On 4 January, von Maercker invited Ebert and Noske to inspect his troops at Zossen, and, as they were driving away, Noske turned to Ebert and said: 'Don't worry. Everything's going to be alright now.'[2] Now, in reaction to the events of 6 January 1919, Majority Socialist leaders set about trying to isolate the Spartacists from their support. They succeeded in getting the People's Naval Division to declare its neutrality, mainly through bribery, but also by sowing seeds of doubt in the sailors' minds that the Spartacists would end up the victors. Garrisons outside Berlin were similarly persuaded. With the knowledge that their salvation lay in the *Freikorps*, the government now approached Colonel Wilhelm Reinhard, who was in the process of forming a Freikorps at Moabit Barracks, to turn the Spartacists out of various newspaper offices. He gathered up other embryo *Freikorps* and, on 10 January, fiercely attacked the *Vorwarts* offices with machine guns, artillery, armoured cars and one of the few surviving German tanks, forcing the defenders to surrender. In the meantime, an *ad hoc* band of armed civil servants, raised by Ebert to guard those government buildings not yet in Spartacist hands, drove the revolutionaries from off the Brandenburg Gate. The tide was beginning to turn.

Noske had set up his headquarters in the well-to-do suburb of Dahlem and quickly summoned von Maercker's men. They now advanced, personally led by Noske, into the centre of Berlin and then linked up with Reinhard's force in the Moabit Barracks. All this was achieved by the evening of 11 January without a shot being fired. Now began the process of reducing the revolutionary strongpoints. On 13 January, realising that they had lost, the Revolutionary Shop Stewards called off the general strike. With Berlin secured, Noske's men now hunted down the revolutionaries. Radek and Eichhorn fled, while Luxemburg and Liebknecht tried to go to ground in the city. They were captured on the evening of the 15th and both were killed before they could be brought to any form of trial.

In spite of what had happened, Noske was still determined to go ahead with elections for the National Assembly on the agreed date of 19 January. However, instead of convening the Assembly in Berlin, he selected Weimar, 150 miles to the south-west, on the grounds of its historical associations with the German arts. This would help create a new atmosphere of liberalism, and,

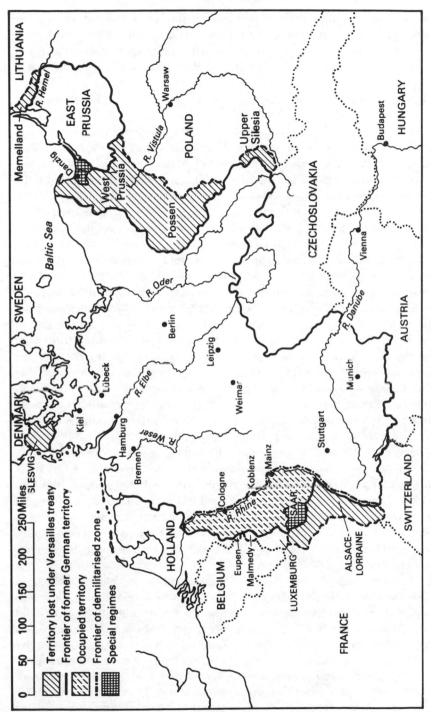

MAP 3 Germany, 1919.

more practically, being smaller in size than Berlin, it was easier to secure. The Majority Socialists emerged as the largest party, but, in order to secure an overall majority, an alliance was forged with the Catholic-based Christian People's Party and the German Democratic Party. The Weimar Republic was now born.

In Munich, the events in Berlin had been watched with interest, but Kurt Eisner was, from the start, concerned to make Bavaria as independent from the 'Prussianism' of Berlin as possible. At the end of November, in an effort to curry more favourable peace terms from the Allies, he published documents from 1914 purporting to show that Bavaria had had no responsibility for the outbreak of war. He also resented the concept of the National Assembly on the grounds that it would remove the power of the workers' and soldiers' councils. Faced with what he saw as Ebert's intransigence, Eisner now severed diplomatic relations with Berlin. Yet, his policies were by no means wholly accepted by Bavarians. The Majority Socialists in Bavaria followed the Ebert belief that power should be concentrated in an elected assembly, in this case the Bavarian *Landtag*. They got their way and elections were scheduled for 12 January. On the extreme left, Spartacist elements and revolutionary soldiers did not believe that Eisner was consolidating the revolution fast enough and, on the night of 7 December, attempted a putsch, which failed. The middle ground of Bavarian opinion was also against him, being unhappy about the concept of what they saw as a totally independent Bavaria, and also fearing that the church was coming under threat. It was thus inevitable that when the elections to the *Landtag* were held, Eisner and his Independent Socialists should find themselves humiliated. Eisner attempted to hold onto power, but on 21 February was forced to resign. As he left his office for the last time he was shot dead by a right wing extremist, Count Anton Arco-Valley.

The reaction to this was immediate. The Munich workers, convinced that a right wing counter-coup was under way, began to take revenge. A butcher's apprentice entered the *Landtag* and badly wounded the leading Majority Socialist, Erhard Auer. Members of the nobility were seized as hostages and the city went into mourning for Eisner's death. Munich was now in a state of anarchy, but there was little that Ebert, with his thinly stretched military forces, could do about it. The problem was further accentuated by another flurry of serious unrest.

In Bremen, Independent Socialists and Communists had combined in January to seize the municipal government and a Republic of Oldenburg was proclaimed. Noske organised his Freikorps to restore order, which they did here and in the other North Sea ports during early February. Then there was trouble in the Ruhr, whose vital steel and coal industry was now put under threat by strikes. Luckily for Noske, since he did not have sufficient troops to control the area, the miners and steelworkers were persuaded to return to work in exchange for a promise of no reprisals against them. Unrest followed in other cities and it became clear to the Communists that they now had another chance of effecting the desired revolution. Rather than direct confrontation in the military sense with Noske's *Freikorps*, they relied on the strike weapon in the belief that the *Freikorps* would not fire on unarmed workmen. On 4 March, a general strike was proclaimed throughout the country. Within hours, however, it became clear that the Communist Central Committee could not control its followers, many of whom armed themselves once more. Noske did not hesitate. Once again the *Freikorps* entered Berlin and, with great severity, crushed the uprising after ten days fighting. For the Communist Party, its organisation now in ribbons, it marked the end of hopes for an immediate revolution and, for the time being, it went underground. It would, however, have one last flourish in Bavaria.

It is difficult to gauge what effect these momentous events had had on *Vize-Wachtmeister* Sepp Dietrich. True, he had been the Chairman of *Abteilung* 13's short-lived *Soldatenrat*, but there is no evidence that on his return to Bavaria he became involved in any revolutionary activity. Rather, seeing himself now as a professional soldier with a good war record, he probably had hopes of being allowed to remain in the post-war Bavarian Army, but this was not to be. Yet, he probably viewed the anarchy in Munich with increasing distaste, perhaps echoing the words of an anonymous fellow Bavarian *Frontsoldat*:

'After the retreat [1918] I returned to Munich with my regiment in December 1918. The sad picture of Red rule made a most painful impression on us front-line fighters. We could not and would not believe that this issue of the war was what we had fought and striven for through four and a half years. We would not be reconciled to the apparent fact that all our struggles and sacrifices had been in vain.'[3]

Thus, with a career in the Army no longer possible, it was probably with these thoughts running through his mind that Dietrich set out for Munich just over a week after his discharge from the Bavarian Army. He arrived there on 4 April 1919, on the eve of Munich's greatest bout of turmoil.

On 6 April a group of men met in what had been a bedroom in the former Queen of Bavaria's palace in Munich and declared a Republic of Councils. They were led by Ernst Toller, an artistically-minded *avant-garde* poet and playwright, who had assumed the mantle of leadership of the Independents after Eisner's death. What had inspired them to do this was the successful and bloodless coup in Hungary on 21 March by Bela Kun, a Russian trained agitator, who immediately declared a Hungarian Socialist Republic. Toller and his followers declared that their intention was to ally themselves with Hungary and Austria in a revolutionary confederation. They gained immediate support from the workers' and soldiers' councils, so much so that Adolf Hoffmann and his Majority Socialist government immediately fled north to Bamberg and declared allegiance to Ebert in Berlin. Toller and his followers now stepped into the vacuum. The result was a government of pure anarchy and a complete farce, with attempts to introduce the concept of free money and even a declaration of war against Switzerland on the grounds that a request for a loan of locomotives had not been immediately granted. It is not surprising that, after six days, other forces stepped in.

It was, in fact, the Communists who now took over the reins of government. The three leading figures were Towia Alexrod, Max Levien and Eugen Leviné, all of whom were Russian born and had only arrived in Munich in the past few months. Undaunted by the fate that had befallen the Communist cause elsewhere in Germany, they had set to with a will to reorganise the Communists in Bavaria. In the midst of the gathering chaos created by Toller and his associates, they called a meeting of the Workers' and soldiers' councils at the *Hofbräuhaus* in Munich at which Leviné was elected Chairman of the new Central Council. He now declared a Bavarian Soviet Republic with the *Hofbräuhaus* as its new parliament building. The police force was disbanded and its place taken by Red Guards. Responsibility for these lay with Rudy Egelhofer, a former sailor and veteran of the Kiel Mutiny. Within two weeks he had raised a Bavarian Red Army of 20,000 men, largely by bribing would-be volunteers with vastly inflated pay, free food and alcohol and even free prostitutes. Weapons were obtained partly by plundering the barracks of the old Bavarian Army and, when that failed to produce enough, by ordering all privately owned weapons to be handed in on pain of death. This Red Army now began wholesale arrests of suspected counter-revolutionaries and seizures of hostages from among the bourgeoisie. The Central Council had called a general strike in order to throw up manpower to form the Red Army, but the money required to maintain it quickly crippled the Bavarian economy. Matters were not helped when Hoffmann organised a blockade of all foodstuffs into Bavaria.

The Majority Socialists, aware of the rapid raising of the Red Bavarian Army, were in something of a quandary. While they recognised the need to strike quickly in order to regain Munich, they had serious reservations over calling in Noske's *Freikorps*, who were predominantly Prussian, since this would probably be unacceptable even to moderate Bavarian public opinion. Their first effort, therefore, was with a scratch force of their own, which clashed with a superior Red Army force under Toller at Dachau, twenty-five miles north of Munich, on 20 April 1919. The result was the scattering of the Majority Socialist force, but Toller, who during the past two weeks had been arrested and freed twice, refused to carry out Egelhofer's order to butcher his prisoners and returned to Munich, only to be arrested and then released once more.

For Hoffmann this failure meant that he had no option but to rely on the *Freikorps* and soon they were on the march. Under the overall command of General von Ovens, they converged on Munich, crushing any Red Army resistance encountered on the way and, by 30 April, had reached the outskirts of the city. The final assault was launched, appropriately or not, on 1 May. By the early hours of the 3rd, it was all over. While the Reds had undoubtedly committed atrocities, including the murder of twenty of Munich's most prominent citizens in the Luitpold Gymnasium, in the belief that all were members of the right wing and anti-Jewish Thule Society, the *Freikorps* now set to with a vengeance to root out all elements of the revolutionary left. In the course of one week no less than one thousand people died at their hands. When, on 13 May, the *Freikorps* allowed Hoffmann's government to return from their short and self-imposed exile, it was to a subdued city. From now on there would be greater determination in Bavaria than anywhere else in Germany to ensure that never again would the Red Flag be allowed to fly.

It would seem that Dietrich played little or no part in these momentous events. Neither he himself, nor the Nazi propaganda machine, ever made any claims that he had an active part in the civil war and only one secondary source states that he did so,[4] as a member of *Wehrregiment* 1, a volunteer body of Civil Guards raised in Munich by the Majority Socialists. Yet his name does not appear on the nominal rolls of this unit.[5] A mystery therefore surrounds what he did do. He must have taken some part, since, if he had not wished to do so it is unlikely that he would have gone to Munich when he did. It is, of course, possible that he sided with the Reds and, finding himself on the wrong side, had to lie low and keep quiet about it for the remainder of his life since it would have hardly fitted in with his later image. The fact that he had been Chairman of a soldiers' council could support this, but otherwise there is no evidence one way or the other. It is also clear from his Munich registration papers[6] that he remained officially at the same address from his arrival in Munich until his marriage in February 1921.

The next concrete fact about Dietrich is that he joined the Bavarian Landpolizei. The date of his joining is open to dispute. According to the *Bayerisches Hauptstaatsarchiv* the date was 1 October 1919 and this was based on an application he made in 1963 to the *Bayerisches Kriegsarchiv* for a certificate of military service to support a claim for an annuity insurance.[7] The most accurate of the published *curriculum vitae* of Dietrich states, however, that he joined on 24 February 1920[8] and this seems to tie up with the information given in his Munich registration forms. It may be, though, that the earlier date refers to when he joined for training and that it was almost five months before his position as a *Wachmeister* commanding the reconnaissance platoon of *Gruppe* 1 in Oberschliessheim, a northern suburb of Munich, was confirmed.

The situation can be slightly clarified by explaining the position and organisation of the police in Bavaria at this time. Almost immediately after the crushing of the Red Revolution in May 1919, Bavaria was brought under the emerging *Reichswehr* and became *Wehrkreis* (War District) VII under General Franz Ritter von Epp, whose *Freikorps*, containing a number of Bavarians, had taken a leading part in the events of late April-early May 1919. Those recruited into the *Reichswehr* from Bavaria were almost all former members of the old Bavarian Army, but were still looked on with suspicion in Bavarian governmental and public circles as being servants of the central government in Berlin. What Bavaria could, however, call her own was her police who were under direct control of the Bavarian Government through the Ministry of the Interior. There were three types of police. The municipal police, as their name implies, were responsible for the town and cities, while the gendarmerie looked after the rural areas. Most important, though, was the *Landespolizei*, familiarly known as the 'Green Police' from the colour of their uniform. This was a paramilitary force organised along the lines of an infantry division; it even had its own armoured cars and three air squadrons, but no artillery. Indeed, as far as the Bavarian Government was concerned, it was a means of circumventing the rigid 100,000 man army restriction imposed by the Treaty of Versailles in June 1919 and was seen as the basis of a future Bavarian Army.

No detail exists on Dietrich's life as a policeman,[9] but it can be assumed that it was his tank experience which made him a natural selection for the reconnaissance role, especially since it involved work with armoured cars. One interesting point is that he claimed, to one of his American interrogators,[10] that on discharge from the Bavarian Army, he was commissioned as a Lieutenant in the Reserve. In 1923 he was promoted Oberleutnant, and the following year to Captain before being discharged. If this was the case, it was no more than a 'paper' commission and, especially bearing in mind the terms of Versailles, he would not have been assigned to any unit or expected to undertake any training under Reichswehr auspices. It was merely a means of ensuring that experienced personnel could be quickly called up in the event of a national emergency.

During this period, though, Sepp met and courted a Munich girl, Barbara, known as 'Betti', Seidl, whom he married on 17 February 1921. She was four years younger than him and they took up residence in the same apartment block in which he had been living as a bachelor.

For Weimar Germany the year 1919 was dominated by Versailles. In the aftermath of the troubles of late 1918 and early 1919, a new constitution had been worked out. From henceforth Germany would have a President, with Ebert being elected, and a government headed by a Chancellor, with Philipp Scheidemann being the first to occupy this post. Legislative power was vested in the *Reichstag*, with members being elected to it every four years. The franchise was given to all males and females over the age of twenty and proportional representation operated. The traditionally semi-autonomous states of Prussia and Bavaria kept their own parliaments and retained control over education, police and the church, but the supremacy of the central government over the states or *Länder* was made very clear. Nevertheless, the *Länder* did have some say in central government through the *Reichsrat*, a second chamber to the *Reichstag*, although its powers were very limited.

Germans of all political persuasions believed in the spring of 1919 that the Allies would be lenient, especially since the Hohenzollerns had been expelled and democratic government set up. When the peace terms were received on 7 May there was horror at their harshness, especially in the context of the territory that Germany was being asked to surrender. For a time, opinion was that the terms should be rejected, but this would mean a state of war once more and Groener warned that the armed forces would not be able to withstand an Allied invasion. Eventually, under pressure from the Allies and after a new government of Socialists and Centrists under Gustav Bauer had been formed, the treaty was signed. While the centre and leftist parties accepted the treaty with the best grace that they could, the right, led by the Nationalists, could not accept Germany's military defeat. Testifying in November 1919 before a government commission set up to enquire into the reasons for Germany's defeat, von Hindenburg declared that: 'An English general has said with justice: the German army was stabbed in the back. No blame is to be attached to the sound core of the army. Its performances call like that of the officer corps for an equal admiration. It is perfectly plain on whom the blame lies.'[11] Thus the 'stab in the back' idea was created and the Right lost no time in using this to villify their political rivals whenever possible.

The first positive threat to the Government over Versailles did not come, however, until the spring of 1920. Angered by the progressive reduction of the *Reichswehr* to the agreed 100,000 man ceiling, a group of officers and *Freikorps* men determined to overthrow the central government and hold fresh elections. They were led by no less than the military commander in Berlin, von Lüttwitz, who had taken a leading part in the crushing of the revolutions in Berlin, and Wolfgang Kapp, a right wing extremist. Matters came to a head when the Inter-Allied Military Control Commission demanded the disbandment of two Baltic *Freikorps*, one of which was the now legendary Ehrhardt Brigade. Von Lüttwitz refused to disband the latter and, although his arrest had been ordered, led it and his own men into Berlin on 13 March. They were greeted by a large crowd which included no lesser a personage than Ludendorff. While General Reinhardt, commanding the *Reichswehr*, was prepared to use force, his superior, General Hans von Seekt, newly appointed as Head of the *Truppenamt* (Troop Office – cover name for the old Ministry of War), refused to countenance the idea of members of the *Reichswehr* firing on one another. Faced with this, Ebert and the government retired to Dresden. Kapp now attempted to assume the reins of government, but the carpet was swept from under him when a general strike was declared and, after four days, both he and von Lüttwitz were forced to flee from Berlin. In the Ruhr, the Communists, in an effort to capitalise on the Ruhr *putsch*, led an uprising, but this was quickly put down by the *Reichswehr* and the *Freikorps*, as were similar disturbances in Saxony and Thuringia. The Republic could breathe again.

Nevertheless, it was clear that the *Freikorps* had to be disbanded and the Central Government succeeded at least in driving them underground during the course of 1920. Others were absorbed by the *Reichswehr*. In May 1921, however, the *Freikorps* took to the field once more.

Under the terms of Versailles, the rich industrial region of Upper Silesia was earmarked for Poland, in response to Polish demands, on the grounds that, although it had not belonged to her for 700 years, it was ninety per cent Polish in terms of the population. The German government lodged strong objections to this, and the Allies agreed that a plebiscite should be held. This revealed that sixty per cent of the population wanted to remain in Germany. The results were published on 20 March 1921 and were, understandably, a bitter disappointment to the Poles and the French, who had consistently supported the demands of Poland. In order to forestall restoration of the region to Germany, Polish irregulars under Wojciech Korfanty crossed the frontier with Silesia on 3 May 1921, with the intention of seizing the territory and presenting the Supreme Council in Paris with a *fait accompli*. The German government protested to the Allies and proposed that the *Reichswehr* be sent in to restore order. This, thanks to the French, was turned down, but British Prime Minister Lloyd George called the Polish action 'a complete defiance of the Treaty of Versailles' and stated that 'either the Allies ought to insist upon the Treaty being respected, or they ought to allow the Germans to do it'.[12] Since they had been forbidden to use the *Reichswehr*, this gave the German Government an excuse to give support to the *Freikorps* who were already making their way to the province.

Sepp Dietrich always asserted that he was a member of the Freikorps Oberland, which he joined in 1920, and took part in the fighting in Upper Silesia.[13] The Oberland was formed by Rudolf von Sebottendorf, leader of the Thule Society in Bavaria, on 19 April 1919, against the background of the Red revolution in Munich and the desire of the Bavarian Government, in temporary exile at Bamburg, to raise an indigenous force to act as a balance to the external *Freikorps* coming to its assistance. A distinguished Bavarian Army officer, Major Ritter von Beckh, was selected as the military commander. By the time that the advance on Munich was under way at the end of April, the Oberland could boast of a strength of 600 men. It took only a minor part in the pacification of Munich, but by the end of May it had grown to 1150 men. It was now subordinated and then absorbed by one of the Bavarian brigades in the new Reichswehr, *Schützenbrigade* 21 and, on 27 July 1919, became the 3rd Battalion of *Schützenregiment* 2. This arrangement lasted, however, for less than a month. On 19 August, the disbandment of the 3rd Battalion and the handing in of all its weapons was ordered – a reflection of Allied insistence on rigid adherence to the 100000 man Reichswehr ceiling. Nevertheless, Noske recognised that there was a continuing requirement for quickly available trained manpower in the event of further unrest in the country. As a reflection of this, it was decreed that *Schützenbrigade* 21 should form a seven-battalion temporary volunteer corps, and the Oberland provided one company for this force. The volunteers took part, in a minor capacity, in putting down the Communist uprising in the Ruhr after the Kapp *putsch*, but on their return were disbanded. The need to circumvent the rigid Versailles restrictions still remained, however.

As early as November 1918, a concept of territorial defence, *Einwohnerwehren* or 'resident defences' had been established on a non-political basis as the Civil

Guard in Bavaria. The idea was that local residents should voluntarily band together to defend their local neighbourhood in time of war. In Spring 1920, a certain Georg Escherich, a Bavarian forester, proposed that all these defence associations be brought together under one umbrella, but that it should operate as a club called *Organisation Escherich* and hence be independent of the state and thus not vulnerable to the provisions of Versailles. This was approved by the Bavarian Government in May, with equipment and training unofficially provided by the Reichswehr. This created an ideal opportunity to keep the Oberland in being and was the situation when the crisis in Upper Silesia erupted a year later.

The Silesian Germans had hastily formed self-protection units, *Selbstschutz Oberschleisen,* but it was clear that these were not strong enough to do more than temporarily hold the Poles. A call thus went out for help. Among those to receive it was the *Organisation Escherich,* or 'Orgesch' as it was more commonly known. Major Horadam, the military commander of the Oberland, immediately went to Upper Silesia to see for himself, arriving there on 7 May. Horadam was singularly unimpressed by the headquarters of the *Selbstschutz Oberschleisen,* which seemed vast and plush but lacked any organisation or direction. He then went and saw General von Hülsen, who commanded the southern sector, and the latter asked him to bring the Oberland to Silesia immediately. On his return to Munich, the Orgesch agreed to the request. Indeed, it seems they did so readily since, as far as the other more conservative elements of the Orgesch were concerned, the Oberland had proved a rather bumptious bedfellow.

Officially the Bavarian Government could not give any support for the venture and hence Horadam had to organise the move himself. Members were called to his house and given money for the journey. As he later recalled:

> 'Collective travel was impossible because the government and authorities were not allowed to know anything officially . . . It proved to be very difficult to have to take with us rifles and machine guns to Upper Silesia; these were just not available there. It could not of course be done openly, but everybody had to take a rifle or part of a machine gun hidden in his personal baggage. . . A battery of field guns were stored in Freising on the River Jsar. They were hidden underneath the straw of four big straw wagons and thus brought to Upper Silesia, where they arrived safely. Communist workers' councils caused us a lot of difficulties at the train stations, especially in Dresden. Numerous transports were stopped by them and sent back to Hof. Matters only slightly improved after a workers' representative, who wanted to search the wagons for arms, was thrown out of the moving train by our people and fell under the wheels.'[14]

Ernst von Salomon, a veteran *Freikorpskämpfer,* also remembers that during his journey from the Saar to Silesia:

> 'At Leipzig some young fellows got in, wearing feathers in their caps, talking in the Bavarian dialect and bringing curious luggage: cart wheels, heavy rollers tied up in cloth and odd pieces of iron packed in boxes. I wandered past them, touched some of the rollers and murmured: 'Guns?' The man standing nearest to me grinned.'[15]

The first members of the Oberland arrived, wearing traditional Bavarian clothes since they were not allowed uniforms, on 11 May, and this represented the 1st Battalion. Meanwhile, back in Bavaria, two further battalions had been

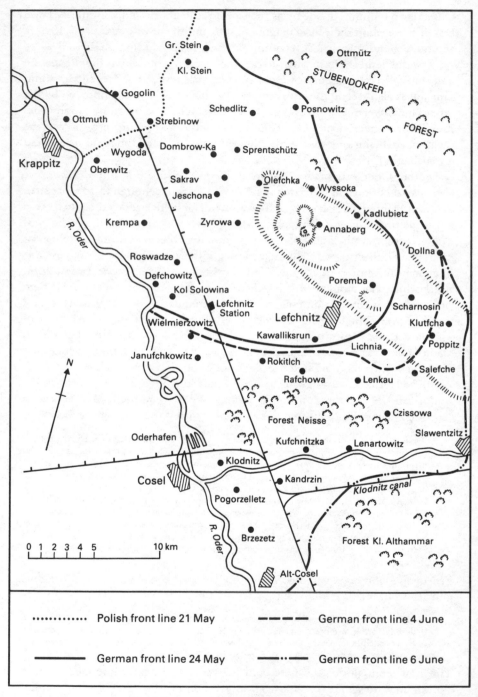

MAP 4 Upper Silesia 1921 – Annaberg and after.

raised from volunteers, although weapons for them were sparse, with only two out of three platoons in each company having rifles and no one having more than ten rounds of ammunition.

How did Sepp Dietrich fit into all this? According to Krätschmer, who is the only source to give any precise details, Sepp was a member of the 1st Battalion, which was also known as the *Sturmflug Teja*, and was in the 2nd Company. He would have therefore been an early arrival in Silesia. He also took leave from the Landespolizei in order to go and paid his own way to get there.[16] Hans Weber, who was in the 1st Company of the *Teja* and who says that he knew Sepp Dietrich from 1919 onwards, recalls Dietrich arriving in Upper Silesia with other Oberlanders, all dressed in 'ruffians' clothes'. He states that there were two other former tankmen in the 1st Battalion of the Oberland at the time and that Dietrich 'showed enormous military knowledge and both bravery and initiative in the face of the enemy'.[17]

The three battalions of the Oberland were commanded respectively by Captain Oestreicher, Captain Ritter von Finsterlein and Captain Sie-bringhan. They were placed under General von Hülsen's Group South. Meanwhile, the Poles, who had now been reinforced by a regular Polish brigade and were also being helped by French advisers, were being held on the line Krappitz-Gross Strelik-Kreuzburg. There was, however, a clash of opinion between the overall commander General Hoeffer and von Hülsen. Indeed, when Horadam, his force now fully arrived, went up to ask whether he could attack, explaining that his men were thirsting for a fight and could not be held back, von Hülsen explained that Hoefer had made an agreement with the senior French representative with the Poles that he would not make any counter-attacks until the International Commission had ruled on the situation. Nevertheless, Horadam seems to have successfully persuaded von Hülsen that an attack should be mounted and the objective was agreed to be the Annaberg, on which stood the ancient convent of St Anna and which commanded the hills on the right bank of the River Oder. During 19 and 20 May the Oberland were transported to Krappitz. En route they stopped a car carrying a man with a lot of money on him, which they took and used to buy off some Polish informers. During the night 20/21 May, the attackers successfully crossed the Oder. At 0230 hours, the attack began, with the Oberland on the left and a force of other *Freikorps* battalions on the right.

By 0930 hours, having successfully repulsed a Polish counter-attack, inflicting many casualties, the Oberland had reached and secured its first objective at a cost of eight killed and fifty wounded. Now came the assault on Annaberg itself. This was preceded by a skirmish between Horadam and his staff and about thirty Poles, whom they drove off a vantage point from which Horadam wanted to spy out the country around Annaberg. A battery of guns previously captured from the Poles was deployed here and, supported by their fire, Horadam now led the 1st Battalion through the woods in front of Annaberg. The 2nd Battalion managed to get round to the rear of the village and, by just after midday, Annaberg was surrounded. Both battalions now stormed it and within twenty minutes it was all over. The surprised Poles fled, leaving one hundred prisoners. The cost to the Oberland had been two killed and twenty wounded.

The repercussions were immediate. In view of the fact that the monastery was a popular place of pilgrimage, the Poles felt its loss deeply and wasted no time in protesting to the French Military mission. As a result, on 21 May, the Allied Control Commission warned the Weimar Government that if any further advances were made, French troops would be withdrawn from Upper Silesia, thereby leaving the ethnic Germans there at the mercy of the Poles. The central command of the *Selbstschutz Oberschleisen*, embarrassed by the Oberland's success, began to hold up supplies to it. Ebert issued an edict stating that those forming military units without official authority would be fined 100,000 Marks or imprisoned and the Prussian Government closed its border with Silesia. On 24 May, reflecting government opinion, the *Berliner Tageblatt* stated that 'the disbandment of the Upper Silesian gangs is in the interest of the Fatherland and an urgent task of the Reichs-Landes authorities'. The day before, however, the Poles had made a strong attack just south of Annaberg but were repulsed, thanks to an Oberland counter-attack in the right flank. For the first time, the Poles fought at close quarters and the Oberland suffered heavy casualties. On the night of 30/31st, having brought in further reinforcements, the Poles subjected the Annaberg area to intense mortar fire. Convinced that this was in preparation for another attack, the Oberland decided to pre-empt it and again drove the Poles back. The only prisoners they captured were twelve French officers and men, whom they handed over to British Control Commission representatives. Horadam noted that the British, who took a dim view of the French support for the Poles, were 'exceptionally pleased'. [18] A further clash with the French on 7 June led to five French soldiers being killed and the Weimar Government, which was in an impossible position, had to make an official apology to the Control Commission.

Throughout June, the Oberland continued to mount attacks against the Poles in order to liberate Ratisbon. Eventually, at the beginning of July, the British, through their French opposite numbers, managed to persuade the Poles to pull back from Upper Silesia and, on 5 July, General Hoefer ordered the *Selbstschutz Oberschleisen* to be disbanded. The Inter-Allied Military Control Commission had ordered all weapons to be handed over to them, but the Freikorps objected to handing them over to the French. Many were therefore buried. Later, some of those belonging to the Oberland were smuggled back to Bavaria. While the majority of Oberlanders returned home, others stayed in Upper Silesia masquerading as forest and agricultural labourers.

All those who fought with the Self-Protection Forces in Silesia were awarded the Silesian Eagle. This unofficial award had been instituted by General von Freideburg, commander VI Army Corps, in June 1919 as a means of rewarding those who were prepared to defend German interests in Upper Silesia.

Dietrich was awarded both 1st and 2nd Classes of the order and, since the laid down qualifications were three months' service for the 2nd Class and six months for the 1st Class, one can only assume that he remained in Upper Silesia under cover until at least mid-October 1921. How he could have reconciled this extended leave of absence with his police duties is not clear.

Those who fought in Silesia genuinely felt that the Weimar Government had betrayed them and could not reconcile this with the fact that they had been defending Germans. Unfortunately, they did not appreciate that, in the face of Versailles, Ebert was in a straitjacket. There was also a suspicion that the Oberland, especially, had a wider motive that mere defence of ethnic Germans in the region. The editor of the *Hamburger 8 Uhr-Abendblatt* visited Upper Silesia in mid-July and stayed at the headquarters of the Oberland. Listening to conversations among its members led him to believe that they were intending to restore the Hohenzollerns, that Silesia was merely a start and that they planned to overthrow the Weimar Government. He reported this to the Ministry of the Interior and an inquiry was initiated, but no substance was found to support this allegation. Indeed, the Oberland themselves denied that they had monarchist sympathies.[19] Nevertheless, it reinforced the 'stab in the back' belief among the *Freikorps* members. As one who took part in the assault on Annaberg wrote later:

> 'In the hearts of *Freikorps* fighters and the stormers of Annaberg, the realization became increasingly clear that any great German War of Liberation presupposed the overthrow of western parliamentarianism and the whole Liberal-Marxist system.'[20]

It is thus hardly surprising that the majority of *Freikorpskämpfer* would eventually fall in behind Hitler. He, in his turn, was to recognise the meaning of Annaberg when, on the twelfth anniversary of its capture, a celebration was held at the convent of St Anna and SA *Obergruppenführer* Edmund Heines, another Annaberg veteran, but who a year later was to be a victim of the Night of the Long Knives, declared: 'Your soul, SA men is the same as that of the men who twelve years ago. . . stormed the Annaberg.'[21] At the same time, the Silesian Eagle became an official decoration, together with the Baltic Cross, awarded to those *Freikorps* members who took part in the Baltic campaign of 1919-20, and the Roland of Bremen or 'Iron Bremen' for those who put down the Red insurrection there in February 1919.

The Ebert decree against the paramilitaries also applied to those in Bavaria. The Minister President, Gustav von Kahr, had successfully resisted demands from Berlin to disband the *Wehrverbande* up until this time but, in June 1921, he had to give in and the Orgesch went underground. The returning Oberlanders were forced to do the same, although the Bavarian paramilitaries were not formally dissolved by the Bavarian Government until late November 1921. The previous month, however, the *Bund Oberland* had been founded in place of the *Freikorps*. This was a civilian political association in the main and, in order to be allowed to operate, the military element faded into the background. The other *Wehrverbande* generally combined under a rival organisation the *Bund Bayern und Reich*. The main difference between the two was that while the latter organisation thought merely in terms of putting the clock back to the Bavaria of pre-1914, and this included the restoration of the Bavarian monarchy, the *Bund Oberland* was much more outward looking. Their three main objectives were the rescinding of the Treaty of Versailles, which they viewed as the root of Germany's current miseries, the preservation and unity of the German Reich as a whole and the rejection of the class struggle in the belief that national reconstruction could only effectively come about if all classes combined together. Yet, evolving this platform was not achieved without much internal dissension and many of the original leading figures, including Horadam, were expelled in the process. While the *Bund Bayern und Reich* supported von Kahr, the *Bund Oberland* found themselves moving closer and closer to Hitler and his young *Nationalsocialistiche Deutsche Arbeiterpartei* (National Socialist German Workers' Party or NSDAP).

Sepp Dietrich stated after the war that the first time that he came across Hitler was in 1921, when the latter was giving a 'patriotic lecture to the troops', presumably members of *Schützenbrigade* 21, which made up the Reichswehr garrison of Münich. [22] In the summer of 1921, Hitler had succeeded in gaining the undisputed leadership of the NSDAP and now proceeded to imprint it with his own particular brand of politics. Viewing the other right wing parties as being too theoretical and narrow in their approach, he laid down that the NSDAP should be 'a nationalist movement with a firm social base, a hold over the broad masses, wielded together in an iron-hard organisation, filled with blind obedience and inspired by a brutal will, a party of struggle and action'. [23] Supported by the efficiency of his stewards, the *Sturmabteilung* (SA), his close contacts with his former commander, Ritter von Epp, now commanding the Reichswehr in Bavaria, and his ADC, Ernst Roehm, together with his own powers as an orator, Hitler gradually gained adherents. Yet, Dietrich, even if he did hear Hitler speak in 1921, which is more than likely, was not yet ready to join him. In any event, he would have been deterred by the attitude of the Landespolizei commander, Colonel Ritter von Seisser. While von Seisser generally maintained good relationships with the *Wehrverbände*, and indeed was authorised by the Bavarian Government to give them military training, which would have enabled Dietrich to officially maintain his links with the Oberland, he was suspicious of Hitler and believed that he had to be kept in check. Thus, members of the Landespolizei would not have been encouraged to side with the NSDAP. In any event, while Dietrich may well have shared many of Hitler's beliefs, he would not easily have deserted his comrades in the Oberland.

Germany at this time was still in a very unsettled state, not as a result of the Leftist agitation of 1918-19, but from the rift between the moderates who, in spite of Versailles, supported the democratic values of Weimar and those who had become mesmerised by 'the stab in the back'. With the paramilitaries now driven underground, sinister organisations arose who became responsible for a large number of successful and attempted political assassinations of leading Weimar figures. Most notorious of these groups was the so-called Organisation Control, or 'C', which had been founded by Hermann Ehrhardt of Ehrhardt Brigade fame after the Kapp *Putsch*. It was fiercely anti-semitic, but also dedicated to fermenting unrest in order to overthrow the Weimar Government, and soon began a programme of assassinations. The first victim was Matthias Erzberger who had signed the Treaty of Versailles and the campaign culminated in the death of Walter Rathenau, the Weimar foreign minister, on 24 June 1922. Majority Socialists, Independents and Communists combined together to demonstrate vociferously against the activities of the Right and a general strike was called for the day of Rathenau's funeral. To this the government was forced to react and enacted the Law for the Protection of the Republic which was directed towards the state governments, ordering them to suppress anti-Weimar groups and to prosecute those engaged in such activity. Led by Bavaria, whose government objected to being dictated to in this way and which believed that it needed the support of the paramilitaries, there were Right wing demonstrations throughout Germany, and often clashes with the Left.

This, of course, was exactly the type of atmosphere which Hitler wanted. Matters elsewhere also played into his hands. In Italy Mussolini and his Fascists attained power at the end of October 1922, which served to inspire him. Germany, too, was suffering from the financial reparations imposed by the Allies. When the Reparations Commission finally produced its report in April 1921, the demand was for Germany to pay £6,600 million in annual instalments of £100 million, together with payments amounting to a quarter of all German exports. Given a six day ultimatum to accept this, the Weimar government resigned. It was replaced by a centrist coalition led by Joseph Wirth, with Rathenau as his foreign minister. They believed that only by attempting to pay could Germany demonstrate how impossible the terms were, but the Right merely saw this as another 'stab in the back' and it was this which led to Rathenau's assassination. The only way in which the reparations could be paid was by raising foreign loans and this weakened the Mark. Germany inevitably fell behind with payments as inflation rose, but France under Pioncaré was determined to extract the last pfennig. Eventually, in January 1923, French and Belgian troops moved in and seized the Ruhr. This produced a wave of anti-French feeling in Germany and many *Freikorps*, including the Oberland, were covertly reactivated and sent men to the region to carry out a campaign of sabotage. Dietrich, however, was not involved in this. Only Hitler stood out against the popular feeling, declaring that the Weimar Republic must first be brought down before dealing with France. Now that Germany's prime industrial area had been confiscated, inflation rocketted to new heights. The government tried to resist by refusing to make further reparation payments, but it was to no avail and, in August 1923 it fell, to be replaced by a fresh administration under Gustav Stresemann, which received support from all parties in the Reichstag, apart from the Nationalists and Communists.

Stresemann realised that Germany had reached economic breaking point and could not stand up to the Allies. He therefore called off the campaign of passive resistance and announced that he was willing to resume reparation payments. In Bavaria, especially, there was violent reaction to this. The Knilling government declared a state of emergency and appointed former Minister President Ritter von Kahr as State Commissioner with dictatorial powers. Von Kahr was, of course, closely connected with the nationalist groups in Bavaria and these included Hitler and his NSDAP.

On 2 September, some four weeks before the state of emergency had been declared, Hitler had formed the *Deutscher Kampfbund* (German Fighting Union). This was an alliance of the Bund Oberland, Hitler's SA and the *Reichsflagge*, a more conservative *verband* which looked to the re-establishment of the German Empire, but was also anti-semitic. The occasion of the founding of the *Deutscher Kampfbund* was a rally to mark the anniversary of the Prussian defeat of the French at Sedan in 1870. Its members pledged themselves to the overthrow of the Weimar Republic and the tearing up of the peace treaty.

Hitler also had the advantage of continuing to enjoy close links with the *Reichswehr* in Bavaria, now under General Otto von Lossow. When the latter was ordered by Berlin to suppress the NSDAP newspaper *Voelkischer Beobachter* (it had been partially founded with *Reichswehr* funds, thanks to Ritter von Epp), because of its attacks on the Republic, von Lossow refused. On 24 October von Seekt sacked him, but von Kahr refused to recognise this and made all Reichswehr officers and men in *Wahrkreis* VII take an oath of allegiance to the Bavarian Government. At the same time, there had been Communist disturbances elsewhere in Germany and Stresemann had immediately sent the *Reichswehr* in and put them down. This impressed moderate Bavarian opinion. Von Seekt now warned that any revolt in Bavaria would be put down by force. This was sufficient to convince von Kahr, von Lossow and the *Landespolizei* commander, von Seisser, that they must proceed with caution. Thus, when Hitler agitated for a march on Berlin, he was told that any decisions rested with this triumvirate. Fearful that they aimed merely to separate Bavaria from the rest of Germany, Hitler now decided on unilateral action.

The initial plan was to mount the coup on 4 November 1923, celebrated as *Totengedenktag* (The Day of Remembrance for the Dead) throughout Germany. In Munich the Crown Prince Rupprecht of Bavaria, von Kahr, von Lossow and von Seisser would be taking the salute at a *Reichswehr* parade, and the intention was to pre-empt it by sealing off the street in which the saluting base was situated. Hitler would then mount the dais, declare a revolution and make the dignitaries join it. This plot was abandoned, however, when a reconnaissance showed that the *Landespolizei* were out in too much strength. Hitler now decreed that it should take place on the 11th, the anniversary of the armistice, but then he heard that von Kahr was to address a meeting at the

Bürgerbräukeller, a large beer hall in the south-eastern outskirts of Munich, on the evening of 8 November. Convinced that von Kahr was about to proclaim an independent Bavaria and restore the monarchy, Hitler felt forced to act.

Dietrich is supposed to have taken part in the Beer Hall *Putsch* as a member of the Oberland. Certainly, his SS personal file reflects this and he wore the Nazi Blood order, which was struck at Hitler's command in 1933 to reward all those who had taken part. The Nazi propaganda machine also made much of the fact that he had been in the 'front ranks'.[24] Yet, as with his service as a whole with the Oberland, there is no first-hand documentary evidence to confirm this.[25] In any event, whether he took part or not, the Oberland fielded some 800 men in two battalions. On 7 November Dr Friedrich Weber, the leader of the Bund Oberland, called its military commanders together at a *Gasthaus* and handed them orders in sealed envelopes which were to be opened at 2030 hours on the following evening. The orders simply read:

> 'Just now the national dictatorship of Kahr, Hitler, Ludendorff and Lossow has been proclaimed in Munich. You have to come to Munich as soon as possible with all available men and report to OberstLt Kriebel.'
>
> Signed Dr Weber[26]

Knowing that von Lossow and von Seisser would also be present at von Kahr's meeting, Hitler planned to literally hijack it and, using Ludendorff, who was sympathetic to his cause, to persuade them, if necessary at gun point, to fall in behind him.

The events in Munich of 8/9 November 1923 have been described many times[27] and it is not necessary to go into them in any detail. Suffice to say that Hitler did enter the *Bürgerbräukeller* and force von Kahr, von Lossow and von Seisser to support him, but then departed, foolishly leaving the three unguarded. They quickly changed their minds and made their escape. Consequently, when Hitler made what should have been his triumphant march to the *Felderrnhalle* next morning, he found the Landespolizei in his path. Firing took place and fourteen of Hitler's followers were killed. That the *putsch* had been too hastily and badly organised can be illustrated by the experience of the Oberland. The 1st Battalion, under Captain von Müller, had a rendez-vous in front of the barracks of the 1st Battalion of Infantry Regiment 19, where they carried out their normal military training. They demanded arms and ammunition, but these were refused. Even when von Müller announced the setting up of the Hitler-von Ludendorff dictatorship, it was to no avail. The Oberlanders and some SA men, who had also arrived, were detained within the barracks throughout the 9th before being released. It was much the same story with other detachments who attempted to occupy the barracks of Engineer Regiment 7, the police praesidium, main railway station and the telegraph office. The 2nd Battalion, under Captain Oestreicher, went first to the monastery of St Anna to collect a cache of arms and then took them to the *Bürgerbräukeller*. Here they found a festive atmosphere with bands playing *Oberland* songs to greet them. One company remained there while the remainder went to Munich's most famous beer hall, the *Hofbräuhauskeller*, where they waited for orders which never arrived. The company in the *Bürgerbräukeller* remained there until the afternoon, when they moved out, but the route away from the city was blocked by *Reichswehr* troops. They turned back towards the city centre and went into a *Gastatte* where they had a meal. They then surrendered peacefully to a *Reichswehr* NCO and were allowed to go home.

In the aftermath, von Kahr and von Lossow came to terms with Berlin and von Lossow retired from the *Reichswehr*. The NSDAP, *Oberland*, and *Reichsflagge* were immediately proscribed by von Kahr as part of his deal with Berlin, and Hitler, Ludendorff and eight others stood trial at the end of February 1924. Hitler was sentenced to five years' imprisonment, subsequently reduced to nine months, which he spent in the fortress of Landsberg above the River Lech (a place subsequently to become well known to Sepp Dietrich) writing *Mein Kampf*. If Dietrich himself did take part in the *putsch*, and only a very few officers and men of the Landespolizei did clearly support it, it is likely that, like the others, he would have resigned or been dismissed in the days following it. Certainly, as a platoon commander, his absence from duty on 9 November would have been noticed. His SS personal file and a statement that he made to his American interrogators in 1945[28] indicate that he did leave the police at this time. But other sources contradict this, stating that he remained a policeman until 1927.[29] Like so much of this period of Dietrich's life, it is difficult to establish the facts one way or the other.

CHAPTER 3

Hitler's Bodyguard
1927-33

When Sepp Dietrich left the Landespolizei, he remained in Munich and obtained a job as a clerk with the Austria Tobacco Company. This did not last long and he went to work for the Customs Service. He was then employed in the filling station, the *Tankstelle-Blau-Bock* (Blue Buck Filling Station), as the garage manager by a well known local Nazi, Christian Weber, an early Hitler follower and former horse dealer and night club bouncer. It was through Weber that Dietrich eventually joined the NSDAP on 1 May 1928. (Party No 89015, which later entitled him, as one of the first 100000 members, to the Gold Party Badge.) Five days later, he became a member of the SS (No 1177) and, just short of his 36th birthday, he could finally be said to have embarked on a full career.

With the banning of the NSDAP in November 1923, the Right wing elements in Bavaria combined together in early 1924 to form the *Völkischer Block*. In the April 1924 state elections this grouping did comparatively well, finishing third behind the Bavarian People's Party and Social Democrats with a 17 per cent share of the vote. Much of its success was attributed to the 'martyrdom' of Hitler at his trial after the Beer Hall putsch. The Reichstag elections held the following month also echoed this trend, but to a lesser extent. Although the *Völkischer Block* was unable to gain representation in the new Bavarian government led by Dr Heinrich Held, its success was sufficient to alarm the latter enough to cause him to consider seriously how the Right in Bavaria could be contained in the future. Nevertheless, within the *Block* itself, splits soon developed. In essence, it was a question of whether or not the *Block* should enter candidates for parliamentary elections since this was tantamount to recognising a system which the radical elements had vowed themselves to change. Those who believed that elections should be boycotted were members of the *Grossdeutsche Volksgemeinschaft* (Greater German People's Community) created by Julius Streicher and Herman Esser from former members of the NSDAP after it had been dissolved, and by autumn 1924, the GVG had broken away from the *Block*. It refused to participate in the Reichstag elections of December 1924. As a result of this, and the lack of issues to exploit – the Dawes Plan had put reparations payments on a sound and sensible footing and brought about the French evacuation from the Ruhr – the Rightist vote fell dramatically.

On 20 December 1924, Hitler was released on probation from Landsberg and, a month later, the Bavarian government removed the ban on the NSDAP. It was formally relaunched at a rally held at the *Bürgerbräukeller* in Munich on 27 February 1925. Hitler made a two hour speech during which he stressed the importance of discipline within the party, was contemptuous of parliament and laid down that 'we will in future conduct our fight against person and object, namely against the Jew as person and Marxism as object'.[1] Although somewhat moderate in tone compared to some of his 1923 speeches, it was enough to worry the Bavarian government and they imposed on Hitler a ban on speaking in public. This meant a severe brake on the expansion of the NSDAP during the next two years, since Hitler had a recognised ability to attract and sway audiences. As it was, shortage of funds and lack of popular appeal meant that the Party was little more than a fringe grouping on the Right. Indeed, by early 1927, the Bavarian government considered that the Nazis offered no serious threat for the future and rescinded the ban. When Hitler did begin to make speeches in public once more, he was careful not to say anything that might lay him open to further government action. Furthermore, he now decided that the NSDAP would contest elections on the grounds that: 'we want Parliament in order to supply ourselves, in the arsenal of democracy, with its own weapons. We become members of the Reichstag in order to paralyse the Weimar sentiment with its own help.'[2] The fact that deputies to the Reichstag were paid a salary and had free rail passes was also attractive to a party which was desperately short of money.

It was in the Reichstag elections of May 1928 that the NSDAP had its first opportunity. Hitler himself could not stand since he was still technically an Austrian citizen. He was concerned that support for him in Bavaria might be weakened by the fact that Gustav Stresemann, the Weimar government foreign minister, was standing in Bavaria in order to strengthen the position of his German People's Party (DVP). Hitler therefore persuaded Ritter von Epp, that hero, in Right wing eyes, of the Bavarian Civil War of 1919 and also holder of Germany's highest decoration the *Pour La Mérite*, not only to join the NSDAP but also to stand against Stresemann in the electoral district of Upper Bavaria-Swabia. Since von Epp joined shortly before Sepp Dietrich, it is very likely that it was this and the demise of the *Bund Oberland* that finally persuaded Sepp to commit himself to the Nazi cause. As it was, although Ritter von Epp was elected, the NSDAP performance was disappointing in that it only secured twelve out of the 491 seats available in the Reichstag.

Dietrich himself could never be called a political animal *per se* and while he obviously did his bit during the election campaign, he was much more concerned about the specific organisation which he had joined, the SS or *Schutzstafflen* (Protection Squads). The circumstances of its founding were later explained by Hitler as follows:

'Being convinced that there are always circumstances in which élite troops are called for, I created in 1922-3 the 'Adolf Hitler Shock Troops' They were made up of men who were

ready for revolution and knew that some day things would come to hard knocks. When I
came out of Landsberg everything was broken up and scattered in sometimes rival bands. I
told myself that I needed a bodyguard, even a very restricted one, but made up of men who
would be enlisted without conditions, even to march against their own brothers, only twenty
men to a city (on condition that one could count on them absolutely) rather than a dubious
mass. It was Maurice, Schreck, and Heiden who formed in Munich the first group of toughs,
and were thus the origin of the SS. . .'[3]

In April 1925 this body was given the name of *Schutzstaffel*, but while the
Sturmabteilung (SA) continued to grow in numbers – it had 72,000 members by
1927 – the SS was restricted to little over 200 men. Hitler, however, while he
recognised the value of the SA as a means of demonstrating the disciplined
power of the Nazi movement, was increasingly concerned by the fact that its
leaders, especially Captain Pfeffer von Salomon, believed that it was primarily
the military arm of the movement and parallel to, but not subordinate to the
political wing. Thus, the SS assumed growing importance as a small but
entirely political counter to its big brother.

Sepp quickly impressed and was promoted *Sturmführer* on 1 June 1928 and
two months later, on 1 August, was appointed commander of the Munich SS
detachment or *Standarte*. Since Hitler was, of course, based in Munich it was
inevitable that Dietrich would soon come in close personal contact with him.
That Hitler quickly took to Sepp is without doubt. It is probable that he saw in
Sepp's rough and open Bavarian manner and his proven war record someone
who was utterly dependable and straightforward, whose ready sense of humour
could cheer at the darkest moments.

On 6 January 1929, Hitler appointed Heinrich Himmler *Reichsführer* of the
SS, an appointment that he would hold until the Third Reich was crushed in
May 1945. At the time, the SS still consisted of 280 men only, but Himmler
soon embarked on a scheme of gradual expansion. Dietrich obviously
impressed Himmler and on 18 May 1929 assumed command of *SS Brigade
Bayern*, which meant that he was in charge of the SS throughout Bavaria. At
this time, though, SS men received no pay – the Party could not afford it –
and even had to provide their own, now to become increasingly familiar, black,
as opposed to the SA brown, uniform. In order to bring Dietrich closer to the
centre of things, he was given a job as a packer, echoing his father's trade, in
the Nazi publishing firm of Eber-Verlag, whose boss, Max Amann, was later
described by Sepp as 'ill-mannered and brutal, but a hard worker who paid his
men well'.[4] During this time, Dietrich was very active in recruiting in Bavaria,
but was also being used increasingly by Hitler, together with his chauffeur
Julius Schreck, as a personal bodyguard.

On the wider front, Germany had been admitted to the League of Nations in
1926. Perhaps more important was the implementation of the Young Plan in
1929. The Dawes Plan for the payment of reparations had only been seen as a
temporary measure until Germany was on a sound economic footing. When it
became clear that she still could not meet her payments in full, a committee of
financial experts, representing the victorious Allies of 1918, met in early 1929

and drew up a plan extending reparation payments until 1988, but reducing the total amount to be paid. Foreign control of reparations was ended and the British and French agreed to withdraw their troops from the Rhineland by June 1930, five years ahead of the timetable laid down at Versailles. While this would certainly give Germany a much needed breathing space, as was recognised by the moderates, the Nationalists campaigned vociferously against the Young Plan, seeing it as merely prolonging the 'enslavement' of the German people. They attempted to introduce a 'freedom' bill in the Reichstag. This demanded an immediate repudiation of Germany's war guilt and evacuation of occupied territory and that ministers who signed such agreements as the Young Plan should be charged with treason. It was overwhelmingly defeated and a subsequent referendum showed that less than fifteen per cent of the German people supported such an action. As a result, the more moderate Nationalists withdrew into the background, leaving Hitler as virtually the sole spokesman for the Right.

The days of the Weimar Republic were now, however, to become numbered. The Wall Street Crash of 1929 soon reverberated across the Atlantic and, by the end of that year, Germany was suffering from rising unemployment, falling tax receipts and a serious budget deficit. Differences over how the problem could be solved led to the resignation of the coalition government and von Hindenburg, who had been President of the Weimar Republic since the death of Ebert in 1925, appointed Heinrich Brüning as Chancellor at the end of March 1930, with the Presidential emergency powers to back him should the Reichstag not be co-operative. Brüning survived until July when he attempted to introduce a fiercely retrenching budget by decree. A Socialist motion demanding its withdrawal was narrowly carried and Brüning was forced to seek a fresh mandate.

During this time, there had been growing concern over the increasing violence generated at NSDAP rallies and meetings. Much of the blame for this must lie with the SA. Typical evidence of their disregard for the sensitivities of others came in April 1930 at Oberammergau. The famous Passion Play was to be performed that year and the village elders had asked for a ban on political meetings some weeks beforehand so that it could be performed against a peaceful background and visitors would not be deterred from attending. The local Nazis decided to hold a meeting at a local inn and provoked a brawl which clearly shocked the local people. It was incidents like this that caused the Bavarian Government to issue a decree at the beginning of June banning the wearing of party uniforms at meetings and rallies. Similar bans were enacted in Prussia and Baden. This was, of course, deeply resented by the NSDAP, but there was little that they could do about it, especially since Hitler was fearful that he might be deported if he antagonised the establishment too much. That the SA was speedily getting out of control was also clear. Matters boiled over during the run up to the September 1930 election. SA resentment that they were the shock troops of the campaign and taking the casualties, but that they had little say in its overall conduct, and the fact that they were receiving little or no financial recompense for their efforts, manifested itself in Berlin at the end of August. Walter Stennes, the SA Commander East, and a band of his men broke into the party offices in Berlin and beat up the SS men who were guarding them. This marked the end of Pfeffer von Salomon, who resigned next day and also represented a further feather in the cap for the SS in Hitler's eyes, since they had demonstrated that they put loyalty to the Party above all else.

The election itself proved to be a triumph for the National Socialists. They won no less than 107 seats in the Reichstag, with a total vote of six and a half million. This made them the second largest party. The Communists, too, increased their seats from fifty-four to seventy-seven and it was significant that forty per cent of the electorate had voted for Parties standing against the principles of Weimar. Much of Hitler's support came from those who had become disillusioned with the other Nationalist parties, but also from the youth – there were an additional four million voters over the 1928 election. Hitler had now arrived as a national figure.

Among those elected on the NSDAP ticket was Sepp Dietrich, who was returned for Electoral District No 5 – Lower Bavaria. He had, in the meantime, been promoted from packer to despatch clerk (*Expedient*) for Max Amann and this was what he gave the electoral authorities as his profession. It is unlikely that he would have been paid much in this lowly post and the additional money and perks that he was entitled to as a Deputy must have been more than welcome. Indeed, it is probable that Hitler invited him to stand as a reward for services rendered, especially since he appears to have done little in the Reichstag other than vote.[6]

Earlier, on 11 July 1930, Dietrich had been promoted to SS Oberführer Süd, which gave him charge of all SS activities in Southern Germany. This and being a Deputy made him a person of note in Party circles. Thus, reporting a speech made by Hitler at Nuremberg at the beginning of November 1930, the Nazi *Illustrierter Boebachter* showed a photograph of Sepp seated in the front row, with Prince August Wilhelm, fourth son of the Kaiser Wilhelm II and a fanatical Nazi, on his left, and described him as one of the 'notable listeners'.[7] The truth was that Dietrich had now become very much part of Hitler's inner circle, together with Julius Schaub, Hitler's Adjutant and Heinrich Hoffmann, his personal photographer. As Otto Wagener, who headed the Party's economic section at this time, recalled:

'If one wanted to call his [Hitler's] attention to a mistaken view, an error in reasoning, or a contradiction with basic concepts of his own programme or the law, morality, or ethics, it was essential to avoid doing so in the presence of outsiders. Only the presence of people closest to him – Hess, Schaub, Sepp Dietrich, and the rest – could be tolerated in such a situation, though even then Hitler did not like to be spoken to in a way that might appear as instruction, let alone as a reprimand.'[8]

The problem of the SA had still not been solved. Ernst Röhm, disillusioned by the failure of the Beer Hall *putsch*, had retired to private life. He was subsequently recalled to the *Reichswehr* and had spent the past two years with the German military mission to Bolivia. He had now been brought back into the fold as Chief of Staff of the SA. He could not, however, control Stennes. The latter had allied himself to Otto Strasser, and his brother Gregor, leader of the North German wing of the NSDAP. Gregor Strasser had been with Hitler in Landsberg, but had since diverged gradually from him in viewpoint. He became increasingly critical of Hitler's abandonment of the socialist ideals of the Party and his flirtations with the industrialists, aristocracy and conservative politicians. His organisation in North Germany became independent of that in the South and he felt, as did Otto, that the power base should be in Berlin and not Munich. It was, however, Otto, who was prepared to join Stennes in a *putsch* to bring this to reality. On the evening of 31 March 1931 Stennes' men once again occupied the National Socialist offices in Berlin and published an appeal in the weekly Nazi newspaper, which had been founded by Goebbels, *Der Angriff*. A deputation was sent to Weimar, where Hitler was holding a meeting, in order to win Goebbels over to the cause, but without success. The plot then collapsed through lack of money and desertions by Stennes' followers and, a month later, Otto Strasser was expelled from the Party. According to Goebbels,[9] Dietrich played a leading part in crushing the attempted putsch and another source[10] praises Dietrich for the way in which he prevented bloodshed by the 'rational and balanced way' in which he acted. What he actually did is not clear, but Hitler did pay the SS in Berlin a significant tribute when he said to them: "SS Man, your honour is your loyalty".[11] This later became the SS motto.

The unruliness of the SA sparked off a further, but much larger expansion of the SS and its strength rose from 2,700 at the end of 1930 to 30,000 by April 1932. Yet, the same was also happening to the SA, which rose by 100,000 men during 1930-1, largely thanks to the unemployment situation. Himmler now reorganised the SS into fifty-five *Standarten* which were organised into 18 *Abschnitte* (sectors) within the four *Gruppen* – North, East, South and West. On 11 July 1931, Sepp Dietrich was posted to *Abschnitt* IV in *Gruppe Nord*, with his headquarters at Hildesheim. Presumably this was to maintain SS morale in the aftermath of the unrest created by Stennes and also to help keep an eye on SA activities. Nevertheless, this did not mean that Dietrich was distanced f. m Hitler and, indeed, probably spent more time with him in Munich and elsewhere than he did in his own sector.

It was at about this time that Goebbels met his future wife Magda. Recently divorced from her husband, the industrialist Günther Quandt, she had become an admirer of Hitler's and was working part-time as an unpaid secretary in the Party's Berlin offices. Hitler, on a visit to Berlin, was staying in a suite at the Kaiserhof Hotel, which represented his personal headquarters in the capital, and first met her through her son, then eight years-old, but dressed in 'a blue musical-comedy uniform'. Hitler invited her to tea and also present were Otto Wagener, Goebbels, Sepp Dietrich and Schaub. He was much taken with her. Later that night Hitler and Wagener were in conversation with Schaub, Dietrich and Schreck entered the suite 'somewhat noisily'. Hitler asked where they had been and they replied that in response to an invitation to visit her at sometime, they had been to Frau Quandt's, 'where we gradually drank up everything that she had in the icebox'. As they were about to leave her apartment, Goebbels entered and they were astonished that he had got in without ringing the door bell. It was Sepp who then said: 'He has a key. We'd better leave.'[12] This illustrates Sepp's liking for liquor, his ability to hold it and his native wit.

In the meantime, Brüning, who had clung to office after the 1930 election, was doing his best to restore the German economy by the implementation of deflationary policies. These did improve the situation, but also led to even greater unemployment, thus inevitably yielding new recruits for the extremist parties. In order to placate Nationalist opinion he attempted to set up a customs union with Austria in order to demonstrate that he, too, and not just the Right, favoured *Anschluss* (union) with Germany's southern neighbour. The International Court at the Hague, however, blocked this as being incompatible with the Versailles Treaty. He also retackled the problem of reparations and succeeded in obtaining in July 1931 a year's suspension of payments through the Hoover Moratorium and eventually, through the Lausanne Conference of June 1932, abolition of them all together. However, this was too late to save his personal position.

In the spring of 1932, von Hindenburg's term as President expired. While Brüning wanted him to stay on, seeing his presence as the best safeguard against a Nazi takeover, this was blocked by Alfred Hugenberg, leader of the German National People's Party and an ally of Hitler, and the National Socialists. Von Hindenburg was therefore forced to stand for re-election and Hitler and Ernst Thaelmann, leader of the German Communist Party, stood against him. Hitler was able to do so as he had finally acquired German citizenship and now embarked on a hectic electioneering trip around the country.

Because of the frequent clashes with Communist paramilitary organisations, which in December 1931 had banded together to form the *Eiserne republikanische Front zur Abwehr des Faschismus* (Republican Iron Front for Defence Against Fascism), Hitler's personal security was a constant problem. By the beginning of 1932 it had become too much for Dietrich and Schreck to manage on their own and so, on 29 February, the *SS-Begleit-Kommando 'Der Führer'* came into being. It consisted of twelve men personally selected by Sepp and these were presented to Hitler at his Berlin headquarters in the Kaiserhof Hotel. One who was close to Hitler at this time described them as:

'. . . fine, athletic German types. They had zipped motor-car overalls over their black-coated uniforms. . . and wore close-fitting aviators' helmets. Armed with revolvers and sjamboks – hippopotamus whips, terrible weapons, capable of knocking a man out with one blow – they looked like men from Mars.'[13]

Sefton Delmer, who was the *Daily Express* correspondent in Berlin at the time, recalls accompanying Hitler on a flight in a Rohrbach Roland, which Hitler had chartered from Lufthansa, the airline, for his campaign. They were flying from Berlin to Pomerania.

> 'In the stern nearest the door sat Sepp Dietrich, the gay little fighting cock of a Bavarian ex-cavalry sergeant who was chief of the bodyguard. With him his men. Four or five of them there were. But I can remember only Durr by name, a thick-set, flat nosed, fairhaired boxer with cauliflower ears. Some of the other men looked strangely delicate for bodyguards – almost effeminate. When they took photographs out of their wallets and started showing them round with remarks like "Isn't he sweet!", I began to wonder whether the *Stabschef* [Röhm] had had a hand in their selection. But delicate though they looked, they were tough alright – as they showed us a few hours later that evening.'

Hitler's car was waiting for him at the airport. On their way to the third meeting of the day, in the Baltic port of Elbing, they ran into a Communist ambush. Julius Shreck managed to serve the car round and through it.

> 'But Hitler's leathercoated bodyguards had already leaped out of their car and were lashing out at the overalls with rubber truncheons and black jacks. Stones started to fly and pistol shots rang out. Then the Dietrich men were back in their cars and on we went.'[14]

Delmer also noted that the police took no notice of what was going on. The election took place on 13 March and when the results were published they showed that von Hindenburg had won with forty-nine point six per cent of the vote. Hitler was second with 11,339,446 votes, representing thirty per cent, Thaelmann was third with thirteen per cent and Theodor Dusterberg of the German National People's Party last with just under seven per cent. Because Hindenburg had failed, although only just, to secure an outright majority, there had to be a second poll. This was held on 10 April and, with Dusterberg having dropped out, Hindenburg managed to secure fifty-three per cent, while Hitler increased his vote by some two million and gained thirty-six point eight per cent. Thaelmann, on the other hand, dropped over a million votes. It was a considerable triumph for Hitler, who had now almost doubled the vote which he obtained in the 1930 election. It also marked the end of Brüning's political career.

The *eminence grise* of the Weimar Republic at this time was General Kurt von Schleicher, who as Head of the Reichswehr *Ministeramt* (Ministry Bureau), was in charge of naval and military political and press affairs. He had close contacts with von Hindenburg, into whose old regiment, the Third Foot Guards, he had been commissioned, and with General Groener, the Minister of Defence, on whose staff he had served at the end of the war. It was he who had been largely responsible for the selection of Brüning as Chancellor and now, in view of Hitler's recent election success, believed that the only way to avoid a Nazi uprising was to come to terms with him. This could only be done with a more Right-looking Chancellor. Brüning himself had, in von Schleicher's eyes, compounded the serious situation that prevailed by imposing a ban on the SS and SA immediately after the election. Von Schleicher now made a deal with

Hitler that, in return for not opposing the new Chancellor, the ban on the SS and SA would be lifted. He then told von Hindenburg, who insisted that Brüning form a more Right wing cabinet, at which he resigned. In his place came a close friend of von Schleicher, Fritz von Papen. His selection, however, was greeted with hostility by all political parties, including the National Socialists, Hitler having broken his word not to oppose him. There was no option but to call a general election.

The election was set for 31 July and for Sepp Dietrich it marked the opportunity to represent his own home area, since he was moved across to stand in Electoral District No 24 – Upper Bavaria/Swabia. As a result of the 1930 election, the strongest party in Swabia was the Bavarian People's Party, as it had been after the 1928 election, with seven members returned. Next came the Social Democrats with four seats, followed by the National Socialists with three and the German Peasants' Party with two seats. The only other party to have a seat was the Communists. The Nazis maintained a roll of prospective candidates for each electoral district. This was drawn up by the party leadership, with most of the candidates being proposed by local party groups, trades unions and other associations. Dietrich's name did not, however, appear in the lists until the end of June 1932 when he was inserted into fourth position behind Ritter von Epp, who had been representing the district for the Nazis since 1928, a school director and a lawyer from Memmingen. Nobody seems to have sponsored Dietrich [15] and his name was probably put up by Hitler in person. It was obviously desirable that Sepp should stand in the electoral district in which was his birthplace, but for the 1930 election, in view of the strength of the Bavarian People's Party, there were others like Ritter von Epp, who had more political stature and hence Dietrich had to stand elsewhere. That he was moved at such relatively short notice probably reflects persuasion of Hitler on Dietrich's part and increased NSDAP optimism that they would gain additional seats in this district.

Dietrich probably had little time to carry out much personal electioneering since he was too busy with his escort duties. During the campaign, there were a number of brushes with Left wing factions. In June, Hitler ran into an ambush at Stralsund near Freiburg im Breisgau. Rocks were thrown at his car, with one grazing his head. Then, on 30 July, there was an assassination attempt against him in Nuremberg. Indeed, throughout Germany the scale of violence during the campaign reached unprecedented heights, with many riots and street battles. The worst was perhaps in the Altona district of Hamburg, a notorious 'Red' area, on 17 July. When Nazis under police escort staged a march through it, shots were fired and, by the end of the day, nineteen people had been killed and 285 wounded. As an additional precaution, it was now arranged that Dietrich and some of his men should fly on ahead of Hitler, arriving at the destination airfield some hours before, in order to check security arrangements. It was probably at about this time that Dietrich learnt to fly. Certainly, Hitler later recalled that during the election campaigns of 1932:

47

'Often I had to use a little Junker single-motor that had belonged to Sepp Dietrich. It was rather an unstable aircraft.'[16] Dietrich was also awarded the very rare Pilot's and Observer's Badge in gold and diamonds. Wolf-Dieter Dietrich, Sepp's eldest son, now possesses it.

Another cause of security concern was the Party's headquarters in Munich, in the Brown House at 16 Prinzregentenplatz. Sepp had been registered as living there since 15 March 1932, although he still had an apartment elsewhere in Munich, together with Hitler, who was described as a 'writer'.[17] On 25 June 1932, Himmler was made personally responsible for Brown House security. Guards were to be found from both the SA and SS, but were not to be mixed. Appointments to the guards would be made from lists prepared by Sepp Dietrich for SS members and Wilhelm Helfer, leader of the SA in Munich. Preference would be given to those with long membership and who were unemployed. No changes could be authorised except by permission of Röhm or Himmler. Obviously it was an honour to be a member of the Brown House guard, but Hitler did not want to antagonise the SA by relying solely upon SS men.

As for the election itself, it was a victory for the National Socialists, who secured 230 seats out of the 609 available in the Reichstag. In Swabia, while the Bavarian People's Party remained top, this time with eight seats, the National Socialists returned six deputies, including Dietrich. Hitler now had a constitutional right to form a government and Schleicher and von Papen accepted that he must come into the cabinet. Hitler, however, was not interested in power-sharing and told von Hindenburg so. The latter was unimpressed and, since no other grouping could form a government, there was deadlock. Thus, when the Reichstag met in September, von Papen was forced to dissolve it and call another election, to be held on 6 November.

Once again, Sepp stood for Upper Bavaria-Swabia, lying in fourth position behind von Epp, Fritz Reinhardt, *Gauleiter* of Upper Bavaria, and Wilhelm Schwarz, a Memmingen lawyer and local party leader. This time the National Socialists did not do so well, losing some 60,000 votes and one of their six seats. Indeed, all parties suffered, apart from the Communists, who doubled their vote, increasing their deputies from two to four. This fall in the National Socialist vote was reflected country-wide. The NSDAP lost some two million votes overall and were reduced to 196 seats. The cause of this was partly to do with an improving economic situation – the legacy of Brüning – and also because von Papen had withdrawn Germany from the Disarmament Conference running at Geneva until she was given equality in arms, a step which pleased the Nationalists and increased their vote by fifty per cent. Hitler, too, was very short of money by this stage and, because he had failed to seize power after the previous election, many of his more radical supporters had deserted him for the Communists. Some middle-class voters, on the other hand, were also scared away because of his efforts to attract the working class.

PLATE 1 77-mm field gun FK 96 n.A. with which Dietrich went to war in 1914.

PLATE 2 7.6-cm Krupp Ll6.5 infantry gun used by Dietrich when he was supporting storm troops with Infantry Gun Battery 10.

PLATE 3 Storm troops in training at Beuville.

PLATE 4 Bayerische Sturmpanzerkraftwagen Abteilung 13 at Roux, near Charleroi, late June or early July 1918. Dietrich is sitting on the right of *Bob's* driver cab.

PLATE 5 Mark IV booty tanks, made in front and female behind, possibly *Abteilung* 14, waiting to move up, Rheims. June 1918.

PLATE 6 The monastery at Annaberg, where the *Freikorps Oberland* covered itself with glory in May 1921 during the fighting in Upper Silesia.

PLATE 7 Oberlanders in Upper Silesia, summer 1921. Their badge, which can be seen on their collars, was the Edelweiss flower.

PLATE 8 Review of the Frekorps Oberland late September 1923. Ludenorff is to left in *pickelhaube*, and Goering in right foreground.

PLATE 9 9 November 1923. Himmler, with flag, helps to man a barricade outside the War Ministry in Munich.

PLATE 10 SS-Standartenführer Dietrich when commanding the SS Standarte München.

PLATE 11 New recruits to the *Leibstandarte* take the oath of allegiance, Feldhermhalle, Munich, 9 November.

PLATE 12 SA and SS on parade at the 1934 Nuremberg Rally.

PLATE 13 Dietrich, Hitler and Himmler listen to the band of the *Leibstandarte* playing in the gardens of the Chancellery, Berlin, on Hitler's 48th birthday, 21 April 1937.

PLATE 14 Dietrich, unusually on horseback, reviews the *Leibstandarte* at Lichterfelde.

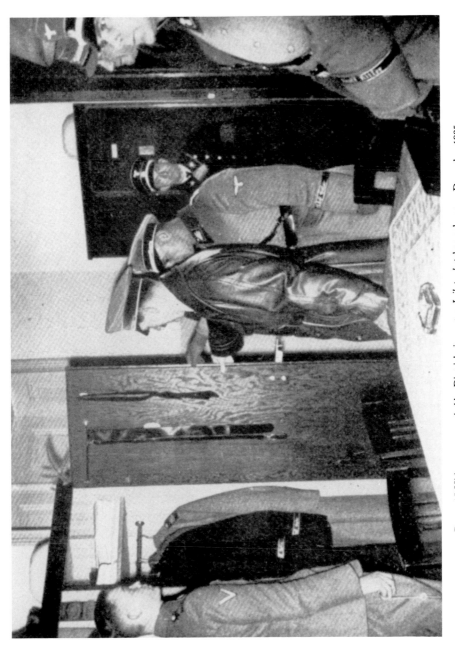

PLATE 15 Hitler, accompanied by Dietrich, inspects a *Leibstandarte* barrack room, December 1935.

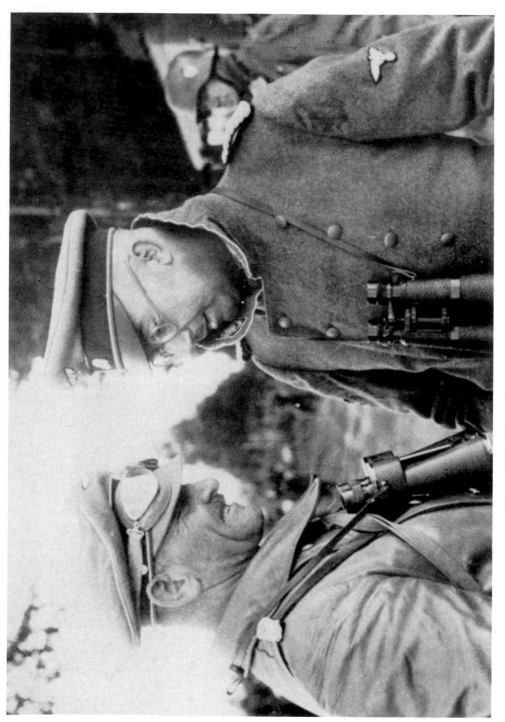

PLATE 16 Poland, September 1939. Dietrich and Himmler in a rare moment of *bonhomie.*

There was, however, still a deadlock and von Papen decided to break this by resigning on the assumption that Hitler would not be able to form a government. Hitler, though, was still insistent on all or nothing, but von Hindenburg remained obturate. Von Papen now proposed to declare martial law, dissolve the Reichstag and rule by decree until a new and more authoritarian constitution could be drawn up. At this point, von Schleicher stepped in once more. He reckoned that he could split the Nazis by drawing away the left wing grouping under Gregor Strasser. He therefore got rid of von Papen by pretending to von Hindenburg that the *Reichswehr* objected to his policies because they would lead to civil war. The President swallowed this and, on 2 December 1932, von Schleicher became Chancellor, and the scene was set for the last act.

Before the November election took place, Sepp had received another promotion. He had already been promoted to *Gruppenführer* on 18 December 1931, but now on 1 October 1932 he was appointed to the command of the SS *Gruppe Nord* with headquarters in Hamburg. He did take up residence in Hamburg, although he was to be in the post for only little over five months, but he still kept his apartment in Munich and his billet in the Brown House.

Von Schleicher's ploy to draw Strasser away from Hitler was to offer him the Vice-Chancellorship and make him Prime Minister of Prussia. Strasser tried to prepare his way by asking Hitler to tolerate von Schleicher's cabinet. Hitler, who had sensed what was up, ordered him to refuse the offer and Strasser gave way, resigning all his offices in disgust and leaving politics for the directorship of a chemical combine. Von Schleicher now turned to the Left, trying to bribe them with a radical programme of public works, wage and relief reforms and land resettlement on the large and inefficient estates in East Prussia. This turned the Right against him, but also failed to win over the Socialists. Von Schleicher was therefore left with no option but to do as von Papen had done and rule by decree. Hitler, in the meantime, had opened negotiations with von Papen and reached agreement with him over the Nazis and Nationalists working together. The possibility now existed that a government could be formed, and von Hindenburg, realising that von Schleicher was totally isolated, withdrew his support for him, forcing the latter's resignation on 28 January 1933. Two days later, the President appointed Hitler as Chancellor.

Hitler's cabinet contained, in fact, only two National Socialists – Wilhelm Frick as Minister of the Interior and Hermann Goering as Minister without Portfolio. This gave von Papen, who was Vice-Chancellor, cause to believe that he could now isolate the Nazis. He reckoned without Hitler's artfulness. On the pretext that the government did not have a reliable majority in the Reichstag, Hitler called for fresh elections, which were set for 5 March. This time he was in a position to control the state apparatus, of which he took advantage, especially in Prussia, where the police were purged and SA and SS men drafted in as auxiliaries and encouraged to use violence against Left wing opponents.

For this election, Sepp Dietrich stood once more as a candidate for Upper Bavaria-Swabia. This time, however, he was only No 8 on the list of NSDAP candidates. Determined to overthrow the supremacy of the Bavarian People's Party, the National Socialists brought in their 'big guns'. Heading the list was Hitler himself, followed by Frick, Goering and von Epp, and while Reinhardt and Schwarz continued to stand, Max Amann, Sepp's former boss, also joined the platform, together with Artur Holzmann, a local landowner and the Party's agricultural specialist. All these nine, including Sepp, were elected, although the total NSDAP vote of 385000 only entitled them to directly return six members and the Bavarian People's Party were still the winners, with over 570000 votes.[19]

Just before the election, on the night of 27 February, the Reichstag building was set ablaze. Whether this was the work of the mentally disturbed Dutch Communist Marianus van der Lubbe, as the Nazis claimed, or was deliberately engineered by them, has never been conclusively proved one way or the other. Nevertheless, it was opportune and enabled the Nazis to claim that a Communist uprising was about to take place, Hitler had little difficulty in persuading von Hindenburg to issue a decree which drastically restricted civil and political liberties. Hitler himself was in Berlin at the time, together with the faithful Sepp, and Sefton Delmer recalls how Sepp allowed him to tag on the end of Hitler's entourage when he entered the Reichstag to inspect the damage.[20]

Yet, in spite of the advantages which the Nazis had, they still failed to obtain an overall majority in the Reichstag, polling only 43.9 per cent of the vote and obtaining 288 seats. This forced them to combine with the Nationalists, with their fifty-two seats, at least for the time being. On 23 March Hitler managed to steer an enabling act through the Reichstag which gave the government extraordinary powers to do as they wished in order to consolidate the 'National Revolution', whether it infringed the constitution or not. This was the death knell of democracy in Germany and, by the end of the summer, all political parties, other than the National Socialists, had dissolved themselves.

CHAPTER 4

SS Leibstandarte
1933-39

On 17 March 1933, Hitler personally ordered Sepp Dietrich to form a guard for the protection of the Reich Chancellery. Three days later Sepp relinquished his appointment as commander of SS Gruppe Nord and was made a *Führer zur besonderen Verwendung* (zbV or Leader on Special Employment) to the Reichführer SS and the *SS-Stabswache* (Staff Guard) Dietrich came into being. Its initial strength was 117 all ranks. Among the junior officers who joined were three who would later become famous in the Waffen-SS, Wilhelm Mohnke, Theodor Wisch and Fritz Witt. The *Stabswache* was based at the Kaiserin Augusta Victoria Barracks on Friesenstrasse, Berlin-Kreuzberg, near to the Chancellery. Within a few weeks the unit title was changed to the *SS-Sonderkommando Berlin* and moved to Lichterfelde, site of the old Imperial Officer Cadet School of that name. Rather than being kept directly under Himmler's control, it was placed technically under the command of the *Polizeiabteilung Wecke*, with whom it shared the barracks. Major Walter Wecke himself was one of Hermann Goering's key subordinates in his capacity as commander of the Prussian police and the members of the *Sonderkommando* were made police auxiliaries, in the same way as those SA and SS men who had been drafted in before the March 1933 Reichstag elections. This apparent splitting of Dietrich's unit from the main body of the SS, which was unique, was to prove a continual source of friction between Dietrich and Himmler.

Dietrich's opinion of Himmler given to his American interrogators after the war was that:

'This guy tried to imitate the Fuehrer. His appetite for power just could not be satisfied. On top of this he was a great hand at hoarding and scrounging. He received money from everywhere and everybody . . . I had quite a number of rows with Himmler.'[1]

Karl Wolff, who was to become Himmler's Adjutant and later the German military governor of northern Italy and had, like Sepp, been a *Frontsoldat*, stated that

'Himmler . . . had nothing in common with the front soldier; his whole bearing was rather sly and unmilitary, but he was very well read and tried to engage our interest with his acquired knowledge, and to enthuse us with the tasks of the SS.'[2]

Indeed, Willi Frischauer, one of Himmler's biographers stated that he was happy discussing SS matters with 'such rough types as Dietrich' and his men 'because he could impress them with his superior knowledge and articulation'.[3] According to Dietrich's son,[4] his second wife claimed that Himmler was the only person whom Dietrich really hated and he would do anything possible to circumvent any inconvenient order emanating from him.

By June 1933 two other SS *Sonderkommandos* had been organised, at the Reichswehr training bases of Jüterborg and Zossen. These camps were also used specifically to give three months' basic military training to the personnel posted to *Sonderkommando Berlin*, the instruction being carried out by the Army with police and SS assistance. These three *Sonderkommandos* marked the foundation of the Waffen-SS, the SS's military wing. Dietrich's command itself had now been expanded to some six hundred men. The fact that the unit was being trained by the Army, although this had been done to some SA units in order that they might swell the 100,000 man Reichswehr in the event of a national crisis, began to give it and the two other *Sonderkommandos* a singular character when compared to the rest of the SS and SA. A further demonstration of this came in July when a small detachment under Theodor Wisch, 1 *Wachkommando*, was sent to guard Berghof above Berchtesgaden on the Obersalzberg, Hitler's summer retreat, which he had recently bought, although he had been in the habit for some years of renting it for his summer vacations. This was an early indication that Hitler saw *Sonderkommando Berlin* as a personal guard, rather than merely being responsible for the physical security of the Chancellery. Up until this time, all members of these *Sonderkommandos* were borne on the books of the Prussian Police, in their capacity as police auxiliaries, and hence were paid by them. In August 1933, however, the police auxiliaries were dissolved. While the other auxiliaries reverted once more to being dependent on National Socialist party funds for their pay and allowances, it was decided that Dietrich's unit should be paid from state funds, and on equivalent scales to the Army.

It was this which caused Dietrich to have his first brush with the authorities. If his *Zonderkommando* was to be paid like the *Reichswehr*, then its members should also be entitled to half price rail fares, just as soldiers were. To begin with, the Ministry of Transport was unwilling to recognise a branch of the SS as being equivalent to the armed forces of the State. Sepp pointed out, however, that his unit was 'uniquely a special troop alongside the Reichswehr'.[5] Apart from the fact that it was now paid by the Reich treasury and not the Party, he could also demonstrate that it was personally responsible to Hitler and not Himmler. On 3 September 1933 all three *Sonderkommandos* had been brought together under the new title of the *Adolf-Hitler-Standarte*. The status of the unit was further enhanced on 9 November, the tenth anniversary of the Beer Hall *putsch*. Hitler conferred yet another new title on the unit, and it was now to be known as the *Leibstandarte SS Adolf Hitler*. Furthermore, on that very evening, the whole of the Leibstandarte paraded and personally swore an oath to the Führer: 'We swear to you Adolf Hitler, loyalty and bravery. We pledge to you, and to the superiors appointed by you, obedience unto death. So help us God.' It was significant that the remainder of the SS was represented solely by the *Abschnitt* leaders and *Gruppenführern*. Under these circumstances, it was inevitable that the Ministry of Transport was eventually forced to give way over the question of concessionary rail fares.

Dietrich also irritated the SS hierarchy in the way in which he established close relations with the Army. For a man whose efforts to become a professional soldier had been twice frustrated, by his riding accident and then by the end of the war and the events of 1918-19, it is understandable that he would do everything he could to get back to being a soldier. During the early days of the *Leibstandarte*, he did all he could to further a friendly relationship with the Army. He got on well with Werner Freiherr von Fritsch, commanding the Berlin based *Wehrkreis III*, which had overall responsibility for giving the *Leibstandarte* its military training. At the lower level, a close rapport was struck up with all ranks of Infantry Regiment 9. At the end of August, Sepp personally invited an officer and six NCOs of the training cadre of the regiment to spend a few days at Lichterfelde and, a few days later, a company of the regiment specially requested signed photographs of Sepp's officers in memory of the 'close co-operation' enjoyed at Jüterborg.[6] Sepp also adopted military terminology in the Leibstandarte. The officers were called *offiziere* rather than *führern*, although this did not last very long. Dietrich, however, liked to use *Batallion*, *Kompanie* and *Zug* instead of the Nazi paramilitary *Sturmbann*, *Sturm* and *Truppe*. Himmler tried to get Dietrich to use the latter terms, but without success.

In order to bring Dietrich back into the fold, Himmler appointed him on 24 November 1933 as commander of SS *Gruppe Ost* back-dated to 1 October, the day on which it was decided that the *Leibstandarte* should be paid by the Reich Treasury. He transmitted his orders to Sepp in this capacity, rather than as commander of the *Leibstandarte*, but this appears to have made little difference to Sepp's attitude.

By the time that the title of *Leibstandarte* had been conferred on the unit, it had grown in size from the original single company of the *Stabswache Dietrich* to two battalions. Each had two line companies, but the 1st Battalion had a machine gun company and the 2nd a transport company in addition. Also, at the beginning of August, a band had been formed. This, under the direction of Hermann Müller-John was soon to become nationally famous and to add considerably to the *Leibstandarte*'s reputation as a showpiece unit. It had 835 all ranks on strength, of which some 110 were employed on guard duties in Berlin at any one time. The guard on the Reichs Chancellery took up almost forty per cent of this commitment, but the Leibstandarte also had to have a presence at, among other places, Berlin's three airports – Tempelhof, Staaken, Johannistal – Lichterfelde itself, the SS headquarters, the Treasury and Ministry of Food. Furthermore, it was also responsible for the security of the private residences of both Himmler and his sinister chief of the *Sicherdienst* (SD or Security Service) Reinhard Heydrich, which must have given Himmler further cause for frustration in that he was guarded by a body over whom he did not have total control.

Because the *Leibstandarte* was a showpiece, very rigid entry standards were laid down. Those wanting to join, and it was made up entirely of volunteers, had to be aged between 17 and 22 and be of a minimum height of 1.80m (5ft 11 inches), which was later raised to 1.84m (6ft ½ inch) and have a high standard of physical fitness. Himmler, with his obsession with racial purity, also insisted that a man should be truly Nordic in appearance and from 1935 onwards he had to demonstrate a pure Aryan ancestry back to 1800, with 1750 for officers. Himmler's argument was that: 'The point is that in his attitude to discipline the man should not behave like an underling, that his gait, his hands, everything should correspond to the ideal which we set ourselves.' By the same token, an applicant had to be perfectly proportioned physically on the grounds that otherwise he would be unable to face up to the intense physical demands made of him, and it was Himmler's boast that 'until 1936 we did not accept a man in the *Leibstandarte* . . . if he had one filled tooth'. While Sepp was happy to accept rigid physical entry standards, he was less enthused by the race qualification. 'Some forty good specimens at least are kept from joining the *Leibstandarte* every year due to doubt concerning ancestry', as he complained at one point.[7]

In terms of ideology, it must be pointed out that, initially, Dietrich's unit consisted of a mixture of SS and SA men and a return dated 8 September 1933 shows that the unit was made up of 463 men with SS numbers and 262 without.[8] Once it was established as the *Leibstandarte SS*, however, all members joined the SS. In theory, every man was supposed to be a member of the Party, but in practice this did not work out. As early as March 1934, a strength return showed that out of a total strength of 968 there were forty-five who were definitely not Party members and a further 136 who had no Party number.[9] Dietrich himself had little interest in this subject and at one point was seriously in arrears over the payment of party dues.[10] During the course of 1934, the *Reichs Sicherheitshauptamt* (RSHA or Race and Settlement Office) worked out a programme of indoctrination for all SS units and the Leibstandarte had a permanent education officer for this purpose from 1934, who in his own words said of his programme that:

> 'Its main point is to influence the *Leibstandarte* so that it can at any time be the shock troops of the regime in ideological struggles. That is to say, it must recognise no other ties than to the Führer and his orders . . . We must and can so use the time . . . to weld the units of the *Leibstandarte* together and make them into a stout tool in the hand of the Führer.'[11]

In order to forge this spirit every man in the *Leibstandarte* had to undergo a weekly indoctrination session.

Sepp Dietrich had given up his Munich apartment at the end of April 1933, but retained his room in the Brown House until towards the end of September

1934. The Munich City Directory for 1934 described the occupants as 'Adolf Hitler, Writer' and 'Reich Chancellor', 'kitchen-master – Zaske, Ernst [member of the SD]' and 'Merchant, Dietrich, Jos', but from 1935 onwards there were no further listings of either Hitler or Dietrich. [12] Now that he was permanently based in Berlin, Dietrich had two places of residence in the capital. He had rooms at Lichterfelde, but also gave as his address Rothenburgerstrasse 12, which was the headquarters of *SS-Oberabschnitt Ost*, and it is probable that he had an apartment here. He also appears to have rented a property at Bad Saarow, some 50 kilometres east of Berlin and near Frankfurt-on-Oder, and to have used this as his country retreat. [13] Apart from continuing to be a member of Reichstag, Dietrich also became a member of the *Presse Staatsrat* (the State Press Chamber), which was headed by Max Amann and was responsible for ensuring that the Press toed the National Socialist line. What it really meant was that Amann could close any newspaper at will and then could buy it for the Eher-Verlag. Indeed, Hitler was to later (1942) describe Amann as 'the greatest newspaper proprietor in the world' owning seventy to eighty per cent of the German Press. [14] It cannot be believed, however, that Sepp played a very active part in this and it is probable that Amann merely wanted him as a way of 'guarding his back' since Sepp was so close to Hitler. Likewise, also in 1934, Dietrich was apparently made a judge of the Supreme Disciplinary Court of Dr Robert Ley's German Labour Front (*Deutsche Arbeitsfront*) which was responsible for organising the German work force. [15] This was another sinecure, which probably brought in some useful income. Nevertheless, Dietrich liked Ley. He told his American interrogators that, having been an '*armer Hund*' (poor dog), it was the good points about improving the lot of the worker that attracted him to the National Socialists. Ley himself was 'an old dreamer (*Fantast*), but he was good natured and would not hurt a fly – he only wanted the best for the working-class'. [16] Indeed, there is only one recorded occasion when Dietrich had an outburst against Ley (see Page 135). In spite of this increasingly busy life, Sepp did find time for recreation. He became increasingly addicted to game shooting and also began to gain a reputation as a competent cross-country rally driver, the equivalent to today's motocross. It was probably for his prowess in this that he was awarded the *SA-Sportabzeichen* (SA Sports Badge) in Gold and likewise the *Deutsches Reichssportabzeichen* (German Reich Sports Badge), also in Gold. All motor sports in the Third Reich were much encouraged, especially with regard to creating a modern fighting machine. [17]

Throughout 1933, Hitler worked to consolidate his position in power. During that summer, the other political parties gradually dissolved themselves and, on 14 July, a law came into effect which stated that, from now on, Germany was a one party state. He then tackled the paramilitary organisations. The until now conservative old comrades association, the *Stahlhelm* (Steel Helmet), was incorporated with the SA and eventually, in November 1935, formally dissolved. Then, on the tenth anniversary of the Munich *putsch*, a ceremony at the Brown House marked the formal end of the *Freikorps*, whose standards were laid up there. Yet, if there was significant opposition to this growing dictatorship among the German people it remained muted and a plebiscite held by Hitler in November 1933 showed that eighty-eight per cent of the population supported his policies. Admittedly, Catholic opinion had been appeased when, in July 1933, Hitler signed a concordat with the Vatican, and his withdrawal of Germany from both the Geneva Disarmament Conference and the League of Nations in October met with general approval. Also, Hitler had no intention of upsetting the economic Establishment of the country. It was the industrialists like Krupp who had helped him to power with their money and the services of the economic experts were still needed if the problem of unemployment was to be solved. Likewise, he did not wish to upset the Army and wanted the generals to be on his side. It was this, in particular, which caused a widening rift between him and Roehm.

Ernst Roehm had become dissatisfied with many aspects of Hitler's policy. While Hitler had announced in a speech on 4 July 1933 that 'the stream of revolution released must be guided into the safe channel of evolution' and that 'in the long run our political power will be all the more secure, the more we succeed in underpinning it economically',[18] Roehm had always believed in the short, sharp and violent revolution which would, at one blow, overthrow the existing order. Since his SA had been in the forefront of the struggle, he believed that its members should now be rewarded by being given proper jobs. Yet, especially with the disbandment of the police auxiliaries in August 1933, the majority were still out of work. In particular, he looked at the *Reichswehr* and argued that the SA should absorb it and become the revolutionary militia army of the future. Hitler, however, saw the Army as the main means of furthering his foreign policy goals in the future, whereas the SA was merely the tool of the Party. Yet, even if Roehm's views were dramatically at variance with his own, and his blatant homosexuality was common knowledge, Hitler decided, conscious that Roehm had two million men behind him, that he must be humoured. This Roehm took as a sign that Hitler agreed with his concept of a new revolutionary army. The result was an open rift betwen him and General Wernher von Blomberg, the Minister of Defence. Sitting as fellow members of the Reich Defence Council at a meeting on 1 February 1934, Roehm told von Blomberg of his plan for the SA to relieve the Army of its responsibility for defence of the country.

Up until this time the Army had become surprisingly acquiescent to the SA, largely thanks to von Blomberg's admiration for Hitler and his desire to avoid clashes. Soldiers and SA men had been instructed to salute one another when in uniform; on joint parades, the SA was allowed to march in front of the Army; volunteers for the Army would come from the ranks of the SA and, once conscription was introduced – essential if Hitler was to expand the armed forces – all pre-military training would be an SA responsibility. Horrified, however, at Roehm's wholesale takeover plan, von Blomberg now called a meeting of the *Wehrkreis* commanders and told them that, from now on, they were not to cooperate with the SA, but at the same time must be careful not to provoke open clashes. As the meeting was taking place, a letter arrived from Roehm stating that he regarded the *Reichswehr* as no more than a training establishment and that from henceforth the SA was to be responsible for the conduct of war and mobilisation for it. This was the last straw and von Blomberg immediately took the letter to Hitler. The result was a meeting called on 28 February 1934 at which Hitler confirmed that the expanded army which he wanted was to be built on the existing *Reichswehr* and not on the SA militia model. As a sop to Roehm, however, it was agreed that, in the meantime, the SA could be used for frontier protection and pre-military training. Both von Blomberg and Roehm signed this agreement, but Roehm soon made it clear that he had little intention of observing it and spoke disparagingly of Hitler as an ignorant World War Lance-Corporal (*Gefreiter*). News of this reached Hitler's ears.[19] In the meantime, the Army braced itself for what it thought would be a *putsch* by Roehm.

Hitler now realised that something would have to be done to curb Roehm and his resolve to do so was strengthened by agitation from both Goering and Himmler, both of whom wanted to see the power of the SA crushed so as to strengthen the police and SS. At the beginning of June 1934, Hitler had a raging debate with Roehm and it was this which probably finally decided him to act. In order to disguise his intentions, he ordered the whole of the *Leibstandarte* on leave for the first part of the month and a few days later told Roehm that the SA should be stood down for the month of July. On the 7th, Roehm said that he was going to take sick leave, but did so declaring that those who hoped that the SA would not be recalled after their leave would be permitted to 'enjoy this brief hope. They will receive their answer at such time and in such form as appears necessary. The SA is and remains the destiny of Germany.'[20] At the same time, he invited Hitler to attend a conference of SA leaders at Wiessee, a resort near Munich, on 30 June and Hitler accepted.

The tension was further relaxed by the fact that Hitler now flew to Venice on the 14th in order to meet Mussolini for the first time. Dietrich was also to be present, perhaps not just to look after security but also because he did have at least a smattering of Italian,[21] picked up on his pre-1914 travels. He was to accompany the baggage which was flown there the day before and that indefatigable newshound Sefton Delmer also managed to wangle a seat on the aircraft.

'When Sepp Dietrich arrived, he welcomed me like an old comrade. And it was not his fault that it was a far from comfortable flight. As the plane climbed higher and higher over the Alps, breathing became painfully difficult. Cabins were not pressurised in those days and the oxygen apparatus was not functioning properly. I felt terrible. "Hope we don't have the unpleasant experience Hermann Göring had when he was flying back from Rome the other day," gasped Sepp Dietrich.
"What was that?" reporter Delmer just managed to gasp back.
"Every one of them, passengers and crew alike passed out," Dietrich said.

"Passed out while the plane was at high altitude over the Alps. Trouble with the oxygen supply it was."

Göring's pilotless plane, said Dietrich, had then swung round, and flown out over the Atlantic. As it started losing height, the pilot regained consciousness.

"Another thirty seconds, and they would have been in the drink.'''

Another example of Dietrich's rough humour, but at the same time he revealed his naivety. On arrival at the Grand Hotel, Delmer continued:

'Sepp Dietrich and his men did not enlighten the Italians. Sepp probably thought that I, whom he had seen with Hitler on so many election flights in Germany, was accompanying his Führer yet once more in Venice. But when at last the Italians did discover their mistake and realised that I was not one of Hitler's "lads", the cold formality broke with a bang.'[22]

Hitler's meeting with Mussolini did not go especially well and, on his return, he called a meeting of party leaders for the 17th at Gera in Thuringia in order to report back and also to review the domestic situation.

It so happened that, on that same day, von Papen, who was still, at least in name, Vice Chancellor, delivered a speech at the University of Marburg in which he called for an end to the violent excesses of the regime and a return to the decencies in relations between fellow Germans. What had prompted him to do this was a recent audience which he had had with von Hindenburg, now in his dotage and a sick man, who said that the country was in a mess and asked him to sort it out. Goebbels tried to have reports of the speech suppressed, but von Papen had largely forestalled this, Hitler was livid. Von Papen complained to him about Goebbels' actions and said that he would report them to von Hindenburg. At which point Hitler decided that he, too, should go and see Hindenburg in order to calm the waters and flew to Neudeck on 21 June. He was met by an unusually frosty von Blomberg who told him that the President had declared that unless the current tension in the country was quickly terminated, he would declare martial law and bring the Army in. The message was clear; Hitler must choose between the Army and the SA, and do so now.

The Army made it clear, however, that it was not prepared to become actively involved and the only other weapon Hitler had was the SS. Consequently, it was to them he turned and the plan of what was to happen a few days later was undoubtedly drawn up by himself and Himmler. For Dietrich the first inkling he probably had that something was in the wind came on 22 June. He reported to the Chancellery and then, at 1030 hours, telephoned Lichterfelde Barracks with instructions for the *Leibstandarte* to be warned off for a practise alert. Next day, which was a Saturday, all *Leibstandarte* leave was cancelled, but at midnight the alert was lifted, although just prior to this the guards on the Chancellery, SS headquarters and the Lichterfelde Barracks were strengthened. Nothing more then happened until the following Wednesday, the 27th, when Dietrich visited von Reichenau, the Army Chief of Staff, to request transport to help lift the *Leibstandarte* to southern Germany, as well as rifles and machine guns.[23] This was granted. Next day, at 1600 hours, exit from Lichterfelde was barred to all members of the *Leibstandarte* and at 2000 hours there was a silent alert.

In the meantime, the Army had been taking its own precautions against a pre-emptive move by the SA. General von Fritsch, the Commander-in-Chief, placed his troops on full alert on the 25th, stopping all leave and confining them to barracks. Three days later, it was announced that Roehm had been expelled from the German Officers' League and, on the following day, von Blomberg placed a signed article in the *Voelkischer Beobachter* affirming that the Army was behind Hitler. Hitler himself had left Berlin on the 28th for Essen, where he attended the wedding of the local Gauleiter, spending the next day touring Labour Service camps in Westphalia and staying the night of the 29th/30th at a hotel run by an old wartime comrade at Bad Godesburg on the Rhine. Significantly, Dietrich was told of Hitler's intention to stay at Bad Godesberg only at 1500 hours on the 29th and then the information came via the War Ministry and he was ordered to join Hitler there.[24] Later that evening, Goebbels joined Hitler, having flown from Berlin, bringing with him the news that the SA leader in Berlin had placed his men on alert, although this appears to have been in the belief that a right wing coup was about to be mounted. In his explanatory speech to the Reichstag on 13 July, Hitler stated that he had received other disquieting reports – that the SA had occupied government buildings in Berlin and were mustering in Munich on the evening of the 29th. Whatever information he did or did not receive, he took off from Bonn with Dietrich[25] at 0200 hours on the 30th, arriving at Munich two hours later. In the meantime, two companies of the *Leibstandarte* had been organised and sent by train overnight from Berlin to Kaufering outside Munich.

Even before Hitler and Dietrich arrived at Munich airport, things had begun to happen. August Schneidhuber, the SA commander in Bavaria, his adjutant and other local SA leaders had already been arrested on the orders of the Gauleiter of Munich, Adolf Wagner, who had had them brought to the airport, accompanied by some of Hitler's old comrades from the early days of the party, Christian Weber, Joseph Berchtold, commander of the 1923 *Stosstruppe Adolf Hitler* and Emil Maurice, who had formed the first Nazi 'strong arm' squads in 1921. Having torn off Schneidhuber's insignia and sent him and his confreres to the Stadelheim prison in Munich, Hitler set off for Bad Weissee with a column of cars and lorries. From what can be gathered, and the evidence is conflicting, Dietrich did not accompany Hitler on this drive, but went instead to meet his two companies at Kaufering. He expected to take them to join Hitler at Bad Weissee, but bad roads, which proved difficult for the light vehicles which were all his men were able to bring by train, and the need to refuel, held him up. He thus did not arrive until noon when the operation was over. Hitler, in the meantime, arrived at Bad Weissee and surprised Roehm and his comrades in bed. They were dragged out and driven back to Munich, where they joined the others in the Stadelheim.

Hitler had left orders for Dietrich and his men to return immediately to Munich, which they did, and Sepp himself reported to Hitler at the Brown House. Hitler gave him a list of six prominent SA men and told him to organise an execution squad and go to the Stadelheim and shoot them for high treason. It is very likely that Sepp blanched when he saw the names. Two, Peter von Heydebreck and Hans Hayn, had been prominent *Freikorps* leaders. Others were Schneidhuber, who was also a former Army colonel, Edmund Heines, the SA leader in Silesia and, like Roehm, notorious for his homosexual activities, and Graf Hans-Joachim von Spreti. The final name on the list was Wilhelm Schmid. Here there was a tragedy of mistaken identity. Not knowing that he had already been arrested, a group of SS men burst into the house of Willi Schmidt, the well known music critic of the *Muenchener Neueste Nachtrichten*, and dragged him away from his wife and children. Four days later, his coffin was returned to his widow. The majority of these men Sepp had regarded as comrades and yet, since it was a direct order from the Führer, he obviously felt that there was nothing he could do but to obey. The prison itself was being guarded by the *Landespolizei* under Hans Frank, the Bavarian Justice Minister and later the notorious governor of Poland. When Dietrich and his men arrived at 1900 hours, Frank was at the prison and Dietrich showed him the list, but Frank said that no executions could be carried out without a legal warrant. Apparently, Dietrich then telephoned the Brown House and Hitler told Frank that the matter was of no concern to him. Frank now telephoned Rudolf Hess, Deputy Leader of the Party, in Berlin and asked him to remonstrate with Hitler. Later, Hess telephoned back to state that Hitler had obtained emergency powers from von Hindenburg and the executions went ahead. Dietrich himself later testified at his Munich trial in 1957 that he had left after the 'fourth or fifth shot', not being able to stand any more. [26]

Other executions followed, as they did also in Berlin. Here these were ordered and managed by Goering and Himmler, who remained there, the actual executions being carried out by the *Leibstandarte* at Lichterfelde under the direction of *Sturmbannführer* Martin Kohlroser who had been left in charge there. Hitler's decision to execute Ernst Roehm was not made until the afternoon of 1 July and he passed the order to Himmler. He, in turn, contacted Theodor Eicke, commandant of the already infamous Dachau concentration camp, and told him to carry it out. Assisted by his adjutant, Michael Lippert, Eicke went to the Stadelheim and they carried out the deed. Eicke himself was to be killed in Russia in February 1943 while commanding the SS-*Totenkopf* Division, but Lippert would survive to join Dietrich in the defendants' box in 1957.

Hitler flew back to Berlin on the evening of 1 July and on that same day the two *Leibstandarte* companies also returned by train, Dietrich going by plane. On arrival he reported to Hitler at the Chancellery, who immediately promoted him to *Obergruppenführer*, but said to Sepp: 'Do you know you were also on the list?' [27] Those who took part in the Night of the Long Knives, as it came to be called, were sworn to an oath of secrecy, indeed it was not until the 1957 Munich Trial that anyone who had taken a direct part in it spoke directly about it. All documents relating to it were systematically destroyed and no one has been able to arrive at an exact total of those who lost their lives during that weekend. Certainly, the figure runs into hundreds and it included not just key SA figures, but many leading figures from Weimar days. Among the other victims were General Kurt von Schleicher, Gregor Strasser, Ritter von Kahr, Erich Klausener, leader of Catholic Action and General Kurt von Bredow. Indeed, anyone who could possibly be seen as a threat to Hitler was eliminated. Even von Papen was lucky to escape with his life. His leading adviser, Edgar Jung, who had been arrested by the Gestapo a few days earlier, was murdered in prison, and his principal secretary shot as he sat at his desk. There is no doubt either that Himmler, Goering, Bormann and others also took the opportunity to settle private scores and, indeed, added many names to the lists without Hitler's authority.

Apart from some who were horrified at the deaths of von Schleicher and von Bredow, the military hierarchy was generally delighted with what had happened, seeing the SA as a dangerous threat to the Army. Von Blomberg issued an order of the day on 1 July praising Hitler for his courage and von Hindenburg, too, sent him a telegram the next day congratulating him. The matter, too, was sealed on 3 July when a new law was announced stating that the executions were legitimate acts of self-defence taken against traitors. The Army, however, unwittingly or not, had to pay penalties. On 2 August 1934, von Hindenburg finally passed away. Hitler immediately combined the offices of President and Chanceller, calling himself *Führer* and *Reichskanzler*, and ordered von Blomberg and von Fritsch to swear a personal oath of loyalty to him. A short time later, all officers and men in the *Wehrmacht* were required to do the same. Hitler now had the Army morally in his thrall. The SA itself was not disbanded, but was placed under command of Viktor Lutze, an early SA member who had demonstrated his loyalty to the Fuhrer prior to and during the Night of the Long Knives. The SS was removed from its theoretical control, to the delight of Himmler, and the SA became a body without teeth. Apart from being granted its independence, the SS as a whole was also rewarded for its loyalty through von Blomberg's agreement to provide a division's worth of arms and military equipment for it. Out of this would arise the Waffen-SS.

Sepp Dietrich, though, in spite of his promotion, which 24 others, including Eicke, also received, and the ceremonial daggers with which all were awarded, remained shocked over what had happened for some days. The evidence for this comes from Ernst 'Putzi' Hanfstaengel, noted wit and Hitler's Foreign Press Chief, who was on his way back from a visit to Washington DC at the time of the Night of the Long Knives. He was amazed over what had happened and, on his return to Berlin, approached Sepp, whom he regarded as 'a rought-and-ready fellow, but not as personally hostile to me as the others', perhaps because Hanfstaengel himself was also a Bavarian.

'Dietrich as good as admitted that he had been out at Wiesse [sic] with Hitler, but he was not talking. I really think that even he was shattered by what he had taken part in. "You have no idea," he muttered, "thank your lucky stars that you were not around. I got my orders signed but I had to practically force him [Hitler] to put his signature on them.'' I thought I saw a chance of breaking him down but before I could continue Schaub loomed up from somewhere in the gloom and joined us, suspicious and surly as ever. The conspiracy of silence descended again.'[28]

Yet, shocked as Dietrich may have been, he had no practical or realistic option but to 'soldier on'. He could not wash the blood from his hands and any thoughts in this direction that he might have had were quickly erased by the memory of what Hitler had said to him in the Chancellery on the evening of 1 July.

Some months before von Blomberg gave his agreement to Army support for a military wing of the SS, Himmler had already begun to lay plans for such an eventuality. In May 1934 he had established, on paper at least, four *Standarten* (regiments), one in each *Oberabschnitt*, with the *Leibstandarte* being that for *Oberabschnitt Ost*. Now that the Army was prepared to make the arms available, his concept could be realised. In September 1934 the formal announcement was made of the creation of the *SS-Verfügungstruppe* (SS Special Purpose Troops or SS-VT) and two new *Standarten* were created, one based in Munich and the other in Hamburg. There were not, however, the resources available to form the fourth *Standarte* at this time. In parallel with this step, Himmler also combined the SS elements running the growing number of concentration camps into the *SS-Totenkopfverbände* (SS Death's Head Units) under Eicke. Thus, taking into account Heydrich's SD, there were now three specialist groupings within the SS as a whole and, in order to differentiate the main body from these, it was henceforth titled the *Allgemeine* (General) SS. With regard to the SS-VT, Himmler hoped to be able to use this organisation as a means of bringing Dietrich and the *Leibstandarte* to heel. With this in mind, he intended to call the *Standarten* SS Regiments 1-3, with the *Leibstandarte* as SS Regiment 1. Hitler, however, thwarted this by insisting that the *Leibstandarte* retain its unique title, thus providing Dietrich with ammunition for his argument that, although his unit was part of the SS, its special status meant that Himmler must treat it with deference. Thus Himmler was forced to call the new units SS Regiments 1 and 2, although they soon became better known as SS-*Deutschland* (Munich) and SS-*Germania* (Hamburg). Himmler also set up an SS Officers school at Bad Tolz and another school at Brunswick in order to standardise what had until now been a somewhat haphazard training for potential leaders in the SS. It was also clear that if the SS-VT was to become militarily efficient it needed an injection of professional soldiers. Among the early arrivals was General Paul Hausser, who had retired from the Army in 1932 at the age of 52. He set up the SS training academy at Brunswick before going on to become Inspector of the SS-VT. Another was Felix Steiner, who stepped across from being Director of Education at the War Ministry. Yet another was Willi Bittrich, former World War I pilot who had spent eight years teaching the Russians how to fly under the secret agreement arranged between the Weimar and Soviet governments in 1922.

This injection of military experience would help the SS-VT be less dependent on the Army but, at the same time, in order to make Dietrich, who had up until now forged his own contacts with the Army, both in the Ministry and with the formations in the Berlin area, come to heel, Himmler and von Blomberg drew up new guidelines for the relationship between the SS-VT and the Army. From now on, all dealings between the two would be at the level of Himmler's own staff and the War Ministry and Himmler's headquarters would control issues of military equipment. If Dietrich resented this he gave no outward sign and concentrated on making the *Leibstandarte* a showpiece of National Socialism. Lichterfelde was transformed, being given the most up-to-date facilities, including a dining-room that could feed 1700 men at one sitting, riding stables, which for a time included the favourite mare of the late Ernst Roehm (until she was purloined by Goering), a 200 metre underground indoor shooting range, and an indoor swimming pool. Many foreign delegations were taken round it. Overall, the presence of Sepp Dietrich permeated. This visitor also noticed a glow in his men's eyes when they saw Dietrich. He often ate with his men rather than in the Officers' Mess and addressed them with the familiar '*Du*' rather than formal '*Sie*'. His standing was nowhere better reinforced than when an NCO charged a recruit for throwing a rifle at him in a fit of pique. Sepp immediately charged the NCO for failing to sort the matter out himself. As he once said to a visitor to the barracks, when asked about the affection in which he was held: 'Well yes, it makes them happy when they see me.'[29] One material token of this affection came in March 1937. To mark the fourth anniversary of the formation of the *Leibstandarte*, Sepp's men presented him with a suitably inscribed solid platinum ring. He clearly treasured this, often wearing it, and it is still in the possession of his eldest son to this day. Yet, strict discipline on the one hand and paternalism on the other did not necessarily produce the ideal Party soldier. During the course of 1935 there were a number of complaints by the Reich Chancellery about the juvenile behaviour of the *Leibstandarte* guard, such as riding the lifts to pass the time, loud radios in the guardroom and tearing off the clothes hooks outside Hitler's offices.[30] Later, in summer 1940, Hitler was to sack two of his *Leibstandarte* servants for theft. Not only were they dismissed from the SS, but sent to Dachau Concentration Camp as well.[31]

In a secret order dated 2 February 1935, Hitler clarified the position and organisation of the SS-VT. He confirmed that it was to be made up of three *Standarten* or regiments, together with an engineer and signals battalion, but that no decision had as yet been made over giving it its integral artillery and reconnaissance detachment. In wartime, the SS-VT was to be 'incorporated into the Army. They are then subordinated to military laws which also apply to matters of recruitment.' The intention was that the SS-VT should be fielded as a complete division, with the Army supplying the necessary supporting arms, services and staff. Preparation for its wartime role was to 'proceed even in peacetime under the responsibility of the *Reichswehr* Minister, to whom they are

63

subordinate in this respect.'[32] For the *Leibstandarte*, however, the opportunity to carry out its wartime role came quicker than anyone could have expected, although, in truth, it was little more than a deployment exercise.

On 12 January 1935 a plebiscite was held in coal rich Saarland, marking, under the terms of the Versailles Treaty, the end of fifteen years under League of Nations auspices. The population voted, with a ninety per cent majority, to be reunified with Germany. Hitler was naturally delighted, declaring that this brought to an end his differences with France, and the date for bring the Saarland back into the fold was fixed for 1 March 1935. Instead of choosing the Army to enter the Saar, Hitler ordered that the *Leibstandarte* should carry out the task, probably to demonstrate to the Saarlanders all that was best about National Socialism. On 28 February, Dietrich mustered the *Leibstandarte*'s motor-cycle company (established in November 1934), two line companies of the 1st Battalion, two companies from the 2nd Battalion and one from the 3rd, a total of almost 1600 men. They moved by road that afternoon, arriving in Saarbrucken at the stroke of midnight. For the next five days, there were speeches and parades in which the *Leibstandarte* featured prominently. So impressed were the Saarlanders with its appearance and conduct that one local newspaper was moved to comment: 'Hitler's men – they are as gods come to show the way for the new Germany.'[33] Indeed, so touched were Sepp and his men by their reception that on their departure he issued an open letter to the local press thanking everyone for the warmth of their reception.[34]

This success further encouraged Sepp in his campaign to resist Himmler's attempts to bring him to heel. The fact that the *Leibstandarte*'s uniform had noticeable differences to the remainder of the SS-VT also helped. Only the *Leibstandarte* was allowed to wear white accoutrements with its black uniform and bear the SS runes on the collar tab without a unit number. According to his eldest son, Dietrich personally designed the *Leibstandarte*'s uniform. Furthermore, in 1935 the *Syndikat Film GmbH* made a documentary about the unit which was shown as a supporting film to the box office success *Fridericus Rex*. All this gave Sepp additional muscle in his battles with Himmler, besides the fact that he remained a member of Hitler's personal staff and, indeed, largely controlled key figures in it, including Hitler's chauffeur and his personal pilot, Hans Baur, whose names were on the books of the *Leibstandarte*. For Himmler, this continued to make difficulties. Thus, when an obligatory six-month tour of duty with Ley's Labour Service was introduced for all young males, Dietrich chose to ignore it. Himmler's staff were forced to issue a directive to Sepp that October reminding him of the rules, but this only resolved matters for a short time and the problem arose again three years later. Dietrich also continued his unofficial contacts with the Army, in spite of the directives stating that he must go through Himmler's office. Thus, in January 1935, he tried to secure tanks for the *Leibstandarte*, although without success.[35] In all this, Hitler, rather than making sure that Dietrich obeyed Himmler, seems to have encouraged him to resist.

As for Dietrich's personal life, by the mid 1930s he and Betti had grown apart. The reasons for this are not clear, but it may have been that Betti was unable to have children and also because Dietrich had an eye for a pretty girl. Thus, when the contents of his pocket book came up for auction in the United States a few years ago, among the items on offer was a pencil drawing of a scantily dressed girl on paper from the *Weinstube Kempinski* in Berlin. It was inscribed '*Sepp Dietrich von Maxi Herber, Berlin 2.4.37*'. Maxi herself was quite a well known skater and Sepp himself was a member of the *Berliner Schlittschuklub*, a fashionable skating club in Berlin. [36] Dietrich's frequent absences from home once he joined the Party cannot have helped, even though Betti clearly tried to take an interest in what he was doing, herself becoming a Party member (No 233700). It is probably unlikely that she accompanied him to Berlin and it may be, too, that she felt ill at ease in the company that Sepp was now keeping. He had become good friends with the industrialists Alfred Krupp and Friedrich Flick, both presumably a good source of hunting invitations, as well as with the owner of Berlin's premier restaurant, Horcher's, and it is probably here, at least according to Wolf-Dieter Dietrich, [37] that he first met the girl who would become his second wife. Her father, Heinrich Moninger, owned the famous brewery of that name in Karlruhe, which still exists. He was also President of the *Vorstand des Brauereiweres Veruchs und Lehrenshalt*, a brewers' association whose headquarters were in Berlin. Hence he had to go there quite frequently and took his daughter Ursula, who was twenty-two years old in 1937, with him. Dietrich and Moninger became good friends and he was much attracted by Ursula. The two fell in love and the result was the birth of a son, Wolf-Dieter, in 1939. He was, however, born out of wedlock and it may have been that Dietrich was unable to obtain a divorce from Betti. Certainly, she was still officially his wife until at least April 1937. [38] How Ursula's parents reacted to the birth is not known, but she certainly had the baby at home in Karlsruhe and they did not stand in the way of her marriage to Sepp in January 1942. It is thus probable that Heinrich Moninger's close friendship with the man who was to become his future son-in-law overrode any qualms which they might have had over the social mores. It may have been, too, that Wolf-Dieter's birth finally persuaded Betti to give way over the matter of divorce. By then, however, war had broken out and Sepp was to be seldom in Germany long enough during the early years for his marriage to Ursula to be organised.

Detachments of the *Leibstandarte*, and often Dietrich himself, continued to accompany Hitler during his travels about Germany. The responsibility for the Führer's security was, however, now shared with the SD. Thus, during the Winter Olympics held at Garmisch-Partenkirchen in February 1936, Dietrich and Rattenhuber of the SD co-operated together, with Dietrich having some 200 of his men there. They were put up in a local schoolhouse and given the freedom of the local inns, except one whose landlord was not a National Socialist. The Nuremberg Rallies held in September each year during the

mid-1930s also entailed a large *Leibstandarte* commitment, as did the commemoration of the 1923 *putsch* in Munich. There is no doubt that the *Leibstandarte*
had by now gained a reputation second to none for the standard of its drill and
turnout, but also the nickname 'asphalt soldiers' from the remainder of the
SS-VT and especially by the SS *Deutschland* from 1937, when Felix Steiner took
over command and concentrated on turning it into a crack fighting force. Otto
Weidinger, who was in the 4th Battalion at the time, recalls how when he was
in a command of a guard of honour from the *Deutschland*, when Hitler was
visiting Stuttgart, he was personally berated by Dietrich for reporting his
guard present and correct direct to Hitler rather than through his staff. Having
told Dietrich which unit he was from, Sepp said 'with a gesture of resignation
with his hand: "Oh well – the peasant battalion."'

'Years later, during the Ardennes offensive, 44/45 I was decorated with the Oakleaves to the
Knights Cross by the commander-in-chief of the 6 Pz Army Sepp Dietrich at the battle
headquarters of *Das Reich*, together with the commander of the Regiment *Deutschland*
Obersturmbannfuhrer Wisliceny.
When later on, during a short drinking session, I was sitting beside Oberstgruppenführer
Sepp Dietrich, I reminded him of that episode in Stuttgart 1937 which he found thoroughly
amusing and laughed hearily.'[39]

Nevertheless, this is an indication that during the 1930's at least, Dietrich
looked down on the other two SS-VT regiments.

In spite of the fact that the *Leibstandarte* ceremonial and guard duties left little
time for military training, the regiment was gradually motorised. In July
1936, the trench mortar company (No 13) was converted into an infantry gun
company, and an armoured car platoon was added at the end of the year. It is
also worthy of note that *Oberst* Erwin Rommel, then an instructor at the War
Academy at Potsdam and fresh from publishing his book on infantry tactics,
Infanterie Greift An, lectured the officers of the *Leibstandarte* one evening in
November 1937.[40] This was probably the first time that Sepp Dietrich came
into direct contact with him. Later, in Normandy, they would come to know
one another very well. Nevertheless, relations between the SS-VT as a whole
and the Army were not especially good. The Army quickly began to see the
SS-VT in the same light as it had Roehm's SA and was concerned that it might
usurp the *Wehrmacht*'s prerogative to be the nation's sole bearer of arms. While
the Army was prepared to allow the SS-VT to share its training areas, it found
it hard to swallow that it was not given the privilege of guarding the Führer
when he visited manoeuvres. This duty remained the responsibility of the
Leibstandarte, and it seemed that the Army could not be trusted. This certainly
was the view of many members of the SS-VT, who saw themselves as an elite
with an ideological fervour which the Army could never have. No wonder that
General von Fritsch noted in early February 1938, just before his downfall as
chief of the Army High Command: 'All sources agree that the attitude of the
SS *Verfügungstruppe* towards the Army is frigid, if not hostile. One cannot avoid
the impression that this hostile attitude is deliberately cultivated.'[41] This

accusation could not be laid at the door of Hausser, Steiner and the other former professional soldiers and, indeed, Sepp Dietrich himself, but Himmler, an empire builder *par excellence*, certainly felt this way, as did many of the more junior officers, especially once they had graduated from Bad Tolz. When Hitler issued a new decree in August 1938 redefining the role of the SS-VT and stating that he reserved for himself 'the decision as to the time, strength, and the form of the *SS-Verfügungstruppe*'s absorption into the Army at the time of mobilization according to the then existing political situation'. If the threat was internal, the SS-VT was under Himmler's control and if external, under the Commander-in-Chief of the Army, but even then it still remained 'politically an arm of the Nazi party' [42] thus ensuring that he and Himmler still retained a sizeable degree of control over it. No clearer indication of how the SS-VT regarded the Army is given than in the reactions of one member of the SS *Hauptamt*, *Brigadeführer* Leo Petri, to this decree: 'The Wehrmacht has been forced to recognise that the pertinacity of the *Reichsführer-SS* in the pursuit of his aims is stronger than its own resistance to the innovations of the Third Reich.' [43] Nonetheless, the Army was able to persuade Hitler not to turn the SS-VT into a fully fledged division, which was why it was still not allowed its own artillery. The Army retained the right to inspect SS-VT units, as well as forbidding it to place recruiting advertisements in the newspapers.

During 1938, there were continual ructions between Dietrich and Himmler and also with Hausser in his capacity as Inspector of the SS-VT. At the beginning of March, Dietrich was in trouble with Himmler once more over publicity for the fifth anniversary of the formation of the *Leibstandarte*. Instead of clearing it through Himmler, Dietrich dealt directly with the Press over publicity, which earned him a stiff rebuke.

> 'You officers are good enough to recognise me personally, but otherwise the Leibstandarte SS Adolf Hitler is an undertaking for itself and does what it wants without bothering about orders from above and which thinks about the SS leadership only when some debt or other, which one of its gentlemen has incurred, has to be paid or when someone has fallen into the mud and has to be pulled out of the mess . . . Please do not forget that what you do as first commander of the *Leibstandarte* SS Adolf Hitler will naturally be taken as right by the next twenty commanders. You don't seem to have thought that this would be the beginning of the end of the SS.' [44]

In July, Sepp was in trouble for procuring his own volunteers and issuing his own call-up orders. This brought about a complaint from no less than General Wilhelm Keitel, now *Chef des Oberkommando der Wehrmacht* (OKW). Himmler saw this as yet another example of Dietrich's arbitrariness, but was chiefly concerned that he would be seen by the *Wehrmacht* as having no control over the *Leibstandarte*. [45] Furthermore, Dietrich was again in hot water for ignoring the six months' labour service rule. Then, in August, it was over a more personal matter. Himmler was concerned that Sepp had been accepting hunting invitations from a certain von Palombini, who was regarded as suspect by the Party. In future he was to have all such invitations cleared through Himmler's adjutant, Karl Wolff. 'You have to realise that most people inviting us don't do it for generosity.'[46] Paul Hausser was also frustrated by Dietrich's behaviour, especially since Dietrich used the ploy of his seniority in rank to prevent Hausser carrying out formal inspections of the *Leibstandarte*, something that he was only able to do if he accompanied Himmler. Matters came to a head in May 1938 over the final formation of the fourth SS-VT regiment, *Der Führer*, which was to be based in Vienna. Hausser ordered Dietrich to provide a cadre for it, but Sepp refused point blank. Hausser now wrote to Himmler offering his resignation. The matter was resolved by Himmler, who made Dietrich go and see Hausser. After this there was, in fact, no more trouble between the two and Dietrich did provide some personnel for the new regiment.[47]

The raising of the *Der Führer* also made the Army anxious once more. Major Engel, who was Hitler's Army adjutant during 1938-43, recorded a discussion between Hitler and Dietrich on 19 April 1938.

> 'Occasion was the creation of the 4th Standarte in Vienna "*Der Fuhrer*". Fuhrer said that the establishment of the VT would be finished now. He wanted to keep this "elite" small. Otherwise it would no longer be an elite. It had to be a political state formation, blindly obedient to the Fuhrer and State. Riots could always occur; the force would intervene brutally. He saw it as a pure "Praetorian Guard" which does away with all who kick against the pricks, even within its own ranks. That's the reason for equipping it with the best and most modern weapons . . .'

Engel was very worried over this since he saw the danger of the Army being pushed aside in Berlin and believed that perhaps a similar military force should be formed.[47] It also illustrates, too, the close relationship which Dietrich continued to enjoy with Hitler in that the latter was prepared to discuss SS policy matters direct with Dietrich without Himmler being involved.

Nevertheless, 1938 saw the *Leibstandarte* deployed for the first time as it would be in war. The occasion was the 'liberation' of Austria in March. For some months the Schuschnigg government had been under increasing pressure from Hitler to accommodate the Nazi movement within the country. In a last desperate measure to try and retain a measure of independence for his country, Chancellor Schuschnigg announced in early March 1938 that he intended to hold a plebiscite on the 13th so that the Austrian people could decide whether they wished to remain free and independent of Germany. Hitler now threatened invasion if the plebiscite was not cancelled and Schuschnigg did not resign. Both these things happened but, on 10 March, Hitler decided that he would invade in any event and bring Austria firmly under his control. The Army received only forty-eight hours warning of this and Dietrich was told that the *Leibstandarte* would take part. The bearer of this news was General Heinz Guderian, who had recently assumed command of XVI Panzer Corps and who had already established the reputation of being Germany's leading expert on armoured warfare. He told Dietrich that the *Leibstandarte* would be under his command. There is no doubt that the two men took an immediate liking to one another. While Guderian probably respected the fact that Dietrich had fought in tanks in 1918, which he himself had not done, having been on the staff for most of the war, and enjoyed Sepp's robust humour, Sepp saw in Guderian a man of purpose and directness unfettered by pomposity, unlike many of the more conservative German senior officers. Establishing that Dietrich had an appointment with Hitler later that evening, 10 March, Guderian took advantage of this to ask him if he would pass on a request to Hitler that the vehicles should enter Austria bedecked with flags and greenery so as to demonstrate to the Austrians that the troops were friendly and had no feelings of enmity. This Sepp did and Hitler agreed to the idea.[48] This was the first occasion on which a Wehrmacht general had taken advantage of Dietrich's special relationship with Hitler and it was a practice that others would adopt in later years.

The *Leibstandarte* itself was to be the rearguard for Guderian's corps and appears to have performed satisfactorily, crossing the Austrian border at 1400 hours on 12 March and then making for Hitler's birthplace, Linz. From here it moved to Vienna, where it took part in a parade for Hitler, which also included 2nd Panzer and 27th Infantry Divisions. It remained in Austria for a further three weeks before returning to Berlin.

A month after the successful conclusion to the *Anschluss*, Hitler turned his eyes on Czechoslovakia. Although, as early as 21 April, he discussed with Keitel the possibilities of a lightning strike on the country, it was not until 20 May that he issued a directive for Operation *Green*, as it was codenamed. Some six weeks later, he decided that the SS-VT would take a role in the invasion, with the *Leibstandarte* once more coming under Guderian's command in XVI Panzer Corps. At the end of September, the *Leibstandarte* deployed to the training area at Grafenwöhr, with 1st Panzer Division, to carry out intensive training. It seemed that Operation *Green* could be mounted at any time.

The absence of the *Leibstandarte* from Berlin, however, gave encouragement to a group of conspirators built round such as General Ludwig Beck, who had recently resigned as Chief of Staff of the Wehrmacht as a protest against Hitler's plans to invade Czechoslovakia, Karl Goerdeler, formerly Lord Mayor of Leipzig, General Erwin von Witzeleben, commander of III Army Corps and Ulrich von Hassell, formerly German ambassador to Italy. They planned to arrest Hitler and his close confederates and put them on trial. One essential precondition to this was that the *Leibstandarte* should be away from Berlin. They planned to strike on 28 September, but they were forestalled by Hitler's decision to treat with the British Prime Minister, Neville Chamberlain, the French Prime Minister Eduard Daladier, and Mussolini and by the subsequent Munich Agreement, by which they recognised the German right to annex Sudetenland without a plebiscite in return for Hitler calling off his invasion plans. Since the conspirators' pretext was the threatened invasion of Czechoslovakia and the resultant European war, which they believed would follow in its wake, they cancelled their plans. What all this did indicate, however, was how widely regarded the *Leibstandarte* was as a linchpin of the Nazi regime. Then, at the beginning of October, Guderian's XVI Panzer Corps, with the *Leibstandarte* still under command, moved in and peacefully occupied the Sudetenland. Six months later, the *Leibstandarte* also took part in the occupations of Moravia and Bohemia which marked the final dismemberment of Czechoslovakia.

During the spring and early summer of 1939, the *Leibstandarte* was back in Berlin carrying out its normal round of guard and ceremonial duties, but Hitler's territorial ambitions in Europe were still not satisfied. By mid-August, war clouds were once more looming over the horizon, but this time neither peaceful negotiation nor occupation without bloodshed were there to dispel them.

CHAPTER 5

Blitzkrieg
1939-41

In June 1939, Hitler finally overrode the objections of the Army and declared that the SS-VT would now be organised as a division. To this end, an SS artillery regiment was raised at Jüterborg, with drafts from the *Leibstandarte*, *Deutschland* and *Germania*. His decision to invade Poland, however, came too quickly for the division to be properly constituted and the three regiments were placed piecemeal under army command. For the *Leibstandarte* this meant coming under command of XIII Corps, part of Blaskowitz's Eighth Army. Blaskowitz's task was to cover the left flank of von Reichenau's Tenth Army in Army Group South.

On 24 August, Dietrich received his orders. At dawn the next day, the *Leibstandarte* left Berlin and deployed to Kunersdorf, east of Breslau, leaving a guard battalion under *Sturmbannführer* Bertling at Lichterfelde. On arrival at Kunersdorf, Dietrich was formally placed under the command of General Freiherr von Weichs, commanding XIII Corps and received a motorised battalion of 46th Artillery Regiment to provide him with the close fire support which he lacked. The *Leibstandarte*, however, was the only motorised element in XIII Corps. The other formations, 10th and 17th Infantry Divisions had little other than horse drawn transport and were mainly reliant on their feet. Sepp himself, was now well used to commanding a regiment in peace time and had attended a course for motorised regimental commanders at Zossen in 1936 and one for all Panzer division commanders at the Tank School at Windsdorf in 1938.[1] Yet to command a regiment in war, when his previous combat experience had been as an NCO, was a quantum jump. Luckily, Willi Bittrich had been appointed his chief of staff in June 1939 so that at least he had a relatively experienced officer at his right hand, although, of course, most of Bittrich's military experience *per se* had been as a pilot. Bittrich's opinion of Dietrich's intellect, however, was low: 'I once spent an hour and a half trying to explain a situation to Sepp Dietrich with the aid of a map. It was quite useless. He understood nothing at all.'[2] Under the German system, whereby the chief of staff provided the brains and the plans while the commander was the figurehead, it did not matter as much as it might have in other armies. As for the men of the *Leibstandarte*, there is no doubt that their morale and self-confidence could not be bettered. It was not so much formal ideological

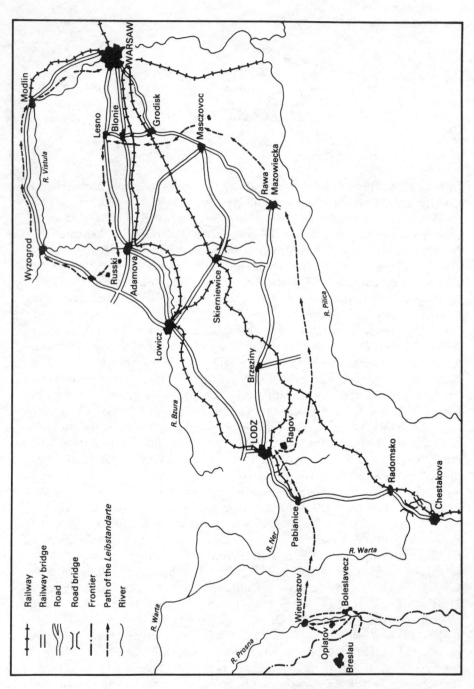

MAP 5 Poland. September 1939.

Railway
Railway bridge
Road
Road bridge
Frontier
Path of the *Leibstandarte*
River

WARSAW
Modlin
Lesno
Blonie
Grodisk
Masczovoc
Rawa Mazowiecka
Wyzogrod
Russki
Adamova
Skierniewice
Lowicz
Brzeziny
LODZ
Ragov
Radomsko
Chestakova
Pabianice
Wieuroszov
Boleslavecz
Oplatov
Breslau

R. Vistula
R. Bzura
R. Ner
R. Pilica
R. Warta
R. Warta
R. Prosna

instruction which made the SS-VT man what he was. As Ernst-Günther Krätschmer recalled: 'The rules of Germanness were not read out; one learned them by leaps from ten-metre towers, by thirty-kilometre marches and by the most severe training on the exercise grounds.'[3] Yet, as we shall see, this often bred a dangerous over-confidence.

Hitler's original intention had been to kick off the invasion, or *Case White*, as the plan was called, shortly before dawn on 26 August, but the signing of the Anglo-Polish mutual assistance pact and Mussolini's refusal to join in the fighting until Hitler had delivered him vital raw materials, caused a postponement. Orders to the troops to halt were not sent out until the evening of the 25th, in one or two cases, they did not reach forward units in time and there were isolated incidents of the border being crossed and fire being opened on the Poles. The *Leibstandarte* was on its approach march and received the order to about turn and withdraw to Kunersdorf at about midnight. On the next evening, they adjusted their bivouac areas in order to cater for the fact that they might be in them for at least a few days and, rather than be idle, the majority occupied themselves in helping to gather in the local harvest.

In the meantime, the new date for the attack had been laid down as 1 September and Hitler spent the intervening days fruitlessly trying to strike a bargain with Britain, so that she would stay out of the war, and in attempting to persuade Mussolini to reconsider. By 31 August, to Hitler at least, war was now inevitable and confirmatory orders were sent out. Using the fake attack by SS man Alfred Naujocks and concentration camp inmates dressed in Polish uniforms, on the German radio station at Gleiwitz and a customs post and forestry station as his pretext, Hitler released his armies at 0445 hours on the 1st.

The first objective of the *Leibstandarte*, which had deployed overnight from its leaguer areas to the border, was the village of Boleslavecz on the River Prosna. Brushing aside light resistance met in a village in front of it, the *Leibstandarte* closed on Boleslavecz, which was stoutly defended. In spite of a desperate Polish counter-attack with the bayonet, the village fell shortly after 1000 hours and the *Leibstandarte* continued northwards towards the town of Wieuroszov, where it was to link up with 17th Infantry Division operating on its left. Stiffening resistance by 19th Polish Division prevented it from getting any further forward by nightfall than four kilometres north of Boleslavecz, which was still six kilometres short of the objective. 17th Infantry Division had by that time already entered Wieuroszov. Nevertheless, Dietrich could feel reasonably satisfied with his men after their blooding in combat and pleased that casualties had been only seven killed and twenty wounded.

Next day, having finally linked up with 17th Infantry Division, the *Leibstandarte* turned eastwards, its objective Burzenin on the River Warte, the next major water obstacle in that sector. The sandy soil, which created problems for the heavy troop carrying vehicles, and continued Polish resistance, made the advance a slow one. Not until 0900 hours on the 4th was Burzenin reached. By that time elements of Tenth Army were already crossing the river and hence Eighth Army was not really fulfilling its role as flank guard. Since the *Leibstandarte* had been in the lead, there was a certain amount of criticism about its performance in this phase. *Generalmajor* Loch, commanding 17th Infantry Division, was especially disparaging and complained about the *Leibstandarte*'s wild firing and tendency automatically to set villages alight as they passed through them. Indeed, 'trigger happiness' was to be a marked characteristic of the *Leibstandarte* and other SS-VT formations during the first year of the war.

As far as the overall picture was concerned, pressure on the Poles from von Küchler's Third Army advancing from East Prussia and von Kluge's Fourth Army from Pomerania was forcing them back towards Warsaw and the Vistula. While the southernmost army of von Rundstedt's Army Group South, the Fourteenth under the command of List, was progressing well and would reach Lwov on 12 September, the Eighth and Tenth, having forced the defences on the River Warte, were now faced with another defence line on the Widawka. Between this and the Warthe the *Leibstandarte* was involved in further stiff fighting during the 5th and 6th and had another tough battle at Pabianice, a road-rail junction on the River Ner, along which the Poles were defending the approaches to Lodz, the next Eighth Army objective. The battle for Pabianice began on the morning of the 7th, when the *Leibstandarte*'s 1st Battalion, supported by a battalion from 23rd Panzer Regiment, attacked and penetrated the western outskirts, but was then repulsed. The other two battalions were now brought up, but they too failed to make much headway. The Polish defenders were helped by reinforcements from other troops withdrawing in the face of Tenth Army's advance and launched fierce counter-attacks; at one point Dietrich's own command post was in very real danger of being cut off. Finally, Loch, under whose command the *Leibstandarte* still was, was forced to send a complete infantry regiment to Dietrich's assistance and this succeeded in getting round the north of the town. By the early hours of the 8th, it had finally fallen.

Once again, reservations were expressed about the *Leibstandarte* and the first indications of this came with orders from HQ XIII Corps on the 8th. While 10th and 17th Infantry Divisions were to push on to Lodz itself, the *Leibstandarte* was merely given the subsidiary task of clearing the area between Pabianice and Ragov, which lay to the south of Lodz. Its artillery battalion was taken away from it and given to 10th Division. The general view of the SS-VT was that their training was insufficient and that they were rather a liability and should be withdrawn into reserve. It was recognised by the Army High Command, however, that such a step was unlikely to meet with Hitler's approval. Indeed, he took a personal interest in how the SS-VT were progressing, especially the *Leibstandarte*, whose position he kept charted on a map in the Chancellery using the notation 'Sepp'.[4] Instead, therefore, it was decided, probably to Blaskowitz's intense relief, that the *Leibstandarte* be transferred to Reinhardt's 4th Panzer Division, then part of XVI Corps in von Reichenau's Tenth Army, under the pretext that Reinhardt needed more motorised infantry for the drive on Warsaw.

This move took place on 9 September, and the *Leibstandarte* joined Reinhardt on the south-western outskirts of Warsaw that evening. By this stage, the battle of Warsaw was about to begin, but strong Polish forces in the shape of Poznan and Pomorze Armies now launched a counter-attack southeastwards across the River Bzura which ran west of Warsaw and into the Vistula. On the 10th, Blaskowitz was forced to turn back from his attack on Warsaw to deal with this threat and, that night, von Rundstedt ordered von Reichenau to assist him. In the meantime, on the 9th, 4th Panzer Division had been involved in heavy fighting on the outskirts of Warsaw and had been forced back with heavy losses, half its tanks being destroyed. The *Leibstandarte* now joined it and 31st Infantry Division, the other formation in XVI Corps, in helping to beat back and destroy the Polish counter-stroke. Indeed, the *Leibstandarte* was committed in the Piastow area on the 9th and, for the next few days, fought a bitter battle, gradually pushing westwards in the face of repeated Polish attacks. Von Rundstedt now took personal control of the battle and ordered Eighth and Tenth Armies to annihilate all remaining Polish forces between the Bzura and Vistula. In this operation the *Leibstandarte* attacked northwards on both sides of the Bzura up to its junction with the Vistula in order to seal off the eastern exit of the large pocket which had now been created, a task which it completed by the 19th.

Two days earlier, on 17 September, the Russians began to invade Poland from the east. This, and the reduction of the Bzura pocket, effectively marked the end of Poland, but it was not quite the end of the campaign for Dietrich and his men. They were now ordered to join XV Corps to assist in the reduction of Modlin, to which the northern Polish forces had withdrawn. The *Leibstandarte*'s role in this was essentially static, however, investing the southern part of the fortress while the main attack on it was launched from the north. While this operation was taking place, Dietrich and No 15 (motorcycle) Company went to Guzow on the 25th and met Hitler. On 27 September, Warsaw finally fell and, two days later, Modlin did as well and the campaign was over.

The *Leibstandarte*'s casualties during the campaign had been 108 killed, 292 wounded, 14 lightly wounded, 3 missing and 15 accidental deaths.[5] The Army considered these casualties, like those of the other SS-VT units which took part in the campaign, *Deutschland*, SS Artillery Regiment, SS Reconnaissance Battalion, as part of von Kempf's composite Panzer division in Third Army, and the *Germania* in Fourteenth Army – to be unnecessarily high and an indication of the poor standard of training. Certainly, the *Leibstandarte* had proved disappointing in the early days of the campaign, although Sepp Dietrich later put most of the blame on his transport, 'which was useless in rough terrain'.[6] Nevertheless, its performance did improve in the later stages and it did all that was asked of it. As for the enemy, Dietrich considered that the Polish Army was well led and that the Poles were a 'worthy opponent'.[7]

To the disappointment of its members, instead of going back to Berlin at the end of the campaign, the *Leibstandarte* received orders that it was to go to Czechoslovakia, where it was to relieve the *Der Führer*, which was being sent to the West Wall. There was, however, one unpleasant matter which the *Leibstandarte* left in its wake. Ulrich von Hassell recorded in his diary on 19 October 1939: 'I hear that Blaskowitz, as commander of an army, wanted to prosecute two SS leaders – including that rowdy Sepp Dietrich – for looting and murder.'[8] It is not clear whom the other SS leader was and there is no specific record of exactly what Blaskowitz wanted to charge Dietrich for, although it may have been for the indiscriminate shooting in and burning of Polish villages. What, however, the generals were more concerned over were the activities of Eicke's SS *Totenkopf* regiments, who followed in the wake of the armies in their 'cleansing and security' role,[9] which meant the murder of members of the Polish Establishment and Jews. In Blaskowitz's case, this would have been the *Brandenburg* under *Standartenführer* Paul Nostiz. No SS-VT members were ever convicted of these crimes by the Army or SS. Indeed, by a decree dated 17 October 1939, SS-VT members could no longer be tried by court-martial. While they remained theoretically under the military penal code, they were from now on to be tried by special SS courts. In any event, it would have been very difficult to bring charges against Dietrich in view of his special relationship with Hitler. As for Blaskowitz, he did eventually submit a report on SS activities, in his capacity as military governor of Poland, to von Brauchitsch the Wehrmacht Commander-in-Chief early in 1940. Von Brauchitsch discussed the report with Himmler, who assured him that matters would be corrected, but nothing more was done about it.

The *Leibstandarte* arrived in Prague on 4 October, after a two day drive and was greeted by the Reich Protector of Bohemia and Moravia, Constantin Freiherr von Neurath. The duties given to Dietrich's men were mainly guards over public buildings, but there was an opportunity to relax, which was much helped by the warm welcome given by the ethnic German population. Sepp, himself, did not stay in Prague for long and was back in Berlin before the end of October. His short stay was sufficient, though, to form strong views on how the protectorate was being governed. He spoke to Goebbels of the 'psychological errors' being made. 'We are too inconsistent in our methods. Above all, the old-school bureaucrats have a tendency to cause annoyance where none is necessary.'[10] Two weeks later, Goebbels was noting that 'Sepp Dietrich . . . confirms my views on the Protectorate'.[11]

Immediately after the victory over Poland, Hitler turned his attention to France and Britain. Initially, he hoped that they might come to terms, but it was quickly made clear to him that they intended to fight on. Invasion of France was therefore the only option. The first plan for this was published on

9 October and called for a repeat of the 1914 von Schlieffen Plan, the only difference being that Holland was included in the northern wheel. Hitler declared that *Case Yellow*, as it was called, was to be implemented on 12 November. This brought about another conspiracy to remove Hitler, this time led by General Georg Thomas, Chief of War Economy and Armament, and Colonel Hans Oster of the Abwehr. They believed that any attack in the west would be to Germany's fatal detriment in the long run, and resolved to go into action when Hitler gave the final confirmatory order to launch the offensive. They would then arrest Hitler, Ribbentrop, Himmler, Heydrich, Goering and Goebbels and, among others, Sepp Dietrich. Von Brauchitsch and Halder were brought into the plot and the former attempted to persuade Hitler that the Army was not ready to carry out such an operation, which in many respects it was not, but more on the grounds of equipment and organisational deficiencies rather than the picture of low morale which von Brauchitsch tried to paint. At this Hitler flew into one of his customary rages, which so stunned von Brauchitsch that the plot collapsed. Even so, Hitler did postpone *Case Yellow*, but only week by week.

Dietrich, however, was more directly involved in the next attempt on Hitler, which happened a few days later. It was at the annual commemoration of the 1923 Munich putsch at the *Bürgerbräukeller* in Munich on the evening of 8 November. Shortly after Hitler had finished speaking and left the hall, a bomb went off, killing seven and wounding sixty-three of those present. Who was behind it has never been satisfactorily established, although a Communist, Georg Elser, was arrested for it. At the time, however, Hitler, Dietrich and others of his inner circle had retired to the *Löwenbräu* Restaurant and so escaped it.

Sepp's men did not stay much longer in Czechoslovakia. In mid-November the *Leibstandarte* returned to Germany and was quartered in the Bad Ems-Nassau area near Koblenz, being placed under command of Guderian's XIX Panzer Corps, which must have pleased Dietrich. The main tasks were training for the impending attack on the Western Allies and regrouping. In autumn 1939 Himmler achieved his long held ambition to form SS divisions. In all, three were created. The first was the SS-V Division made up of the *Deutschland*, *Germania* and *Der Führer*, together with the SS Artillery Regiment, pioneer and Reconnaissance Battalions, with Paul Hausser being given command. Then there was Eicke's *Totenkopfverbände*, which, based on the three regiments which had been in Poland, formed the SS *Totenkopf* Division at Dachau. Finally, Himmler also managed to produce an SS Police Division, which was formed in the main from the conventional police force. Since there was little allowance made for the SS-VT in the recruiting quotas for the armed forces, Himmler and his chief of recruiting, Gottlob Berger, had to bend the regulations and resort to subterfuge in order to find the manpower, but they were successful. The final change came in March 1940 when the SS-VT was renamed the Waffen-SS.

The *Leibstandarte*, in view of its special status, was kept out of this reorganisation, but did receive additions to its strength in spring 1940 in order to make it a fully independent motorised infantry regiment. The engineer platoon was enlarged into a company, an additional infantry gun company (No 16) was added, as was an assault gun battery. A new battalion (4th) of the SS Artillery Regiment was also created and, commanded by *Sturmbannführer* Otto Staudinger, came to the *Leibstandarte* with three batteries of 105mm field guns. Before this happened, Hitler paid a Christmas visit to his troops in the west. He went to a celebration of the *Leibstandarte* at the Kurhaus in Bad Emms on 23 December, with every man present having Christmas cake, cigarettes or tobacco and a bottle of wine. In his speech, Hitler declared: 'As long as I stand at the forefront of the battles, it is for you, men of my *Leibstandarte*, an honour to be at the forefront of the battles.'[12] This was reciprocated by Sepp Dietrich in his New Year's Day order: 'We will always be his most loyal soldiers.'[13]

Meanwhile, *Case Yellow* had been going through a number of changes, with increasing attention being paid to the centre, largely thanks to the efforts of von Rundstedt and Guderian, who argued that the heavily wooded Ardennes region was, contrary to popular opinion, passable to armour and had the advantage of splitting the Allied armies. Gradually, the weight of the attack was shifted to this area and would have involved the *Leibstandarte*, as part of Guderian's corps. On 28 December Hitler ordered that the operation was to be mounted on 17 January, but six days before this a German light aircraft lost its way and made a forced landing at Mechelin in Belgium. On board was a Luftwaffe liaison officer carrying a map with the latest version of the plan on it. Not certain whether the officer had managed to destroy it or not, Hitler ordered an indefinite postponement. Not until the fifth and final version of the plan was issued, on 24 February, was it confirmed that von Rundstedt's Army Group 'A' would launch the main and decisive thrust through the centre, but by that time the *Leibstandarte* had been moved out of his command. On 29 February, it joined von Bock's Army Group 'B' in the north, coming temporarily under the command of Hausser's SS-V Division and quartered in the Ludinghausen area near Münster. Then, for a few days, it was placed under X Corps, before joining XXXIX Panzer Corps on 13 March and coming specifically under command of 227th Infantry Division. It was now in the Neuenkirchen area, just south-west of Rheine and some thirty kilometres from the Dutch border, and was to remain there until 10 May. It was also during this time that the major part of the enlargement of the *Leibstandarte's* supporting arms took place.

The task of General Frederick Zickwolff's 227th Division and the *Leibstandarte* was to cross the Dutch border and seize and capture all road and river bridges up to and including the River Ijssel. For this they formed *Schnelle Gruppe Nord* (Fast Group North) and *Schnelle Gruppe Mitte* (Fast Group Centre). These were respectively built round the 2nd and 3rd Battalions, with Regimental HQ accompanying *Schnelle Gruppe Nord*. 1st Battalion, strengthened by

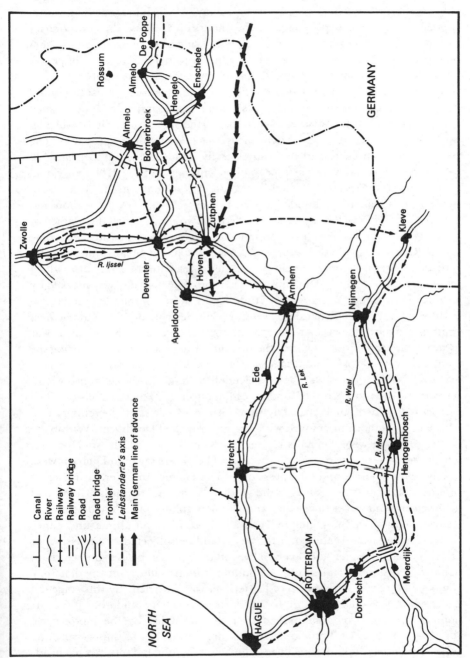

MAP 6 Holland, May 1940.

some supporting arm elements of 227th Division, was in reserve. Warning of the operation was given at 1300 hours on 9 May. At 0205 hours next morning, the codeword *Danzig* was passed. At 0535 hours on 10 May, the two *Leibstandarte* battle groups crossed the border on either side of Enschede. Facing them was an enemy whose army had become run down over many years of peace, with obsolete weapons and equipment, and whose forces were thinly spread. It is therefore hardly surprising that the *Leibstandarte* advanced almost fifty miles by noon – in contrast to the early days of the Polish Campaign. Indeed, such was the speed of the advance that when the northern group reached Zwolle on the Ijssel at 1400 hours, they caught the troops there totally unprepared. The bridges here, however, had been successfully demolished, but *Gruppe Mitte* managed to force a crossing further south at Zutphen and, by 2100 hours, had also crossed the Apeldoorn Canal just south of Apeldoorn itself. At a cost of nine killed and nineteen wounded, the *Leibstandarte* captured over one thousand prisoners, apart from the casulaties in killed and wounded which they inflicted.

On the 11th, Group North was brought down from Zwolle to Zutphen, while Group Centre exploited over the Apeldoorn Canal. Meanwhile, the 1st Battalion found itself operating in the Arnhem area with the *Der Führer*, which was under command of 207th Infantry Division. The next day was marked by a dramatic foray by *Obersturmführer* Hugo Kraas, who commanded the motor-cycle company. He penetrated as far as Harderwijk on the Zuider Zee, capturing over 120 prisoners and a number of weapons. For this he was awarded the Iron Cross 1st Class, the first officer to be so decorated during the campaign in the West. The *Leibstandarte* now received fresh orders. It was to assist XXXIX Corps under General Rudolf Schmidt in the assault on Rotterdam and was to be placed under command of 9th Panzer Division. The *Leibstandarte* joined 9th Panzer Division north of Breda on the evening of 13 May and, next morning, moved with it to north-west of Dordrecht. Within the Rotterdam area were elements of General Kurt Student's 7th Air Division, which had been dropped there on the 10th. The orders given to Dietrich were to relieve these forces and then press on to The Hague. In order to accelerate progress, especially since, away to the south in France, Guderian's armour had achieved crossings over the Meuse and was now splitting the Allied armies, it was decided to give the Dutch defenders of Rotterdam an ultimatum; either they immediately surrendered or the city would be subjected to a massive air attack. The surrender did eventually come, but not before the German bombers had already taken off. A communications failure meant that they could not be recalled and much of Rotterdam was flattened. By this stage the *Leibstandarte* was in the southern outskirts of the city and, once the air bombardment was over, it dashed over the Maas led by the motor-cycle company and the 1st Battalion. By this time Student was supervising the surrender of the Dutch troops, using the Dutch Kommandantur as his headquarters. *Leibstandarte* elements passed by, saw armed Dutch troops further up the street and immediately opened fire. Student had gone to the window to see what had happened and was chipped by a bullet in the head. Only when Lieutenant Colonel von Choltitz, commanding a battalion of the 16th Infantry Regiment, which was under Student's command, dashed outside and herded the Dutch into a church, did the firing cease. There is no record of how many surrendering Dutchmen became casualties, but the wounding of Student marred what had until then been an excellent performance by the *Leibstandarte* and, once again, demonstrated that the SS men were often far too 'trigger happy'. Long after the war, the *Leibstandarte* old comrades approached the German Paratroop Association (*Bund deutsche Fallschirmjäger eV*) in order to absolve themselves of the blame for Student's wounding. The reply they received was disappointing in that it stated that Student's recollection of the event was that it was an exchange of fire from an 'unknown source' which attracted him to the window. 'He never suggested by a single word that he was hit by a shot from members of the Waffen SS.'[14] On the other hand, he did not say that the *Leibstandarte* did not do it. Under the circumstances it would have been remarkable if he had been able to identify where the shot had come from, but, from the evidence available, the blame must rest with Dietrich's men.

By the evening of the 14th, the *Leibstandarte* had pushed on towards Delft and its bag for the day had been 3500 prisoners at a cost of one killed and ten wounded. Next day, the Dutch capitulated and the *Leibstandarte* and 9th Panzer Division were ordered to make a 'Cook's tour' of southern Holland in order to impress the degree of German military might upon the Dutch. Dressed in their best uniforms, their route took them from Leyden to Harlem and Amsterdam and then through Utrecht, Arnhem, Nijmegen, Venlo and Roermond and finally across the border into Belgium, where they arrived at Tongeren on the 18th. Here the *Leibstandarte* passed once more under the temporary command of Hausser and the SS-V Division.

At this stage, the battle for France was going increasingly badly for the Allies. The thrust through the Ardennes and across the Meuse had, by the end of 18 May, reached Péronne, thus virtually isolating the French First Army, British and Belgians and forcing their backs to the English Channel. On the 20th, the Germans reached the mouth of the Somme and then began to squeeze the resultant pocket. For the time being, however, the *Leibstandarte* was not to be involved in this. Instead, it moved with the SS-V Division to the Valenciennes area, where it helped guard the northern flank of the German penetration against possible French attempts to cut it. During 23 May, Dietrich was relieved of this task by 1st and 8th Infantry Divisions and was ordered to join *Panzergruppe von Kleist* which was now in contact with the British Expeditionary Force (BEF) along the La Bassée Canal. Arriving west of St Omer at dawn on the 25th, the *Leibstandarte* was told that it was to come under command of Guderian's XIX Panzer Corps once more. The *Leibstandarte* came into the line in the Watten area of the Aa extension of the La Bassée Canal, with the Regiment *Gross-Deutschland* on its left and 6th Panzer Division on its right.

The time of the Leibstandarte's arrival coincided with the issue of Hitler's controversial order to the Panzer formations to halt their drive on Dunkirk and leave the destruction of the BEF to Goering's Luftwaffe. Dietrich, even though he had been informed of this, immediately chose to send his 3rd Battalion across the canal in order to capture the dominant height of Watten the other side. This was successfully accomplished at a cost of two killed and twenty wounded. When Guderian visited Sepp's headquarters to ask him why he had flagrantly disobeyed orders, Sepp's reply was that the enemy on this feature had been able to 'look right down the throat of anyone on the other bank',[15] which was sound military sense and perfect justification for making the attack. The remainder of this and the following day were taken up in consolidating the newly won bridgehead. It also gave Dietrich the opportunity to do some tightening up on discipline. He was especially concerned by the fact that some men were wearing civilian clothes and that the vehicles were festooned with all types of loot acquired during the previous two weeks.[16] The pause did not last long, however. In the face of representations from von Rundstedt and others, Hitler agreed that the advance on Dunkirk could continue. For this the *Leibstandarte* was placed under command of 20th Motorised Division and was ordered to advance from Watten towards Wormhoudt.

The *Leibstandarte* was faced by the British 48th Division, which was largely made up of Territorials. They proved a much more formidable foe than the *Leibstandarte* had so far met during the campaign. The attack was first delayed by problems in throwing a bridge across the canal. As soon as this was finally completed there was a pre-emptive British attack. Eventually, at 0830 hours, the attack at last got underway. Slowly it made progress, dogged much of the time by heavy artillery fire. By 1600 hours, Guderian was forced to commit 2nd Panzer Division to the battle. Each village contained enemy strongpoints which had to be reduced and, by midnight, the *Leibstandarte* was still one kilometre short of Wormhoudt. Nevertheless they had captured over 250 British and French prisoners, but twelve of its members had been killed and twenty-four wounded, including four officers.

At 0100 hours on the 28th, Dietrich received fresh orders. He was to secure Wormhoudt and then advance to La Bellevue and thereafter towards Heerzeele. He would be assisted in this by 2 Panzer Brigade. The attack was launched at 0745 hours, but soon ground to a halt in the face of heavy fire from Wormhoudt and Esquelbecq. The defenders were the divisional machine gun battalion, the 4th Cheshires, and the 2nd Royal Warwicks, one of the four Regular battalions in 48th Division. It was Sepp's birthday and one that he would remember.

At 1150 hours, 1st Battalion HQ, which was situated at the western edge of Esquelbecq, reported back to Regimental HQ that Dietrich had been cut off on his way from 1st to 2nd Battalions, together with Obersturmführer Max Wünsche, at the south-eastern edge of Esquelbecq. His car had been shot up and he was only fifty metres away from the British positions. Max Wünsche, who was commanding No 15 (motor-cycle) Company at the time, had gone to Sepp's headquarters before dawn in order to wish him a happy birthday and be briefed on his task for the day. Sepp had kept him with him and together they went round the battalions to establish what was holding them up. Max Wünsche:

> 'When we drove along, we noticed neither battle noises nor contacts. That's why we approached a street barrier in an unsuspecting and inoffensive way and wanted to remove it. Suddenly we received machine gun fire from several machine guns and anti-tank gun fire, so we had to take cover (in the ditch beside the road).
> Fortunately, the ditch was deep, but they literally shot the edge of the ditch away with machine guns. We tried to escape to the rear. That was unsuccessful as a path from a field joined the road and we would have to go through a drainage pipe. Meanwhile, our car (Kfz 15, Mercedes cross-country) had been shot out of action; the petrol tanks leaked and a tracer round set light to the lot. I finally tried to go through the drainage pipe, but got stuck in it. I lost consciousness through what happened next. Behind me and in front of me was the burning ditch; artillery fire from friend and foe; attacks by our own troops, sorties by the enemy.'[17]

Eventually, in late afternoon, they were rescued by elements of 2 Panzer Brigade and, as Guderian wrote, Sepp 'soon appeared at my headquarters covered from head to foot in mud and had to accept some very ribald comments on our part'.[18]

In the meantime, Dietrich's men continued to struggle against the British defences and eventually, at about 1500 hours, the 2nd Battalion managed to get into Wormhoudt itself. Fighting house by house, they reached the centre of the village at 1700 hours. During this time, however, the commander, *Sturmbannführer* Schutzeck, received severe head wounds from a grenade, and Wilhelm Mohnke, as the senior company commander, took over the battalion. According to evidence collected after the war from the villagers of Esquelbecq, the men of the *Leibstandarte* had become enraged by the trapping of Sepp Dietrich, Schutzeck's wounding and the stiff resistance they were meeting, and there was much talk of revenge.[19] From the British side, the 2nd Royal Warwicks intelligence summary for the twenty-four hours from 0700 hours on the 28th noted that most of the *Leibstandarte*'s attacks were accompanied by tanks and that the infantry 'attacked in large numbers and, in some cases, shoulder to shoulder. In the rear they were urged on by the cry of 'Heil Hitler!' Large numbers were undoubtedly mown down by our fire.' Furthermore, 'many of the enemy were dressed in civilian clothes, others wore uniforms of the British, French and Belgian Armies. As they came they shouted: "Hullo, boys! We're here, don't fire."'[20] It would thus seem that Dietrich's efforts to restore discipline when in the Watten bridgehead had not been successful, but that also there was definite intent to contravene the laws of war, but at what level this was ordered or condoned cannot be established.

Wormhoudt was eventually secured at about 2000 hours, after what the *Leibstandarte*'s definitive history called 'the up until then hardest day in the West'.[21] There had been a number of prisoners captured during the course of the day and indeed many were reasonably treated – one source even says that

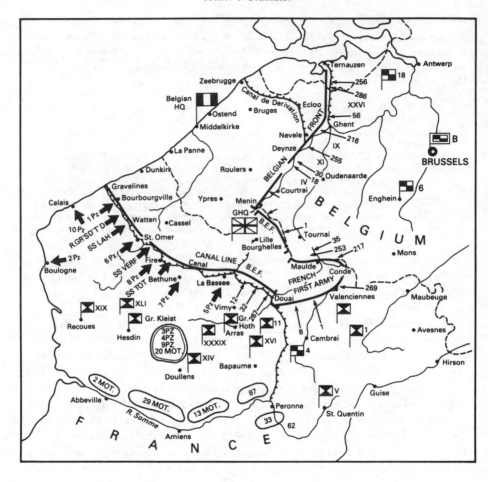

MAP 7 Dunkirk Pocket.

Dietrich entertained some captured British officers and presented them with armbands and flashes as souvenirs.[22] One group were not so lucky. As the author of the Royal Warwickshire Regimental History wrote:

'. . . a batch of 80-90 men (made up of the 2nd Battalion, the 4th Cheshire, and some artillerymen from a passing convoy) were murdered by the SS in a barn on the outskirts of Wormhoudt. Of the Battalion prisoners, there seem to have been about 50 men from D company (together with Captain Lynn-Allen, the only officer in the group) and some from A Company. They were double-marched to the barn, and thrust at with bayonets on the way. Wounded and unwounded alike were then herded into the barn. Captain Lynn-Allen immediately protested. He was answered with taunts, and several hand-grenades were thrown among the crowded troops, killing and wounding many of them. Survivors were taken outside to be shot, in batches of five. After this had happened twice, those left behind refused to come out; whereupon the Germans fired indiscriminately into the barn until they judged that none were left alive. They judged wrongly; a few men did survive, thanks

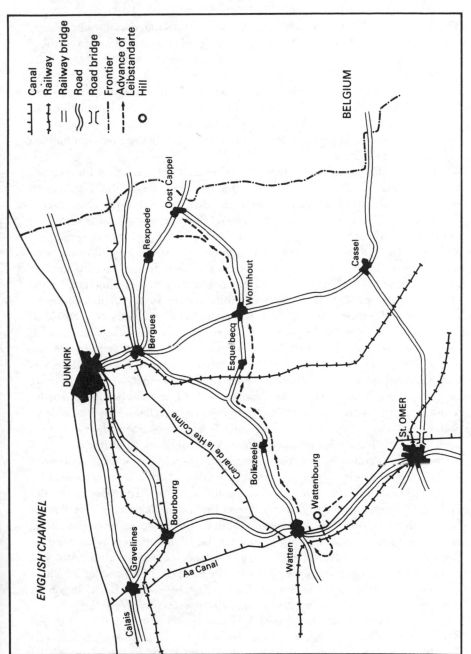

MAP 8 The Leibstandarte in the battle for Dunkirk.

perhaps to the self-sacrifice of CSM A. Jennings and Sergeant J. Moore, who threw
themselves on the top of grenades and were killed instantly by the explosion.'[23]

There were indeed four survivors, who, being incapacitated as a result of their
wounds, were returned to Britain in an exchange of prisoners of war in October
1943. It was from them that the details of the crime were first learnt. An official
investigation was launched, which continued after the war, as will be related in
Chapter Ten. There was another atrocity against British troops at this time in
France by the Waffen-SS. This was the massacre of some 100 Royal Norfolks
prisoners at Le Paradis by the *Totenkopf*. There were two survivors, however,
and their testimony resulted in the officer responsible being tried and hanged
after the war (see Page 210).

By this stage, Operation *Dynamo*, the evacuation of the Allied forces from
Dunkirk, was in full swing. During the next two days, the *Leibstandarte*
continued its slow push against the perimeter defences in the area south-east of
Berques. It achieved an advance of some eight kilometres and came to rest on
the Berques-Poperinghe road. Then, at midday on 31 May, *Panzergruppe von
Kleist* sent Dietrich orders to take his regiment by road that night to the area
south-west of Calais so that it could have the chance to rest and refurbish. The
Leibstandarte arrived in the Cap Gris Nez area in the early afternoon of 1 June
and the men were able to take the opportunity to swim in the English Channel.
It was also at this time that the *Leibstandarte* adopted its distinctive key emblem,
which from now on would be painted on its vehicles, *Dietrich* being the German
for skeleton key.[24] The rest, however, was to be short-lived. While the
evacuation of the bulk of the BEF, and a large number of French soldiers as
well, had continued and finally ended on 4 June, the French were still fighting
on and hoped to be able to hold the Germans on the line of the Somme. In order
to overcome this, von Bock's Army Group B was to attack towards the Seine on
both sides of Paris, beginning at dawn on 5 June, followed four days later by a
blow from von Rundstedt's Army Group A on von Bock's left flank.

On the afternoon of 3 June, the *Leibstandarte* was told that it was to carry out
a march the following night to the Marcoing area, where it would come under
von Reichenau's Sixth Army, the left-hand army of Army Group B. On
arrival, Dietrich was placed under General Erich von Hoepner's XVI Panzer
Corps. Initially, the *Leibstandarte* followed in the wake of von Hoepner's
armour, crossing the Somme at Péronne on the 7th and then moving south to
Roye on the River Avre. Here French resistance proved stubborn and von
Hoepner had to plan a set-piece attack for the morning of 8 June for which he
intended to commit the *Leibstandarte* for the first time. Von Bock, however,
cancelled it since he now wanted to use *Panzergruppe von Kleist* further east,
where the going was better. Dietrich was now detached however, and joined
Koch's XXXXIV Corps for a thrust towards the Marne west of Chateau
Thierry. For this, the 3rd Battalion was placed under command of 1st
Mountain Division, which was to advance astride the Soissons-Chateau
Thierry road, while the remainder of the *Leibstandarte* was to operate with 72nd

Infantry Division on the right. This attack was launched at 0330 hours on the 10th and by the end of the day had progressed some twenty kilometres, coming to rest on a tributary of the Marne, which runs west of Chateau Thierry. Nevertheless, French resistance had been surprisingly stiff and the *Leibstandarte* suffered fifteen killed and fifty-seven wounded. During the next two days, the advance continued and eventually the heights overlooking the Marne to the south-west of Chateau Thierry were secured. The *Leibstandarte* managed to establish a bridgehead across the river on the morning of the 12th. By now, von Bock had brought back von Kleist and his armour and this now crossed over the Marne. The *Leibstandarte* came back under von Kleist's command, which was transferred to Army Group A. On the 14th Paris fell. The *Leibstandarte* heard the news while snatching a brief rest in the village of Etrépilly, and members of No 11 Company celebrated by ringing the bells of the village church, which cannot have been much welcomed by the locals.

The end was in sight. Now under command of 9th Panzer Division, the *Leibstandarte* found itself in the forefront of Panzergruppe von Kleist's advance across the Seine and on southwards. Beginning on the 16th, the *Leibstandarte* advanced rapidly, meeting little other than small isolated pockets of resistance. Late on the evening of the 20th, Clermont-Ferrand was reached after a brief brush with the French at Riom, ten kilometres to the north, which cost the 1st Battalion two killed and twelve wounded. Here the 2nd Battalion seized the airfield which had on it, among other booty, no less than 242 aircraft and eight tanks. On 22 June, Dietrich was placed under command of XVI Corps. The reason for this was the Italian invasion of the French Riviera, which had finally begun the day before. There was an opportunity to take the French Army of the Alps in the rear and thus make life easier for the Italians. This operation began on the 23rd and, by the evening of the following day, the *Leibstandarte* had reached St Etienne, south-west of Lyons, having experienced stiff resistance on the approaches of the town from a force built round some First World War vintage French tanks. At 0135 hours on the 25th, Dietrich received a message from von Bock to say that hostilities were over, as stated in the armistice terms which had been signed by the French on the 22nd. The campaign in the West was over. It had cost the *Leibstandarte* 111 killed and 390 wounded.

Dietrich's views on the campaign were that the British 'were a formidable enemy, and superior in their equipment'. The French were 'variable'. 'Often they fought very courageously, while at other times they hardly resisted at all, even when their forces were superior to ours. Their equipment compared with that of the German Army, was satisfactory. The German troops made good use of the battle experience gained in the Polish campaign, and the supply system of the German Army was satisfactory everywhere.'[25] He was clearly delighted with the way his regiment had performed, especially since it had done everything asked of it, and issued a special order of the day to his men: 'I, as your Regimental Commander, am proud of you and grateful that I have been allowed to lead this Regiment, the only one in the German Army with the

Führer's name.'[26] This indicated that Dietrich definitely saw himself and the *Leibstandarte* as part of the Army rather than as a separate entity within the Waffen-SS. That Hitler was also pleased with the *Leibstandarte*'s performance was reflected in the award of the Knight's Cross to the Iron Cross (he had already won the 1939 Iron Cross 1st and 2nd Class in Poland) to Dietrich on 4 July. He was the 40th winner of this decoration. The citation read:

> '*Obergruppenführer* Sepp Dietrich through independent resolve in his sector during the gaining of the bridgehead over the Aa Canal near Watten decisively influenced the speedy pursuit of operations in northern France and further – as before in Poland – has demonstrated special personal bravery and close comradeliness with panzer and motorised formation headquarters.'[27]

One detects the hand of Guderian in this. In any event Dietrich was decorated with the Knight's Cross on the following day by von Brauchitsch. At this time, the *Leibstandarte* had just moved up to Paris, where it came under the direct command of Second Army and was engaged in general occupation duties. Hitler himself had intended to stage a victory parade in Paris, which he had visited immediately after the signing of the armistice, but then thought better of it, since it would probably cause too much offence to the French and would not help his attempts to persuade Britain to come to terms. The *Wehrmacht* did hold a parade in Paris on 23 July, after it became clear that Britain was going to fight on, but Hitler did not take it, being still in Berlin, and the *Leibstandarte* was not involved. Nevertheless, the delights of Paris, even though the inhabitants were still in a state of shock after the momentous defeat which their country had suffered, provided a welcome reward to the men of the *Leibstandarte* after their exertions of the last few weeks.

On the same day that the *Wehrmacht* parade was held in Paris, the *Leibstandarte* was informed that it was to move to Metz, where it would come under command of XLI Corps. It began its march there on the 26th, arriving two days later. Almost the first news received, once the regiment had settled into its new home, was that it was to be expanded to brigade strength. This meant an enlargement of its supporting arms and services and during the next few months its organisation became as follows:

Three rifle battalions (each of three rifle companies, a machine gun company and a heavy company – two anti-tank gun platoons (37mm and 50mm), one mortar platoon, one engineer platoon) (1st, 2nd, 3rd Battalions)

One heavy battalion with one light infantry gun company (75mm), one heavy infantry gun company (150mm), one field gun company (75mm self-propelled), one air defence company (37mm) (5th Battalion)

Reconnaissance detachment with two motor-cycle companies, one armoured car company (Sd.Kfz 222 and Sd.Kfz 233)

One artillery regiment with one field artillery battalion (three batteries of 105mm) and one mixed battalion (two batteries of 150mm and one of 88mm anti-aircraft guns)

One engineer battalion (two field companies, one bridging company)
One signals battalion (two companies)
One repair workshop
Transport unit with three transport columns
One bakery company
One butchery platoon
One food supply office
One post office
One medical company

In addition there was the guard battalion (4th), which remained in Berlin, but was on the same establishment as the rifle battalions. The continuing problem over recruits for the Waffen-SS meant, however, that much of the rein-forcement had to be carried out at the expense of the two Waffen-SS divisions. For example, two of the additional artillery batteries came from the *Totenkopf*. This may well have been a move by Himmler to clip Eicke's feathers, since the latter's arrogance and complaints over the racial purity of new recruits was creating increasing irritation among the staff of the SS Operations Office (SSFHA) and its executive branch the *Kommandoamt der Waffen-SS*, which had been set up by Himmler in August 1940 to coordinate all Waffen-SS activities. [28]

While grappling with the problems of expansion, the *Leibstandarte* was also engaged, in the late summer of 1940, in preparations for Operation *Sealion*, the invasion of Britain. This included amphibious exercises on the Moselle and intelligence briefings on Britain, but with the failure of the Luftwaffe to achieve the necessary air superiority over the skies of the South of England *Sealion* had receded into the background by the end of September. This enabled the men of the *Leibstandarte* to take home leave. Sepp Dietrich himself was frequently away in Berlin, spending much time trying to hurry along the reorganisation. Thus, Goebbels noted in his diary on 31 October 1940: 'Chat for a long time with Sepp Dietrich. He is an amiable, solid fellow. Has all sorts of complaints. Nice to chew the fat with an old Party warhorse like him.' [29]

At Christmas 1940, the *Leibstandarte* was once more honoured by a visit by the Führer. He was present at the Regiment's Christmas celebration, which took place on 26 December and was accompanied by a performance by the Regimental Choir and the Band. Dietrich presented the Führer with a record of the operations of the *Leibstandarte*, and Hitler, in his speech, said much as he had done the previous Christmas, reminding the men that the honour they had in wearing his name was to be at the forefront of the battle. [30] It would not be long before this became so, once more.

In October 1940, Mussolini, affronted by the German occupation of the Rumanian oilfields, which he considered to be in the Italian sphere of influ-ence, invaded Albania and then Greece. By Christmas 1940, the Italians had suffered disaster, being driven out of Greece and almost back to their start line.

Hitler, whose attention was now turned eastwards towards the Soviet Union, which he intended to attack in the spring, was concerned over the effect that a Balkan front might have on his plans. At the same time, Mussolini's forces had also been driven back in North Africa. While Rommel was sent to Africa, other forces were massed to deal with the Balkans. These were built round the Second and Twelfth Armies. Indeed, a plan already existed, in the shape of Operation *Marita*, to deny the Balkans to the British. The first indication that the *Leibstandarte* received that its services might be required came on 14 January when an advance party entrained at Metz for a secret destination – Rumania. Orders for the main body were, however, cancelled, and during February, while other formations were deployed from France, the *Leibstandarte* remained at Metz. Eventually, on 5 March, came the order to move. After a three day journey by train through Germany, Czechoslovakia and Hungary, it came to rest north of Bucharest. Ten days later, Dietrich's men were moved to south-western Bulgaria.

On 27 March, the Yugoslav Government, which had been prepared to allow the German forces passage through its territory, was overthrown and in its place, under the titular leadership of the 17 year-old King Peter II, a government of national unity, with a strong anti-Axis stance, was formed. Hitler immediately decided that Yugoslavia must be invaded and *Marita* was hastily revised to reflect this. At the same time, in the realisation that it was now going to take longer to subdue the Balkans, *Barbarossa*, the invasion of the Soviet Union, was postponed for a month. Ten days later, on 6 April, the attack on Yugoslavia was launched.

The *Leibstandarte* formed part of Field Marshal List's Twelfth Army and was placed under the command of Georg Stumme's XL Corps, which also had the *Leibstandarte*'s old friends 9th Panzer Division and 73rd Infantry Division. Stumme's task was to advance from Kustendil, seize Skopje and clear down through Monastir southwards to the Greek border. Initially, 9th Panzer and 73rd Infantry Division were in the lead, with the *Leibstandarte* in reserve. Thus, it was not until the 7th that the *Leibstandarte* crossed the border, although they suffered a Yugoslav air attack the day before which seriously wounded Wilhelm Mohnke, commanding the 2nd Battalion, and one of the battery commanders. Skopje fell to 9th Panzer Division on the 7th and the *Leibstandarte* advanced, first westwards and then south, passing to the east of Skopje. Prilep was reached in the early hours of the 9th and Bitola, some forty kilometres to the south, at 1700 hours that evening. Here the first significant resistance was met and Bitola was only secured after house-to-house fighting. The reconnaissance battalion which was under command of Kurt 'Panzer' Meyer was now split. While one part continued to probe the defences of the Monastir Pass, the other turned west to link up with the Italians on the Albanian border. The latter was successfully achieved on the 11th. On the Greek border attention was now concentrated on the Klidi Pass. The *Leibstandarte*'s reconnaissance detachment got as far as Vevi, at the entrance to the pass, late on the evening of the

9th. Here they ran into elements of General Sir Henry Wilson's British and Commonwealth forces which had been sent to Greece in March to help defend the country against Axis attack. Wilson, himself, realised that should the Germans get through the pass, they would cut him off from the Greek forces fighting the Italians in the west and also open his own defensive line to envelopment. List also recognised this and Dietrich was given orders to seize it.

On the morning of 10 April, a battle group under *Sturmbannführer* Fritz Witt, commander of the 1st Battalion, began to attack the pass. The defence, by a brigade from 6th Australian Division was determined and had the advantage of operating on dominating ground. Witt's men struggled slowly forward in the face of machine gun nests, mines, demolitions, air attacks and even a fall of snow. Every height they captured was dominated by another further on, but finally, on the morning of the 12th, the key to the defences, Height 997 was captured by *Obersturmführer* Gert Pleiss and his 1st Company after a hand-to-hand fight. Next morning, the battle group was through the pass and, having faced a counter-attack launched by tanks of the British 1st Armoured Brigade Group, was relieved by elements of 9th Panzer Division, who then carried on with the pursuit of the now retreating enemy. The three days fighting had cost the *Leibstandarte* 37 killed, 98 wounded and two missing, but they had captured 450 prisoners and a number of weapons, including eight light tanks. More important, the road into Greece was now open. It was an impressive performance and Stumme, in a special order of the day, thanked the *Leibstandarte* for its efforts 'which resulted from the same unshakeable spirit which the *Leibstandarte* constantly displays. The present victory signifies for the *Leibstandarte* a new and imperishable page of honour in its history'.[31] Pleiss was awarded the Knight's Cross and no less than fourteen other members of Witt's battle group received the Iron Cross 1st Class.

While Witt's men paused for breath, the reconnaissance battalion under *Sturmbannführer* Kurt Meyer was involved in an equally spectacular victory. It was ordered to advance south-west from Klida, through the Klissura Pass to Lake Kastoria in order to impede the Greek withdrawal from the Albanian front. In the Klissura Pass, they met fierce resistance from elements of the Greek 20th Division and, like Witt at Klidi, found it difficult to get forward. One method of getting the men moving was described by Meyer, who found himself pinned down by heavy machine gun fire with his men gone to ground and unwilling to continue the attack:

> 'In my distress, I feel the smooth roundness of an egg hand grenade in my hand. I shout at the group. Everybody looks thunderstruck at me as I brandish the hand grenade, pull the pin, and roll it precisely behind the last man. Never again did I witness such a concerted leap forward as at that moment. As if bitten by tarantulas, we dive around the rock spur and into a fresh crater. The spell is broken. The hand grenade has cured our lameness. We grin at each other, and head forward toward the next cover.'[32]

By the afternoon of the 14th, the pass was secured. Over 600 prisoners had been captured, including a regimental and three battalion commanders, and

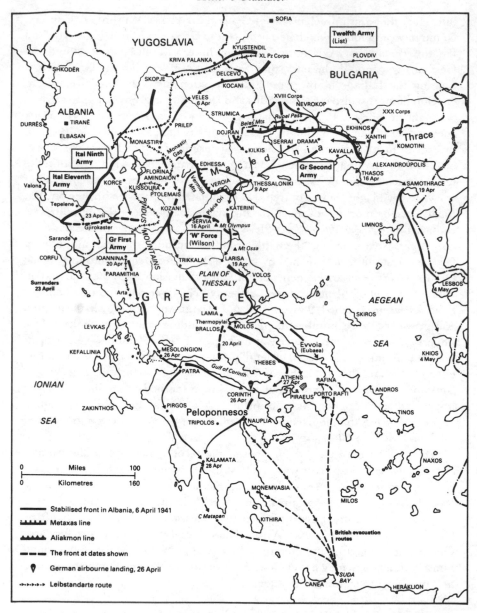

MAP 9 Yugoslavia and Greece, April 1941.

all this achieved at a cost of nine killed and 18 wounded. Meyer, followed up by a battle group based on the 3rd Battalion, then moved round the southern shore of the lake, turned north along the western side of it and seized Kastoria, taking a further 1200 prisoners and 36 guns, throwing the Greek forces into total confusion and forcing them to the west side of the Pindus Mountains. XL

Corps was now directed to the south-east, to deal with the new defence line set up by Wilson's troops through Servia to the Gulf of Salonica.

The *Leibstandarte* was now ordered to assist this operation by turning the right flank of the enemy's defence line. Dietrich was told to send a force from Kastoria towards Elasson, which lay south-south-west of Mount Olympus. By this time, however, Wilson, fearing that all was up had begun to withdraw his forces further to the south and to arrange for the Royal Navy to evacuate them from Greece. Dietrich had already despatched his force, a battle group built round the 2nd Battalion, which had so far not been heavily engaged in the campaign, under its commander *Hauptsturmführer* Horstmann. By the end of 18 April, it had advanced as far south as Grevana, when Dietrich received further orders to turn south-west, get through the Pindus mountains and cut off the Greek forces retreating towards Epirus. Consequently, Horstmann continued south to Kalampaka and then turned west towards the Katarra Pass. His leading elements arrived here at 0900 hours on the 20th and secured it after a brief fire fight. At 0945 hours, Dietrich received a slightly garbled wireless message from Horstmann which stated: 'The point of *Kampfgruppe* Horstmann 0915 hours Katarra Pass after short fire fight. Greek delegate offers surrender of whole Greek Army, General Tsolakoglou, the reinforced 2nd Battalion holds the Delegation, keeps the Army under surveillance and requests Commander send back instructions.' Sepp's reply was: 'Commander on the march and underway.'[33] He had not waited to inform Stumme or List, believing that a great opportunity might slip if the Greeks were allowed time to change their minds. In any event, Hitler had given an order prior to the campaign that enemy surrenders should be accepted by local commanders.

Heavy traffic and twisting mountain roads meant that Dietrich did not arrive at the pass until 1600 hours. Having congratulated the troops, he immediately set out for the Greek lines for a personal interview with General Tsolakoglou. The two of them arranged the surrender between them, which covered the whole of the Greek Army and, indeed the ending of hostilities between not just Germany and Greece, but Italy as well! Dietrich also chivalrously allowed the Greek officers to return to their homes because he feared that otherwise the Greeks might change their minds about surrendering. (Full text is given in Appendix 1.) Dietrich's men were too few to prevent what amounted to sixteen Greek divisions from having second thoughts. It was obviously vital that List be informed immediately and Max Wünsche, who was now Dietrich's adjutant and had accompanied him, was despatched by light aircraft to Larrissa to do this, almost crashing it in to a river such was his hurry to get there.[34] List passed details back to OKW and Jodl informed Hitler. He, in turn, told Mussolini, who somewhat understandably flew into a rage, considering the terms far too generous and that he had been betrayed by his ally. Accordingly, on the 21st, the Greeks had to sign another surrender agreement, which contained much harsher terms than the first, all soldiers being now transferred to prisoner of war camp, although officers were still allowed to keep their sidearms, and Mussolini grudgingly accepted it two days later. In the meantime, elements of the *Leibstandarte* were sent up to the Albanian border in order to ensure that the Italians did not interfere. Rather unfairly, in view of Dietrich's initiative which had done much to shorten the campaign, but also with some right on his side, given the sweeping nature of the terms, Hitler later admonished him: 'You are a good, brave soldier, but no diplomat, and still less a politician. You forgot that we still have a friend called Mussolini.'[35] Still, there was much sympathy for Sepp. Goebbels recorded a discussion which he had had with the Chief Editor of the SS weekly periodical *Das Schwarze Korps* (The Black Corps), Gunter d'Alquem, who had been covering the campaign. 'He is furious at the Italians who behaved in an impossible fashion during the surrender negotiations. But Sepp Dietrich, whose conduct has been marvellous, was not slow to express his opinion of them.'[36]

All that there was now left to deal with were Wilson's forces, who were now pulling back from their defence line around Thermopylae to ports in the Peloponnese. Not, however, until the 25th, did the *Leibstandarte* begin to take part in the final phase of the Greek campaign, namely to prevent the embarkation of the British and Commonwealth forces. Leaving the 2nd Battalion to police the Epirus area, the Corinth Canal was reached at midday on the 26th. Here Meyer and his reconnaissance battalion seized a couple of fishing boats and captured the port of Patras and then moved down the west coast of the Peloponnese, while the 3rd Battalion cleared the north coast towards Athens. A number of British, Australian and Indian prisoners were captured, but not as many as had been hoped, as the majority had been taken off by the Royal Navy during the period 24-29 April. One who was captured was Sir George Kennard Bt, serving with the 4th Hussars. He paid a special tribute to the *Leibstandarte*, which perhaps runs counter to the popular view of it as a Waffen-SS formation: 'Over the entire fighting they had been brave, chivalrous and, towards the end, they would go out of their way, at considerable risk to themselves, to take prisoners rather than take lives.'[37]

The campaign in Yugoslavia and Greece was the maturing of the *Leibstandarte*. There was undoubtedly delight among circles close to Hitler at its performance. Kurt Daluege, Commander-in-Chief of the German Police and, like Sepp, an old fighter, wrote to congratulate him and spoke to him of 'the great joy here [Berlin] once again at what one, as an *alter Kämpfer*, is able to perform without staff training. Once again, proof for the Wehrmacht that they must change their opinions once and for all.'[38] Kietel, later referred to the way in which 'Sepp Dietrich roared right through them with his division'.[39] Max Wünsche, who was by Sepp Dietrich's side all the time, pays a special tribute:

'If our men had not been motivated and if Sepp Dietrich had not been at the right places at the right times during the decisive phases, with his orders and decisions, the campaign would have gone a different way.'[40]

Dietrich himself later recalled that 'the difficult terrain could only be overcome with great skill and untiring efforts' and praised his men, stating that 'it is due to their qualities alone that the campaign in Greece was finished so quickly'.[41]

Dietrich and his troops had little opportunity to celebrate their victory. True, there was a parade in Athens on 3 May, which was taken by List and in which the *Leibstandarte* took part, and a few days to enjoy the Greek sunshine. On 8 May, however, the *Leibstandarte* was ordered to move to Bohemia to prepare for a test on an altogether different scale than the *Blitzkrieg* campaigns of the past twenty months.

CHAPTER 6

The Eastern Front 1941-43

The *Leibstandarte* moved by road up through Greece and Yugoslavia and eventually arrived at Brno in Czechoslovakia at the beginning of June. It now entered a period of frenzied activity. Not only was *Barbarossa* scheduled for the 22nd, less than three weeks away, but also the *Leibstandarte* had to cope with not just refitting but another reorganisation as well. As Hitler had rewarded the *Leibstandarte* after the French campaign by decreeing that it should be expanded to brigade size, so now he ordered that it become a division. This was done by forming a fourth rifle battalion, which was, in essence, the guard battalion from Berlin. This became the 4th Battalion, while the refurbished guard battalion became the 5th, and the heavy weapons battalion became known merely as the Heavy Battalion, *Leibstandarte*. The artillery regiment now had three battalions, one being air defence with two 37-mm and one 20-mm flak batteries. It was also given a survey battery. The medical company was expanded into a field hospital. Yet, the Leibstandarte was still little more than a strong brigade and had only just over half the strength of *Das Reich*, *Totenkopf* and the newly formed SS *Viking* divisions, with a total strength of just over 10000 men as compared to 19000. This, however, was compensated by the fact that the *Leibstandarte* was allowed to retain its rigid entry standards, and indeed its reinforcements, as in 1940, were creamed off from the other divisions, who were now being forced to recruit *Volksdeutsche* (those living outside the borders of the Third Reich who had German ancestry). Admittedly, though, the *Waffen-SS* was still composed entirely of volunteers, unlike the *Wehrmacht*. This continued racial purity in the *Leibstandarte* was not only done to maintain it as an elite, but also because it was still seen to have an internal security role. Indeed, plans were drawn up in the autumn of 1941 to construct a new barracks for it in Berlin, large enough to take the whole division, although these never came to fruition.[1]

It is hardly surprising that the reorganisation was not completed in time for the *Leibstandarte* to take part in the opening day of *Barborossa*. Nevertheless, the idea was that it should join von Rundtedt's Army Group South, which had been given the task of seizing Kiev, everrunning the Ukraine and advancing towards the heavily industrialised Donetz Basin. To carry this out, von Rundstedt had been given three infantry armies (Sixth, Eleventh, Seventeenth) totalling 38 divisions, *Panzergruppe* 1 under command of the *Leibstandarte*'s old friend, von

Kleist, and two Rumanian armies with a total of fourteen divisions. The *Leibstandarte* was to come under von Kleist's command as one of his three motorised divisions. He also had five Panzer divisions. During the second half of June, the *Leibstandarte* had moved northwards to an assembly area in the region of Lublin and joined XIV Panzer Corps, which was under command of von Wietersheim.

The Soviet forces in the Ukraine, under Colonel General M P Kirpones, were better equipped and prepared to meet the German onslaught than their counterparts in the north. Initially, though, von Kleist had had little difficulty in breaking through the Soviet defences, choosing an inter-army boundary for his axis. However, on 23 June, he started to run across the concentration areas of a number of Soviet mechanised corps, which significantly delayed his progress and by 1 July, when the *Leibstandarte* was first committed to battle, von Kleist had reached a line Rovne-Dubno-Krzenienic. He was now facing fierce counter-attacks and the Leibstandarte's initial task was to repel these. Heavy rain now fell. The men of the *Leibstandarte* were surprised how primitive the Soviet tactics were. As one recorded in his diary:

> 'Their counter-attack . . . was launched while we were still getting our breath back. Their infantry came in mounted on open lorries which swayed from side to side with the speed. It looked as if all the Ivans on the trucks were standing up and firing their guns at us. The whole thing was quite primitive. The lorries just drove straight at our positions . . . a shell hit a lorry and killed many of the infantry mounted on it, but the others sprang over the side and charged us on foot. . . There was no cover at all. . . They had no hope of reaching our positions, but they still came on. . .[2]

There was thus little difficulty in repulsing these attacks and they died away with the decision by Kirpones to withdraw to behind the River Sluch, where the defences of the so-called Stalin Line lay.

This enabled von Kleist's armour to get moving once more and the *Leibstandarte* was now placed under Eberhard von Mackensen's III Corps. Von Kleist quickly closed up to the River Sluch and succeeded in penetrating the Stalin Line in the area of Berdichev on 8 July. As 13th Panzer Division pushed on towards Zhitomir, the last major town before Kiev, the *Leibstandarte* was brought up in its wake in order to repulse another series of fierce counter-attacks from the north-east. 13th Panzer Division continued, however, to advance and took Zhitomir on 10 July. Next day, now reinforced by 14th and 25th Panzer Divisions, it reached the River Irpen, less than ten miles from Kiev. In the meantime, the counter-attacks on the northern flank of this drive continued and at one point even cut the corps main supply route, which was the highway passing east-west through Zhitomir. The *Leibstandarte*, advancing slowly behind the Panzer divisions, was often hard put to resist these, being unsupported and thinly stretched and also have to face numerous air attacks. Nevertheless, hold they did and, as the Soviet attacks gradually died away, they were able to advance and by the 17th were in front of Kiev. Even then, the Soviet attacks did not cease. Indeed, during the first three weeks that the

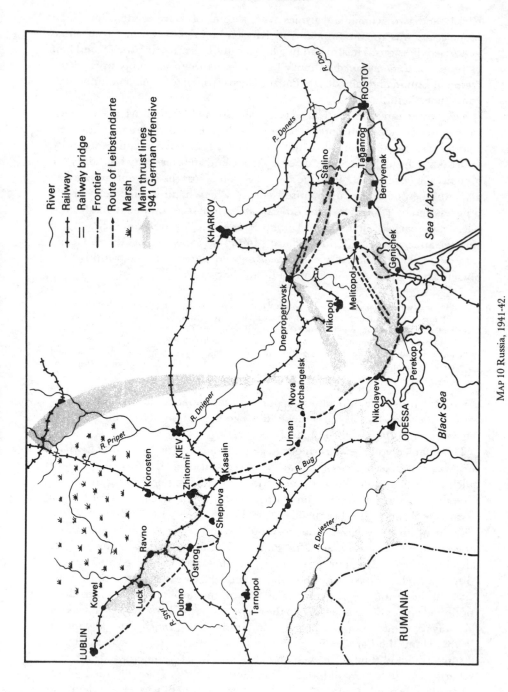

MAP 10 Russia, 1941-42.

Leibstandarte was in combat on the Eastern Front it suffered no less than 683 casualties, both killed and wounded, as well as some one hundred vehicles destroyed. No wonder that one SS man said of the Russians at this time, 'they are the best fighters we have ever met'.[3]

Von Rundstedt had failed to trap Kirpones in a pocket as the two army group commanders to the north had succeeded in doing to the opposition in front of them and both he and Hitler were becoming frustrated. Hitler even suggested that he split up his Panzer group into three and try and create smaller pockets, but von Rundstedt rejected this on the basis that it would be breaking the cardinal principle of keeping armour concentrated. Instead, he resolved to form a pocket south-east of Kiev by driving the Russians onto von Schobert's Eleventh Army which was advancing in concert with the Rumanians in the south. The arrival of Sixth Army in front of Kiev relieved von Kleist and he set off down the line of the River Bug on 24 July. Dietrich was removed from von Mackensen's command to that of Kempf's XLVIII Corps, which was ordered to advance directly on Uman. The *Leibstandarte* reached Uman on the 31st, spearheading the corps advance, with 11th and 16th Panzer Divisions on its left and right flanks respectively. The corps then moved south-east and wheeled round to face westwards in order to deal with the Soviet Sixth and Twelfth Armies, which were now desperately trying to break out of what had by now become a major pocket. The *Leibstandarte* itself was directed to seize Archangelsk. There followed a week's desperate fighting but, by the end of it, no less than 100,000 Russians marched into captivity. The *Leibstandarte* had occupied a key point, which represented the main axis of the Soviet Twelfth Army's attempted escape route. Time and again, the Soviets attacked until by the end, as one SS man recorded: '. . . we are all exhausted from lack of sleep. We seem to have been fighting without adequate sleep for weeks now. . . I have lost all track of time.'[4] Yet, the contribution that Sepp Dietrich's men had made to this victory was recognised by a special order of the day issued by Kempf on 8 August:

'Since coming under command of the Corps on 24.7, the *Leibstandarte* SS *Adolf Hitler* has taken the most glorious part in the encirclement of the enemy around Uman. Committed at the focus of the battle for the capture of the key enemy position at Archangelsk, the *Leibstandarte SS Adolf Hitler*, with incomparable dash, took the city and the heights to the south. In the spirit of the truest brotherhood of arms they intervened on their own initiative in the arduous struggle of the 16th Infantry Division (Motorised) on their left flank and routed the enemy, destroying numerous tanks.
Today at the conclusion of the battle of annihilation around Uman, I want to recognise and express my special thanks to the *Leibstandarte SS Adolf Hitler* for their exemplary effort and incomparable bravery. The battle around Archangelsk will be indelibly recorded and forever in the war history of the *Leibstandarte SS Adolf Hitler*.
In respect to the memory of the fallen of the *Leibstandarte SS Adolf Hitler*, it is giving up your lives that lets the Fatherland live.'[5]

There was, however, to be no chance as yet to be able to rest and enjoy the fruits of this victory.

Panzergruppe von Kleist, now that the infantry divisions had caught up and could sort out the prisoners in the Uman pocket, was free to advance once more, this time on to the lower Dneiper. Still under Kempf's command, the *Leibstandarte* advanced towards Kherson on the Black Sea. Once again, Dietrich's men proved themselves in spectacular fashion, throwing off Soviet attacks on both flanks as they advanced. It was, however, during this time that the question of atrocities against the Russians raised its head for the first time. The origins of this lie in a book written by Erich Kern, a Viennese journalist who at the time was serving in the 4th Battalion of the Leibstandarte. The book was first published in Switzerland in 1948. It was entitled *Der Grosse Rausch* (The Great Ecstasy) and was three years later published in English as *Dance of Death*[6]. Kern recounts the drive on Kherson in some detail, although his dates are rather awry. He describes how, at the end of one day's fighting, it was reported that two companies from the formation on the right, presumably 16th Infantry Division (Motorised), could not be contacted and Kern's battalion was ordered to try and find them. At about midnight, having had no success, they halted in the village of Gejgova, or Grejgowo as Lehmann calls it,[7] five miles east of Nowo Danzig. At dawn they discovered what had happened to the two companies; the bodies of 103 officers and men were strung up in a cherry orchard. That night, the Battalion leaguered in Nove Danzig and discovered the bodies of six other German soldiers who had clearly been shot after surrendering. As a result of this:

> 'At noon next day an order was received by Division to the effect that all prisoners captured during the last three days were to be shot as a reprisal for the inhuman atrocities which the Red Army had committed in our sector. It so happened that we had taken very many prisoners during those fatal days and so the lives of four thousand men fell forfeit. They scarcely looked up when our interpreter told them of their fate.'

He then went on to describe how they were shot at the edge of an anti-tank ditch in batches of eight men at a time.[8]

Gerald Reitlinger, in what is now generally held to be his classic history *The SS: Alibi of a Nation 1922-1945*, which was first published in 1956, seizes on this as an example of the brutality of the Waffen-SS, stating that it was Sepp Dietrich who gave the order for the 4000 prisoners to be massacred,[9] disregarding the fact that Kern had written 'an order was received by Division'. Other authors have followed this line, notably George Stein, who manages to twist the original account still further. According to him it was the discovery of the bodies of six members of the *Leibstandarte* in what had been the headquarters of the GPU in Taganrog which provoked Dietrich to give his execution order, and he quotes Reitlinger as his source. The bodies in Taganrog were not, however, discovered until the end of March 1942 after the town had been recaptured (See Page 108), as Stein admits.[10] Thus between Reitlinger and Stein there is a seven month gap at least as to when Dietrich's supposed order was given and neither accurately reflects what Kern had actually written. Significantly, Heinz Höhne in his *The Order of the Death's Head*, also regarded as a 'classic', while describing the discovery of the bodies at Taganrog, does not mention any reprisals ordered by Dietrich, neither then nor earlier. Indeed, in order to give a balanced picture, he quotes a letter he received from Wilhelm Keilhaus, who commanded the *Leibstandarte's* signal battalion and then was the *Leibstandarte's* Chief of Staff during 1941 campaign, that Dietrich did everything he could to prevent reprisals on prisoners – 'We owe it to the title on our sleeve', as he said. [11] This supposed slur on the name of the *Leibstandarte* was taken up by Rudolf Lehmann when writing its definitive history. Having scoured the records held in the *Bundesarchiv-Militararchiv* at Freibung im Breisgau and found no evidence of any such order having been given, he then went to the length of placing the matter before the State Justice Administrative Department (*Landesjustizverwaltungen*) in Ludwigsburg and obtained the reply from them that no such execution had taken place between 16-18 August 1941, the dates which related to Kern's description. He described *Der Grosse Rausch* as a ' "commentary" [*Reportage*], a free representation by the author (and with no documentation).' [12]

This is not to say that the *Leibstandarte* was blameless on the Eastern Front and it may well be that Kern took another incident and wove it into his story. The figure of 4000 prisoners does, however, have some connection with what actually happened during the fighting in that, on 16 August, the *Leibstandarte* captured 4283 Russians and the next day a further 4643. What must be realised, though, is that, to use Max Wünsche's words, 'somebody who did not participate in the Russian campaign cannot know or have any concept of what it meant'. [13] It was not just the physical conditions, but the sheer intensity of the fighting between the representatives of two ideologies diametrically opposed to one another. There was barbarism, in the Western sense, on both sides. It should also be pointed out that, on the German side, the atrocities were not confined just to the SS, Waffen or otherwise, but were committed by the Wehrmacht as well, as a recent study has convincingly demonstrated. [14]

To return, however, to the main story. Kherson fell to the *Leibstandarte* on 19 August after fierce street fighting with the Soviet Marine defenders. During the fighting, the anti-tank and flak elements of the Division took on some unusual targets, shipping in the river. On the afternoon of the 20th, the *Leibstandarte* was relieved and, now, for the first time during the campaign, was given the opportunity to rest. They retraced their steps northwards and went into leaguer areas around the town of Ssedrewka. One of the places which they occupied was the Rosa Luxemburg Collective Farm, but there is no record of what the men of the Leibstandarte had to say about this. There was much to be done. Over fifty per cent of the vehicles were off the road and, on 31 August, no less than 674 reinforcements arrived and had to be assimilated.

The battle of the Uman pocket and the subsequent exploitation had caused Hitler to have a major change of mind on 21 August. He now saw a golden opportunity to trap no less than one million men of the Soviet South-West Front in the Kiev area. In order to carry this out, he ordered von Bock, commanding Army Group Centre, to divert Guderian's *Panzergruppe* 2, despite vehement protests from Guderian, southwards from its drive on Moscow. It was to come under von Rundstedt's command and, in conjunction with von Kleist's Panzer Group, create the pocket. On 16 September, Guderian and von Kleist linked up at Secha, one hundred miles east of Kiev and well to the Russian rear and during the next ten days, a desperate battle was fought as the Russians struggled in vain to escape. The final yield was well over 500,000 prisoners alone, with Kirpones himself being killed.

The *Leibstandarte* did not take part in this spectacular victory. On 3 September it left XLVIII Corps, with another laudatory order of the day from Kempf, and joined von Schobert's Eleventh Army, which had been given the task of spearheading Army Group South's drive to the Crimea and Donetz Basin, an operation which was to be carried out in tandem with the creation of the Kiev pocket. On 8 September, the *Leibstandarte* began its move back to the Lower Dnieper, deploying to Berislav, where Eleventh Army had established a bridgehead across the river. On 11 September, under command of Hansen's LIV Corps, the *Leibstandarte* Reconnaissance Battalion, still commanded by Panzer Meyer, was loosed from the bridgehead; its target the Perekop Isthmus, gateway to the Crimea. Meyer's route took him across the trackless Nogay Steppe, a new sensation for the men of the *Leibstandarte*: '. . . this is true desert country. Movement is visible for miles; clouds of choking, red brown dust hang over our moving columns and pinpoint our exact positions. Paradoxically, the only sign of life are the dead tree trunks of telegraph poles. Without them it would be difficult to orientate oneself.'[15] Hopes, that Perekop could be seized quickly were dashed, however, when Meyer discovered that the Soviets had erected a comprehensive system of defences across the isthmus. In the meantime, von Schobert was killed in an air crash on the 11th and, a few days later, Erich von Manstein arrived to take charge of Eleventh Army. He ordered a frontal assault, but despite fierce fighting over the period 24-26 September only a partial penetration was achieved, even though the *Leibstandarte's* Engineer battalion particularly distinguished itself.

Von Manstein now had his attention diverted. The remainder of his army, together with the Rumanians, had been advancing in pursuit of the withdrawing Soviet South Front along the shores of the Sea of Asov. On the evening of 23/24 September, the Soviets launched a limited counter-attack against part of the Third Rumanian Army, tore a large gap in the line and threatened to cut off the Eleventh Army on the Negay Steppe. Von Manstein was therefore forced to halt his break-in operation against the Crimea and divert forces to restore the situation. It was inevitable that the *Leibstandarte*, which was now beginning to get the reputation of a 'fire brigade' called in to deal with critical problems, would be involved. Now under the command of Kübler's XLIX Mountain Corps, the *Leibstandarte* moved to the Gavrilovka area near Melitopol. Dietrich's men first held the Russian attacks and then counter-attacked, restoring the German-Rumanian Line. At this stage, von Kleist, his command now designated First Panzer Army, had been freed from the battle of the Kiev pocket and moved south to join the fray. He cut round behind the Soviet forces and linked up with von Manstein at Orechov on 6 October and at Berdyansk on the Sea of Asov on the following day. Here, it was the *Leibstandarte* which achieved the link up.

There was to be no rest. While this pocket had netted another 100,000 prisoners and vast qualities of material it also meant that von Rundstedt could now resume his offensive. Eleventh Army was to continue its operations to seize the Crimea, a task which would not finally be completed until the fall of Sevastapol the following July, while First Panzer Army was to push on to the Lower Don. Hitler now stepped in and insisted that the *Leibstandarte* rejoin von Kleist, probably because his role was a more glamorous one, and so Dietrich once more found himself under von Mackensen's command in III Corps. Indeed, Hitler was paying close attention to the doings of the *Leibstandarte* and even at one point gave Dietrich specific advice as to how he should use his guns against the threat of Soviet gunboats operating on the Don.[16] On 16 October, the *Leibstandarte* captured Taganrog, which had been mainly evacuated by the Russians, although, once again, the 88mm's had good sport against shipping.

Now came an ominous development. Fierce winds and heavy rain marked the prelude of the Russian winter. This, and increasing Russian resistance, wore down the combat power of III Corps. Given the vast distances involved, the supply problem became immense and many vehicles were immobilised because of shortage of fuel. Sickness, especially dysentery, was also rife. At the end of October, the *Leibstandarte's* rifle companies were down to one third effective strength.[17] The campaign, too, seemed to have no end in sight. However many prisoners were captured and however deep the German forces penetrated, there still seemed to be more Russians and their resistance was often stronger rather than weaker. This had an effect on morale, even in the *Leibstandarte*, and this even reached the ears of von Brauchitsch.[18] Nevertheless, the offensive had to be maintained and von Rundstedt now had his eyes on Rostov. By the beginning of November, XIV Panzer Corps, having captured Stalino, was poised to strike from the north. The *Leibstandarte*, still with III Corps, had, in the meantime, reached the River Tusloff, fifteen miles north of Rostov and was now to turn south to clear the way for XIV Corps' attack. On 7 November, however, renewed heavy rain, which turned the area into a sea of mud, put paid to the chances of XIV Corps making the decisive thrust. Then, on the 13th, winter arrived with a vengeance. The temperature suddenly dropped to - 20° Celsius, which added to the suffering of the men, who had not been issued with any winter clothing - the result of Hitler's belief that the Soviets would be defeated before the onset of winter. Nevertheless, the resultant frost did firm up the ground and enable the attack on Rostov to be mounted. Von Manstein, however, decided that III Corps should now carry it out since it was closer to the city. In turn, von Mackensen, who had for some time held a high opinion of Dietrich's division, earmarked the *Leibstandarte*, reinforced by a regiment of 13th Panzer Division, to carry out the main attack. This kicked off on the 17th, amid falling snow. By the 20th, the *Leibstandarte*, accompanied by 14th Panzer Division, had broken into the city, which was secured by the end of the following day, after bitter fighting in the streets. 10,000 prisoners, 159 guns, fifty-six tanks and even two armoured trains fell into the hands of III Corps and von Mackensen understandably crowed with delight. 'We have cut to pieces the only efficient Russian communications centre in the Caucasus', as he declared in a special order of the day on 21 November.[19] However, his optimism was to be shortlived.

Almost as soon as Rostov was secured, it came under heavy Soviet artillery fire. There had also been Soviet pressure on the north flank of the Rostov salient since the 18th and it was this which had caused von Kleist, fearful that his army could be cut off from the rest of Army Group South, to begin a gradual withdrawal to the River Mius. The attacks then eased, which caused von Kleist to countermand his order, but on the 25th they were renewed, not just in the south, but also towards Rostov itself. Here the *Leibstandarte* defended with a desperate bravery:

> 'It is not possible in words to describe winter on this front. There is no main battle line, no outposts, no reserves. Just small groups of us depending on each other to hold defended points. . . We are here in the sunny south, how frightful it must be for the comrades up North. Here life is paralysed . . . you would never believe the lavatory procedures. . . And the food . . . we live on a sort of thick soup made of ground buckwheat and millet. We have to strip the fallen, theirs and ours, for warm clothing. I don't think I will ever be warm again and our tame Ivans say that this is a mild winter. God preserve us.'[20]

During the 26th and 27th, the *Leibstandarte* reported 31 deaths from frostbite[21] and it was not just the men, but the officers as well who suffered. It was probably at this time that Sepp Dietrich himself succumbed to first and second degree frostbite to the toes of his right foot.[22] He fought on, however, as did his men. For example, on the first day of the renewed counter-offensive, the *Leibstandarte*'s reconnaissance battalion, under the command of Kraas, who had been the first Iron Cross 1st Class winner in the 1940 campaign in the West, since Meyer was laid up with dysentery, repulsed an attack by elements of two Soviet divisions. This moved von Kleist to comment that 'a bold self-assured unit will be master of the strongest mass attack'.[23] The writing was on the wall, however. The Rostov bridgehead was too extended and too vulnerable against increasing Soviet determination and, on 28 November, von Rundstedt gave orders that von Kleist should now definitely withdraw behind the Mius. This accordingly took place and, by Christmas, the *Leibstandarte* was occupying a defensive line with its right flank on the Sea of Azov, just east of Taganrog. It would remain in this position until June 1942.

When Hitler heard the news of von Rundstedt's withdrawal from Rostov he was furious. It had been the first German withdrawal on the Eastern Front and had been carried out without his permission. Von Rundstedt was immediately sacked and von Kleist branded as a coward. One of the first actions that Hitler took when he first heard the news was to ask for a combat strength return from the *Leibstandarte*. This showed that, as at 30 November, the Division had 157 officers and 4556 men, against an establishment of 290 officers and 9704 men. Worse, only fifteen per cent of its vehicles were on the road.[24] This must have given Hitler a clear indication of how weak the troops holding the Rostov salient had become, but his dismissal of von Rundstedt stood and von Reichenau was summoned from Sixth Army to take over, although he did not last long, dying of a stroke in mid January. Nevertheless, Hitler did decide to come and see for himself and flew out to Mariupol to speak personally to Dietrich. As to the interview itself, Keitel recorded how Dietrich 'stood up honourably and incorruptibly for his Army superior, and it was he who succeeded in eliminating the Führer's lack of confidence on this occasion'.[25] It would not be the last time that Dietrich found himself defending the generals against Hitler's wrath. Indeed, Dietrich later claimed that he had instituted the withdrawal from Rostov on his own initiative.[26] This, however, is an exaggeration although he undoubtedly supported the correctness of von Rundstedt's actions. As for von Rundstedt himself, he did not remain long without another job, being appointed Commander-in-Chief West in March 1942.

In spite of its forced withdrawal, the *Leibstandarte* had performed excellently in the eyes of its Wehrmacht commanders. Von Mackensen even took the trouble to write to Himmler on 26 December:

> 'I can assure you that the *Leibstandarte* enjoys an outstanding reputation not only with its superiors but also among its Army comrades. Every division wishes it had the *Leibstandarte* as its neighbour, as much during the attack as in defence. Its inner discipline, its cool dare-devilry, its cheerful enterprise, its unshakeable firmness in a crisis (even when things become difficult or serious), its exemplary toughness, its camaraderie (which deserves special praise) – all these are outstanding and cannot be surpassed. In spite of this, the officer corps maintains a pleasant degree of modesty. A genuine elite formation that I am happy and proud to have under my command and, furthermore, one that I sincerely and hopefully wish to retain.'[27]

For Dietrich came a personal award on 31 December when it was announced that he had won the Oak Leaves to the Knight's Cross, the 41st Soldier to be so decorated. Hitler, in a reply to Dietrich's New Year greetings, stated that the award was 'demonstrable recognition of my pride in your and my Regiment's achievements'.[28] By this time, however, Dietrich himself had gone to Berlin to receive his reward in person from the Führer.

He was to spend the whole of January away in Berlin and was lionised by the Party establishment. Immediately on arrival he stayed at the Chancellery as Hitler's special guest for three nights[29] and the Führer was fulsome in his praise:

> 'The role of Sepp Dietrich is unique. I have always given him the opportunity to intervene at sore spots. A man who's simultaneously cunning, energetic and brutal, Dietrich is a serious, conscientious and scrupulous character. And what care he takes of his troops! He's a phenomenon in the class of people like Frundsberg, Zeithen and Seydlitz. He is a

Bavarian Wrangel, someone irreplaceable. For the German people Sepp Dietrich is a national institution. For me personally there is the fact that he is one of my oldest companions in the struggle.'[30]

The *Völkische Beobachter* ran a banner headline on the award[31] and there was a long article on him in the *Schwarze Korps*.[32] Von Hassell also recorded that on the occasion of Goering's birthday, 12 January, 'when the usual fantastic tributes were brought to him, Goering . . . brought Sepp Dietrich to the fore and introduced him as the "pillar of the Eastern Front". At the same time he hurled verbal barbs at the stale old generals.'[33] Goebbels, too, commented, after hearing of Dietrich's experiences: 'in sharp contrast to the leading gentlemen of the Army, the leaders of the Waffen-SS have had National Socialist training. For them difficulties exist only to be overcome.'[34] Two days later he wrote:

> 'Sepp Dietrich is a real comrade and makes one think of a Napoleonic general. If we had twenty men like that as divisional commanders we wouldn't have to worry at all about the Eastern Front. He told me in great detail how the bourgeois generals on the southern front lost their nerve and how this weakness of character naturally communicated itself to the troops. . .'[35]

It is unlikely, however, that this was actually what Dietrich said. If he had in truth thought this way, he would not have stood up for von Rundstedt as he did. The truth was that the leadership was suffering from a crisis of confidence. The withdrawal from Rostov and, even more important, the rebuff in front of Moscow, where Soviet counter-attacks had also forced withdrawals and cost, among others, Guderian his command, were the first major reverses that German arms had suffered, at least on the ground, since the outbreak of war, and they were hard to swallow. Scapegoats had to be found and it was easy to pick on the Army generals. Yet, there had to be optimism for the future and it is clear that all this adulation was a determined attempt to build up Dietrich as the epitome of the National Socialist soldier, who could achieve results where the Army was unable, because the generals lacked the necessary ideology. It does not seem, however, that Dietrich was taken in by this. Guderian records that, while at home in Berlin, he received a telephone call from Sepp at the Chancellery to say that he was coming to see him in order to show 'the people at the top' that Guderian had been unjustly treated. Indeed, Dietrich was one of his few visitors at this time.[36] Yet, there were people in the Army who did not like Dietrich and the prominence being given to him. According to Berger, the OKW was now accusing Dietrich of 'charging into Rostov' contrary to orders 'purely to gain a prestige victory'.[37] Here again, this hardly reflects von Mackensen's testimonial on the *Leibstandarte* and was totally unfair. On the other hand, it may have been a fabrication on Berger's part, constantly wrestling as he was with the Wehrmacht imposed recruiting restrictions on the Waffen-SS, in order to fuel the antagonism against the Army.

Apart from being used as an internal propaganda weapon, Dietrich undertook what was for him a far more important and intensely personal undertaking while he was in Berlin. On 19 January 1942 he married Ursula. The fact, though, that he only obtained Himmler's permission to do so on the previous day[38] indicates that it was probably a spur of the moment decision although, by leaving it until the last moment, it could have been a way of having a sly dig at Himmler. He did not, however, have long in which to enjoy a honeymoon, for on 30 January he was on his way back to Russia, being lent one of Hitler's personal aircraft for his trip. Albert Speer, who was then working for the Labour Front, but was about to take over as Minister of Armaments and War Production, recorded how he hitched a lift in this aircraft as he wanted to visit German railway gangs operating in Southern Russia. They landed at Dnepropatrovsk, but could not take off again for some time because of the snow. He noted how Sepp was immediately at home with the workers. 'Socializing with our construction workers filled the time; get-togethers were held, songs sung. Sepp Dietrich made speeches and was cheered.'[39]

During the early winter months of 1942, the *Leibstandarte* and, indeed, most of First Panzer Army were not committed to any major operations. Von Manstein did, however, have sufficient to occupy him. In the second half of January, the Russians launched an attack south of Kharkov, across the Upper Donetz, and succeeded in creating a salient fifty miles deep. This required elements of First Panzer Army to help contain the attack, but the *Leibstandarte* was not called upon. In the extreme south, in the Crimea, there was little let up. Hitler had ordered that it be reduced and time and again Eleventh Army, and especially XLII Corps, attempted to both break into the defences of Sevastopol and also drive eastwards to secure the Strait of Kerch. Again, though, the *Leibstandarte* was left undisturbed, probably because Hitler wanted it to be fully fit again for the spring 1942 offensive. Indeed, he decreed that it be increased in size. To this end, there were a number of additions. Most significant of these was the formation of a Panzer battalion at the *Wehrmacht* training area at Wildflecken. This consisted of three tank companies, and a total strength of thirty Pz Kw Mk IVs, two Mk IIIs and twelve Mark IIs. A new guard battalion, the 7th, was formed in Berlin, and the 5th Battalion was flown out to the Leningrad front towards the end of February. The reason for this is not clear, but presumably Hitler felt that the injection of a *Leibstandarte* element would stiffen the resolve of von Küchler's Eighteenth Army, which was tasked with capturing the city. Its arrival was quickly spotted by the Russians, who, using propaganda loudspeakers, declared: 'We greet the *Leibstandarte*, think about Rostov! We'll smash you here just as we did in the south.'[40] Under the command of Hugo Kraas it fought well and joined the rest of the division in June. Further additions at this time included a Panzerjäger battalion and an assault gun battalion, both of which were formed at Sennelager. It would be a few months, however, before these new units were properly incorporated in the Division.

For the rest of the *Leibstandarte* it was a lengthy period of static warfare. For most of the time the division was back under command of XIV Panzer Corps.

Until the end of March, the temperature remained well below freezing point, apart from a brief spell in mid-February when it did rise to just above zero. There was a steady trickle of casualties. Thus, in March alone, eight men were killed, forty-two wounded and 221 admitted to hospital. On 28 March, the bodies of the six members of No 3 Company (1st Battalion) were discovered in the former GPU headquarters in Taganrog, presumably uncovered by the thaw, since it was believed that they had been captured the previous October and a detailed report on the tortures which had been inflicted on them was forwarded direct to Himmler. [41]

Finally, towards the end of May the *Leibstandarte* was withdrawn into reserve in the Mariupol area so that it could absorb the additional units which had been assigned to it. During this time, a member of one of the *Leibstandarte*'s 37mm flak gun crews recorded that his battery had been deployed to the coast of the Sea of Azov. Life was pleasant, with the opportunities to swim, but they were very short of food. So much so that they put a sign outside their quarters, a half collapsed earth dug-out, which said 'hunger tavern'. Russian aircraft often flew over, but normally at too low a height to hit. One day, to their intense surprise, Sepp Dietrich visited them.

> 'He emanates a calmness which is felt by his soldiers and which is carried over to them. When he sees the sign he wants to know its purpose. Then he goes to the gun; he wants to know how it is operated. He takes the gunlayer's seat and moves the gun up and down. He asks whether he can fire it. The soldiers think that he wants to put them in a trap as it is forbidden. They explain this and tell him of the Russian planes which regularly fly over. Before he leaves, he gives them a packet of cigarettes. He orders them to send two men to Divisional HQ. To the gun commander he says that during World War I he had always taken care that his men had had something to eat, to keep morale high.
> When the two men came back from Divisional HQ they could hardly carry the food. They changed the sign to 'Flak recreation centre'.
> And really, Dietrich comes back the following day to have a go with the gun. But he misses as well.' [42]

This illustrates Sepp Dietrich's greatest attribute, the constant concern he showed for the well-being of his men. Having been an ordinary soldier in combat himself, he knew only too well what kept a soldier going and this was a major contributory factor to the *Leibstandarte*'s high reputation in battle.

On 28 May 1942, Sepp Dietrich celebrated his 50th birthday. Apart from receiving greetings from his comrades in arms, he was given a very special birthday present by Hitler. This was a cheque for 100,000 Reichsmarks in recognition of his 'special services'. [43] Given the fact that Sepp Dietrich's salary as an *Oberstgruppenführer*, a rank which he was not to achieve until 1944, was RM1420 per month, and one realises the size of the gift, especially since it was tax free, apart from interest on any investment and being considered for property tax. This way of rewarding individuals who, in Hitler's eyes, had served the Third Reich well, was not uncommon during the war years, however. The recipients ranged from the elderly hero of the First World War, Field Marshal von Mackensen, on his 90th birthday, through distinguished military figures of the Second World War like Guderian, von Brauchitsch and von Milch, through his personal staff, for instance Baur, his pilot, and the Party 'faithful' to, in one case, a family that had produced five children in sixteen months![44] For Dietrich, who had never had much money, it must have been very welcome, although Ursula, of course, did have money of her own.

The main impetus of the German 1942 offensive on the Eastern Front was to be directed towards the capture of the Caucasus. However, the Russians struck first on 12 May when Timoshenko's South-West Theatre launched an attack south of Kharkov. Once again, First Panzer Army was called north to deal with this, but the *Leibstandarte* did not go. Von Kleist cut through the Soviet salient and achieved a significant victory, capturing 214,000 prisoners and much equipment. In the meantime, von Manstein continued with his efforts to clear the Crimea. Then, on 28 June, the main German offensive began, with Hoth's Fourth Panzer Army attacking north of Kharkov towards Voronezh. The attack then moved down the line of the Don, but Hitler became increasingly mesmerised by Stalingrad. At the same time, he was becoming concerned over a possible Allied invasion of France. The build up of US forces in Britain and Soviet agitation for the Second Front to be opened in order to relieve some of the almost unbearable pressure from the Germans seemed to point in this direction. He therefore decided that his forces in the West must be strengthened. Accordingly, at the beginning of July, the *Leibstandarte* was ordered to France. It began its move by rail on 11 July and arrived at Fontainebleu, outside Paris two weeks later. Here, on 29 July, Dietrich's men paraded through Paris itself, the salute being taken by von Rundstedt, with Paul Hausser, in his capacity as Commander SS Panzer Corps, beside him.

Hitler had agreed to the setting up of a Waffen-SS Corps headquarters in May 1942 and this was organised by Hausser at Bergen-Belsen, north of Hannover and soon to become infamous for the concentration camp there, moving to France in July. The plan was for the *Leibstandarte*, *Das Reich*, which had also moved to France in July, having received a heavy battering during the winter fighting around Moscow, and the *Totenkopf* to be placed under its command. The last-named, in spite of Eicke's desperate pleas on account of the consistently heavy casualties that it was suffering in the Demyansk Pocket south of Lake Ilmen, was not, however, withdrawn from Russia until October 1942. Indeed, Hausser's command was to remain a headquarters without troops until the new year, with responsibility merely for the conversion of the three divisions from motorised to Panzer Grenadier establishments, with operational control being retained by Army commands. While the *Das Reich* was sent to the south-west of France, the Leibstandarte moved to the Evreux-Dreux area, west of Paris, where it came under the operational command of Kuntzen's LXXXI Corps.

On 13 August, von Rundstedt came to visit Dietrich and stayed talking to him until midnight. Von Rundstedt's opinion of Sepp, which he gave to his interrogators after the war, was that he was 'decent but stupid'.[45] Certainly, in view of the way in which Dietrich had defended him against Hitler after the withdrawal from Rostov, von Rundstedt would have obviously considered him 'decent'. Lehmann, however, argues that von Rundstedt would not have spent so long talking to him on this occasion if he really thought that Dietrich lacked brains.[46] Yet, von Rundstedt's view was shared by many others and it is likely that he was prepared to spend time with him because he recognised, like others, the value of having Sepp as an ally in view of the special relationship which he enjoyed with Hitler. He would also be concerned, bearing in mind that the *Leibstandarte* was now a quick reaction reserve in the event of an Allied attack across the Channel, that Dietrich knew exactly what his role was and understood it. Dietrich, too, was good company, with an ability to get on with people at all social levels, even a Prussian Junker like von Rundstedt. This did not mean, though, that he was endowed with great intellect.

For some days, German intelligence had been certain that some form of amphibious operation was to be mounted across the Channel and von Rundstedt's forces were prepared for it. Consequently, when the Canadians attacked at Dieppe on 19 August they were thrown back into the sea with little problem. The *Leibstandarte* took no part in this, although it stayed on full alert for twenty-four hours. Nevertheless, Hitler remained convinced that a full scale invasion was likely. In mid-October the *Leibstandarte* was moved to Normandy, in what would be a preview of the ground that it was to fight over two years later. Further alarms came with the Allied invasion of North Africa, Operation *Torch*, on 8 November. As a result, the Germans moved in and occupied Vichy France, but the *Leibstandarte* was not directly involved in this, although *Das Reich* was.

In spite of these alarms, the *Leibstandarte* continued with its reorganisation during autumn 1942. The most significant element in this was the enlarging of the Panzer battalion into a regiment of two Battalions, each of three tank companies, a heavy company equipped with the new Tiger tank and a Panzer engineer company. The infantry was now organised into two Panzer Grenadier regiments, each of three battalions, together with supporting arms, and equipped with half-track personnel carriers. The artillery regiment now had four battalions, two with 105mm guns, one with 150mm guns and a mixed battalion. Finally, on 10 December, Hitler decreed that from henceforth the division's title was to be *SS-Panzer-Grenadier-Division Leibstandarte SS Adolf Hitler*. All this reorganisation resulted in a massive increase in strength to just under 21,000 men, significantly higher than that of Army divisions, but there was a penalty to be paid. The rigid entry standards had finally to be relaxed and gradually during the next year it lost much of its racial 'purity'. Indeed, a number of Russian volunteers, the so-called 'Hiwis' (*Hilfsfreiwillige* or 'auxillary volunteers'), recruited from POW camps, gradually found their way into the Division, which also boasted of two members of the British Free Corps, a London taxi driver and Midlands lorry driver,[47] during the 1943 campaign in Russia.

Dietrich continued to put the welfare of his men as a high priority. An example of this was in November 1942 when an *Unterscharführer* told him that his wife, who was living and working in Dresden, had been arrested by the Gestapo for carelessness at work. She had been held by them for three weeks and was badly treated. Dietrich, very angry about this, immediately wrote a stiff letter of complaint to the Higher SS and Police Leader (*Höher SS-und Polizeifuhrer* or HSSPF) Elbe (Dresden), *Obergruppenführer* Udo von Woyrsch, who had originally been responsible for raising the SS in Silesia and had in 1939 led an *Einsatzgruppe* (operational group) against the Polish Jews in Upper Silesia. At the same time he also wrote to Martin Mutschmann, Gauleiter of Saxony, demanding that von Worysch be disciplined. This produced a rebuke from Himmler saying that in future he must act more rationally and try to resolve problems like this within the SS.[48] Himmler also became concerned about another problem relating to the *Leibstandarte*. On 5 January 1943, he wrote to Carl Oberg, HSSPF France, saying that Dietrich told him that day that 7000 of his men had caught gonorrhea during their time in France. While he understood the human sexual problems of men who had come from a long spell on the Eastern Front, it was necessary to introduce properly controlled military brothels. Dietrich then came back and reassured Himmler that in fact there were only 244 cases, but Himmler then wanted him to carry out further investigations, as 'the question is of basic interest to me'.[49] Indeed, Himmler, with his obsession for racial purity could not leave the topic alone and in May 1943 there was a meeting of SS legal officers to discuss reports that the rule that SS men should not have sexual intercourse with women of other races was being flouted. The Chief Legal Officer of the *Leibstandarte* accepted that such intercourse was 'very frequent' and was brought about by the fact that many of the logistic units had incorporated female auxiliaries of many races. Indeed, 'some men more or less kept a concubine'. To compound this, *Sturmbannführer* Heinz of the Kiev SS and Police Court told the meeting that Dietrich had said to him that the order did not apply to his division. 'This order has been issued by theoretical experts', as Dietrich scathingly declared.[50] Once again, it was an example of Sepp displaying the 'blind eye' to orders with which he did not agree, especially if they were to the detriment of his men's interests.

The *Leibstandarte*'s sojourn in France was, however, only temporary, and at the end of December 1942 it received orders to return once more to the Eastern Front. This time the concept of a Waffen-SS Corps was at last to be realised and Hausser had the *Leibstandarte*, *Das Reich* and *Totenkopf* placed under his command, although the *Totenkopf* did not move until the end of January. Hausser was ordered to the Kharkov region and, indeed, initially set up his headquarters in the city. The situation facing him was grim. Paulus's Sixth Army lay totally beleaguered in Stalingrad with no prospect of relief and the sands of time running out. Even more serious was that, on 12 January, the Russians had launched a massive attack from Orel to Rostov designed to recapture all the territory which they had lost the previous summer. By the

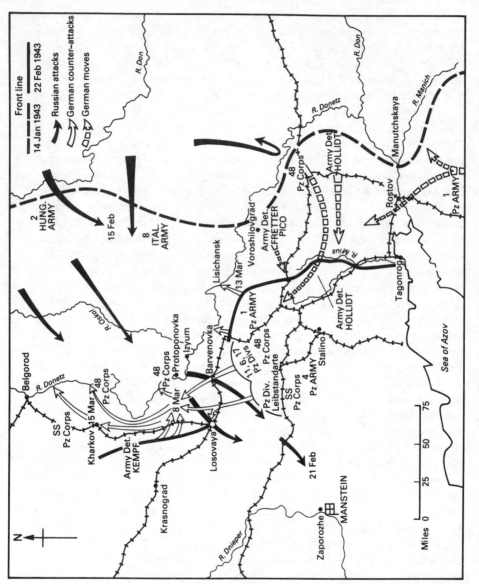

MAP 11 The battles in the Donetz Basin, January–March 1943.

beginning of February, Rostov had been lost once more and the line in the south was back on the Mius. Further north, the Germans and their allies were now behind the Don. The SS Panzer Corps was subordinated to what was called Army Detachment Lanz, commanded by General of Mountain Troops Hubert Lanz, which also had the *Grossdeutschland* Division and elements of two other German divisions under command. Lanz was given the task of defending Kharkov by von Manstein, now commanding Army Group South, and this lay in the path of Golikov's Voronezh Front. On 11 February, this was backed up by a personal order from Hitler that, at all costs, Lanz was to hold the city.

By 31 January, Lanz had deployed his forces on a thinly stretched line fifty kilometres east of Kharkov, with the *Das Reich* in the north, then the *Leibstandarte*'s reconnaissance battalion and, further to the south, 298th and 320th Infantry Divisions. The bulk of the *Leibstandarte* was located in reserve at Chegevayev on the Donetz itself, under the temporary command of Fritz Witt, since Dietrich had been ordered to report to Hitler on his way to Russia from France, presumably for a 'pep' talk, and did not arrive until 5 February. During the first week of February, Lanz's troops were forced back to the Donetz amid frequent fierce snowstorms. By the end of it the *Leibstandarte* was fully committed, with its back to the Donetz and with a dangerous gap appearing between it and 320th Infantry Division to the south. Indeed, 320th Infantry Division was cut off for a time and had to be extricated by the *Leibstandarte*'s 3rd Battalion of 2nd SS Panzer Grenadier Regiment. Led by Joachim Peiper it penetrated some forty kilometres into hostile territory and then formed a protective screen for the remnants of the 320th so that the 1500 wounded with which they were encumbered could be brought back to safety. At much the same time, Dietrich himself led a battle group to cut through the enemy thrust which had now got well beyond Kharkov in the south, leaving the city in grave danger of being enveloped. The axis of the counterstroke ran through Merefa and then on as far south as Dietrich could get. In spite of the extreme cold and constant snowdrifts, Dietrich and his men drove some thirty miles down through the Soviet VI Cavalry Corps, but then found themselves cut off. In the meantime, Hausser realised that to try and hold onto Kharkov, in view of the fact that it was virtually surrounded, was to achieve nothing more than send men needlessly to their deaths. In spite of a further order received from Hitler the day before, that Kharkov must be held, Hausser informed Lanz on the afternoon of the 14th that he intended to evacuate the city that night. Lanz told him to stand fast. He did so for the moment, but by the morning of the 15th the Russians were well into the north-western and south-eastern areas of the city and only one narrow corridor remained. At 1300 hours Hausser therefore took the inevitable step and the *Das Reich* and *GrossDeutschland* fought their way outwards to the south-west. Not unexpectedly, Hitler was furious and immediately flew out to von Manstein's headquarters at Zaprozhe, determined to sack him. He could not help realising, however, that the situation was impossible and von Manstein's neck was saved. Lanz was made the scapegoat, being replaced by Kempf, and Hausser escaped immediate censure, although, as we shall see, Hitler did see it as a black mark against his name. Dietrich probably helped to save Hausser as he had done over von Runstedt at the end of 1941. Certainly, when asked by Hitler's headquarters what reserves he had at the time of the evacuation of Kharkov, he replied, in characteristic fashion, 'behind me are 400 kilometres of wind'.[51] Understandably, though, the sacking of Lanz did create some bad feeling in Army circles.

By 22 February, some semblance of order had been restored. Hausser's corps, now strengthened by the arrival of the *Totenkopf*, managed to link up with Fourth Panzer Army under whose command it was placed. What von Manstein had in mind was to hold the Soviets west of Kharkov and then use Hausser from the north and XLVIII Panzer Corps from the south to destroy the continuing south-west drive of the Soviet VI Cavalry Corps, with a similar operation being mounted just to the east against Popov's armoured group which was heading directly south. This was totally successful, with both Soviet formations being virtually destroyed. Now he could turn his attention to the recapture of Kharkov, for which Hitler was agitating. While XLVIII Panzer Corps turned east towards the Donetz, the SS Panzer Corps drove on to Kharkov, with Dietrich's Tigers arriving on the outskirts of the city on 8 March. This thrust prised open a gap between the Soviet Sixty-Ninth Army, in the vicinity of Kharkov, and Third Tank Army to its south and there were no reserves immediately available to plug it. Hoth, commanding Fourth Panzer Army, now ordered Hausser to seal off the city from west and north and to take any opportunity to seize it. Hausser thus sent the *Leibstandarte* and *Totenkopf* round to the north and began to probe into Kharkov itself. While the latter went round to the east to block the exits, the *Leibstandarte* began a break-in operation. *Das Reich* had also begun to do the same from the west when Hoth ordered it to follow the *Totenkopf*. It was thus left to Dietrich to capture Kharkov which he did on 14 March, at the end of four days bitter fighting. Dietrich later claimed that he had recaptured Kharkov on his own initiative,[52] but this was not so. Indeed, according to Paul Carell,[53] Hausser was criticised for beoming involved in costly street-fighting in the city when he could have forced its surrender through encirclement. It seems that it was for this reason that there was a delay in him receiving recognition in the form of a decoration, while Dietrich was awarded the Swords to his Knights Cross (26th soldier to be so decorated) on the day that Kharkov finally fell.

There may well be truth in this, but it is also likely that Hausser's previous withdrawal from the city still rankled with Hitler. Many others, including the commanders of the *Grossdeutschland* and 320th Infantry Divisions, were also decorated at the same time as Dietrich, and Hausser, understandably, did feel snubbed. A little while later, however, Hausser was awarded the Gold Party Badge and Sepp's sympathetic comment was: 'That will please him.'[54] As for Sepp, Hitler was clearly delighted with what he had personally achieved. Just before the fight in Kharkov began, Goebbels had noted in his diary: 'Sepp Dietrich enjoys his (Hitler's) unlimited confidence. He considers him one of our best troop commanders and expects miracles from him. He is, so the speak, the Blücher of the National Socialist movement.'[55] Yet, in spite of the eulogies broadcast on the radio and in the *Schwarze Korps* and other publications to mark the award of the Swords, Hitler still did not think that sufficient effort was being made to build Sepp up as a hero of the Third

Reich. Goebbels noted that 'the Führer desires that Sepp Dietrich's achievements be given more publicity. He is not to be classed as a mere "also ran" among the generals.'[56]

Perhaps personally more important to Sepp was the birth of his second son, Lutz, in Professor Lingemeier's private clinic in Karlsruhe on 20 March 1943. This time Himmler took a personal interest and a telex was sent by his headquarters to *Oberabschnitt Südwest* instructing them to purchase flowers up to a value of RM50 for Ursula in his name. Furthermore, the baby received the Himmler substitute for a baptism present, a silver candlestick inscribed 'Lutz 20,3.43'. Normally, in order to encourage SS men to raise large families, each newly born baby received a gift of a silver beaker, silver spoon and blue shawl, all made at the SS owned factory at Allach near Munich. Indeed, Himmler became Lutz's godfather and for Christmas 1943 gave him a 'little brown bear' (presumably a toy!), on his first birthday a silver spoon and a toy hare on a string and, for Christmas 1944, a large toy car made of wood, chocolates and sweets.[57] Wolf-Dieter, on the other hand, was never recognised by Himmler.

It would be some time, though, before Sepp could see his second son. There was no pause after the recapture of Kharkov. It was vital to secure the line of the Donetz once more. To this end, Peiper's 3rd Battalion of the *Leibstandarte*'s 2nd SS Panzer Grenadier Regiment was sent north, in conjunction with elements of the *Grossdeutschland* and *Totenkopf*, to seize Belgorod. This achieved and the German line now restored, the *Leibstandarte* could withdraw for rest and refitting. This was urgently needed. During the little over two months that the SS Panzer Corps had been in action its casualties had been over 11000 and the *Leibstandarte* alone had lost 4500 men during the recapture of Kharkov. The Division remained in the Kharkov area for its refit, also helping to repair the Kharkov defences. In April, while here, it received an unusual gift on the occasion of Hitler's birthday, 20 April, a cheque for over two million Reichsmarks. This, according to the message that Hitler's courier brought with the money, had been collected in three months through the offices of the Winter Relief Fund to mark the *Leibstandarte*'s battles in the East and would be used for welfare purposes.[58] Yet, in spite of the honours heaped on Sepp and his men for their achievements during the recapture of Kharkov, a black mark against them was later to appear.

After the Soviet recapture of Kharkov in August 1943, the Russians discovered several mass graves in the area. During September a commission was set up to investigate these. It concluded that:

'. . . during the occupation of Kharkov and the Kharkov region, the German command and Gestapo agents savagely exterminated, by means of poisoning with carbon monoxide in *Dushagubbi* (murder vans), shooting and hanging, tens of thousands of Soviet citizens, including women, old men, children, wounded Red Army men under treatment in Kharkov hospitals, as well as arrested persons incarcerated in Gestapo prisons.'

The finger of accusation was pointed at Dietrich, Max Simon, who had taken over command of the *Totenkopf* after Eicke had been killed while conducting an air reconnaissance in the Kharkov area on 26 February 1943, *Sturmbannführer*

Hamlitter, head of the Kharkov SS *Sonderkommando*, and Hans Ritz, a member of the Gestapo.[59] Matters became clearer when the Kharkov War Crimes Trial was held 15-18 December 1943. Those who stood trial were Hans Ritz (not to be confused with the officer of the same name who was on the staff of the *Leibstandarte* during the first part of 1943), Wilhelm Langer of the German counter espionage service, Reinhard Tizlaff of the Gestapo and a Hiwi driver. During the trial, three witnesses, a professor, a doctor and a nurse stated that:

> 'On 13th March 1943, three automobiles with SS men of the 'Adolf Hitler' division drove up to the hospital [First General Evacuation Hospital of the Sixty-Ninth Army, in Trinkler Street, Kharkov]. They shut the door of Block No 8 and threw an incendiary shell [grenade?] into the building. It caught fire. When the wounded tried to save themselves by jumping out of the windows, they were shot down by SS men with automatic rifles. The next day, a group of nine SS men came into the hospital and, driving the medical personnel out of the wards, shot all the remaining wounded in the other blocks of the hospital.'

A widow of one of the wounded visited the hospital on 15 March and found the body of her husband 'mutilated and covered in blood, lying on the floor between the beds. The head was bashed in, one eye had been knocked out, the arms were broken, and blood flowed from still gaping wounds.' In all, some 800 men had been done to death. The accused were all found guilty and were hanged, but in the summary of the trial it was declared that Dietrich, Simon and five others were equally guilty and had 'to bear criminal responsibility for the crimes committed by them against Soviet citizens on Soviet territory in accordance with the criminal laws of the USSR.'[60]

Whether Dietrich's men were guilty or not of this crime, it brought him into prominence with the intelligence agencies of the Western allies. A British intelligence report published before the end of 1943, commenting on the Waffen-SS, spoke of 'a strong element of the worst type of Nazi thuggery [that] still exists and has probably been fostered by such divisional commanders as Sepp Dietrich, an old SS beer-cellar gangster of Munich, or the late Theodor Eicke of the Concentration Camp Guards'.[61] A War Office MI 14 paper on the senior commanders of the Waffen-SS dated April 1944 noted specifically that Dietrich was listed by the Soviets as a war criminal[62] and a memorandum by Anthony Eden, the British Foreign Secretary, of June 1944 listed Dietrich as one of the top thirty-three Nazi war criminals on the grounds that he was 'the most prominent figure' in the Waffen-SS.[63] Likewise, an American biographical report on Dietrich also noted the Kharkov war crimes and quoted a source which described him as retaining 'many of the qualities of the bullying NCO'.[64] As we shall see, though, unlike the other crimes of which he was accused, the Kharkov massacre was only pursued by the Soviets long after the war.

All this, however, lay in the future. In the meantime, in April 1943, Dietrich was summoned by Hitler, both to receive the Swords and also to be told of a new assignment. Hitler had agreed in February, after representations by Himmler, that a new SS division should be raised from the *Hitlerjugend* and that it should be trained by a cadre from the *Leibstandarte*. It was decided to raise a new Panzer corps with these two divisions and that it should be designated I SS Panzer Corps, while Hausser's corps was demoted to II SS Panzer Corps. Dietrich was to command I SS Panzer Corps and supervise the raising of the *Hitlerjugend* Division and, when told the news, expressed himself very happy.[65] Meanwhile, the *Leibstandarte* was preparing for a new offensive on the Eastern Front, Operation *Zitadel*.

The story of *Zitadel*, the attempt to pinch out the Kursk salient, which was launched at the end of June 1943, has been told many times and it is not proposed to go into it in any detail. Suffice to say, Hausser's II SS Panzer Corps was part of Hoth's Fourth Panzer Army, which was responsible for the thrust from the south, and attacked from west of Belgorod on 5 July and, after initial good progress, was forced to a halt on the 12th. The Allied landings in Sicily on 10 July presented a threat to Italy and Hitler now ordered Hausser's corps to be withdrawn and sent there in order to stiffen Italian resistance. On 12 July, the Soviets mounted an offensive from Kursk in towards Bryansk, followed three weeks later, also from the Kursk salient, by another aimed at Kharkov and the region to the west of it. This prevented the whole of Hausser's corps going to Italy and, in the end, only the Corps Headquarters and *Leibstandarte* were sent.

Dietrich himself did not take part in *Zitadel*. On 4 June 1943[66] he handed over command of the *Leibstandarte* to Theodor Wisch. It was the end of a long era. Rudolf Lehmann, who had been close to Sepp as his principal staff officer, summed up the feelings of his men when he wrote:

> 'For sure – our old commander, to us under him 'Obersepp' – he was no strategic genius, but a leader of the highest quality of soldiers and of men. He could not use this gift as a commanding general nor as the commander-in-chief of an army; it suffered a lot because of this. Neither was it his strength to formulate perfect tactical judgements on a situation. But he possessed a special sense for what would become crisis points, especially how to favourably develop them.
> His very rare and then very short speeches to his men did not contain any strokes of genius, but they were, as one realised, meant to come from his heart, and they went from heart to heart. This man had an extraordinary charisma. Somebody who experienced him can only recall with astonishment and admiration how he set himself against a human wave in a night of crisis, during which everything fled towards the rear. With the collar of his coat turned up, both his arms in his coat pockets up to the elbows, uttering incomprehensible sounds, but angry in tone, he managed not only to stop the wave of men but to reverse its direction. Also his warning to his troop leaders will never be forgotten: "Bring me back my men!"'[67]

He would be much missed and a difficult act for Wisch to follow. He returned to Germany, where presumably he was able to obtain leave so that he could meet his new son for the first time. Himmler now proposed to Hitler that Dietrich be promoted to *Oberstgruppenführer*, but Hitler considered that this might offend the Army since Dietrich was really only a divisional commander and would not be commanding an active corps for some time yet and the rank of *Oberstgruppen-führer* equated to an army commander. Instead he honoured him on 23 June 1943 with the unique rank of *SS-Obergruppenführer und Panzergeneral der Waffen-SS*. Dietrich now began to collect a staff for his new command. The first to join was a transfer from the *Wehrmacht*, Colonel Fritz Kraemer, who had been selected for Dietrich as his chief of staff. Kraemer was a fully fledged staff officer, having graduated from the Berlin War Academy in 1934, served on the staff of 13th Panzer Division until the end of 1942 and latterly had been the senior logistics staff officer to I Panzer Corps. He thus had a comprehensive staff background, was experienced and was just what Dietrich needed to help him grapple with the complexities of running a corps. Indeed, apart from one brief period in autumn 1944, when Dietrich was forming Sixth Panzer Army, Kraemer was to remain at his side for the remainder of the war and also during the Malmédy Trial. Finally, on 27 July, Headquarters I SS Panzer Corps was activated at Berlin-Lichterfeld. During the next two months, elements of the *Hitlerjugend* and the *Leibstandarte* cadre began to join.

It was at this time that Dietrich first publicly voiced his disillusionment in public over how the war was going in the East. It appears that he declared that, in view of the sheer numerical superiority in men and material which the Soviets enjoyed, decisive victory over them was now no longer possible. This was picked up by Alfred Rosenberg, Minister for the Occupied Eastern Territories, who in turn, perhaps with some relish, as he was a rival to Himmler in the struggle for power and influence, informed Himmler. The result was another rebuke for Dietrich. Himmler wrote to him:

> 'I am sure that this remark of yours about the combat value of the Russians was misunderstood. Please take the opportunity when you come to Berlin to go and see Rosenberg or write him a few words.
> Whatever you think about the war in the East, I know best. That it is not easy is clear to all of us. But at the same time we are sure that the Russians can and will be defeated.'[68]

It is, however, most unlikely that Dietrich made any contact with Rosenberg. It would not have been in his character to go on 'bended knee' to him. Others, too, were expressing discontent over the way in which the war was being conducted. Indeed, General Henning von Treschow, Chief of Staff of Army Group Centre and a key participant in the plots against Hitler, is supposed to have told Carl Goerdeler in August 1943 that von Manstein, von Kluge and von Kuchler would support an anti-Hitler coup and that Hausser and Dietrich would go along with it.[69] Whether he had heard of Dietrich's utterance is not known, but he was probably aware of Hausser's resentment of Hitler's treatment of him over Kharkov. Nothing came of it and, in any event, Dietrich now had another task.

Towards the end of July 1943, both the *Leibstandarte* and Sepp Dietrich received orders that they were to move to the Innsbruck area prior to being deployed to northern Italy. On 31 July, Dietrich, Wisch and Rudolf Lehmann, still the Leibstandarte's Chief of Staff, flew from Berlin to meet Rommel, now commanding Army Group B, at his headquarters in Munich, to be briefed on their task. At this time, the battle for Sicily was continuing, but invasion of the Italian mainland could only be a matter of time. On 25 July, the Fascist Grand Council passed a vote of no confidence in Mussolini and he was arrested. In his place, a new government was formed by Marshal Badoglio and Hitler, fearing that he might seize the passes through the Alps, especially as his government contained no Fascists, immediately ordered that they should be guarded, giving this task to Rommel. Consequently, the *Leibstandarte* was to be deployed to South Tyrol with special responsibility for the Brenner Pass. The division's advance party arrived in Innsbruck on 1 August, but then there was a change of plan. For a start, Hitler now decided that Hausser's headquarters should be sent to take command of the *Leibstandarte*. There were also fears that the Allies might attempt a landing in northern Italy. Hence, the *Leibstandarte*, which had left all its armour in Russia and had to be re-equipped en route, was now sent through the Brenner Pass to the Verona area, coming under Hausser's command, together with 25th Panzer and 65th Infantry Divisions, on 14 August.[70] Dietrich's headquarters, however, seems to have been left at Merano just south of the Brenner Pass and presumably made responsible for its security. What this seems to indicate is that in the delicate situation that existed Hausser was more to be trusted than Dietrich, although Rommel approvingly noted in his diary on 3 August that Dietrich was 'fully prepared to play hell with the Italians and make them dance to his tune'.[71]

In the event, the Italians stonewalled and, in the meantime, put out surrender feelers to the British and Americans. The Allied landings in Italy went ahead and, on 8 September, the Italian surrender became fact. There now follows some confusion among historians as to what Dietrich actually did in Italy. David Irving gives the impression that it was he who commanded the SS Panzer Corps, which had the *Leibstandarte* under command, and he quotes an entry from Rommel's diary for 4 September 1944: 'Himmler wants to send us Hausser in exchange for Sepp Dietrich. At my request this plan is dropped.'[72] While this is flattering to Dietrich, it makes little sense since Hausser already had the *Leibstandarte* under command in Italy. In any event, Manfred Rommel, Rommel's son has stated that his father's diary for this period was lost.[73] The confusion is compounded by Goebbels. Mussolini had been imprisoned firstly on two islands near Sardinia and then in the Albruzzi mountains, from where he had been rescued by German parachute troops, accompanied by Otto Skorzeny, in a spectacular *coup de main* glider operation on 13 September. From here he had been taken to meet Hitler and had then declared a new Italian Socialist Republic, basing himself near Lake Garda. He arrived here on 25 September and was given a company of the Reconnaissance battalion and a flak battery from the *Leibstandarte* to protect him.[74] William Shirer assumed that, because the *Leibstandarte* was involved, Dietrich was in charge of guarding Mussolini, not realising that the *Leibstandarte* was no longer under his command.[75] Also, on 13 September, Wisch received orders from Hitler to send an officer to escort Mussolini's wife to Forli, a task which was undertaken by *Hauptsturmführer* Steinert, commander of the *Leibstandarte* engineer battalion.[76] From here she and their children had been taken to Munich, where they were re-united with Mussolini. She eventually joined Mussolini on

Lake Garda. Mussolini's mistress also went there, but was placed in a villa a few miles away. This was organised by Karl Wolff, now German military governor and plenipitentiary to Mussolini, and she was given an SS escort officer, *Obersturmführer* Franz Spögler.[77] Many historians, seem to have confused these two stories and to have asserted that it was Dietrich had to escort Claretta Petacci from Lake Maggiore, where she and her family had fled after Mussolini had been deposed. The origins of this lie in an entry in Goebbel's diary, which stated that this was what had happened, but he must have been under a misapprehension. Under the same entry he does, however, note that Dietrich, who, accurately summing up Mussolini's unpopularity with the Italian people as a whole, had told him that Mussolini's wish to make a public speech in Milan could only be achieved 'under the protection of German arms; otherwise he would be booed off the stage'.[78]

It would thus seem that Dietrich and his headquarters did very little in northern Italy. At the end of October, the *Leibstandarte* was ordered back to the Eastern Front, as were Hausser and his headquarters, in order to help stem the tide of the Soviet autumn offensive. Here, under command of XLVIII Corps in Fourth Panzer Army, rather than Hausser, the *Leibstandarte* quickly became embroiled in the fighting south-west of Kiev. Dietrich also left Italy at much the same time and returned to Berlin. At this stage, the *Hitlerjugend*, still under training, had been sent to Beverloo in Belgium, and, without an effective combat command, Dietrich was sent, in his own words, 'to observe the third winter campaign' in Russia,[79] although Goebbels, for some reason, was under the mistaken impression that he was going to take command of 'more than 220,000 men and a total of 1000 tanks', which would equate to a good sized army, and conduct an advance up to Melitipol.[80] While there he did pay a visit to his old division during the afternoon of 2 December. Although inflicting significant damage on the enemy, the *Leibstandarte* had suffered heavily itself and Dietrich passed this back to the commander of XLVIII Corps. It was this that probably later prompted him to complain to Hitler on his return towards the end of December that 25th Panzer Division, which had performed very badly in its first action, had been issued with brand new transport while, 'we've [*Leibstandarte*, presumably] only got broken down old lorries',[81] an indication that the widely held belief that the Waffen-SS took priority over the *Wehrmacht* for equipment was not necessarily always true.

At the beginning of 1944, Sepp Dietrich returned once more to take up command of I SS Panzer Corps, which still had only the *Hitlerjugend* and would not receive additional formations until April. His task was to prepare his troops for the Allied invasion from across the English Channel which was now seen as inevitable. The only question was where and when the main landings would be made.

CHAPTER 7

Normandy 1944

For the first few months of 1944, I SS Panzer Corps consisted of just the *Hitlerjugend* and it remained in Belgium. In April, however, Dietrich was delighted to see the *Leibstandarte* arrive once more, although it was not placed directly under his command. This division, after its desperate battles during 1943 and again in the winter 1943-44, especially during the fighting around the Cherkassy pocket in February 1944, was urgently in need of a long rest and refit, and would be non-operational for some time to come.

In the meantime, as winter gave way to spring, Dietrich became indirectly caught up in the controversy over how best to repel an Allied landing on the shores of France. It was a question of how to employ the armour. Rommel, commanding Army Group B, and responsible for actually fighting the battle on the beaches, wanted the Panzer divisions to be positioned on the coast so that they could be used to drive the invaders back into the sea before they could consolidate the beachhead. His superior, von Rundstedt, as Commander-in-Chief West, believed that the tanks should be held back, on the grounds that it was by no means clear where the Allies were intending to strike, Normandy or the Pas de Calais. In this he was supported by Hitler, who laid down that no armour could be moved without his express permission. In order to reinforce this, the Panzer divisions were placed under command of the new formed Panzer Group West under Geyr von Schweppenburg. I SS Panzer Corps was now given 2nd Panzer Division, based at Arras and 17th SS Panzer Grenadier Division, which was in the Le Mans area, to add to the *Hitlerjugend*, leaving the *Leibstandarte* to carry on undisturbed with its refit. The tasks of the Corps were to be prepared for commitment in the event of enemy air landings or a surprise amphibious landing in the Antwerp-Cherbourg area – a wide brief. Dietrich himself now moved his headquarters from Brussels to the Paris area. This was partly to be more central, but also because, although he was under Geyr von Schweppenburg's command for training, he was put under von Rundstedt's direct operational control, and it made sense to have his headquarters close to that of High Command West. At the beginning of May, as a slight concession to Rommel, the *Hitlerjugend* was moved from Belgium to the Evreux area.

Dietrich, like most others on the German side, was taken by surprise when the Allied landings did eventually take place in Normandy early on 6 June

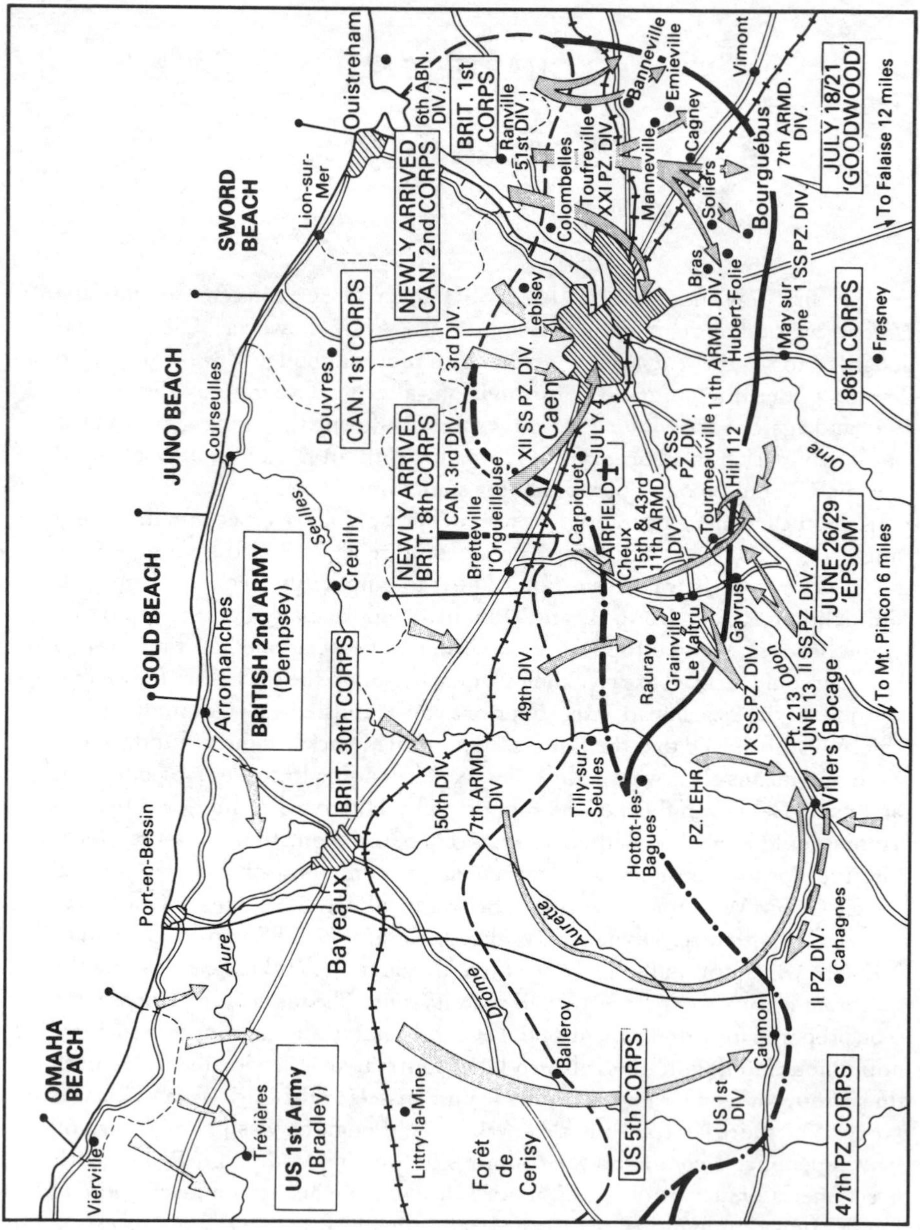

MAP 12 Normandy, June–July 1944.

OMAHA BEACH

Vierville

Trévières

US 1st Army (Bradley)

Port-en-Bessin

Arromanches

GOLD BEACH

JUNO BEACH

Courseulles

Creuilly

SWORD BEACH

Douvres

Lion-sur-Mer

Ouistreham

6th ABN. DIV.

BRIT. 1st CORPS

NEWLY ARRIVED CAN. 2nd CORPS

CAN. 1st CORPS

51st DIV.

Ranville

Colombelles

Touffreville

XXI PZ. DIV.

Banneville

Emieville

Vimont

JULY 18/21 'GOODWOOD'

7th ARMD. DIV.

To Falaise 12 miles

Manneville

Cagney

Bourguébus

Soliers

May sur Orne

1 SS PZ. DIV.

Fresney

86th CORPS

Bras

Hubert-Folie

11th ARMD. DIV.

3rd DIV.

XII SS PZ. DIV.

Lebisey

Caen

AIRFIELD

JULY 4

X SS PZ. DIV.

Tourmeauville

Hill 112

NEWLY ARRIVED BRIT. 8th CORPS

CAN. 3rd DIV.

Bretteville l'Orgueilleuse

Carpiquet

Cheux

15th & 43rd DIV. 11th ARMD.

Gavrus

Grainville

Le Valtru

IX SS PZ. DIV.

II SS PZ. DIV.

JUNE 26/29 'EPSOM'

Orne

Odon

To Mt. Pincon 6 miles

Seulles

BRITISH 2nd ARMY (Dempsey)

BRIT. 30th CORPS

49th DIV.

Rauray

Pt. 213

JUNE 13

Villers Bocage

50th DIV.

7th ARMD DIV

Tilly-sur-Seulles

Hottot-les-Bagues

PZ. LEHR

Bayeaux

Aurette

Drôme

Aure

Balleroy

US 5th CORPS

Littry-la-Mine

Forêt de Cerisy

US 1st DIV

Caumon

II PZ. DIV.

Cahagnes

47th PZ CORPS

122

1944. He was, in fact, in Brussels, where he had been visiting Theodor Wisch and the *Leibstandarte*. On hearing the news, he immediately returned to Paris to receive orders from von Rundstedt. In the meantime, Kraemer and the Corps staff had already been alerted by von Rundstedt and had begun to set the deployment of the Corps to the battle area in train. Dietrich's orders were to counter-attack from the direction of Caen and drive the Allies back into the sea. Hitler had, for once, allowed the General Staff to persuade him, against his personal hunch to the contrary, that the landings in Normandy were a feint. They insisted that the main effort would be made in the Pas de Calais. Hence, 2nd Panzer Division was to stay put, while 17th SS Panzer Grenadier Division was to be released to Dollmann's Seventh Army, which was facing the American landings towards and on the Cherbourg Peninsula. Dietrich was therefore told that he could have Feuchtinger's 21st Panzer Division, the only one of its type which had been deployed forward near the Normandy coast, and which was now trying to combat the British airborne landings in the area of Caen, and Fritz Bayerlein's *Panzer Lehr*, which was at Chartres. In due course, he would also receive the *Leibstandarte*, once its refit was complete.

The move of Corps Headquarters and Corps troops began at 1600 hours on the 6th, with the former reaching Rouen that night. This move gave a foretaste of what was to come.

'Already there were burning vehicles of all kinds on the road. No considerable flak formations or air forces were available for defence against enemy fighter planes so these were able to attack as though carrying out exercises. Air attacks had a paralysing effect on some of our drivers. German soldiers were not accustomed to this type of attack and it was several days before they became accustomed to it. . .'[1]

Overwhelming Allied air supremacy was to dominate events in the days and weeks ahead.

Dietrich's initial plan was to counter-attack with the *Hitlerjugend* and 21st Panzer at first light on the 7th, but events soon convinced him that this was over-optimistic. En route to their new headquarters site in the woods south of Falaise, Dietrich and Kraemer met with Fritz Witt. He reported that Panzer Meyer's 25th SS Panzer Grenadier Regiment, whose initial objective had been Houlgate, east of the River Orne, in the belief that the main invasion attempt would be made in this area, had now been diverted to report to Headquarters 21st Panzer Division, which was now at St Pierre sur Dives. The remainder of the division had been delayed by air attacks and it was agreed that it should take a new route, avoiding major roads, and make maximum use of the hours of darkness. It would not, however, be completely in position until midday on the 7th. Dietrich and Kraemer now went on to Headquarters 21st Panzer Division and arrived there at 2000 hours. Unfortunately, Feuchtinger himself was away at the headquarters of 716th Infantry Division. He had foolishly failed to take a radio with him – as Kraemer remarked: 'For a commander of a panzer or motorised division to leave his headquarters without a radio set was considered tantamount to travelling without his head'[2] – and the landline available was poor, with frequent interruptions and with speech, at times, almost inaudible. Nevertheless, by this means and by talking to the chief operations officer, Dietrich and Kraemer were able to gain some idea of the situation.

21st Panzer Division had been committed piecemeal during the day in support of 716th Infantry Division, which was holding the coastal sector immediately west of the Orne, but, because of communications problems, Feuchtinger had little idea where his units were. What was clear was that his reconnaissance battalion was in contact with elements of the British 6th Airborne Division south of Ranville, one regiment had turned back the advance of British infantry on Caen and the remainder were advancing towards Luc sur-Mer, between the *Sword* and *Juno* beachheads. 716th Infantry Division was still fighting, but again there was little idea of unit locations and the division appeared to be split into groups. Meanwhile, *Panzer Lehr* had still not been formally placed under Sepp's command and there was no means of contacting it.

Since the sector in which I SS Panzer Corps was now operating was under Dollman's Seventh Army, Dietrich was under command of this formation, but it took time to establish communications with them. Eventually, at midnight, a teleprinter message was got through asking for *Panzer Lehr* to be subordinated to I SS Panzer Corps immediately. It also told Dollman that Dietrich had taken 716th Infantry Division under command but that, in view of the confused situation, a counter-stroke was not possible before 8th June, especially since it was clear that the *Hitlerjugend* would now not be complete in its assembly areas before the night of the 7th/8th.

Dietrich and Kraemer had now returned to their own headquarters, and the next visitor to Headquarters 21st Panzer Division was Panzer Meyer. Feuchtinger had returned and the two discussed the situation. While Feuchtinger considered that a counter-attack was not feasible until *Panzer Lehr* had arrived, Meyer exuded confidence, terming the invaders 'little fish', who would soon be driven back into the sea.[3] Consequently, it was agreed that the two should launch a co-ordinated attack next morning. They clashed with advancing elements of the 3rd Canadian Division, but after two days' bitter fighting had made no progress. Meyer blamed his lack of success on a shortage of fuel for his tanks, complaining that Feuchtinger had refused to give him any. Feuchtinger later said that he would have made some available if Meyer had asked for it. Dietrich's view was to laugh and to say: 'It is easy for Feuchtinger to say that now, but on 7th June his answer to such a request would have been "I haven't got any"'.[4] Indeed, it is probable that Feuchtinger, numbed by the events of D-Day, during which he had reacted very slowly, took an immediate dislike to Meyer, especially his arrogance, and, not believing that an immediate attack would be successful, was dragging his feet.

Back at HQ I SS Panzer Corps, Dietrich and Kraemer continued to try and sort out the confusion. Telephone links remained at best intermittent, with lines being destroyed by Allied bombing, and they did not want to use radio for fear that this would give away their presence in the battle area. Liaison officers were despatched to neighbouring corps headquarters, but the key task was to bring *Panzer Lehr* firmly under command. To this end, a signals officer was sent to a bridge at Thury-Harcourt over which it was known that *Panzer Lehr* would pass. He had the necessary codes and signals instructions to hand over. Unfortunately, at about 0500 hours on the 7th, Kraemer himself found this officer dead on the road, victim of a traffic accident. Not until late in the afternoon did Bayerlein report to Corps Headquarters, which had now shifted to May sur Orne. The news he brought was not good. A delay had been caused by the destruction of the bridge at Thury-Harcourt by Allied bombers and, as a result, the division would not be complete in its assembly areas before the early hours of the 8th. Furthermore, the remaining armour of the *Hitlerjugend* was also delayed because of mechanical breakdowns. Worse, rumours were rife that Caen had been taken and that enemy armoured columns were driving on Falaise. Most of these originated from members of the rear services of the coast divisions, Todt Organisation and railway and supply workers, 'faint-hearted rabble who had grown unaccustomed to war during their stay in the west', as Kraemer drily remarked.[5] Nevertheless, although these reports proved groundless, it was clear to Dietrich, after a visit to HQ 716th Division, that that division was no longer a viable fighting force. There was also a gap on his left flank, but it took time to establish that it was some seven to ten kilometres wide because Dietrich's liaison officer had been unable to find HQ LXXXIV Corps. In view of this gap, the strengthening of the enemy forces to the front and worries over the effects of bombing on the approach marches of the *Hitlerjugend* and *Panzer Lehr*, Dietrich determined that the counter-stroke must go ahead on the morning of the 8th with whatever he had to hand by then.

It was at this stage that Rommel stepped in. While he liked Dietrich, as his views on him in Italy have shown, he did not trust him with so crucial an operation as this counter-attack. He therefore decided to subordinate him to Geyr von Schweppenburg's Panzer Group West, but such was the state of communications, that it seems that Dietrich continued to think that he was still under Dollman's command. Curiously, though, in his Canadian post-war interrogation, Sepp was very disparaging about Rommel, stating that he was not a proper soldier because he had not fought in Russia. 'What did he know of war? He constantly had himself photographed by Dr Berndt, his publicity man, for the newspapers back home. All he could do was stand on a tank, baton in hand and shout "I am the King of Africa".'[6] Events during the next few weeks were to belie this view of Dietrich's.

The attack itself went in at 1000 hours on the 8th. Only one battle group of *Panzer Lehr* was available because of the delays and shortage of fuel, and much of 21st Panzer Division could not be committed because it was too tied up in defensive tasks. The *Hitlerjugend* continued to battle away, but little progress was made. The weight of artillery fire, the overwhelming Allied air supremacy, which resulted in an entire lack of Luftwaffe support, and the nature of the terrain, which was intersected by numerous streams and hedgerows, thus providing the advantage to the defender, together with the continuing lack of fuel, proved too much. All that was really achieved was to clear the approaches to Caen from the north. Casualties were heavy and it was becoming very obvious to Dietrich and Kraemer that they would need reinforcements if they were to have any chance of success. The situation was not helped when a garbled message was received that night from HQ Seventh Army ordering an attack on Bayeux. This was clearly totally impracticable considering the situation, and Dietrich chose to ignore it, contenting himself with firing on the Allied invasion fleet with two 175mm batteries, whose fire was controlled by an observer in the tower of a small chateau on the right bank of the Orne.

By this time, Dietrich had lost sixteen of his twenty radio vehicles as a result of artillery fire and air attack and Geyr von Schweppenburg was in the same situation. It is therefore not surprising that the two could not communicate with one another or that Rommel received no news of the failure of the 8 June attack. As a result, Rommel decided to come and see for himself and arrived at Dietrich's headquarters on the 10th. The situation was that the remnants of 716th Infantry Division had now been withdrawn and the line was held by on the left, *Panzer Lehr*, centre, *Hitlerjugend* and right, 21st Panzer Division. Dietrich stressed to Rommel the overwhelming superiority of the Allied firepower. As Rommel noted in a report:

> 'As I personally and officers of my staff have repeatedly proved and as unit commanders, especially *Obergruppenführer* Sepp Dietrich, report, the enemy has complete control over the battle area and up to sixty miles behind the front . . . As *Obergruppenführer* Sepp Dietrich informed me, enemy armoured divisions carry on the battle at a range of up to 3500 yards with maximum expenditure of ammunition and splendidly supported by the enemy air force.'[7]

Added to this were a severe shortage of defence stores – mines, wire, spades – and close quarter weapons like the *panzerfaust* and grenades. The constant Allied air attacks had destroyed almost all the dumps in the region and fresh stores and ammunition had to come from depots east of the Rhine, with the transport moving them being able to travel only at night. The divisions had by this time suffered twenty-five per cent casualties. Replacements, both of men and equipment, were hard to come by. The gap between *Panzer Lehr* and LXXXIV Corps could only be covered by little more than a reconnaissance screen. In these circumstances a major attack towards Bayeux was out of the question.

Rommel accepted all this, but said that tank attacks must be mounted towards Bayeux none the less. He did, however, offer Dietrich some crumbs of comfort when he told him that the plan was to bring XLVII Panzer Corps, with two divisions, up on the left of *Panzer Lehr*. He also confirmed that Panzer Troops West was taking over the sector between the Rivers Orne and Vire and that Dietrich would be answerable to Geyr von Schweppenburg. This arrangement was to be shortlived. On the very day after Rommel's visit, Geyr's headquarters was hit by an air strike, having been accurately located through Ultra intercepts. The Chief of Staff, Ritter von Dawans, was killed, together with some forty officers and men, and Geyr himself slightly wounded. I SS Panzer Corps therefore reverted once more to under command of Seventh Army.

It was now that the British began at last to attempt to exploit the gap on the left flank of *Panzer Lehr*. On 12 June, 7th Armoured Division, which had been meeting stiff resistance from the *Panzer Lehr* along the line Verrières-Tilly, was ordered to side step to the west, in view of encouraging reports from V US Corps, who were advancing towards Caumont. The target was Villers Bocage and steep and narrow minor roads were chosen, the object being to turn *Panzer Lehr*'s left flank. The advance began at 1400 hours and, to begin with, no opposition was met. Finally, having cleared the village of Livry, where elements of *Panzer Lehr* were finally contacted, 7th Armoured Division halted for the night, with contact made with the 1st US Infantry Division on the Caumont-Caen road. Next morning, at 0530 hours, the advance was resumed and Villers Bocage entered. It looked as though *Panzer Lehr* and, indeed, the whole of I SS Panzer Corps was in danger of being peeled back like the lid of a sardine can.

It was at this moment that five Pz Kw MK VI Tigers of Heavy Panzer Battalion 501 made their appearance. Commanded by *Obersturmführer* Michael Wittmann, a *Leibstandarte* veteran, who had already won the Knight's Cross in January 1944 for having destroyed sixty-six Soviet tanks, they were situated on Hill 213, north-east of Villers Bocage and on the road to Caen. It was fortuitous that they were there, since the spot had been chosen so that they could spend the day carrying out undisturbed and much needed maintenance of their tanks. They saw a squadron of tanks from the 4th County of London Yeomanry (CLY), accompanied by a company of half-tracks of A Company 1st Rifle Brigade, Regimental Headquarters and Reconnaissance Troop of the 4th CLY, debouch from Villers Bocage and come towards them. It was too good an opportunity to miss. Wittman wasted no time and charged down on the column. Within five minutes, it was in ruins, with twenty-five tanks and other AFVs destroyed. Wittman, himself escaping four direct hits from a 17 pounder Sherman Firefly, which caused only superficial damage to his Tiger. This stopped the British exploitation in its tracks and shortly afterwards the long awaited lead division of XLVII Panzer Corps, 2nd Panzer, arrived and launched a counter-attack. This was repulsed, with Wittman, who had joined it, being 'dehorsed', but later he was to be awarded the Swords to the Knight's Cross for his dramatic intervention, which had literally saved the day for I SS Panzer Corps.

Even though 2nd Panzer Division's counter-attack made little progress, the British found themselves virtually cut off in Villers Bocage, and within a short time had withdrawn to east of Caumont. As Kraemer recognised, the British had let a great opportunity slip. Much of the blame was placed on those desert veterans of the 7th Armoured Division, who had by now seen rather too much war and had become somewhat sluggish. The relief of Dietrich that the hole which had worried him so much had now finally been plugged, was heartfelt, but also tempered by the death in action on that very same day, the 13th, of Fritz Witt, commander of the *Hitlerjugend*. Although he had left the *Leibstandarte* in 1935 to join the *SS Standarte Deutschland* as a company commander, he had returned to the *Leibstandarte* in October 1940 and fought with it as a battalion and then regimental commander in the Balkans and Russia, until leaving it finally just before Kursk to command the 12th SS Panzer Division *Hitlerjugend*. Sepp, on hearing of his death, said: 'That's one of the best gone. He was far too good a soldier to stay alive long.'[8] In his place, Panzer Meyer was appointed to command the division.

Dietrich's relief was to be shortlived. The pressure from the enemy was constant, although the impression at HQ I SS Panzer Corps was that these attacks were piecemeal, with no strategic objective in mind. As Kraemer later wrote:

'The fact that the enemy time and again put in breathing spaces between his attacks indicated that he suffered losses. Many attacks certainly could have been successful if there had been better co-operation between the attacking infantry, artillery and air force. We observed, for instance, that enormous artillery activity would start at daybreak and last for several hours. Usually this was considered preparatory to enemy attacks. Sometimes these would not take place or would start much later with less preparation. We ascertained likewise that air force attacks were not coincident with this artillery fire or the subsequent attacks.'[9]

Yet, as much as they might be inflicting losses on the enemy – they had captured a thousand prisoners by 20 June – the continuous fighting was gradually weakening Dietrich's troops. By the same date, the average strength of a company was no more than thirty to forty men, with the best having been killed or wounded. Replacements became harder and harder to come by and often could only be found by stripping logistic units to the bone. The survivors, too, were not the men that they once were. As Dietrich said to Albert Speer about the demoralising effect of the constant Allied bombing: 'The soldiers who had survived were thrown completely off balance, reduced to apathy. Even if they were uninjured, their fighting spirit was shattered for days.'[10] It is thus understandable that, at about this time, he is supposed to have complained to Rommel: 'I'm being bled white and getting nowhere.'[11] On the other hand, Admiral Friedrich Ruge, Rommel's naval adviser, noted at Sepp's headquarters, during a visit by Rommel on 21 June, 'the good spirits there. Sepp Dietrich believed that he could withstand the British pressure in any case.'[12]

A growing irritation to Sepp, though, was his right hand neighbour, General Obstfelder, who commanded LXXXVI Corps. This consisted only of two infantry divisions, the 346th and 711th, and Ostfelder was very conscious that he lacked armour and was worried that, being on the extreme right flank, he would be in the path of a major Allied effort to make an outflanking move against him. He was constantly asking Rommel for tanks, and these had to be loaned by 21st Panzer Division, but were seldom returned. Admittedly, pressure was put on 711th Infantry Division on 23 June as the British tried to expand the bridgehead around the bridge north-east of Blainville, but Dietrich and Kraemer were expecting a major Anglo-US assault on the line Caen-Bayeux and desperately wanted at least some of their tanks back so that they could lengthen 21st Panzer Division's front at the expense of that of the other two divisions in order to produce some form of reserve. They managed to retrieve one tank battalion, in spite of repeated protests from Obstfelder, of whom Dietrich remarked: 'He had more fear than patriotism.'[13]

Dietrich had been told that he could expect some relief for his hard pressed divisions. 16th Luftwaffe Field Division and 276th Infantry Division would be made available to relieve 21st Panzer Division and the *Hitlerjugend*, both of which were now down to some thirty tanks, and that the *Leibstandarte* would be assigned to him. Furthermore, II SS Panzer Corps under Paul Hausser, with 9th and 10th SS Panzer Divisions, was also being deployed, the object being to use the panzer divisions in a concentrated counter-attack. In view of the overwhelming Allied superiority in men and material and the exhaustion of the divisions which had been in the line since 8 June, the prospects for this were not rosy. The move of the *Leibstandarte* was also proving difficult. The tanks had been moved by rail to Paris, with the infantry coming by road, but the division was now stranded at St Germain because of lack of fuel.

The attack which Dietrich was expecting was Operation *Epsom*, a renewed attempt by Montgomery to take Caen by enveloping it from the west. It was launched on 26 June by the three divisions of O'Connor's VIII Corps. It fell on both *Panzer Lehr* and *Hitlerjugend*. The fighting was desperate – Kraemer called it 'the most bitter since the start of the campaign'[14] – and the weakened defenders were forced to give ground. It was also noted that many casualties were suffered from British flamethrower tanks – the Churchill Crocodiles of 141st Regiment Royal Armoured Corps (RAC). Allied air activity and artillery also made life very difficult and, within the first few hours, penetrations of up to a depth of three miles had been made. It was at this stage, in response to desperate appeals by Dietrich, that one regiment of the *Leibstandarte*, Ist SS Panzer Grenadier Regiment, was sent up and fed into the battle under command of the *Hitlerjugend*. It immediately launched a counter-attack in the area north-west of Verson, which helped to stabilise the situation. In the meantime, Dietrich's command post, which was at Baron, had come under artillery fire and was forced to move. Of more concern, however, was the fact that, once again, a gap had appeared, this time between *Panzer Lehr* and *Hitlerjugend*. During the night, Dietrich and Kraemer did their best to seal it off with what troops they could scrape together, but everywhere they were spread too thin. Consequently, Dietrich warned Seventh Army that he could not hold his front west and south-west of Caen for more than a few days. He pleaded for II SS Panzer Corps, which had now arrived from the Eastern Front, to launch a counter-stroke next day towards Bretteville in order to stop the enemy and cut off the head of his advance. Dollmann's reply was that it was not a decision that he could make on his own since it had to be referred to OKW. Thus, there were no prospects of such an operation being carried out on the 27th and Dietrich had to hope that the remnants of his two, now almost decimated, divisions could hold the British attack next day on their own.

In fact, to the surprise of all, this attack did not materialise. Indeed, Montgomery had been keeping a wary eye on II SS Panzer Corps and was expecting it to put in an appearance. Consequently, his VIII Corps spent the 27th preparing to receive this attack. On the next day, however, the British advance resumed, with 11th Armoured Division striking towards the prominent Hill 112, but there was still no decision on the committal of Hausser's corps. Matters were also not helped when Dollman, doubtless as a result of the strain which he had been under for the past three weeks, died of a heart attack. Hausser was selected to take his place and Willi Bittrich, now commanding the 9th SS Panzer Division *Hohenstaufen*, assumed command of II SS Panzer Corps. This complicated the planning for the counter-stroke, which had now been ordered for the 29th. Consequently, the attack did not take the line that Dietrich and Kraemer wanted. Instead of attacking from Caumont directly towards Caen, it came in from Aunay and took a south-west, north-east axis. The divisions, too, had had little chance to look at the ground and Allied air reconnaissance obtained forewarning; during the move into its assembly areas II SS Panzer Corps was subjected to both artillery fire and air attack. 10th SS Panzer Division *Frundsberg* soon found itself halted in almost impossible ground for tanks. Nevertheless it succeeded in linking up with the *Hitlerjugend*, while its sister division, which had suffered heavy casualties from air attacks, did the same with *Panzer Lehr*, west of Villers Bocage. So the gap was finally closed. Once again, panzer divisions, which should have been used in a concentrated counter-stroke, found themselves committed to a defensive battle. Nevertheless, the pressure was sufficient for the British to feel forced to surrender their gains south the River Orne.

There now followed a period of tidying up of the line, but the Allied pressure continued. II SS Panzer Corps was temporarily subordinated to Dietrich and the remnants of *Panzer Lehr* were passed across to XLVII Panzer Corps. It was also decided that Dietrich should now be subordinated once more to Panzer Group West, whose headquarters under Geyr von Schweppenburg, now fully recovered from his wound, had been reconstituted. This meant that Panzer Group West were responsible for Dietrich's supplies. For a number of days they did not receive any, while Hausser, now that Dietrich was no longer under his command, refused to help out. By far the greatest concern, however, was Caen. Under the continuing intensive Allied pressure, it could only be a matter of days before it fell and Dietrich and Kraemer wanted to evacuate it. Indeed, Dietrich had already begun to withdraw his logistic elements from the town. Both Geyr von Schweppenburg and von Rundstedt were in favour of this step, but now Hitler stepped in and refused permission for it to happen and both von Rundstedt and Geyr von Schweppenburg were sacked, although Rommel was left alone, probably because his removal would have caused a wholesale lowering of morale. In their places, von Kluge, who had been commanding Army Group Centre on the Eastern Front, was appointed as Commander-in-Chief West, and General Heinrich Eberbach, Inspector of Panzer Troops, replaced Geyr von Schweppenburg.

Further pressure on Caen itself was not long in coming. On the evening of 7 July, 467 aircraft of RAF Bomber Command dropped bombs on the open ground and northern outskirts of Caen. Although there were few German casualties, those units in the neighbourhood were severely shaken. Next morning the British 3rd and Canadian 3rd Infantry Divisions attacked and once again it was Panzer Meyer's *Hitlerjugend* which took the brunt. The civilian population of Caen also suffered, although Dietrich had arranged with the Mayor for some of the citizens, those who were prepared to, to be evacuated. On Meyer's right, 16th Luftwaffe Field Division, which had been put under command of LXXXVI Corps, began to fold under the pressure and Meyer had to lend them armoured and artillery equipment. On 9 July, the *Hitlerjugend* was partially surrounded and Meyer requested Dietrich's permission to withdraw from the city. Dietrich, conscious of the Führer order that Caen must be defended at all costs, forbade it, but, Meyer withdrew across the Orne nonetheless. As he said, 'We were meant to die in Caen, but one just couldn't watch those youngsters being sacrificed to a senseless order'.[15] The situation was largely saved, however, by the arrival of the *Leibstandarte*, which now relieved Meyer's battered remnants in the southern suburbs of the city and enabled them to go into rest at long last.

Eberbach had by now had the chance of observing Dietrich at close quarters. He recognised that Dietrich relied heavily on Kraemer for the tactical handling of the corps and preferred to leave the latter at the command post, while he spent much of the time forward visiting his troops. There was no doubt that he was an inspiration to them. Indeed, during this fighting, there was little else that he could offer them. As Eberbach said of him at this time: 'Sepp Dietrich is something grand.'[16]

The split between Hitler and OKW and the commanders on the ground in Normandy had not been resolved by the sacking of von Rundstedt and Geyr von Schweppenburg. Indeed, the fighting at Caen merely served to aggravate it. While Hitler and the OKW were still fearful of another landing further eastwards on the Channel coast and hence refused to commit Fifteenth Army, apart, of course, from the wretched LXXXVI Corps, which was trying to contain the left flank of the Allied beachhead, von Kluge, Rommel and Eberbach were convinced that Normandy was the one and only Allied effort and had only to point to the, by now, vast Allied commitment to it in terms of men and material. To Hitler, Normandy must be strongly defended, with all troops, including the panzer divisions, forward, but, at the same time, the enemy must be destroyed. To those in Normandy, on the other hand, the time for a major counter-attack was now long past. All that was happening was that their valuable armour assets were merely being whittled away. Furthermore, the supply position was growing more and more desperate. Yet the Commander-in-Chief had no control over the Luftwaffe and *Kreigsmarine* elements in the area, whose relatively large stocks of transport, which could have done so much to relieve the situation, remained untapped. Rommel and others saw that the only chance of holding on longer in Normandy was through defence in depth, and this meant using von Salmuth's Fifteenth Army, basing it on the south bank of the Orne. The Panzer troops should be relieved by infantry and the Orne line held long enough for another defence line based on the Seine, Yonne and Voges to be organised. Unfortunately, no withdrawals could be carried out without the sanction of OKW. Hence, von Kluge and Rommel were hamstrung.

What of the views of Hausser and Dietrich, the SS generals? Hans Speidel, Rommel's Chief of Staff, records a visit to the front which Rommel made during the period 13-15 July. The situation reports which he was given by both 'sounded particularly serious. They were absolutely frank, and Rommel did not anticipate any difficulties with his SS troops if he decided to act independently.' Furthermore, Dietrich 'had professed his dislike for the war-lord to both Rommel and his Chief of Staff during a visit to La Roche Guyon [Rommel's headquarters]. He, too, demanded "independent action if the front is broken".'[17] By 'independent action' was clearly meant withdrawal from Normandy and had nothing to do with a plot to assassinate Hitler which was then in its final stages of planning. On 17 July, the discussion was taken a stage further when Rommel visited Dietrich once more. According to Rommel's ADC, Helmuth Lang, who witnessed the conversation, Rommel sought Sepp's reaction to the possibility of opening up negotiations with the Allies, presumably with the idea of closing down the fighting in the West so that the Germans could concentrate all their efforts on repelling the Russians. Panzer Meyer, who was also present recalled Rommel saying: 'Something has to happen! The war in the West has to be ended!'[18] Dietrich then shook Rommel's hand and declared: 'You're the boss, Herr Feldmarschall. I obey only you – whatever it is you're planning.' Afterwards, on their way back to La Roche Guyon, Rommel said to Lang: 'I've won Dietrich over.'[19] Whatever was in Rommel's mind, though, never developed further. A short time later, they were strafed by a British Typhoon. Their driver was wounded, the car crashed and Rommel suffered serious head injuries and left the stage.

Dietrich, however, had little time in which to ponder the conversation, for Montgomery was about to launch another major assault on his sector. The aim of Operation *Goodwood* has been hotly contested by historians ever since as to whether Montgomery intended it to be the key to unlock the door of the German defences, thus enabling the Allies to break out of Normandy or whether its purpose was to keep the German armour tied down in the British and Canadian sectors, so as to facilitate a break out by the Americans to the west. While the debate is an interesting one, it lies outside the context of this book. It was, however, Dietrich who had to meet the shock of the attack of 7th, 11th and The Guards Armoured Divisions down the east side of Caen towards the formidable Bourguebus Ridge and the secondary attack by the 2nd and 3rd Canadian Divisions in and on the west side of the city.

By this time, Dietrich had been able to draw his armour off into reserve, having received von Schack's 272nd Infantry Division. 21st Panzer Division had finally been passed across to Obstfelder, but remained on Dietrich's right flank. The withdrawal of the remainder of the armour from the front line was not, however, to give them the chance for rest and recuperation. Von Kluge was planning a spoiling attack in the Caen area. This was forestalled when, after a dawn attack by no less than 942 British bombers on villages held by 21st Panzer Division and the luckless 16th Luftwaffe Field Division, the British armour was unleashed. Dietrich afterwards claimed that, in spite of the artillery barrage, he had warning of the attack by the simple expedient of pressing his ear to the ground and hearing the noise of tracked vehicles, a trick which he had learnt in Russia.[20] Sensing the threat to his right flank, Dietrich immediately deployed the *Leibstandarte* to the area of the Bourguebus Ridge, while Panthers of 501 SS Heavy Tank Battalion were went to Frenouville, where they began to extract a heavy toll on the enemy. The efforts, too, of 21st Panzer Division, especially the Battle Group von Luck (supported by a battery of Luftwaffe 88mm flak guns, whose commander was forced, at the point of von Luck's pistol, to convert his guns to the anti-tank role, in the defence of the villages in the path of the British attack), also played their part in slowing down the British advance. Not until 1600 hours did the leading elements of 11th Armoured Division, which was the spearhead of the attack, get across the Caen-Vimont railway. Here they found themselves looking upwards onto the Bourguebus Ridge itself and straight into the muzzles of the *Leibstandarte*'s guns. Fire from here and from the Panthers in Frenouville produced what one British survivor of the attack called 'a state of chaos',[21] made even more so when it seemed that *Leibstandarte* tanks were about to counter-attack. The British attack was halted in its tracks, with 11th Armoured Division alone losing 126 tanks during the day's action. Efforts to resume the attack next day made no progress, although at one stage the village of Bourguebus was held for a short time before being recaptured by Dietrich's men. In order to stiffen up the resistance on the ridge, the *Hitlerjugend* was also deployed here, and by the evening of the 19th the British armour had had enough, suffering some 400 tank casualties in all.

Dietrich was also under pressure from the Canadians to the west of and in Caen. They succeeded in clearing the southern suburb of Faubourg-de-Vaucelles and, bridging the Orne, they now attempted to seize the prominent Verrières feature on the northern end of the Bourguebus Ridge, overlooking the Caen-Falaise road. This sector was held by 272nd Infantry Division, supported by armour loaned by the *Leibstandarte*. Again, the Canadians met with little success, suffering some 2000 casualties.

Goodwood once more demonstrated the fighting qualities of both the Waffen-SS and the German Army. Dietrich paid particular tribute to his tank repair workshops, without whom, in view of the fact that he received no new replacement tanks, his armoured strength would have been reduced to nothing. Indeed, he paid a visit to the workshops to decorate personally the mechanics with the Iron Cross 2nd Class. [22]

20 July 1944 was, however, dominated by events elsewhere. Colonel Graf Claus von Stauffenburg visited Hitler's headquarters in the East, the famous Wolf's Lair at Rastenburg in East Prussia, and deposited a briefcase filled with explosive under the table around which Hitler was holding one of his routine conferences. Although Hitler escaped the subsequent explosion with minor injuries, the plotters were not immediately aware of this and were convinced that he had been killed. Efforts to secure the garrison in Berlin, a key part of the plan, were foiled, largely thanks to quick thinking by Goebbels, who was able to convince Major Otto-Ernst Remer, commander of the crack Guard Battalion *Grossdeutschland*, that Hitler was still alive and use him to turn tables on the plotters. In Paris, however, the situation was different. General Karl Heinrich von Stülpnagel, the Military Governor of Paris, was deeply implicated in the plot and, on receiving the codeword that the assassination of Hitler had been successful, immediately had all the key Gestapo and SS men in Paris rounded up and arrested. Some of these managed to escape, however, and some accounts state that they got a message to Panzer Meyer – by what means is not clear – and he in turn informed Sepp Dietrich. Meyer later denied this, saying that the only news he received was from radio broadcasts. [23]

Dietrich himself had attended a conference held that day by von Kluge, at which Hausser, Eberbach and Obstfelder were also present. There was at this stage no news of what had happened at Rastenburg and the conference was taken up with a gloomy review of recent events and prospects in Normandy. It was the desperate supply situation, especially over reinforcements – Eberbach stated that his Panzer Group had only received 2,300 replacements for the 40,000 casualties which Panzer Group West had suffered – which dominated all. Dietrich was especially bitter and complained vociferously about 'those back in rear' and their inability to make any realistic decisions. Little, however, came of the conference, apart from a general agreement that the situation was grim and unlikely to get any better unless there was a radical change of heart on the part of Hitler and his military advisers.

This conference may have put Sepp in a depressed mood, but the news from Paris must have thrown him into a complete dilemma. According to von Schramm, Dietrich immediately relayed the news to 'higher authority'. It appears, however, that he had a direct teleprinter or telephone link to Hitler's headquarters and later that night he received a warning order either from Hitler or, more likely, Himmler, ordering him to be prepared to move his

Corps on Paris. This had him looking in two directions at once. According to Eberbach, he was telephoning all night trying to establish which units he could withdraw from the line. In the event, von Stülpnagel, having failed to get von Kluge's support, caved in once he had heard Hitler's radio broadcast of the early hours on the 21st.[24]

There was a belief among the conspirators that Hausser, Dietrich and the other Waffen-SS generals in the West would at least stay neutral in the attempt to overthrow Hitler. Indeed, as late as 1978, Hans Speidel recalled Dietrich saying to him during one of his visits to that front that 'Hitler will have to be *ausgeschaltet* [wiped out].'[25] It is, however, most unlikely that Dietrich, especially, who owed so much to the Führer, would have gone along with the conspiracy in any way. Certainly, Otto Kumm does not believe that Dietrich would have gone this far, particularly as the conspirators lacked 'legitimisation'.[26] Nevertheless, Dietrich, as we have seen previously, recognised that there were criminal aspects to the regime. Rudolf-Christoph Freiherr von Gersdorff, who became Chief of Staff of Seventh Army at about this time, recalls telling Sepp about an uncle of his wife who was arrested by the Gestapo because of his friendship with a Jew. He was sent to Auschwitz and only released after having paid a three million Reichsmark fine. Unfortunately, he caught a fatal fever when in Auschwitz and died two weeks after his release. All that Sepp could say was, 'those pigs'.[27] Another event at this time which gives some insight as to how Dietrich was thinking was his reaction to a speech made by Robert Ley, Leader of the German Labour Front, who spoke during the immediate aftermath of the 20 July Bomb Plot, attacking the German aristocracy as 'blue-blooded swine whose families must be wiped out'.[28] A number of divisional commanders in Normandy objected and Sepp acted as their spokesman, demanding that the speech be withdrawn.[29] Yet, on 22 July, Speidel and Ruge visited Dietrich, after having some difficulty in finding his headquarters.

'He also treated us to fried eggs and brandy. General Bittrich, the Commanding General of the 2nd Panzer Corps, dropped in. Both Bittrich and Dietrich reviled, in the strongest language, the inept leadership and the interference from those at the top. They believed that the breakdown of many things in Germany was due to sabotage.'[30]

David Irving has interpreted this last remark as Dietrich putting the blame on the conspirators for failures of the German war machine.[31] This, however, seems somewhat far-fetched since none of the plotters belonged to Hitler's 'inner military circle' and, in any event, it does not fit in with Sepp's foregoing remarks. It is more probable that he was using the word 'sabotage' in a loose sense, in that it was in the result and not the intent. More likely, Sepp believed that he could, given the right opportunity, talk to Hitler alone, as he had in the old days, and convince him that the military advice which he was receiving was wrong. Events during the next few weeks would tend to bear this out.

Certainly the strain of these few days told on Sepp and von Kluge remarked to Eberbach that he looked 'mighty tired', although, at the same time,

Eberbach considered that Dietrich was 'a little too easy-going', especially with regard to his subordinate commanders. While he was much impressed with Meyer and the *Hitlerjugend*, he felt that not all was well with the *Leibstandarte*, although he recognised Theodor Wisch's worth, and believed that Sepp should be exerting more of a 'grip'.[32]

Luckily, there was a comparative lull for a few days in the immediate aftermath of 20 July, but on the 25th, the Allies renewed their attacks. The main effort was now in the American sector and the day marked the opening of Operation *Cobra*, the break-out from St Lô. Preceded by the now standard bombing attack, which also caused casualties to United States troops, three American corps attacked in line, catching Hausser, who was convinced that the main effort would come in the Caen area, off guard. Nevertheless his troops resisted fiercely, especially *Panzer Lehr*. Simultaneously, the Canadians thrust once more towards Falaise, their precise objective being Tilly la Campagne. This was on the left hand portion of the *Leibstandarte*'s sector. Any concerns that Eberbach might have had about the *Leibstandarte* were quickly dispelled through a series of energetic counter-attacks which drove the Canadians back to their start line by the end of the day.

The situation in the west grew ever more grave. On 30 July, Avranches fell to the Americans, leaving Hausser's left wing in tatters. On this same day, the British mounted Operation *Bluecoat*. This was designed to keep the German forces in the east contained and also to threaten the rear of Seventh Army. The British Second Army attacked on a ten mile front towards the Bény-Bocage ridge and the town of Vire. This covered the extreme left hand sector of Panzer Group West which was covered by General Straube's LXXIV Corps, which had the newly arrived 326th Infantry Division under General Drabisch-Waechter and Feuchtinger's 21st Panzer Division under command. It was Drabisch-Waechter who took the initial brunt, after being driven back some way, which made his left hand neighbour General Meindl, whose II Parachute Corps was trying to contain the left shoulder of *Cobra*, very anxious. Straube ordered Drabisch-Waechter and Feuchtinger to counter-attack. The former did so, and was killed, but Feuchtinger, executing the same caution as he had earlier in June, but tinged with realism, would not do so. In the meantime, Hausser was casting longing eyes on the Panzer divisions in Panzer Group West. However, von Kluge believed that if *Bluecoat* succeeded it was not just Seventh Army that would be lost but that the whole front would collapse. Hence Panzer Group West retained its five armoured divisions.

As yet, *Bluecoat* did not directly affect Dietrich's corps, but next day he was ordered to hand over 9th SS Panzer Division, which had been under his command, to Bittrich. Eberbach's idea was for both this and 10th SS Panzer Division, Bittrich's other division, to be prepared to support 21st Panzer Division in counter-attacks. Indeed, Feuchtinger had at last reacted and was already counter-attacking in the flank. However, the head of the British advance gained part of the Bény-Bocage ridge. This threw Feuchtinger into confusion and his counter-attack petered out. In consequence, on 1 August Bittrich was ordered to restore the situation.

1 August 1944 marked for Sepp his promotion to SS *Oberstgruppenführer*, but backdated to 20 April 1942. This was the date on which Hitler originally wanted to promote him, but had been advised against this, since it would have made him senior to Hausser who was about to form the SS Panzer Corps. On the very next day, the 2nd, Hitler stepped in and ordered von Kluge to use his Panzer divisions to carry out a counter-attack at Avranches. Clearly Bittrich was too tied up with *Bluecoat* to be able to offer up either of his two divisions and, likewise, 21st Panzer Division, which anyway was severely weakened, could not be made available. He therefore turned to Dietrich and orders were sent via Eberbach for him to give up both the *Leibstandarte* and the *Hitlerjugend*. Dietrich was aghast at this, since all that he was offered in their place was 89th Infantry Division, and it would leave him with merely three infantry divisions (89th, 271st, 272nd) to defend against First Canadian Army:

> 'I protested with von Kluge for over an hour about the impracticability of such an operation. I used every argument in the book. There was not sufficient petrol for such an attack; if three armoured divisions were sent west it would be impossible to hold Falaise; it was impossible to concentrate so many tanks without inviting disaster from the air; there wasn't sufficient space to deploy so large an armoured force; the Americans were far too strong in the south and such an attack was only wedging one's way tighter in a trap rather than safely getting out. To each of my arguments von Kluge had only one reply, "It is Hitler's orders," and there was nothing more that could be done. I gave him what he wanted.'[33]

In the event, the *Leibstandarte*, now reduced to sixty tanks, became partially committed to *Bluecoat* and two weak battle groups were all that could be released. These left Dietrich on the 3rd. It prove to be impossible to extricate the *Hitlerjugend* in time because 89th Infantry Division was delayed by Allied bombing and shortage of fuel in its move up to the front.

On 5 August, Panzer Group West was redesignated Fifth Panzer Army and the counter-stroke at Avranches was planned for the evening of the 6th. That day it was announced that Sepp had been awarded the Diamonds to his Iron Cross, the sixteenth soldier to be so decorated and one of only twenty-seven who received this award during the war. Clearly this was in recognition of Sepp's efforts during the past two months, but one also wonders whether the award was not partly made in order to placate him and make him less willing to criticise the High Command. If so, it was to be in vain.

Dietrich was immediately summoned to Hitler's headquarters in the West to receive his decoration. He hoped to raise the problem of Normandy with the Fuhrer. Ushered into Hitler's study he said: 'Mein Führer, I would like to speak to you about what happened in the Ardennes [sic – Normandy].' Hitler replied, 'don't bother me with these details now. I am too tired' and this ended the interview, which had barely lasted two minutes.[34] If Hitler would not listen to Dietrich, then what chance had the *Wehrmacht* generals, especially after 20 July?

The counter-attack at Avranches was delayed for a few hours by a tank battalion which became temporarily trapped in a defile after an Allied fighter-bomber had crashed on the lead tank. The *Leibstandarte* had also been delayed. Not until shortly after midnight did it get going. Darkness and early morning fog aided the attackers and, by noon of the 7th, an advance of six miles towards Avranches had been achieved. By this time the *Leibstandarte* had arrived and been committed, although matters were not helped when elements of the division became bottled up in a dead-end street. Unfortunately, Joachim Peiper, the commander of the Panzer regiment, was absent sick. As Kraemer remarked: 'If Peiper had been there, this would not have happened.'[35] The fog now lifted and the Germans were subjected to the full weight of Allied airpower. This literally stopped the attack in its tracks and the survivors dug in where they were. Von Kluge, whose heart had never been in it, now decided to close down the attack.

The fears of the German commanders in Falaise were realised on the night of the 7th/8th. Operation *Totalize* was launched with a massive bombing attack on I SS Panzer Corps by no less than 1,019 aircraft of RAF Bomber Command. First Canadian Army then thrust southwards from Caen. In their path was the newly arrived 89th Division, which was scattered in panic as a result of the bombing. Luckily, Panzer Meyer, who had been able to withdraw his division to the Liason River on 5 August for a few days rest, had been prepared for such an attack, and had sent a liaison officer to 89th Division to warn him of this eventuality. As soon as the bombing started, Meyer went straight to the headquarters of this division, whose commander could give him little idea of what was happening. He then set off along the Caen-Falaise road to try and establish the true situation.

> 'I got out of my car and my knees were trembling, the sweat was pouring down my face, and my clothes were soaked with perspiration. It was not that I was particularly anxious for myself because my experiences of the last five years had inured me against fear of death, but I realized that if I failed now and if I did not deploy my Div correctly, the Allies would be through to Falaise, and the German armies in the West completely trapped. I knew how weak my Div was and the double task which confronted me gave me at that time some of the worst moments I had ever had in my life.'[36]

Meyer established a blocking position with a mixed bag of Tigers from 101 SS Heavy Tank Battalion, and his own Panthers and Mark IVs, astride the Caen-Falaise road at Cintheaux, and directed another battle group to mount a counter-attack from the east through woods north-east of this position. Although the latter operation failed, the block succeeded temporarily in slowing down the Canadian onslaught. During the next day, surprised that the enemy pressure had slackened (brought about by the fact that the attacking troops, 4th Canadian and 1st Polish Armoured Divisions were inexperienced), Meyer withdrew his battered troops to a new line along the River Laison. By this time, his division had been reduced to a bare 500 men and sixteen tanks, compared with its establishment of 21000 men and 220 tanks. He was thus very thankful when, on the 10th, 85th Infantry Division began to arrive to relieve him.

Dietrich had had little hand in this battle, since on the 9th he had assumed temporary command of Fifth Panzer Army. The reason for this was that, in spite of the failure of the Avranches counter-attack on 7 August, Hitler had decreed that it must be renewed. He did, however, recognise, especially in view of the rapidly changing situation, with Patton's Third Army now not just wheeling east to clear Brittany but also west from Le Mans, thereby threatening to cut off all German forces in Normandy, that this could not be mounted immediately. Eberbach had therefore been ordered by von Kluge to set up a special headquarters to plan and execute the new counter-stroke. Once again, Sepp was aghast:

> 'I warned the Field-Marshal that the Canadians had only been stopped on the Laison River for a short period. Once they resumed the attack, Falaise could not be held more than one or two days. Both Hausser of Seventh Army and Eberbach of the Panzer Group had also urged von Kluge to call the attack off and withdraw. But the Field-Marshal had received a new order from Berlin insisting that he go ahead. There was only one person to blame for this stupid, impossible operation. That madman Adolf Hitler. It was a Fuhrer's order. What else could we do?' [37]

It was Haislip's XV US Corps which was providing the main threat in the west, Eberbach's original intention was to strike it in the area of Alençon on the 14th with 2nd and 116th Panzer Divisions and the *Leibstandarte*, but events moved too quickly for him. Haislip occupied Alençon on the 12th and was now advancing on Argentan, which was only some twenty miles from the Canadians at Falaise. Consequently, Eberbach was forced to commit his forces to the defence of Argentan. This move had also cut Seventh Army's supply lines, since these were based on Alençon, and Hausser now had to rely on Dietrich for logistic support, but Sepp himself was already very stretched for supplies. No wonder that he wrote on the 13th:

> 'If every effort is not made to move the forces toward the east and out of the threatened encirclement, the army group will have to write off both armies. Within a very short time, resupplying the troops with ammunition and fuel will no longer be possible. Therefore, immediate measures are necessary to move to the east before such movement is definitely too late. It will soon be possible for the enemy to fire into the pocket with artillery from all sides'. [38]

This certainly reflects the comment of Lieutenant Colonel Kurt Kauffmann of *Panzer Lehr* who said of Sepp: 'He was no soldier, but he was a realist.' [39] He was also a realist in another way. When asked by Schack, commander of 272nd Infantry Division, why he did not approach Hitler in person, bearing in mind his close relationship with him, Sepp replied: 'If I want to get shot, that's the way to do it.' [40] The truth was that the atmosphere surrounding Hitler was very different to what it had been before 20 July and anyone who disagreed with him was likely to be branded a conspirator and treated as such.

Hitler, in fact, was more determined than ever that the counter-stroke should be mounted and allocated three more Panzer divisions to Eberbach – 21st Panzer and 9th and 10th SS. Meanwhile, on the evening of the 13th, Haislip reached Argentan and was ordered to halt there by Bradley, who was

concerned lest his forces clash with the Canadians who were about to launch
the next phase of their drive on Falaise, Operation *Tractable*. This began next
morning. Once again, it was I SS Panzer Corps, now commanded by
Kraemer, and especially the *Hitlerjugend*, which took the brunt. Desperately
short of armour, especially now that 21st Panzer Division had been taken from
him, Kraemer could not give his infantry divisions any tanks to support them.
Nevertheless, helped by the fact that a copy of the Canadian plan had fallen
into their hands, taken off the body of an officer in a shot-up scout car, the
Corps resisted fiercely so that not until the afternoon were the attackers able to
get across the Laison River. Although von Kluge did relent and allow 21st
Panzer Division to be returned to Sepp, Dietrich was heavily reliant on his
anti-tank guns because of the shortage of armour. He looked to the 88mm's of
Pickert's III Flak Corps to help him:

> 'I constantly ordered these guns to stay forward and act in an anti-tank role against Allied
> armour. My orders were just as often countermanded by Pickert, who moved them back into
> the rear areas to protect administrative sites. I asked time and again that these guns be put
> under my command, but was always told by the High Command that it was impossible.'[41]

Here again he was confronted by the problem of OKW's refusal to place all
Luftwaffe ground formations under command of Army Group B.

Having had no contact with von Kluge for two days, Dietrich was now
informed by him that Eberbach's counter-stroke had proved impossible to
mount and that he had given Hausser orders to extricate himself in five days.
'That's too long', replied Dietrich, 'Falaise is about to fall. He must be out in
three days.'[42] Von Kluge, however, took no notice, but he was by then a
broken man. On the 15th, the day after his visit to Dietrich he was caught in an
Allied air attack and had spent most of the day in a ditch, out of contact with
everyone. Hitler convinced himself that this was because he was negotiating
with the Allies and this, coming on top of von Kluge's foot-dragging over the
Avranches counter-stroke, was the last straw. On the 16th, Hitler summoned
Model from Russia to take over and ordered von Kluge to report to him and
explain himself in person.

In the meantime, the Canadians continued their remorseless pressure on
Falaise, and entered it on the evening of the 16th. This was in spite of fanatical
resistance by the *Hitlerjugend*, a detachment of sixty of whom continued to fight
it out in the *école superieure* for a further three days, with only four out of sixty
eventually surrendering. It was now a question of trying to hold open the ever
diminishing gap between the Canadians and the Americans, so that Seventh
Army and Panzer Group Eberbach could escape. Dietrich did his best but, on
the afternoon of the 18th, the door was closed when the Canadians and
Americans met at Trun.

On that very same day, Model arrived to take command of Army Group B,
and von Kluge sat down to write a farewell letter, knowing that his chances of
survival once he returned to Germany were slim. It was addressed personally
to the Führer and was to reach him by hand of Dietrich, 'whom I have come to

know and appreciate as a brave, incorruptible man in these difficult weeks'. In it he spelt out the impossibility of the counter-stroke against the Americans of succeeding, the impossible supply situation which had dogged Army Group B from D-Day onwards and the refusal of OKW to listen to the commanders in the West. Finally, unless Model was able to 'master the situation' or that 'your new, greatly desired weapons, especially of the air force' did not succeed 'then, My Führer, make up your mind to end the war. The German people have borne such untold suffering that it is time to put an end to this frightfulness.'[43] It would, however, be some days yet before Dietrich could pass on this letter and von Kluge took a cyanide pill on 19 August while flying between Paris and Metz.

The first task facing Model was obviously how best to extricate what remained of Army Group B from Normandy and establish a new defence line further east. It was his initial hope to be able to establish this new line west of the Seine. To this end, he gave Dietrich responsibility for it from the Channel coast to south of Paris. Eberbach's Panzer Group, or what little of it remained, was broken up and he himself went to deputise for Paul Hausser, who had been badly wounded during the breakout from the Falaise pocket, with Dietrich having overall command of Seventh Army. It was, however, wholly over-optimistic. For a start, Dietrich commanded an army only in name, with his divisions being mere broken skeletons and with these he was expected to hold over one hundred miles of front. Furthermore, Haislip's XV US Corps had, after their hold-up at Argentan, continued their mad dash and had already established a bridgehead across the Seine at Mantes by 21 August. This produced a grave threat to the left wing of Fifth Panzer Army, but Model's solution was for Dietrich to launch a counter-attack with four of his Panzer divisions. Sepp protested that they were no more than a few weak Panzer Grenadier units with little more than thirty tanks to support them, but this was of no avail. The attack went in on the afternoon of the 23rd, but was quickly driven back. There was therefore no option but to pull back across the Seine.

Next day Dietrich began to withdraw his troops over the river. As he later recalled:

> 'The crossing of the Seine took place under the greatest difficulties: continuous air attacks, lack of bridges, insufficient numbers of ferries, and continuous pressure of the enemy armies contributed to make the setting up of a front on the E bank of the Seine impossible. Not even the Somme River line could be held because of the rapid advance of the Allies.'[44]

On another occasion he commented: 'From the point of view of equipment abandoned the Seine crossing was almost as great a disaster as the Falaise crossing.'[45] Indeed, by 25 August, while the withdrawal over the Seine was still taking place, Fifth Panzer Army had a strength of 18,000 men, 314 guns and only forty-two tanks and assault guns. On the 28th, there was a conference at Headquarters Fifth Panzer Army attended by Model, Dietrich, Kraemer and the Chiefs of Staff of Seventh and Fifteenth Armies. At this stage Model wanted to set up an intermediate defence line in order to buy time to prepare defences along the Somme and Marne, but von Gersdorf (Chief of Staff Seventh Army) recalls Sepp angrily pacing up and down his room, saying 'do stop this, this is of no use at all', and reviling Hitler and the German leadership.[46] As had been so often the case during the campaign, he was right. On 31 August, the British reached Amiens and Model's plan was in tatters.

Dietrich himself was in the vicinity of Amiens on that day. Model had decided that Seventh Army had been sufficiently revived to be considered a formation in its own right and wanted it to cover the withdrawal of Fifth Panzer Army to Arras, where it was hoped that it could be refitted and reconstituted as a counter-stroke force. Consequently, he ordered Dietrich to hand over to Eberbach. Although the handover was fixed for the afternoon of the 31st, Dietrich, probably impatient to be shot of the business, persuaded Eberbach to bring it forward to midnight. Eberbach himself was aghast at the situation which Sepp left him. They knew, from a captured map, that the main British thrust was towards Dieppe and Abbeville, right in the path of Seventh Army and designed to cut off Fifteenth Army. Yet, all Dietrich left Eberbach as an army reserve was five Tiger tanks. Dietrich rushed off, and an hour later, at breakfast, Eberbach and his staff were surprised by the arrival of tanks of the British 11th Armoured Division and they were all captured. Eberbach felt very bitter over Dietrich's impatience to be off and considered that since there were no further laurels to be won, Dietrich had completely lost interest.[47]

Von Gersdorf did managed to escape, however, and made his way to the headquarters of Army Group B at Hâvrincourt. He reported to Model and, to his surprise, because Eberbach had told him that he had been killed, saw Sepp seated at a desk. Indeed, Dietrich had just been telling Model that both Eberbach and von Gersdorf were dead or taken prisoner. Model was ordering him to reassume command of Seventh Army and Sepp, clearly delighted that he had survived, turned to von Gersdorf and said: 'Now you can say *Du* as well to me.'[48]

Dietrich, however, was not to spend many more days in France. By 8 September, Model had finally accepted that only by falling back to the West Wall did Army Group B have any chance of stabilising the front once more. Hitler reluctantly agreed, on the proviso that a strong armoured reserve be formed so that offensive operations could be resumed. Dietrich was nominated to organise this and, on 11 September, Hasso von Manteuffel replaced him and he returned to Germany with orders to report to the Führer.

Sepp told one of his American interrogators that he considered that the fighting in Normandy had been the hardest of his career.

'The Germans broke down on the invasion front because of the complete failure of our Air Force and Navy, and because of the Allied superiority in men and material. Furthermore, one was not allowed to make decisions of one's own, which led to extreme difficulties in the exercising of command. One's proposals had to go to the GHQ of the Fuehrer. If they were acknowledged at all, replies had to come back by way of army group; but only too often GHQ had no understanding of the situation, or made its decisions hopelessly late.'[49]

His bitterness, too, was accentuated by the knowledge that many of the best of his comrades in the Waffen-SS became casualties. Besides the death of Fritz Witt on 16 June, Theodor Wisch, Dietrich's successor as commander of the *Leibstandarte*, was badly wounded on 20 August and Panzer Meyer, having just been awarded the Swords to his Knight's Cross, was captured on 6 September, Max Wünsche, Sepp's Adjutant in the early part of the war, was badly wounded and captured during the Battle of the Falaise Gap on 11 August 1944 while leading the 12th SS Panzer Regiment, and Michael Wittmann, that hero of so many tank fights on both the Eastern and Western fronts, was killed south of Caen on 8 August. These were the names of just a few who were lost and the SS Panzer divisions would never be quite the same again.

CHAPTER 8

The Ardennes 1944

Dietrich reported to Hitler on 14 September and was told that he was to form the headquarters of what was to become Sixth Panzer Army. On the same day he also had a long conference with Martin Bormann, but what was discussed has not been revealed,[1] but it is probable that Bormann wanted to hear from Sepp exactly what had happened in Normandy. It is also very likely that Dietrich was guarded in his comments in the light of his rebuff from Hitler when he went to receive the Diamonds and his comment to Schack of 272nd Infantry Division. He was also aware that the long arm of the Gestapo had reached General Hans Speidel in connection with the July Bomb Plot.

On 5 September, Speidel had been relieved as Chief of Staff of Army Group B and returned to Germany. Knowing what was in the wind, Speidel next day visited Rommel, who was recovering from his injuries at his home in Herrlingen near Ulm. On the 7th, Speidel was arrested by the Gestapo and spent the next seven months incarcerated in the Gestapo prison on Prinz Albrecht-strasse in Berlin. Constantly interrogated, he never broke. Rommel wrote to Hitler in protest at Speidel's arrest and passed it to Dietrich to hand to the Führer. Rommel never received a reply,[2] but Speidel was convinced that Dietrich had stood up for him and used his influence to ensure not only that he was acquitted by the court of honour convened to try him for his supposed role in the Bomb Plot but also that, while in jail, he was able to have facilities denied to most other prisoners.[3]

Dietrich began to form his headquarters at Bad Salzuflen, near Herford, toward the end of September, beginning with a cadre of just ten officers. Not until October, did Sixth Panzer Army begin to receive troops. When they did come, they belonged to the Panzer divisions which had been so badly mangled in France. Initially, they were organised into I SS Panzer Corps (*Leibstandarte* and *Hitlerjugend*) and II SS Panzer Corps (*Das Reich, Hohenstaufen, Panzer Lehr*). As Chief of Staff, Dietrich had General Gause, whom he knew from Normandy. The two corps commanders were respectively *Generalleutnant der Waffen-SS* Hermann Priess and Willi Bittrich, who had recently done well in the defence of Arnhem against the British airborne attacks. Wilhelm Mohnke, who had distinguished himself as a battle group commander in the last weeks of the campaign in France, now commanded the *Leibstandarte* and Sepp's old

Chief of Staff, Fritz Kraemer, had the *Hitlerjugend*. In II SS Panzer Corps there were two new commanders of the *Das Reich* and *Hohenstaufen*, Lammerding and Stadler, while Bayerlein remained in charge of *Panzer Lehr*. All the divisions except one had been involved in fending off the probes of Hodges' First US Army in the Eifel area of the West Wall. The exception was the *Hohenstaufen*, which had been at Arnhem with Bittrich.

The first step was to concentrate the remnants of these divisions around Heilbronn, to the east of Heidelburg. Once they had got their component parts back together again, for many elements had been detached to other formations, I SS Panzer Corps went into concentration areas around Minden, while II SS Panzer Corps, less *Panzer Lehr*, which left to join Fifth Panzer Army, moved to the east of the Ruhr, Arnsberg in the case of *Das Reich* and Hamm for the *Hohenstaufen*. One problem was that the two corps staffs could not be extricated at the same time as their subordinate divisions. HQ I SS Panzer Corps did not join until 22nd October, and HQ II SS Panzer Corps not until mid-November. This meant that the burden of re-equipping and retraining fell firmly on Dietrich and his staff.

Heavy losses in manpower over the past few months, combined with the general shortage of this commodity with which the Third Reich was now faced, meant that there was no possibility that the strict entry standards of the Waffen-SS in earlier years could be applied. For a start, the Waffen-SS replacements were 'pressed men' and not volunteers and some of these resented not being posted to the *Wehrmacht*. While many were raw 17 year-olds, others were in their forties and even their fifties. Many, too, were ethnic Germans from Rumania, Hungary, Slovakia and places even further afield. Somehow or other, they had to be welded into a shock force by the few veterans that remained.

Shortage of fuel seriously affected the training of tank drivers. Indeed, there was only sufficient for five hours per driver,[4] which also included driving by night. This lack of training was to take its toll later, in December. Many of the recruits, even those who had come from other branches of the armed forces, had little idea of the concept of Panzer units in the attack and their general training had necessarily to be directed towards this. They also had to be educated in the concept of the Waffen-SS as political soldiers, and that the Americans were inferior because they were apolitical. Typical of the propaganda which was put out to these new members was a *Leibstandarte* leaflet:

'The *Leibstandarte* has, in over five years of war, pinned success upon success on its banners. And it has, along with these often decisive victories on all the battlefields of Europe, brought the greatest sacrifices in blood and life, [and] always stands, by the will of the Fuhrer, where things are going hardest. . . .

. . . We want to be the best . . ., because one expects this performance from us and must expect it.'[5]

Doubtless, too, Sepp Dietrich, in his own down-to-earth way, especially his ability to talk to soldiers, appearing as their equal, helped to weld the new Sixth Panzer Army into a cohesive force in which its members believed.

Material also had to be found. The original intention was to give each division 120 tanks. According to Dietrich, some 250 replacements were received during the period October-December 1944, giving his army a total of 500 tanks.[6]

Although Dietrich was not to be made aware of it for a few more weeks, as early as 16 September Hitler had decided on launching a major counter-attack through the Ardennes, with Antwerp as the objective. On 25 September, after Jodl, Chief of the Operations Staff at OKW, had done some initial planning, Hitler expanded on his idea. He envisaged a massive artillery bombardment, followed by an infantry break-in, after which his armour would drive fast and hard to seize bridgeheads over the Meuse. Follow-up armour would then thrust for Antwerp, with the infantry securing its flanks. Hitler looked to Dietrich to provide the main striking force, believing that the SS Panzer troops alone had the necessary dash and dedication to achieve victory. Von Manteuffel's Fifth Panzer Army was to support the main thrust. To his south, Brandenburger's Seventh Army, made up of infantry divisions, would protect the southern flank.

Crucial to the success of *Wacht am Rhein*, as the operation was codenamed, was secrecy. To this end, knowledge of the plan was restricted to OKW for some weeks and all who were privy to it had to sign a pledge of secrecy on pain of death. While the woodlands of the Ardennes would help mask the initial deployment of the attacking troops, bad weather was also considered essential for this and to reduce the effect of Allied air power. Hitler also gave orders that activity against the Americans in the area was to be kept to a minimum in order to lull the enemy into a false sense of security. This was highly successful, in that the Americans used the sector to blood fresh divisions arriving from the United States and to rest others who had been battered in the bitter fighting in the Hürtgen Forest to the north.

Consequently, until mid-November, Dietrich was kept in the dark. While his divisions retrained and refitted in the Minden and Hamm areas their only operational role was as a reaction force against possible enemy airlanding operations in their respective areas. Then, on 9 November, Dietrich received an order to move his divisions westwards by rail. Pleas to delay this move for a further two or three weeks, so that training could be completed, were refused. The move, with each division requiring sixty trains, went ahead and was completed around 20 November. Army Headquarters was now located in Quadrath, west of Cologne, with I SS Panzer Corps deployed on the west side of the city and II Panzer Corps around Bonn, apart from the *Das Reich*, which was at Moenchengladbach, west of Düsseldorf. Training now resumed, with emphasis on night operations. From now on all vehicle moves were to take place at night only and strict orders were given that no one, not even individuals, was to cross to the west of the Neuss-Grevenbroich-Liblar-Euskirchen road. For the officers' map and sand table exercises, the dominant theme was: 'Attacks against the flanks and rear of a motorized enemy who had made a penetration in depth to the main defensive area and even into the interior of the country.'[7] None of the troops on the ground though that they were preparing for a large scale offensive and the general consensus was that they were about to be committed to the desperate fighting around Aachen. Dietrich himself did visit Hitler's headquarters at the end of October, and by then knew what was in the wind, although it was probably not discussed in any detail. Martin Bormann notes that he complained vociferously about the failures of the Luftwaffe[8] – the debacle of Normandy clearly still weighed heavily on his mind. Léon Degrelle, the celebrated, but infamous, Belgian commander of the Wallonia SS Brigade, who was also present to receive the Oakleaves to his Knight's Cross, recalled:

'The Führer's Lieutenant, Martin Bormann, round, plump, and pasty-faced, debated noisily with General Sepp Dietrich of the SS, who arrived in a glider [sic] from the Western front. His legs wide apart, his face as red as a turnip, Sepp expatiated at length on the strength of the Anglo-American air force and on the ravages of the *Tieffliegers* ['strafing planes']. But he wasn't especially worried. He gave everyone great thumps on the back, drank cognac with every breath, and went back to his room at five o'clock in the morning, vigorously supported by four giants of the guard.'[9]

Sepp also had an impending domestic event on his mind. Ursula was expecting their third child and Götz-Hubertus was born on 23 November, again in Karlsruhe. As before, Himmler was to be godfather and sent the baby a silver box with spoon, cup and plate.[10] Ten days after Gotz-Hubertus was born, Ursula took all three boys and their nurse to Bad Saarow. Sepp had finally decided to build a house there and Ursula went to supervise this.[11] Why he should have come to this decision at this late stage of the war is hard to fathom. One can only surmise that perhaps, like others in the Nazi hierarchy, he believed that the Western Allies would shortly come to their senses and join Germany in preventing the Soviet hordes from overrunning Western Europe and that the Russians would be held well to the east of the Oder.

To his American interrogators, Dietrich consistently maintained that the first that he knew of the Ardennes counter-offensive was on 12 December, just four days before it was launched. This totally conflicts with the evidence of all other participants, apart from Guderian, and is clearly wrong.[12] Why he should have done this is difficult to establish, and one can only put forward the theory that he used it as an excuse to help explain away the subsequent failures of Sixth Panzer Army.

The first that anyone outside OKW knew of *Wacht am Rhein* was when Siegfried Westphal, Chief of Staff to von Rundstedt, still Commander-in-Chief West, and Hans Krebs, Chief of Staff to the commander of Army Group B, who was still Model, were summoned to a meeting at the Wolf's Lair on 22 October. They expected to be berated for the loss of Aachen, which had just fallen, but instead Hitler treated them to a briefing on the counter-offensive, stating that it must be launched on 25 November. When their chiefs of staff returned and informed them of what was in the wind, both von Rundstedt and

Model were appalled. With further Allied drives expected, they were now being asked to withdraw some of their divisions from the line in order that they could be added to the attack and were not allowed to use the theatre reserves in the shape of the two Panzer armies now deployed behind the West Wall. Furthermore, Antwerp was a totally unrealistic objective, since it was inevitable that the British and Americans would mount counter-strokes against the long exposed flanks of the thrust towards it. In its place, both commanders came up with more limited suggestions. Von Rundstedt proposed a double envelopment of Aachen, while Model opted for the same, but using just a single encirclement coming up through the Ardennes. This became known as the 'small solution' as opposed to Hitler's 'big solution'.

On 27 October, there was a meeting between von Rundstedt and Model at the latter's headquarters and it was now that the three army commanders – Dietrich, von Manteuffel and Brandenburger – were first brought in. After several hours' discussion they agreed to approach Jodl with the 'small solution'. Jodl met von Rundstedt, Model and von Manteuffel at Model's headquarters on 3 November and listened to their arguments, but replied that the Führer's plan could not be changed. Von Rundstedt and Model now suggested another option. This was to launch an attack from the north into the flank of Simpson's Ninth US Army, which had begun once more to attack in the Aachen sector, but this again was turned down. All Hitler would concede was to put back the date of the attack from 25 November to 10 December in order to allow more time for preparation. At this juncture, Hitler ordered Kraemer to take over from Gause as Dietrich's Chief of Staff, which he did on 16 November. No explanation was given for this, but it is probable that Hitler suspected that Gause, being an Army, as opposed to Waffen-SS, officer did not have sufficient 'fire in his belly', whereas Kraemer had already proved himself in Normandy as Dietrich's Chief of Staff and had been formally transferred to the Waffen-SS. Whatever the reason, Kraemer was quite clear that Gause briefed him on the impending offensive during their handover-takeover.[13]

On 23 November, Hitler held another planning conference in Berlin. Present at this were von Rundstedt, Model, Westphal, Krebs, von Manteuffel, Jodl and Dietrich. Jodl was emphatic that Dietrich was present at this meeting and recalled him asking about the non-arrival of supplies.

> 'Dietrich was present at the meeting on 23 Nov 44. I remember it definitely. We had coffee together. Everything was again explained to the generals, who all had their maps with them. We discussed what still remained to be done. Pressure was exerted to get all the equipment still needed.'[14]

Dietrich, when quizzed by one of his interrogators about this, said:

> 'Yes, now I remember a meeting on that date; however, we only discussed the possibility of committing Sixth Pz Army and whether it would be ready for commitment if needed. Model said it would be, but I said it would not be ready in Dec 44. We talked only in terms of a general winter offensive and did not specify date or time or place. About 4 or 6 Dec 44, Model told me something was coming, but he was very secretive and Hitler had not yet decided the time or place.'

Questioned further, Dietrich said that he was not present for the whole time and it was possible that the details were discussed after he had gone.[15] Given that this was the day on which Götz-Hubertus was born it is reasonable to suppose that he might have been excused for part of the time in order to check up on how mother and son were progressing, but his alleged lack of knowledge on *Wacht am Rhein* cannot be believed.

At this stage, Sixth Panzer Army's role had now been closely defined. It was to break through the enemy's defences in the Monschau-Krewinkel sector, and then send its armoured spearheads across the Meuse south of Liege and, screening its right flank on the Albert Canal, drive on to Antwerp. In order to secure the line of the right flank from his start line to Liège, Dietrich was now lent General Otto Hitzfeld's LXVII Corps (3rd Panzergrenadier Division, 246th, 272nd, 326th Volksgrenadier Divisions) from Fifteenth Army to his north. Once the Meuse had been crossed this corps would once more be subordinated to its parent formation. I SS Panzer Corps was also reinforced with 3rd Parachute Division, and 12th and 277th Volkgrenadier Divisions, who were to carry out the break in operations. Apart from the problems of re-equipment – air raids disrupted the movement of supplies, and weapons and spare parts had to come from a number of different ordnance depots, which complicated matters – Dietrich was, like his brother and superior commanders, filled with gloom over the concept. As he said to his Canadian interrogator, Milton Shulman:

> "'I grew so big with these plans", sarcastically commented Dietrich, flinging out his arms and puffing out his cheeks. "I had merely to cross a river, capture Brussels and then go on and take the port of Antwerp. And all this in the worst months of the year, December, January, February, through the countryside where snow was waist deep and there wasn't room to deploy four tanks abreast, let alone six armoured divisions; when it didn't get light until eight in the morning and was dark again at four in the afternoon; with divisions that had just been reformed and contained chiefly raw, untried recruits; and at Christmas time.'"[16]

It was, however, a Hitler Order and had to be obeyed.

The corps commanders and their chiefs of staff had been briefed in mid-November and on 2 December a map exercise was conducted at Dietrich's headquarters in order to acquaint the divisional commanders with the plan. Von Rundstedt was present, but Dietrich was away at a conference in Berlin – another fruitless attempt to wean Hitler towards the Small Solution and Bittrich deputised for him. There was concern over the infantry divisions which had been assigned to I SS Panzer Corps for the break-in operation. The 277th Volksgrenadier Division was already in the front line, but was weak in terms of experienced personnel. Likewise, 3rd Parachute Division had just been rebuilt after heavy losses in Normandy and was now largely made up of rear echelon Luftwaffe personnel. Only Gerhard Engel's 12th Volksgrenadier Division could really be considered battleworthy, having recently performed very creditably during the fighting around Aachen. It was still considered that the troops were insufficiently trained in night operations and yet it was essential that the infantry started their attack during the hours of darkness in order to give them more chance of making the necessary penetration covered by both this and then fog. In order to help them therefore, some 200 search-lights from II Flak Corps were made available in order to create 'artificial moonlight'. In the event, though, it was found that they were not sufficiently mobile to keep up with the attack. The terrain was such that, during the approach march, it was impossible for the tanks to move off the road and so five routes were selected for the movement of armour only.

One refinement which was agreed at the end of November was the placing of 150 Panzer Brigade, under the newly promoted *Obersturmbannführer* Otto Skorzeny, under command of I SS Panzer Corps. Skorzeny had been ordered by Hitler to carry out a subsidiary operation, *Greif*. This was designed to create confusion behind the Allied lines by using English speaking soldiers dressed in American uniforms and to also try and seize crossings over the Meuse. For this, they were to set off behind I SS Panzer Corps and infiltrate their way through the American lines. Dietrich himself professed not to like Skorzeny, whom he called 'a shady character, always in with Himmler on any dirty work'[17] and probably regarded *Greif* as just another complication which was unlikely to work. This might also explain his attitude to Colonel Graf Friedrich August von der Heydte and his parachute battalion. On 8 December, Hitler suddenly decided that it would be a very good idea to drop a force of a thousand men behind Monschau so as to block the move of American reinforcements from the north until such time as Dietrich could form a hard shoulder. Von der Heydte, a veteran of Crete, was summoned to organise the force, and was told to take elements from all available parachute units. Few of those who were selected had done an operational jump – indeed some had never parachuted – and it was a motley collection with which he found himself. He was told that he would come under Dietrich's direct control and reported to him at his headquarters. When he explained his mission, Kraemer kept uttering: 'It's crazy! What a lunatic operation!'[18] But he and Dietrich had to accept it. They insisted, however, that von der Heydte did a night drop, just prior to the preliminary barrage, about which, given the raw state of his paratroops, von der Heydte was not happy, but had to agree, since otherwise there was a danger of surprise being lost. According to one source,[19] Dietrich had been drinking heavily, which probably meant that he was not at his most polite. Indeed, when von der Heydte asked if he could have pigeons in case his radio failed to operate on landing, Dietrich just laughed in his face[20] and retorted: 'What do you think I am? Running a zoo?'[21] This was understandably upsetting for the aristocratic army officer, and it is not surprising that after his capture he spoke of Dietrich as a 'cur dog'.[22]

The final opportunity that the commanders had to sway Hitler came during a two day conference held at the Eagle's Nest, the concrete bunkers in the Taunus Hills, north of Frankfurt, from which Hitler had directed the French campaign of 1940 and where he intended to supervise this new offensive. All

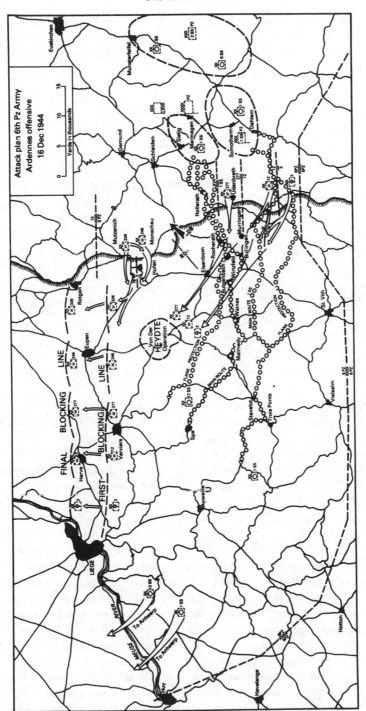

MAP 13 Sixth Panzer Army operational plan for the Ardennes offensive.

levels of command down to and including divisional commanders were invited, with half attending on 12 December and the remainder the following day. Hasso von Manteuffel was present on the first day, as was Sepp Dietrich, and recalled that:

> 'In addition to the army generals, a number of SS generals, commanders of the panzer divisions, had been summoned. The seating accommodation was inadequate and the SS generals politely left the chairs to their senior army colleagues, while they stood. This created the impression on some of the army generals that an SS officer was posted behind each army officer's chair. This was certainly a misunderstanding.'[23]

Much of the time was taken up with speeches by Hitler and his staff and the emphasis was on the potential decisiveness of the forthcoming operation. Dietrich remembered:

> 'Hitler declared at this conference that he had decided on a winter offensive because the Army's continuous setbacks could be tolerated no longer. The Army must gain a victory. He said that all preparations had been made and that thousands of tanks were at their disposal. Hitler continued at great length and referred to former campaigns. "The German people can no longer endure the heavy bombing attacks," he said, and "The German people are entitled to action from me." No one else made a speech. We were not asked. At the end of the conference, the generals were introduced to Hitler and each had an opportunity to talk to him for a few minutes. Hitler asked me, "Is your Army ready?" I answered, "Not for an offensive." To this, Hitler replied, "You are never satisfied." The answers of the commanding generals were similar – "not fully prepared for commitment." After the conference, the generals who had been present met for a birthday celebration at von Rundstedt's house [von Rundstedt was born on 12 December 1875]. No one dared to speak about the offensive. The death penalty hovered over the secret, and it would have been to no avail to discuss it anyway. By midnight, all generals were on the way back to their units.'[24]

Hitler's only concession was to postpone the day of the attack, X-Day, from 15 December, to which it had already been put back, to the following morning, the 16th.

The deployment of Sixth Panzer Army had begun on 8 December, when it took over command of the supply services in its sector. Two days later Dietrich and Kraemer moved their headquarters to Bad Münstereifel, south of Euskirchen, and the next day, the 11th, the Army took over tactical command of the Monschau-Schnee sector. Not until the 14th were commanders below divisional level given their orders, although Joachim Peiper, whose I SS Panzer Regiment was to take a leading and subsequently infamous role in the operation, deduced on the 12th what was in the wind when Kraemer asked him what he thought about the prospects of an attack in the Eifel and how long it would take to move a tank regiment 80 kilometres in the hours of darkness. In typical fashion, Peiper drove a Panther this distance and was able to complete it in one night, but 'with an entire division, that was a different question'.[25]

The supply situation continued to give Dietrich and Kraemer cause for concern. Such was the difficult nature of the terrain in the Eifel that it was calculated that vehicles would consume twice as much fuel to travel the same distances as in normal going. By 12 December, Sixth Army had sufficient fuel for 200 kilometres motoring in the Eifel conditions, but only a proportion of this was actually held by the divisions, the remainder being 'on wheels' or held in dumps west of the Rhine. Contrary to subsequent popular belief, Kraemer asserted that they would only have to rely on captured fuel stocks if there were problems created by the USAAF. Indeed, Sixth Panzer Army had no knowledge of the locations of the American fuel dumps and depots in the area. [26] He also said that ammunition supplies were sufficient, [27] but General Walter Staudinger, commander Sixth Panzer Army Artillery, complained that much of the additional artillery given to support the attack was of many different calibres and there was often an ammunition mismatch. [28] For this, and to allow his newly deployed troops more opportunity to study the ground over which they were about to attack, Dietrich asked for a further postponement of the attack, but this was refused.

Dietrich, now bowing to the inevitable, issued an order of the day to mark the opening of the offensive:

> 'Soldiers of the Sixth Panzer Army! The great moment of decision is upon us. The Führer has placed us at the vital point. It is for us to breach the enemy front and push beyond the Meuse. Surprise is half the battle. In spite of the terror bombings, the Home Front has provided us with tanks, ammunition and weapons. They are watching us. We will not let them down.' [29]

The luckless von der Heydte was supposed to be the first to move, the plan being that his men should drop just before dawn and the opening of the preliminary bombardment on the 16th. Late on the 15th, however, because of transport difficulties, only a third of his force had arrived at the departure airfield and he was ordered by HQ Sixth Panzer Army to wait until all were present. Later that night, he was told to mount his operation before dawn on the 17th, with the dropping zone adjusted slightly to the south-east to overlook the Verviers-Malmédy and Aix-la Chapelle to Malmédy roads. When the operation was finally launched, it was a disaster. Less than a quarter of his men actually landed on or near the predesignated dropping zone and collected at the *rendez-vous*. The supply panniers were scattered and, as he had feared might happen, von der Heydte's radio was smashed. The Panzer relief force promised by Dietrich did not link up with him and, after four days hiding out in woods, he surrendered.

At 0530 hours, the preliminary barrage opened, concentrating on the forward American positions and previously located artillery batteries. Thirty minutes later, the infantry began their attack. Dietrich and Kraemer had allowed for one day to break through the enemy positions, a day to get over the Hautes Vagnes plateau with the Panzer divisions and two further days to get to the Meuse. By 1300 hours the infantry divisions had advanced some four kilometres, but were experiencing difficulties with the terrain. Dietrich and Kraemer considered that all that had been met so far was the American outpost line and that the main US defences still had to be tackled. They therefore ordered I SS Panzer Corps to commit engineers and Panzer Grenadiers but not tanks, because they could not operate off the roads, to the support of the infantry ahead of them.

The plan that Dietrich and Kraemer had drawn up called for the main attack by the armour to be in two echelons. Leading would be I SS Panzer Corps, with the *Leibstandarte* left and *Hitlerjugend* right, while behind them would come II SS Panzer Corps, with the *Hohenstaufen* left and *Das Reich* right. Five routes had been allocated as follows:

Route A – East of Rocherath through Elsenborn camp to Polleur
Route B – Rocherath to Wirtsfeld and then west to Sart
Route C – Losheim – Malmédy – Spa
Route D – Losheim – Stavelot
Route E – Krewinkel – Trois Ponts

Routes A-C were allocated to the *Hitlerjugend* and the other two to the *Leibstandarte*. Route A had just a Panzer Grenadier battalion group and was to link up with von der Heydte's paratroopers, but Routes B and C both had regimental groups commanded respectively by *Sturmbannführer* Siegfried Muller and *Sturmbannführer* Herbert Kuhlmann. Routes D and E also had regimental groups commanded by *Obersturmführer* Joachim Peiper and *Standartenführer* Max Hansen. Also following up behind on these routes were two further regimental groups, one from the *Hohenstaufen* under *Obersturmführer* Bernhard Krause and the other from the *Leibstandarte* under *Obersturmführer* Rudolf Sandig. The idea was that fresh orders would then be given once the line Verviers-Spa-Stavelot-had been reached, depending on how the situation had developed. Hasso von Manteuffel later asserted that one reason for Sixth Panzer Army's failure was that it had attacked on too narrow a front.[30] Kraemer, however, stated that it was because the ground in the initial stages was so bad.[31] This is certainly supported by Peiper who says he pointed out to Mohnke that the *Leibstandarte*'s routes were bad – 'not fit for tanks, but were for bicycles' – but he was told that it was a Führer order and could not be changed.[32]

In the event, in the afternoon of the 16th, the *Hitlerjugend* and the *Leibstandarte* combat groups began to move forward. Route Á became impassable, after ten assault guns had driven over it, and had to be abandoned. To make matters worse, the going off the roads was so soft as to make cross country movement almost impossible. This of course meant that the scattered remnants of von der Heydte's force could not be rescued, another reason for von der Heydte's bitterness towards Dietrich, although Sepp himself later told his American interviewer that I SS Panzer Corps had never had specific orders to contact the paratroopers. It could have been done, however, if the Elsenborn Ridge, which was where he personally wanted them used, had been captured.[33] Resolute defence by Gerow's US V Corps against repeated attacks by 277th and 12th Volksgrenadier Divisions meant that Routes B and C could not be opened. Further south, however, an opportunity did appear in the afternoon. Losheim was seized and Mohnke let loose Peiper's battle group. Unfortunately, the bridge at Losheim had been destroyed and this caused a four hour delay while engineers were moved forward to repair it. Only late in the evening could Peiper really get going. Advancing through the night, he seized Honsfeld at 0400 hours next morning. On Route E, on the other hand, mines prevented Hansen from advancing. Meanwhile, in the extreme north of Sixth Panzer Army's sector, LXVII Corps had failed in its attempts to break through at Monschau, perhaps not helped by an order from Model which stated that artillery was not to fire on it because of its lattice-work houses, which were of architectural significance.[34]

During the 17th, while the *Hitlerjugend* remained tied down in the Rocherath-Krinkelt-Büllingen triangle and LXVII Corps, having been ordered to bypass Monschau and turn south to clear the Elsenborn Ridge, found its route barred by mines and other obstacles, Peiper continued to press forward. The road from Monsfeld south-west to Heppenbach was found to be impassable and since, from the engine noises, it was clear to Peiper that the *Hitlerjugend* was well to his rear, he decided to move up onto Route C by way of Büllingen. This village had another attraction in that Peiper suspected that there was a fuel dump there, and his tanks, especially because of so much low gear work, were running dangerously low. Brushing aside some resistance just north-west of Honsfeld, Peiper reached Büllingen and found his dump, having surprised a group of US L-5 liaison aircraft on the ground. Using US prisoners to help replenish his tanks, he then drove on via Moderscheid towards Stavelot. He saw this as 'a clean breakthrough' and met little opposition, apart from the odd jeeps, which appeared from side roads, an indication that the Americans had no inkling of the depth of Peiper's penetration.[35] Just north of Thirimont, the lead tank fired on an American convoy moving along the Malmédy-Ligneuville road and this marked the beginning of an incident, the eventual outcome of which would haunt Dietrich and many of his men for the rest of their lives.

The convoy was Battery B, 285th Field Artillery Observation Battalion, consisting of about 140 men in thirty soft-skinned vehicles under command of Captain Roger L Mills, and was en route south from Heerlen, in Holland, as part of 7th Armored Division. The first shots struck the lead vehicle in the convoy and others, too, were hit. As the surprised Americans debussed to look for cover, Panzer Grenadiers who were riding on the tanks, dismounted and moved in. The senior surviving American officer, Lieutenant Virgil T Lary, realising that his men had no chance, gave the order to surrender and the survivors were rounded up in an open field by a roadside cafe. Peiper's column then moved on towards Ligneuville, leaving the prisoners under a light guard, and at 1600 hours reached Stavelot. What happened next to the prisoners remains unclear and the details are best discussed in Chapter Ten. Suffice to say that, during that afternoon, the commanding officer of the US 291st Combat Engineer Battalion, which was then defending Malmédy, Colonel David E Pergrin, carried out a reconnaissance southwards and heard machine gun fire and shouting. Four men came stumbling out of the woods and blurted out an incoherent story about a massacre of prisoners which had just taken place. He took them back to Malmédy. During the next few hours, another thirteen survivors, including Lieutenant Lary reached the village. Pergrin had immediately passed details of the massacre back on the radio. Next day the news reached Supreme Headquarters Allied Expeditionary Force (SHAEF) and 12th Army Group in a message from First US Army.

> 'SS troops vicinity L8199 captured US soldier, traffic MP with about two hundred other US soldiers. American prisoners searched. When finished, Germans lined up Americans and shot them with machine pistols and machine guns. Wounded informant escaped and more details follow later.' [36]

SHAEF ordered an immediate investigation, which was initially hampered by the fact that the scene of the massacre was in German hands until mid-January, although the bodies remained frozen and unburied in the snow.

It was Malmédy, more than any other incident, that changed US policy, which up until now had been somewhat ambivalent on war crimes. The massacre was highly publicised and it was now widely believed that there was an overall clearcut plan for the SS and Gestapo to spread terror through atrocities. Peiper's troops were held to be guilty from the start. As US Secretary of War, Henry L Stimson, noted in his diary on 26 December 1944: 'It seems to be clear that their [Germany's] troops have been guilty of many violations of the laws of war against us.' [37] The truth of the matter was that while the troops of the other allies fighting the war in Europe had been victims of war crimes, this was the first direct US experience of it. The resultant investigation would lead Sepp Dietrich and seventy-three of his officers and men to face capital charges in the courtroom at Dachau some eighteen months later.

Throughout this time, Dietrich and Kraemer had had little idea of how Peiper was progressing because of poor radio communications and they only heard that he had reached Stavelot through an intercepted message. Of the massacre they had, not surprisingly, no knowledge. According to Charles Whiting, [38] the first that Dietrich heard of it was on 21 December, when Kraemer handed him the transcript of part of a broadcast put out by the British propaganda radio station *Soldatensender Calais*, which was run by Sefton Delmer. Dietrich ordered an immediate investigation which met with denials all the way down the line. Certainly, Skorzeny later recalled this investigation and that his reaction at the time was that such a crime was 'quite unthinkable in the German Army'. [39] However, when Dietrich was initially interrogated after the war, he denied all knowledge of the massacre and said that if it had happened it must have been in von Manteuffel's sector. [40] Later, he did admit that he had heard about some form of atrocity at the time, since Model asked him if anything had taken place in his army, and it was this that triggered off the investigation. [41] Whatever efforts Dietrich did or did not make to establish exactly what had happened at the Baugnez crossroads on that Sunday afternoon in December 1944, it must be remembered that he was very much preoccupied with his desperate struggle to control the bitter break-through battle in which his army was engaged.

Originally, Kraemer and Dietrich had seen the *Hitlerjugend* making the main thrust towards the Meuse bridges, but by midday on 17 December, with its battle groups still tied down, they decided, in view of the albeit sketchy information which they were receiving, that there were better prospects for the *Leibstandarte*. II SS Panzer Corps was therefore given a warning order to be prepared to pass its lead division, the *Hohenstaufen*, to under command of I SS Panzer Corps and for it to be ready to operate on the left flank of the *Leibstandarte*. The object at this stage was to gain ground in order to prevent the Americans setting up effective defences east of the Meuse and also to provide more room for manoeuvre, since the closer they got to the Meuse, the better the terrain became.

During the 18th, while LXVII Corps continued to inch forward in the Monschau-Elsenborn area, the *Hitlerjugend* and 12th Volksgrenadier Division eventually succeeded in retaking Büllingen, which the Americans had reoccupied after Peiper had passed through it, but then became engaged in a hard fight for the village of Bütgenbach. In the meantime, Peiper had initially been rebuffed at Stavelot, which he found strongly defended. He waited until his Panzer Grenadier battalion further back in the column could be brought forward and then attacked at first light on the 18th, forcing the Americans to withdraw. He now dashed to Trois Ponts to try and seize the bridge there, but it was blown up in his face. He therefore moved via La Gleize to Cheneux, where there was another bridge, and this he captured intact. That afternoon, the skies and fog cleared for the first time and he was subjected to air attack which destroyed some vehicles, including tanks, which blocked the road and caused additional delay. In the evening of the 18th he therefore reverted to his original route and headed for Habiemont, just west of the River Lienne. Unfortunately for him, he was once more foiled when the bridge over this river was blown up just as his vehicles began to cross. He therefore turned north once more towards Stoumont. Concurrent with this, 'Cissy' Hansen's group had been moving slowly along Route E, which proved to be extremely difficult for the armour to negotiate. By the end of the 18th, Hansen had only got as far as Born, still well south-east of Ligneuville.

What was concerning commanders increasingly at all levels was fuel. First line reserves had now been almost exhausted and no other American dumps had been captured, other than the one at Büllingen. I SS Panzer Corps, because of the continued US resistance in the Büllingen area had only one supply route forward and enemy air attacks, although intermittent because of the weather, were interrupting the carriage of fresh supplies from the rear. All that could be done was to strip supporting units, such as artillery, of what fuel they had so that it could be passed to the armoured spearheads.

While reports from Peiper remained fragmentary, mainly because radios kept breaking down, it was clear to Dietrich and Kraemer, that everything must be thrown in to support him if there was to be any chance of reaching the Meuse. Consequently, their orders for the 19th instructed Preiss to disentangle the *Hitlerjugend* from Bütgenbach, move it south and then west for an attack on Malmédy in order to enlarge the salient created by Peiper. Preiss, however, declared that the road Büllingen-Moederscheid-Schoeppen was impassable because of the mud and requested another attempt to seize Bütgenbach, which was agreed. Throughout most of the 19th, the *Hohenstaufen* and 12th Volksgrenadier Division continued their battle for Bütgenbach and it was the mud, as much as the American resistance, which thwarted them. Dietrich therefore once more ordered the *Hitlerjugend* to disengage and assemble in the area Baasen-Losheim-Manderfeld and be prepared to follow on behind either the *Leibstandarte* or *Hohenstaufen*.

It was also becoming clear that the Americans were now recovering from their initial surprise and, indeed, were beginning to mount concerted counter-attacks. This was especially so in the Monschen area to the north and there were signs that they were moving against Peiper as well. He himself had captured Stoumont, after a struggle, and then moved on to secure a bridge over the River Ambleve to the west. He now realised that he had virtually run out of fuel and was unable to cross. At the same time, the Americans began to counter-attack against Stavelot, which they took, and Stoumont, to which Peiper now withdrew his leading elements. Throughout this time he had little radio contact with his divisional headquarters, and Mohnke was almost totally reliant on intercepts of American radio messages for information on Peiper's progress. Realising that there was now a very real danger of the *Leibstandarte* being cut off, Dietrich and Kraemer renewed their efforts to try and give the division more protection, ordering elements of the *Hitlerjugend* to provide a flank guard in the north. At the same time, *Das Reich* was ordered into Fifth Panzer Army's sector in order to widen the *Leibstandarte*'s salient to the south. This move went badly wrong, however, when the *Das Reich* became entangled with elements of von Manteuffel's armour south of St Vith. Matters were not helped by the fact that it was now known that the Americans had captured an order giving complete details of Skorzeny's behind-the-lines deception operations and the remainder of these had to be cancelled. Skorzeny's men, at his suggestion, took on a more conventional role as 150 Panzer Brigade.

With the bad state of the roads delaying the new deployments of the *Das Reich* and *Hohenstaufen*, the fact that the *Leibstandarte* was becoming bogged down and was increasingly vulnerable to counter-attack and the stiff American resistance in the north, meant that matters were now coming to a head. It seemed clear to Dietrich and Kraemer that a new approach was needed. They therefore proposed to Model that all the available armour should thrust in the direction Huy-Dinant or, and this they preferred, advance north, using good roads, in the direction Houffalize-Liège-Laroche. Then, in combination with Fifteenth Army they would attack the American rear in the Liège-Aachen area. Model would not, however, make a decision himself and insisted on referring it upwards to von Rundstedt. No answer was ever received.

The next few days were spent in trying to improve the state of the roads and the supply situation. The latter, however, did not get any better since the weather was now beginning to improve and Allied air power was increasingly making its presence felt. As Kraemer later wrote:

'These air attacks caused definite delays in bringing up supplies, that often had to be carried out during the night. In addition to that, the supply dumps of Army Group B had to be shifted very often and gasoline supply columns arrived very late or not at all. One had to live from "hand to mouth", and it frequently happened that a tactical success could not be exploited, because the gasoline or ammunition did not arrive in time, or in too small quantities. Often the fuel consumption was much higher than anticipated because of the bad road conditions. When some of the supplies arrived at all in the main line of resistance, it was due to the untiring activity of the truck drivers and the energy of the staff of the supply services.'[42]

Most depressing was the fact that Peiper was entirely isolated. His fuel tanks dry and ammunition virtually expended, he received permission to make his way back through the American lines on foot. Before this, in contrast to the way that his men appeared to have behaved at the Baugnez cross-roads a few days earlier, Peiper arranged for the American prisoners on his hands, as well as his own wounded, to be left at La Gleize to be recovered by the Americans. This agreement was formally drawn up with the senior US prisoner, Major Hal D McCown, who had been commanding the 2nd Battalion 119th Infantry, and McCown's praise for the way in which he was treated as a prisoner was later to form part of the defence in the Malmédy trial.

While reserves continued to be fed in to guard the northern flank of the original penetration by the *Leibstandarte*, Dietrich now placed his hopes on Bittrich's II SS Panzer Corps, which by 23 December had both of its SS Panzer divisions committed to a thrust between the Rivers Salm and Ourthe, striking north-west towards Huy. Simultaneously, LXVII Corps renewed its operations to clear the Elsenborn area, but requests that the corps should revert to Fifteenth Army for this, on the grounds that it was now divorced from Sixth Panzer Army's main focus of operations, were turned down. As it was, although Dietrich's headquarters moved to Mayerode, eight kilometres north-east of St Vith, he went forward himself to concentrate on Bittrich's operations, leaving Kraemer to control the rest of the Army's sector. Initially, Dietrich was optimistic that II SS Panzer Corps could get to the Meuse, especially since, on the night of Christmas Eve, the Americans did pull back a certain way in the Trois-Ponts-Manhay area. Degrelle visited Dietrich at this time and, although, as he noted, 'Sepp was far from confirming the dazzling rumours which were running through Berlin like will-o'-the-wisps', he appeared enthusiastic about the Huy thrust.

'Sepp Dietrich showed me the Tongres-Saint Trond area on the map, west of Liege. "See!" he said, "It's here that I'll corner them!" Then, with glittering eyes, he put his big thumb under the name of Aachen, the holy city of the Empire. "Aachen!" he exlaimed, "Aachen! In the month of January I will be in Aachen".'[43]

This implies that he still had, at the forefront of his mind, the idea of trapping the Allied forces between Aachen and Liège, even though Model had not given agreement. Indeed, it would seem that he had given up all idea of the Big Solution. As it was, according to Jodl, if Dietrich had had any ideas of heading towards Liège, rather than bypassing it to the south, then he should have been shot for disobeying orders.[44] Dietrich did, however, say after the war that he was not in the least interested in Liège, or even Huy for that matter, since he did not have the troops to take it and also because it lay on low ground and was therefore difficult to get into to.[45]

Dietrich's optimism was to be shortlived, however. The *Das Reich* had seized the villages of Grandmenil and Manhay on Christmas Eve and then turned westwards on Model's order in order to be better coordinated with the attack of XLVII Panzer Corps of Fifth Panzer Army, which was advancing along the line of the Ourthe. The road to Erezée, *Das Reich*'s next objective, was narrow and with steep banks. The leading tank was immobilised by a bazooka at a roadblock; the others could not get past and withdrew to Grandmenil. The US 7th Armoured Division now counter-attacked and, with extensive air support, had driven the elements of *Das Reich* out of both Grandmenil and Manhay by the early hours of the 27th. In Dietrich's words, after the failure to get to Erezée, which he saw as a 'key position', '. . . I didn't think it was possible to get through. As far as I was concerned, the offensive then was completely stalled.'[46] Any hopes that the Americans were prepared to withdraw voluntarily across the Meuse were now gone and Sixth Panzer Army had 'shot its bolt'.

Others thought so as well, for the attention of higher command now turned to von Manteuffel who, with the advantage of better roads and more trafficable terrain in general, had almost reached the Meuse near Dinant. Only the gallant defence of Bastogne by the US 101st Airborne Division remained a thorn in his flesh and, in order to help reduce it, first the *Leibstandarte* and then the whole of I SS Panzer Corps was placed under von Manteuffel's command. By 4 January, the *Hohenstaufen* had also been passed over, leaving Sixth Panzer Army with just the *Das Reich* as its armour asset. A week earlier it had gone over to the defensive, leaving Dietrich bitterly disillusioned. Albert Speer spent the night of 30/31 December with him and recorded that:

> '. . . in his own plain fashion, he too had parted ways psychologically with Hitler. Our conversation soon turned to the latest batch of commands. Hitler had decreed, with increasing insistance, that encircled Bastogne be taken at "any cost". He refused to understand, Sepp Dietrich grumbled, that even the elite divisions of the SS could not effortlessly overrun the Americans. It was impossible to convince Hitler that these were tough opponents, soldiers as good as our own men. "Besides," he added, "we are receiving no ammunition. The supply routes have been cut by air attack."'[47]

The writing was on the wall, however, for von Manteuffel as well. By Boxing Day Patton's US Third Army was driving up from the south towards Bastogne and, indeed, relieved it that day. The nose of von Manteuffel's drive towards Dinant was being held by the newly deployed British XXX Corps. Hodges'

First US Army was also applying pressure from the north. The Luftwaffe's almost suicidal strike on Allied airfields in France and the Low Countries on New Year's Day 1945, although 156 Allied aircraft were destroyed, it did not reduce the Anglo-American dominance in the air and cost the Luftwaffe some 300 aircraft of the thousand which took part. Likewise, Operation *Nordwind*, the attack by Balck's Army Group G against Patch's Seventh US Army in Alsace, although it forced an American withdrawal, had no influence on the Allied determination to squeeze out the Ardennes salient. By 8 January both Dietrich and von Manteuffel were in full retreat and within a few days they were back on their start line. It was Hitler's last throw in the West.

While all the generals were bitter towards Hitler for the sheer waste of valuable manpower and material in trying to achieve what was, by that stage in the war, an impossible objective, there was also much criticism of his determination to give the lead role in the offensive to Sepp Dietrich, Sepp's handling of the battle and the performance of his SS Panzer divisions. Jodl pointed out that 'the only real weakness in the SS divisions', but a crucial one, 'was the training of the staff and senior officers'[48] and that 'Sixth Panzer Army did not have as many well-trained officers and men who could work out their plans in minutest detail as were available in 1940'.[49] Von Rundstedt stated that a major reason for the failure was 'improper deployment by the Commander of Sixth SS [sic] Panzer Army'.[50] Von Mellenthin commented that 'it was a very great misfortune that Hitler placed his *Schwerpunkt* with the SS Army, whose commander was a very gallant fighter but had no real understanding of armoured warfare'.[51] Bitterest of all was von Manteuffel:

'Sixth SS [sic] Panzer Army . . . proved incapable of a quick advance to the Marne. The unhappiness of its commander was revealed by the fact that he kept silent for days on end. Sixth Panzer Army's staff clearly lacked the ability needed for coping with the situation. The Supreme Commander's folly in creating the Sixth SS Panzer Army and in assigning it its present role, had now to be paid for in every way. Its roads became blocked, nor was its staff competent to sort out the tangle. The junior commanders did not possess the tactical experience needed to ensure that the momentum of the attack was maintained, and fatal delays ensued.'[52]

That there was little direct contact between him and von Manteuffel, Dietrich admitted, 'I had very little communication with him because I was out in the field much of the time, as he was. Our staffs, however, were in constant communication.'[53] One source[54] does, however state that von Rundstedt complained during post-war interrogation that he received few reports from Dietrich and what he did receive was 'generally a pack of lies'. The truth probably lies somewhere in the middle, in that Dietrich with the problems of communication which he had, which would have been aggravated by the hilliness of the terrain, simply had little idea of exactly what was happening, especially with regard to Peiper, whose penetration represented Sixth Panzer Army's only real hope during the early days of the offensive. Peiper himself was clearly very frustrated by the lack of communication which he had with the *Leibstandarte*'s headquarters, as is reflected in his United States Army interview of September 1945,[55] and this must have been reflected up through HQ I SS Panzer Corps and HQ Sixth Panzer Army. If Dietrich had been a Montgomery he would have sent out liaison officers, or at least ensured that Mohnke or Priess did, but then he was not and this is an indication of his limitations as a general.

As for the accusations of the inexperience of the staff and senior officers in Sixth Panzer Army, Kraemer noted that the staff of Sixth Army was in fact two-thirds *Wehrmacht* and only one third Waffen-SS. While Dietrich himself lacked the experience and intellect for army command, this, as has been pointed out previously, did not matter so much under the German system as in other armies, since it was the chief of staff who was the key figure and Kraemer was certainly experienced by now. He also clearly impressed his American interviewers after the war and they noted that he 'obviously had a comprehensive understanding of this operation [Ardennes], and his account should be considered very reliable.'[56] At the corps and divisional levels, Bittrich had already proved himself in Normandy and, more especially at Arnhem, and also, having been Dietrich's regimental chief of staff in Poland, had a good understanding of staff work. Priess was a hardened Waffen-SS soldier, who had commanded the *Totenkopf* on the Eastern Front from October 1943 until July 1944 and also had a thoroughly conscientious chief of staff in Rudolf Lehmann. If there was a weakness, it was probably at divisional and regimental levels that it lay. The staffs here were entirely Waffen-SS and, although good combat leaders, lacked the necessary staff experience and abilities.

Thus the quality of commanders and staff officers may have been a factor in Sixth Panzer Army's failure, but not as significant as the facts of poor terrain, aggravated by the wintry conditions, lack of logistics and, after the first few days, the problem of Allied air power. The whole operation reflected a desperate and unreal gamble by a man whose mind was becoming increasingly unhinged, especially after the attempt on his life in July 1944. Dietrich had seen this increasingly from Normandy onwards, but he was now to have no time to ponder the 'whys and wherefores' of the past few weeks. Hitler still believed he could work miracles.

CHAPTER 9

Last Flourish in the East 1945

By mid-January 1945, most of Sixth Panzer Army was withdrawn from the front and concentrated around Prüm, south-west of Bittburg. The majority of the armour which it still had left was transferred to von Manteuffel and consequently much urgent re-equipping was needed, as well as absorbing replacements to make good the manpower gap, for another, as yet unspecified, task. Towards the end of the month, Dietrich was summoned to Berlin. One of the first people he saw was the Army Chief of Staff, who was none other than his old friend Heinz Guderian, who had been appointed, albeit in an acting capacity, to that post in the immediate aftermath of the July 1944 Bomb Plot. With the last German bolt having been loosed in the West, attention had now turned once more to the Eastern Front. Here the Soviets had launched a major offensive on 12 January. Rokossovski's 2nd Belorussion Front crossed the River Narew north of Warsaw, which itself was encircled and fell on the 17th. South of Warsaw, Zhukov's 1st Belorussian Front advanced rapidly to the Oder and this movement was also taken up by Koniev's 1st Ukrainian Front and Petrov's 4th Ukrainian Front, both on Zhukov's southern flank. Before January was through, East Prussia had been overrun and Zhukov had closed up to the Oder. Guderian believed that it was vital to defend this river and that all available troops should be sent here and Dietrich agreed with him. At the same time, Army Group Vistula, under command of no less than Heinrich Himmler, who had been appointed on 21 January, was coming under threat and Guderian wanted to withdraw it behind the Oder, as well as to deploy Sixth Panzer Army there.

Apart from refusing to allow the Courland to be evacuated, Hitler also would not countenance the deployment of Sixth Panzer Army to the Oder. He had other plans for it. He was looking south-east. In Hungary, by Christmas 1944, the Germans had been surrounded in Budapest. Hitler was determined that the city should hold out and, in order to relieve it, ordered Gille's IV SS Panzer Corps to be transferred from Army Group Centre. On 2 January 1945, Gille launched a counter-attack from the north-west and managed to get within fifteen miles of Budapest before he was forced to halt. He was then withdrawn and brought round in secrecy to the Lake Balaton area and, on 17 January, tried again. This time he gave the Russians a nasty scare, reaching the Danube and almost cutting off most of the 3rd Ukrainian Front. Moving along the west bank of the Danube, he came to within twelve miles of Budapest before the attack was brought to a halt and, at the beginning of February, he was once more forced to withdraw.

It was at this stage that Dietrich was informed that he was to take his army to Hungary in order to try, once again, to relieve the defenders of Budapest. That the Nazi hierarchy still had great faith in him is reflected in a letter from Martin Bormann to his wife Magda: '. . . our greatest asset in the West – Sepp Dietrich and his army – is to be withdrawn and sent to the Eastern Front'.[1] Whatever Dietrich's reservations over the soundness of Hitler's strategy with respect to Sixth Panzer Army, he also had a nagging personal worry. Bormann again:

> 'Dear old Sepp is very worried about his family, who live close to the Oder – very close, that is to the present front. He proposes to shift them to the Upper Danube Gau. A commander of an Army Group [sic] may try to do this, or rather bring it off; but just think how worried the ordinary man – the simple soldier and labourer – must be.'[2]

Dietrich must have been desperately regretting the rush of blood to the head which had caused him to send Ursula and the children to Bad Saarow the previous November and, having put them into a position of danger, had to do everything he could to get them out of it. Indeed, with the stories of Russian atrocities against German civilians in East Prussia and elsewhere now gathering momentum, and the fact that he had a price on his head as far as the Russians were concerned, meant that the fate of his family, if it fell into Russian hands, was awful to contemplate. He did, however, manage to come up with a solution.

The regime had, during the 1930s, set up a number of educational institutes in order to create a Nazi elite for the future. At the lowest level came the *Adolf Hitler-Schule*, which were closely connected with the Hitler Youth. Then came the *Nationalpolitische Erziehungsanstalten* (National Political Training Institutes), known as 'Napolas', and finally there were the *Ordensburgen* (Order Castles). Four of these had been set up as finishing schools for the Party leadership of the future and were located at Crössinsee, Sonthofen, Vogelsang and Marienburg. The students were in their mid-twenties and spent a year at each *Ordensburg* and the concept was a class of one thousand with five hundred instructors. These academies were under the administrative control of Robert Ley and it was presumably through him, and perhaps Himmler, that Sepp managed to arrange for his family to take over one of the instructor's flats at Sonthofen,[3] and he may well have thought back to the time he spent there as a young artilleryman in 1915. By the end of March, the family were settled there, at least temporarily, and Ursula's father had come from Karlsruhe in order to help look after them.

These domestic worries solved, Sepp Dietrich could now pay full attention to the move of his army, which began on 18 February when I and II SS Panzer Corps entrained from Wiesbaden, Koblenz and Bonn. The move itself took

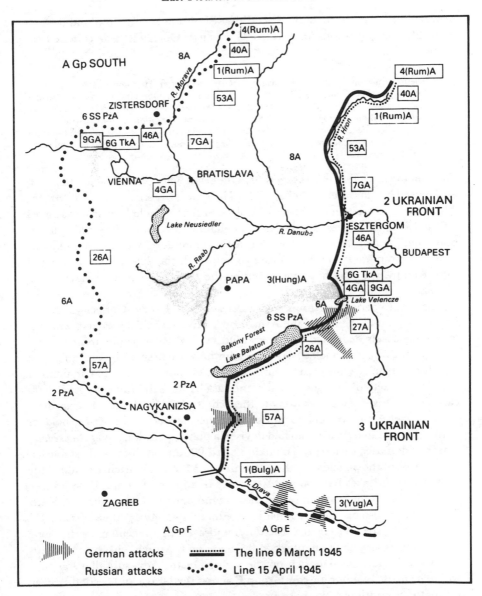

MAP 14 The end in Hungary and Austria, March–April 1945.

two weeks and was much hindered by Allied air attacks and shortage of fuel. In order to camouflage it from the Russians, Dietrich was given the cover name of *Hoeherer Pionier-Führer Ungarn* (Higher Engineer Commander Hungary). The Army's task was to be yet another attempt to regain Budapest, which had been finally turned over to the Russians on 12 February. According to Goebbels, Dietrich appeared optimistic and reckoned that, if all went well, this could be achieved in 'some 10 to 12 days' and that Sixth Panzer Army would then be available for operations in eastern Germany. Goebbels also commented, though, that:

'Dietrich quite openly criticised measures taken by the Führer. He complains that the Fuhrer does not give his military staff a sufficiently free hand and that this tendency has now become so pronounced that the Führer even lays down the employment of individual companies. But Dietrich is in no position to judge. The Führer cannot rely on his military advisers. They have so often deceived him and thrown dust in his eyes that he now has to attend to every detail. Thank God he does attend to them, for if he did not, matters would be even worse than they are anyway.'⁴

One can presume that it was especially Guderian whom Dietrich had in mind, and indeed his days were numbered, for Hitler would retire him on 28 March. This conversation with Goebbels took place in Berlin while Dietrich was on his way to Hungary. It was also the last time that he saw Hitler. It was also at this point that the *Leibstandarte* received its last commander. Wilhelm Mohnke was ordered to remain in Berlin in order to help with the defence of the city and Otto Kumm, who had been commanding the *Prinz Eugen* in Yugoslavia, took his place.

The first to arrive in Hungary was Priess's I SS Panzer Corps, which had gone on ahead of the rest of the Army and arrived in mid-February, where it was immediately dedicated by General Otto von Wöhler, commanding Army Group South, to an attack designed to eliminate a Russian bridgehead across the River Hron. Committed to battle on 18 February, it had, in conjunction with Wehrmacht troops, succeeded in this task by the 25th, but at a cost of 3000 casualties. This was a preliminary to the main task which Hitler envisaged for Sixth Panzer Army. Hitler had now become mesmerised by the need to hold on to the Hungarian oilfields, and had devised a plan Operation *Spring Awakening*. This was designed to destroy Tolbukhin's 3rd Ukrainian Front and establish a barrier east of the oilfields. At the beginning of March, Dietrich assembled his army between Lakes Balaton and Velencze. In addition to I and II SS Panzer Corps, still with the same divisions under command as in the Ardennes, Sixth Panzer Army also had placed under its command two cavalry divisions and IV SS Panzer Corps (*Wiking* and *Totenkopf*) and a Hungarian infantry division. The plan was for the main attack to be made on 6 March with Balck's Sixth Army on the left and Dietrich on the right. On the 5th, subsidiary attacks would be made by Lohr's Army Group E across the Drava and Second Panzer Army to the south of Lake Balaton.

As to what happened to Sixth Panzer Army, Dietrich later recounted:

'My left flank [II SS Panzer Corps] had no success worth mentioning. The emplacements along the western bank of the Danube, the hard, strong enemy, and the marshy terrain, impassable for tanks, prevented our advancing and attaining our goal. The attack bogged down at Sarosd and Sar-Keresztur. The centre [I Panzer Corps and the cavalry divisions] reported good success; yet when tanks were employed to exploit the initial successes, the terrain proved completely impassable. The terrain, which was supposed to be frozen hard, and which General von Wöhler had maintained to be passable, was wet and marshy. For reasons of camouflage, I had been forbidden to make an earlier terrain reconnaissance. Now 132 tanks were sunk in the mud, and fifteen Royal Tigers were sunk up to their turrets, so that the attack could be continued only by infantry. Considerable losses of men followed.'[5]

Goebbels' comment was that: 'I have the impression that our offensive has bogged down, the consequences of which would be fateful. Admittedly, Sepp Dietrich has succeeded in forming a bridgehead across the Sio but it is questionable whether he can advance out of it.'[6] Von Wöhler now committed his reserve, which was built round 6th Panzer Division, but this made little impression. Neither did an attack south of Lake Balaton by Second Panzer Army. Now the Russians, who had been waiting for von Wöhler's attack to bog down, launched their own attack. Dietrich had already, on 11 March, asked Hitler's headquarters for permission to close down the attack because of the impossible nature of the terrain, and again on the 14th, but both requests had been turned down and it was only the launching of the Soviet attack on 16 March which forced a halt to offensive operations. Dietrich again:

'The Russians threw their divisions against the army on my left under Gen Balg [sic – Balck], effecting a large breakthrough. Air reconnaissance announced 3-4000 trucks, with infantry and tanks, coming from Budapest. Army group ordered 12th [SS] Division to march immediately in the direction Stuhlweissenburg, and north from there, to close with the enemy who had broken through in that region. Meantime the Russians reached Zamoly, Osakvar, and the Bakony Forest. The road through Stuhlweissenburg, Varpalota and Veszprem had to be kept open by the 12th [SS] Division, or the original order could not be executed. The southwesterly thrust of the Russian Army was aimed at Lake Balaton, to cut off my army and the army on my left. Hard battles developed. We established that there were four mechanized brigades, five panzer corps and ten guard infantry divisions, all young, fresh troops, excellently trained and armed, among them some older veteran divisions.'[7]

It was an impossible situation and attempts by von Wöhler to use Sepp's army to counter-attack the Russian flank were not sanctioned by Hitler until it was too late. Thus, in danger of being cut off entirely, Sixth Panzer Army, which had now dropped its cover name, was forced to withdraw south-westwards along the shore of Lake Balaton. By 21 March, disillusionment was finally pervading the hierarchy in Berlin and Goebbels was noting that 'even Sepp Dietrich is not in the top class. He is a good troop commander but no strategist.'[8] Even so, two days later, Hitler was rampaging: 'I demand one thing that the *Leibstandarte*, moreover the entire 6th Panzer Army be sent . . . to the last man, available anywhere. I mean immediately! Sepp Dietrich must be informed instantly. Immediately!'[9] Nothing, however, could be done.

The heavy losses suffered by Sixth Panzer Army – and the increasing chaos led to a sharp drop in morale, which also reflected the declining quality of recent intakes into the Waffen-SS. Units began to withdraw without orders, and Balck's left flank became exposed. 'If the *Leibstandarte* can't hold their ground, what do you expect us to do?' he said in exasperation to von Wöhler.[10] News of Sepp Dietrich's withdrawal reached the ears of Hitler. Goebbels again:

'The situation is critical . . . in Hungary. There we are possibly running the risk of losing our vital oilfield. Our SS formations have put up a wretched show in this area. Even the *Leibstandarte* is no longer the old *Leibstandarte* since its officer material and men have been killed off. The *Leibstandarte* bears its honorary title in name only. The Führer has nevertheless decided to make an example of the SS formations. He has commissioned Himmler to fly to Hungary to remove their armbands. This will, of course, be the greatest imaginable disgrace to Sepp Dietrich. The army generals are rubbing their hands at the blow dealt to their rivals. The SS formations in Hungary not only failed to carry their offensive through but withdrew and, in some cases, pulled out. Inferior human material has left its mark in the most unpleasant fashion. Sepp Dietrich is to be pitied, Himmler too however, since he, the Head of the SS with no war decorations, now has to carry out this severe punishment in the face of Sepp Dietrich who wears the Diamonds.'[11]

Hitler raged: 'If we lose the war, it will be his Dietrich's fault'.[12] He accused him of falsifying strength returns and unnecessarily leaving 30,000 of his 70,000 men behind, so that they could be used on the Oder.[13] At the conference when the armband order decision was made, Hitler's personal adjutant, *Obersturmführer* Otto Grünsche recorded that only Goering stood up for Dietrich and Himmler, when told of the decision, meekly accepted it.[14] Originally, Guderian was told to go and discipline Dietrich, but he ducked the issue by saying that it was a Waffen-SS matter. Goebbels, though, was 'seriously worried about Sepp Dietrich for he is not the sort of man to take such a humiliation lying down'.[15]

A signal was sent to Headquarters Sixth Panzer Army, which stated that: 'The Führer believes that the troops have not fought as the situation demanded and orders that the SS divisions Adolf Hitler, *Das Reich*, *Totenkopf*, and *Hohenstaufen* be stripped of their armbands.'[16] What happened when the signal was received has been the subject of differing accounts. The most extreme of these was that the officers of the *Leibstandarte* sent their decorations in a chamber-pot, which also contained a human arm with the *Leibstandarte* armband attached.[17] Dietrich himself told his Canadian interrogator, Milton Shulman, that he first got drunk and then slept for three hours. 'When I awoke I asked myself, "Am I crazy or are they crazy. But I'm not crazy, therefore they must be".' He then summoned his four divisional commanders and threw the signal on the table, saying 'There's your reward for all that you have done the past five years'. He ordered them not to remove their armbands and wrote a 'flaming' reply to Hitler stating that rather than carry out the order he would shoot himself. When no reply had come after a week, he sent back all his decorations to Hitler.[18] The most precise account is that of Georg Maier who was on the staff of Sixth Panzer Army.

'On the day in question, the 27 March 1945, I was on morning duty. It was shortly after 0500 when the orderly officer on duty presented me with a flash teletyped message that had just arrived; the sleeve stripe order. I did not trust my eyes. Filled with anger and indignation, I was on the verge of losing my self control and I was already thinking of waking up the Chief of the General Staff, *Generalmajor der Waffen-SS* Kraemer, and of phoning up the personal adjutant of the Commander-in-Chief *Sturmbannführer Waffen-SS* Weiser, when the door was opened and Sepp Dietrich came in. I reported, briefed on the morning situation and handed over to him the shocking teletyped message. He watched me with a searching look, because he must have noticed the state of my mind; but he did not say anything.

Then he read – turned away slowly, bent over the map table, resting on it with both hands in such a way that I could not see his face. He was deeply shocked and moved and it took him a long time to rally again. Then, after a long interval, still bent over the table, he said in an unusually quiet, almost fragile voice, which reflected deepest disappointment and bitterness: "This is the thanks for everything."

Finally he stood up, looked at me with moist eyes, pointed at his sleeve stripe and said briefly: "This will be kept on." He shook his head again and again, as if he could not believe it all. After a while, now entirely composed again, he asked me "What do you suggest?" Although, in retrospect I was aware of the senselessness of my words, I spontaneously said the following: "I suggest asking the *Führerhauptquartier* whether the sleeve stripes of the thousands of brave soldiers of the Waffen-SS who have been killed between the Plattensee and Danube should be taken off as well. Sepp Dietrich looked at me knowingly, pointed at the message which was on the map table and ordered: "You won't pass on the teletyped message to the corps; inform Kraemer now; we will discuss it when I get back." Then he shook hands with me, a very rare gesture for him. I accompanied him outside the house; shaking his head, he climbed into the car and drove to the front to his soldiers.

Generalmajor Waffen-SS Kraemer was no less shocked and moved when I showed him the order at about 0800 after the morning situation report and also reported the reaction of the Commander-in-Chief. He also became red with anger – we both cut off each other's sleeve stripes with a letter opener. He had that of the *Leibstandarte* and I that of my old mother division, 2nd SS Panzer Division *Das Reich*. We had both had enough.'[19]

Dietrich then visited his divisional commanders and informed them, but told them not to pass the orders on. Nevertheless, everyone quickly knew about it, even the *Totenkopf*, which was no longer under command of Sixth Army. According to Maier, this was because Army Group South, who had also received the signal, transmitted it widely. Whether this was a means of the Army getting its own back on the Waffen-SS cannot be established. But, as Otto Kumm has said,[20] it was only to the veterans, and there were few of them left, that it came as any form of shock. In any event, all armbands of the troops on the ground had been removed on arrival in Hungary as part of the disguising of Sixth Panzer Army. Sepp himself almost certainly removed his own armband, which was distinctive, as was the remainder of his insignia, being in gold rather than the silver worn by all other Waffen-SS members, and was a special distinction which had been conferred on him by Hitler.

The next he knew of the affair was when he was summoned to Vienna to receive his reprimand from Himmler, who was clearly unwilling to go further forward to where the fighting was taking place. Baldur von Shirach, the Hitler Youth leader, who had been sent by Hitler earlier in March to stiffen the resolve of the garrison and inhabitants of Vienna, was present at the interview. It began with Himmler receiving a telephone call from Hitler ordering him to take away the decorations of the officers of Sixth Panzer Army. Himmler, for once, protested: '. . . I would have to drive to the Plattensee to take the crosses off the dead. A German SS man cannot give more than his life to you, my Führer.' Hearing this, Dietrich tore the cross from his neck, threw it in a corner and left the room. One of his adjutants then collected it and followed him,[22] and that was the end of Himmler's mission. This refutes the allegation that Dietrich returned his decorations to Hitler. Indeed, a number of them, including his Knight's Cross with Oakleaves, Swords and Diamonds, are in the possession to this day of his eldest son Wolf-Dieter.

Nevertheless, the whole business was a psychological blow from which Dietrich never really recovered. Erich Kern, who was with Sixth Panzer Army at the time, was probably right when he wrote that Sepp 'had for all practical purposes ceased to have any part in events . . . This was too much for the old warrior. It hit him worse than the now irrevocable collapse.'[23]

In the meantime, in spite of fierce resistance by Angelis's Second Panzer Army, the Hungarian oilfields fell on 2 April. Next day, as a punishment, von Wöhler was relieved of his command, but Dietrich was not penalised further. Instead he was ordered to defend Vienna.

> 'My orders were to get four divisions as fast as possible for the hitherto unprepared defence of the city. We had to defend in, but not in front of, Vienna. The city still had 3,000,000 inhabitants, and no water or supplies for the civilians, but these conditions were not even discussed. General von Buenau was appointed Battle Commander of Vienna, and arrived without bringing any troops for the defence. I put at his disposal the 2 SS Pz Div and the 6 Pz Div, both of which were already pushed back into the city. The battle commander and I had not the least doubt that these troops could sustain the defence for but a few days.'[24]

All this was done on the orders of Rendulic, who had taken over from Wöhler, and had been personally briefed by Hitler to defend Vienna in order to prevent the Russians from getting up the Danube valley or into the Alps. It was at this stage that Dietrich's command was retitled Sixth SS Panzer Army in order to distinguish it from Sixth Army. He set up his command post in von Schirach's house, and when the latter asked him how many tanks he had, he replied: 'We call ourselves Sixth Panzer Army because we only have six tanks left.'[25] Nevertheless, in order to try and bolster the morale of the citizens of Vienna, Vienna Radio announced that Dietrich had taken over the defence of the city[26] and he did his best to make some semblance of defence. He was also conscious, as he explained to one of his American interrogators, of what had happened to General Lasch at Königsberg,[27] who, totally surrounded, was forced to surrender on 12 April. Hitler, in a fury, sentenced him to death *in absentia* and had his family taken as hostages by the SS. As Dietrich said to von Schirach, just before the fall of the city, when the latter visited him in his command post in the grounds of a castle, which was ringed with machine guns, 'I have set up this hedgehog position just in case Adolf wants to wipe me out for not defending Vienna.'[28]

The Russians themselves were on the outskirts of the city by 6 April, with elements of Malinovsky's 2nd Ukrainian Front encircling the city from the east, while the 3rd Ukrainian Front attacked from the south and west. On the 8th, Moscow Radio put out a report that Dietrich had been killed when 'five revolver shots were fired at him at point blank as he was on his way to the broadcasting station to give his usual pep talk on Vienna's invincible resistance' and Western newspapers also reported that the 'free' Austria radio station was stating that Viennese crowds were demonstrating in the streets and throwing hand grenades at German troops.[29] This, however, was clearly propaganda employed to try and bring about the surrender of Vienna. A subsequent account[30] also states that a group of Viennese politicians came to see Dietrich to ask him to declare Vienna an open city and that he promptly hanged them. No source for this statement is given and one suspects that it was merely another piece of Russian propaganda. By 10 April, the Russians were in the centre of the city and, with Vienna now virtually encircled, Dietrich's own headquarters was coming under fire. Otto Kumm recalls that he was awarded the Swords to the Knight's Cross on 4 April (the recommendation had presumably been endorsed by Hitler prior to the armband order) and that he went to Dietrich's headquarters to receive it. 'The very moment that he gave it to me, the door was opened and someone was shot dead just in front of it.'[31] Dietrich was, however, saved from having to take the decision himself as to whether to evacuate the city or not, being ordered to withdraw across the Danube, which he did by the end of 13 April. His last order to von Shirach, whom he had been using as a liaison officer, since Hitler had ordered him to fight with the troops, was to drive to the Tyrol and check on reception centres for the army, refugees and wounded.[32]

Dietrich was now ordered to withdraw his battered remnants to a line along the River Traisen, west of Vienna, down to Traisen itself and then running south-east to Gloggnitz. Ten thousand oddments were scavenged from various training establishments in the area and these were used to strengthen the line. For the next couple of weeks, Dietrich was able to forestall all Russian attempts to break through, although this was helped in some measure by the fact that the Russians now shifted their main focus of attention to Czechoslovakia and the capture of Brno, an important industrial centre. By the end of April, though, Rendulic faced a new threat to his rear. Throughout the past two weeks, Patton's Third and Patch's Seventh US Armies had been racing through Southern Germany and this meant that ammunition and fuel supplies became increasingly difficult to maintain. Dietrich now lost communications with Rendulic and, on his own initiative, ordered the *Hohenstaufen* and *Hitlerjugend* to withdraw to the River Ybbs, where they surrendered to Patton's troops. The *Das Reich* was diverted by Hitler to help prop up the crumbling Army Group Centre in Czechoslovakia and the *Leibstandarte* was left to cover the withdrawal of the other remnants of Sixth SS Panzer Army. Dietrich himself went on 8 May to Zell am See, south of Berchtesgaden and well inside Austria where there was a headquarters under General August Winter. This was OKW South, which had been deployed from Berlin in the second half of April against the event of the Allies cutting off Southern Germany.

In the meantime, Berlin had been taken and the German surrender negotiated. On 8 May 1945 hostilities came formally to an end in the West, although the Russians, intent on securing Prague, did not finally cease fighting for another couple of days. There was concern among the Allies that the Waffen-SS would not observe the cease fire, which was formally to come into effect at one minute past midnight on the night 8/9 May. A broadcast had been made to this effect earlier that evening, but at 1440 hours on the 9th Kesselring was forced to send a repeat to Dietrich reiterating 'the order of the Reich Government that the armistice terms are equally binding on Waffen-SS units'.[33] This was acknowledged by Dietrich's headquarters, but even so, late that night, SS elements in both Army Group Centre and Army Group South were refusing to halt and surrender to the Russians. They had a good idea what might happen to them if they did. Indeed, when the *Totenkopf* surrendered to the US Third Army, who promptly handed it over to the Russians, many of its members were never heard of again.

For Dietrich, news of the surrender reached him at Zell am Zee, where he was also told that Winter had gone to Berchtesgaden.[34] He told his US interrogators that he now made his way there and that he was captured with his wife at Kufstein. Kufstein is a very roundabout way in which to get to Berchtesgaden. It can only be supposed that Dietrich decided to make a dash to Sonthofen in order to pick Ursula up and that they were caught on their return. Reitlinger does, however, suggest that Dietrich may have been trying to smuggle her across into Switzerland.[35] It seems unlikely, though, that she would do this without taking the children with her and it would have been out of character for Dietrich himself to have permanently deserted his men. It is, however, strange that he did not appear to have made any effort to contact Rendulic's headquarters in person, although this may have been out of fear that he might be ordered to stand fast and surrender to the Russians.

As it was, he and Ursula surrendered to the US 36th Infantry Division, which was part of Seventh Army, and, in particular, to Master Sergeant Herbert Kraus of Cleveland, Ohio, who described his prisoner as 'not anything like an army commander – he is more like a village grocer'.[36] It was a somewhat inglorious end to almost six years of often distinguished combat service.

CHAPTER 10

The Malmédy Trial
1945-46

For Sepp Dietrich there now began a period of ten and a half years of captivity, initially as a prisoner of war and then as a war criminal. After his capture he was held in Kufstein for a few days, as was Ursula, although separately. She did however, have at least one opportunity to visit her husband. Yet, although captured on 9 May, it was not until 13 May that HQ Seventh Army released the news that they held Dietrich. At this stage the press release merely spoke of the Russians holding him responsible for the Kharkov atrocities.[1] On 15 May he was transferred to Augsburg, where senior German officers and political figures captured by the Americans were being concentrated. It was now that questions were first asked of him about the Malmédy affair. In the meantime, his father-in-law had also been arrested, leaving his sons temporarily in the care of just their nurse since Ursula had also been brought to Augsburg to help her husband write an account of the war as he saw it. He was taken on the pretext that he had been a colonel in the First World War. The family, however, remain convinced that it was because of his relationship with Sepp.[2]

Dietrich's first interrogation was on 1 June and seems to have been general in nature. His interrogators, Captains Hans Wallenberg and Ernst Langendorf, wrote in their report:[3]

'Sepp Dietrich is a talkative man who takes great pleasure in discussing military and technical matters and constantly refers to his thirty-five years of soldiering in order to evade all political issues. He expresses himself in an original and blunt manner, a form of speech which betrays his working-class origin, and which is not without wit and humour. His criticism leaves little merit with either military or political leaders of the Third Reich. In spite of his sketchy educational background, one cannot deny that he possesses, to a certain extent, sound instinct and "horse sense".'

While he stated that he had been 'completely cured of this [National Socialist] system in which swindle and graft was [sic] rampant', he also said, somewhat contradictorily, 'I have been a member of the Party since 1928 and I intend to stand by it today.' He then went on:

'I could have put a slug through my brains if I wanted to but I have a responsibility for which I must make a stand. I want to speak for the men I once led. I never signed any order providing for the massacre of the Jews or the burning down of churches, nor have I ordered the pillaging of occupied places. I therefore want to clarify things and stand up for my men.'

173

He now went on to give his views on some of the prominent leaders of the Third Reich. Hitler 'knew even less than the rest. He allowed himself to be taken for a sucker by everyone'. Goering 'was a lazy bastard; a clown'. Heydrich was 'a great pig', but Kaltenbrunner, chief of the RSHA and later hanged after the Nuremberg trials, 'was a decent fellow who had to do a lot of things which he did not like to do. He had many a heated argument with Himmler.' Dietrich's views on Himmler have already been given (see Page 51), and it would seem, at least according to his family, that Himmler was the one man that he really hated.[4] Hence, it is understandable that anyone who stood up to him would have Dietrich's sympathy. He also complained that the generals who surrounded Hitler – Keitel, Jodl and others – had no combat experience. 'One ought to beat up the whole bunch of them.' He once again reiterated that he 'found the Party machine simply disgusting . . . I had never anything to do with Party officials as they did not interest me in the least.' He also made the point that Ursula had never had anything to do with the Party. He displayed disbelief that Hitler had been 'killed in action' since he 'never left his air raid shelter.' All these comments were clearly thought to be highly newsworthy and were quickly released to the American newspapers.[5] He also, however, expressed some surprising views on the Russians:

> 'A very intelligent people; good-natured, easy to be led and also adapted in technical matters; on top of that those huge masses. They were poorly led at the beginning but they learnt quickly. These peasants have a lot of brains and are very amenable. Moreover, their tanks were better. They were less complicated and easier to maneuver. Our tanks seem to have been made by a watchmaker; much too complicated and sensitive. I was really taken aback. These tremendous and modern factories, these agricultural institutions, these granaries – that was simply colossal.
> I once had a talk with Molotov and several GPU officers in Berlin. That was highly interesting. They invited me to visit Russia. Too bad I never got around to do it. I spoke to many Russians. They liked it better under Stalin than under the Czar. Even the people on the collectives live all right; they own a piece of land, a cow and they live quite happily.'

It is hard to reconcile this with the atrocities that Dietrich knew had been committed on some of his men, and, while it is understandable that he should have respect for Soviet military power, one can only presume that, fearful that he might be handed over to the Russians to 'face the music' over the alleged Kharkov atrocities, he felt that the best way to avoid the Americans doing this was to be flattering in his comments.

On 11 June, he was given a more thorough interrogation, this time by another interrogator, Lieutenant Rolf Wartenberg. This particular interrogation report[6] has already been quoted at length since it gives Dietrich's detailed comments on the campaigns in which he had taken part. One has the impression that Wartenberg was less taken in than his predecessors or, on the other hand, had a much more hostile attitude to his subject.

> 'The notorious SS general displayed a forceful personality, which at times suggested a brutality which is said to be part of his nature. He seemed, moreover, to be continually conscious of his own personality, his position and his deeds. He spoke freely and willingly, always stressing the subject of honesty, which he presents as an ideal by which he and his

troops were always guided. Though obviously a man with common sense, he showed little intellectual quality during the interrogation. He is very anxious to appear as a purely military man, whose connection with politics was either slight or non-existent. Like so many other German generals, he does not hesitate to blame others for the events which occurred. The playing-down of his own non-military activities, however, does not alter the record of his longtime connections with the Party, with Hitler, and with the Allgemeine-SS.
His interest and devotion to military matters seems to be genuine.'

Details were given in the report of his life history and in it he still maintained one or two untruths about his early life. He claimed that he was a butcher before he succumbed, as a youth, to the *Wanderlust*, and asserted that he had joined the 1st Bavarian Uhlan Regiment in 1911. It is, however, noteworthy that the only decoration specified in the very brief summary of his First World War experience was the *Kampfwagenzeichen* (Tank Combat Badge), which his eldest son still possesses and says that it was one of the awards of which his father was always most proud. The report, however, also says that he commanded one of the 'few German-built tanks', which must imply the A7V, again a total untruth.

It was the first time that he was directly questioned about Malmédy and, as has previously been written (Page 156), he denied all knowledge of it, although he did say that four American prisoners had been killed in his corps at Caen during the Normandy campaign, but that this was after the bodies of similarly killed German prisoners had been found. He had initiated an investigation, but since the commanding officer of the unit responsible had been killed, it did not get very far, but a report had been sent to the Foreign Ministry. This incident presumably referred to the killing of Canadian prisoners by the *Hitlerjugend* for which Panzer Meyer was about to come under investigation. Dietrich concluded his remarks by declaring that 'As an honest soldier, I do not kill prisoners'.

Pressure was already being applied from Washington to locate and bring to book all those involved in the Malmédy massacre. Otto Kumm, who was at Augsburg at the same time, recalls:

'I had to show my hands and the interrogator said: "blood, blood, everywhere." I think he was Jewish; he had a Frankfurt dialect and wore a US uniform. when he realised that I was the commander of the *Leibstandarte* he accused me of being responsible for Malmédy. Then I told him that I was not with the Leibstandarte at the time, but was commanding the *Prinz Eugen*. He said, "then you have killed 500 million Yugoslavs. You are a war criminal." I replied that there never were 500 million Yugoslavs, but if you say 50,000 people were killed, then you could be right, but they were killed in battle and nothing else.'[7]

Gradually all surviving members who had been with the *Leibstandarte* in the Ardennes were gathered together, as well as the staffs of I SS Panzer Corps and Sixth Panzer Army. In the meantime, Dietrich was again moved, on 13 July, to Wiesbaden. Here the interest in him was not so much on account of any war crimes in which he may or may not have been implicated, but more as part of the efforts of the Western Allies to piece together exactly what had happened in the campaigns in Western Europe during 1944-45. For the Americans, it was the Ardennes which was of greatest interest and the Shuster Commission was charged with investigating the battle from the German side. Dietrich had been interviewed prior to the Shuster Commission beginning its work, on 10 July, just before he left Augsburg. This interview[8] appears to have been carried out on behalf of Eisenhower's Chief of Intelligence, General Sir Kenneth Strong and was concerned with the formation of Sixth Panzer Army and its preparations for the Ardennes offensive. The unknown interviewer commented:

> 'Gen Dietrich has been described by interviewers as a crude, loquacious, hard-bitten, tough man whose statements are often inaccurate – yet also a man having a great deal of common sense. His fellow officers, the more class-conscious of whom were often shocked at Dietrich's language and behaviour, attribute his meteoric rise in the Army to his party connections.'

What is significant about this statement is that the interviewer clearly did not differentiate between the Waffen-SS and the Army. The main interview for the Shuster Commission was carried out by 1st Lt Robert E Merriam at the United States Forces European Theater (USFET) Interrogation Center at Oberursel over 8-9 August.[9] Merriam worked through an interpreter and covered the formation, organisation and initial deployment of Sixth Panzer Army, as well as its role in the campaign. He seems to have been even less impressed with his subject than his predecessor:

> 'Gen Dietrich is regarded with low esteem by his fellow officers. He did not seem to have a grasp of the operations of his Army in the Ardennes and was unable to present a comprehensive picture of the happenings, even in the most general terms . . . there are a number of obvious errors in the answers provided by this former chauffeur.'

What made Dietrich's mental shortcomings even more marked was the interview which Merriam had with Fritz Kraemer a few days later, which clearly went extremely well, with much information being gleaned.[10]

Finally, it was the turn of Milton Shulman on behalf of the Canadian Army. He questioned Sepp Dietrich at length towards the end of August 1945, mainly about the Normandy campaign, which was of prime interest to First Canadian Army, but also about his whole life and views.[11] One has the impression that this was a much more relaxed affair than the US interviews, probably because the Canadians were not specifically 'gunning' for Sepp over war crimes, and one can detect a degree of *simpatico* between interviewer and interviewee. Shulman commented that Dietrich's 'position as the senior military officer of the Waffen SS has made him the favourite whipping post of both the Allied press and the German General Staff'. Noting the blame that the press had laid on him for atrocities at Kharkov and in the Ardennes, he observed that the General Staff 'have ridiculed his military skill, his inept leadership, his rough, uncouth personality, his swift climb to high rank with the helping hand of the Nazi Party'. Yet, the Party machine had created an 'almost legendary figure whose exploits as a fighting man of the people rivalled if not surpassed, that other popular National Socialist figure, Erwin Rommel'.

PLATE 17 Hitler, with Dietrich on his right, celebrates Christmas with the *Leibstandarte*, Metz, 26 December 1940.

PLATE 18 'Obersepp' dressed for the Eastern Front.

PLATE 19 Somewhere on the Eastern Front. *Leibstandarte* motor-cycle detachment. Note the divisional sign.

PLATE 20 Marriage to Ursula, 19 January 1942.

PLATE 21 Kharkov, March 1943. Dietrich congratulates Panzer Meyer.

PLATE 22 Russia, April 1943. Dietrich and his commanders. Meyer is on his immediate right. Among others shown are Staudinger (front row, 2nd from left), Theodor Wisch (over Staudinger's left shoulder), who would succeed Dietrich in command, and Rudolf Lehmann (over Sepp's

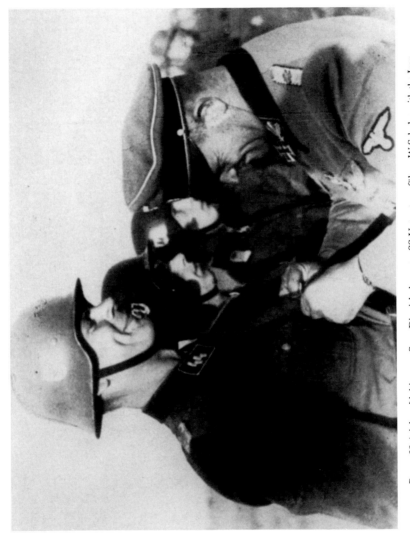

PLATE 23 A joke with his men. Sepp Dietrich decorates SS-Untersturmführer W Schulze with the Iron Cross 1st Class.

PLATE 24 Sepp puts on an act as a Russian peasant woman. Photograph taken by Eva Braun, Hitler's mistress.

PLATE 25 Shaking hands with Wilhelm Mohnke when meeting the staff of the newly formed SS *Hitlerjugend* in Belgium, winter 1943–44.

PLATE 26 Dietrich with Rommel in Normandy, Summer 1944.

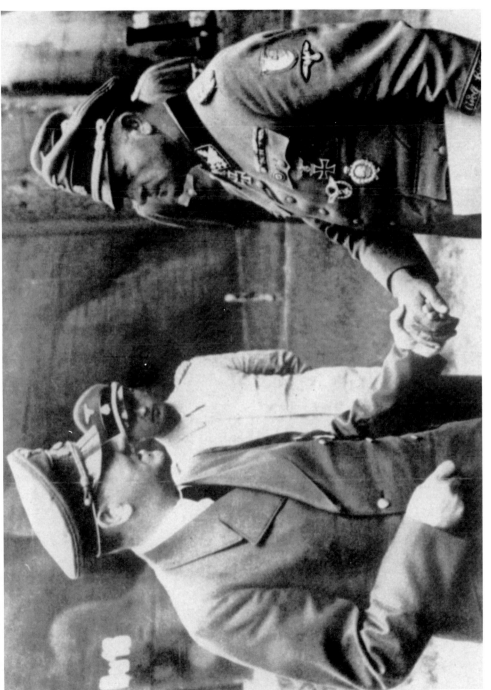

PLATE 27 A grim faced Dietrich receiving the Diamonds from Hitler, August 1944.

PLATE 28: It is understandable why Allied air power made such an impression on Dietrich in Normandy – he very nearly suffered the same fate as Rommel. Gazing at the remains of his car after it had been strafed by an Allied fighter.

PLATE 29 Dietrich, wearing a Waffen-SS camouflage jacket, with an unknown Army general and, in black Panzer uniform, General Heinrich Eberbach, August 1944.

PLATE 30 A *Leibstandarte* Royal Tiger moving up prior to the Ardennes offensive, December 1944.

PLATE 31 Dietrich, with his Adjutant, Hermann Weiser, during the Ardennes offensive.

PLATE 32 Last bow for this *Hitlerjugend* Panther outside the village of Krinkhelt, 17 December 1944.

PLATE 33 The Dachau Trial Dietrich (11), Kraemer (33), Priess (45), Peiper (42).

PLATE 34 Prisoner of War, Nuremberg, 24 November 1945.

PLATE 35 Dietrich's sons, c1950 – (L to R) Götz-Hubertus, Lutz, Wolf-Dieter.

PLATE 36 The Hunter.

PLATE 37 Sepp's tombstone in Ludwigsburg.

'A few moments conversation with the man explains to some extent this reputation. Physically "Sepp" Dietrich is the antithesis of what Hitler would like to have us believe was the Aryan superman. Short, about 5'7" tall, squat, a broad, dark face dominated by a large, wide nose, rapidly dwindling hair, he resembled more the butcher that he started to be back in 1909 than the general he became in 1933. Born near Memmingen, Swabia, he possesses a rich Bavarian accent that no amount of Berlin society has been able to refine of its rough, natural tones. His vocabulary, for which he constantly apologised, is replete with the down-to-earth words of the foxhole and beer cellar, and it is easy to envisage that his language would shock men like Rundstedt and Brauchitsch, who represented the well-educated, class-conscious General Staff. He is garrulous and conceited, and was eager to impress his interrogators as a soldier free from the political intrigues of National Socialism. A flair for the dramatic in gesture and speech, and a crude sense of humour, coupled with a forceful energy that could be hard and ruthless, undoubtedly enabled him to achieve his meteoric rise in the SS.'

He noted that Dietrich's Army colleagues contemptuously referred to him as the *Wachtmeister* [cavalry/artillery sergeant-major], but somewhat curiously likened him to Rommel, in that his education and capabilities could not adequately cope with commands above that of a division. Yet, unlike other Waffen-SS commanders like Meyer and Wisch, 'whose eyes still burn with devotion to their Führer', Shulman saw Dietrich as a disillusioned man. 'His open criticism of Hitler, whom he constantly referred to as Adolf, was not merely that of a man trying to get out from under, but the net result of a bitter and chastening experience.' Once again, he repeated his awe and praise of Soviet military might, but pointed out that the average Russian had almost nothing. Like other captured German generals were saying to their interrogators at the time, Dietrich expressed deep concern over the shadow of the Soviet bear spreading westwards. 'If Germany goes Communist, France will follow. England, Germany and America must create an international organisation to hold the Russians on the Elbe. This can be done if we build up our plane strength, for the Russians are not good fliers.' He made flattering comments about the fighting qualities of the Canadians and said that he wanted to get away from Europe, probably to Canada and start again with the RM 25,000 which he had saved. He concluded by saying: 'You cannot imagine how sick and tired we are of war. You can never know how it felt to fight for three years knowing all the time that your side had already lost.'

Throughout this time, efforts had continued to gather up all those who might have had any connection with Malmédy. During October 1945 some one thousand members of Peiper's command were gathered together in a special annex of the civilian internment camp at Zuffenhausen, near Ludwigsburg. Others, too, like Otto Kumm, were also sent there. He remembers that:

'. . . it was entirely overcrowded. We hardly had any food. We were almost starving. We slept on wooden plank beds. Some of us were so undernourished that they could hardly get up. For months, we had turnip soup for lunch and half a potato for dinner. Deliberately they collected heaps of food outside the fence, which was burnt once a month in front of our eyes.'[12]

If this was so, it was clearly used as a means of breaking down resistance so that concrete evidence of the massacre could be obtained and the culprits identified. It was, however, hard going, for no one was willing to talk. Dietrich was kept separately, spending five weeks at Oberursel before, on 5 November 1945, being sent to Nuremberg. Here it was intended to use him as a witness in the main war crimes trial of major Nazi figures, but he was never, in fact, called. Nevertheless, he remained at Nuremberg until 16 March 1946 when he was removed to Dachau to finally join those on whom suspicion of active involvement or complicity in the Malmédy affair had fallen were now quartered.

Here Dietrich found Kraemer, Priess, Peiper and some 120 of his officers and men. Indeed, the only person missing in the chain of command was Wilhelm Mohnke, whom the Russians would not give up. This was also frustrating for the British, who especially wanted to question him over the Wormhoudt massacre of May 1940. Lt Col A P Scotland, who headed the British War Crimes Investigation Unit, did, however, interview Dietrich at this time and was not impressed, noting that he 'cut a decidedly sorry figure' and 'disclosed a miserable wreck of a personality during his interrogation'.

> 'In wailing tones, repeating his words constantly, all he could say was: "I spent the day in a ditch" . . . "I know nothing of any shootings" . . . "I spent the day in a ditch".'

No case filled Colonel Scotland with greater frustration than this one. He was convinced that Mohnke was the real culprit, but could not obtain prima facie evidence, let alone Mohnke himself. Indeed, Mohnke remained in Soviet captivity until the mid 1950s and now lives undisturbed in Hamburg. The author's efforts to contact him met with a 'wall of silence'. Scotland was convinced that it was this which had made it so hard for the Americans to break down the Malmédy suspects. [13] It was all bound up in the SS oath 'my oath is my loyalty' which meant loyalty not just to the state but also to fellow SS men, and this included not informing on them.

Five days before Dietrich arrived at Dachau, Peiper had made a statement to his interrogators which marked the breakthrough, as far as the prosecution was concerned. He stated that on 14 December 1944 he had visited the *Leibstandarte* headquarters and been handed written orders for the offensive, as well as having a short conversation with Mohnke.

> 'I can remember that in this material, among other things, was an order of the Sixth SS Panzer Army, with the contents that, considering the desperate situation of the German people, a wave of terror and fright should precede our troops. Also, this order pointed out that the German soldier should, in this offensive, recall the innumerable German victims of the bombing terror. Furthermore, it was stated in this order that German resistance had to be broken by terror. Also, I am nearly certain that in this order was expressly stated that prisoners of war must be shot where local conditions should so require it. This order was incorporated into the Regimental Order. . .'

Peiper than went on to say that he held a meeting of his subordinate commanders, but 'I did not mention anything that prisoners of war should be shot when
local conditions of combat should so require it, because those present were all
experienced officers to whom this was obvious'. He recalled that the order had
been signed by Sepp Dietrich. 'I know, however, that the order to use brutality
was not given by Sepp Dietrich out of his own initiative, but that he only acted
along the lines which the Führer had expressly laid down.'[14] Dietrich was
confronted with this testimony and on 22 March made a sworn statement that he
had given such an order in so far that the Ardennes offensive represented 'the
decisive hour of the German people' and that it was to be conducted with a 'wave
of terror and fright' and without 'humane inhibitions'.[15] What had suddenly
broken Peiper and Dietrich down?

On 6 June 1948 Peiper made a sworn statement to his lawyer, Doctor Leer, at
Landsberg.[16] In it he told of the interrogation methods used by the Americans.
At his first interrogation, at the US Third Army Interrogation Center at Freising
in August 1945, he was told that he was 'the GI enemy No 1'. In September he
was moved to Oberursel and confronted with survivors of the massacre, but no
formal interrogation took place. He was, however, placed in solitary confinement for seven weeks and, at one point, spent 24 hours in a cell which was heated
up to 80 degrees Celsius. He was then moved to Zuffenhausen, where the
interrogations began in earnest and were conducted by 1st Lt Perl. The line the
questioning took was that the American people had already found Peiper guilty
and therefore he should do the decent thing and take full responsibility.
Imprisoned for five weeks in a 'nearly completely dark cellar', not allowed to
wash or shave during three weeks of this period, denied food for two days,
'robbed and insulted', Peiper eventually gave way on the condition that his men
would be released unpunished, which was refused. Peiper than asserted that Lt
Perl had warned him that if he chose to commit suicide and left a note claiming
full responsibility, Perl would testify that Peiper had had nothing to do with the
massacre. '"The Führer's Loyal Body Guard" will not come [sic – get] off so
easily.' The fourth phase took place at Schwabisch Hall during December
1945-March 1946. Towards the end of this period, Peiper was told that Dietrich,
Kraemer and Priess had already confessed. But then Perl declared: 'We know
you had nothing to do with the crossroads. We don't want you. We want
Dietrich!' This indicated that Dietrich had not yet confessed. Peiper was now
told that an extract had been found in the Sixth Panzer Army operation order,
which stated that prisoners would be shot under certain circumstances and that
seven or eight of Peiper's officers would confirm it. The extract itself was never
ever produced, even in court. Confronted by his former adjutant, Hans Gruhle,
who admitted the existence of this order, Josef Diefenthal, who had commanded
3rd Battalion 2nd SS Panzer Grenadier Regiment and admitted giving the order
to shoot the prisoners, and others, Peiper finally broke down.

In a further series of sworn statements given at Landsberg in 1948 by some of
Peiper's men, it was asserted that they themselves were broken through

torture.[17] Mock hangings, beatings and hooding, mock trials and threats against families living in the Soviet Zone of Occupation were all apparently employed. Otto Kumm, although he was not himself physically tortured, states that at Dachau he certainly recalled that one Gottlieb Berger, who was not a Malmédy defendant, had had lighted matches forced under his finger nails.[18] Dietrich himself also asserted that he had been kicked while being led to interrogation.[10]

It is extremely unlikely, though, that it was torture or, indeed his treatment by his captors, which made Dietrich break down. More likely, confronted with confessions by Peiper, Kraemer, Priess and others, Dietrich felt duty-bound to shoulder the major share of the responsibility for the atrocities, but, as we shall see, the majority of these confessions, including Dietrich's, would be retracted once it came to the trial. The allegations of torture would also later be a major factor in the subsequent controversy over the trial.

Dietrich, himself, appears to have only spent a short time at Schwabisch Hall (6-25 April), when the Malmédy interrogations were mainly carried out,[20] but while here, on 16 April, he was formally arrested and charged by the United States Counter-Intelligence Corps (CIC) and on 9 May, after his return to Dachau, he lost his Prisoner of War status, as did the other seventy-three defendants. On 16 May the Malmédy massacre trial was formally opened.

Officially known as Case No 6-24, United States versus Valentin Bersin et al – former *Unterscharführer* Bersin was the first man on the alphabetical list of the accused – the trial took place at Dachau before a General Military Government Court. President of the Court was Brigadier General J T Dalbey and the members of the court consisted of seven US Army officers of field rank, assisted by a legal adviser, Colonel A H Rosenfeld. The prosecution team was the same that had carried out the investigation over the previous months, and was led by Lt Col Ellis and included Lt Perl. The defence had seven somewhat unwilling German lawyers, but also a man, who was to be instrumental in later making the case a *cause celebre* in the United States, Lt Col Willis M Everett Jr, an Army lawyer from Atlanta, Georgia. The accused were formally charged with violation of the Laws and Usages of War in that they, as

'German nationals or persons acting with German nationals, being together concerned as parties, did, in conjunction with other persons not herein charged or named, at or in the vicinity of Malmédy, Honsfeld, Büllingen, Ligneuville, Stoumont, La Gleize, Cheneux, Petit Their, Trois Ponts, Stavelot, Wanne and Lutebois, all in Belgium, at sundry times between 16 December 1944 and 13 January 1945, willfully, deliberately and wrongly permit, encourage, aid, abet and participate in the killing, shooting, ill-treatment, abuse and torture of members of the Armed Forces of the United States of America, then at war with the then German Reich, who were then and there surrendered and unarmed prisoners of war in the custody of the then German Reich, the exact names and numbers of such persons being unknown but aggregating several hundred, and of unarmed allied civilian nationals, the exact names and numbers of such persons being unknown.'

Thus, the trial was not devoted merely to the incident at the Baugnez cross-roads on the afternoon of Sunday 17 December 1944, but to a whole series of alleged atrocities. These were detailed by the prosecution and are best represented in a tabular form.

Date	Place	Incident
17 Dec 44	Honsfeld	25 US PW shot in various incidents
17 Dec 44	Büllingen	Some 80 PW and one Belgian woman shot in various incidents
17 Dec 44	Baugnez Cross-roads	Up to 80 PW shot. (The permanent United States memorial on the site of the massacre lists eighty-four names. However, some of these are likely to have been killed before Lieutenant Lary gave his order to Surrender.)
17 Dec 44	Ligneuville	Up to 60 PW shot in various incidents
17 Dec 44	Ligneuville-Stavelot road	15 PW shot
18 Dec 44	Stavelot	93 Belgian civilians shot in various incidents
18 Dec 44	Cheneux	Some 40 PW shot in various incidents
18 Dec 44	La Gleize	50-60 PW shot in various incidents
19-23 Dec 44	La Gleize	Number of unspecified incidents of PW shootings
19 Dec 44	Stoumont	80 PW and one civilian shot in various incidents
20-21 Dec 44	Wanne	Unspecified number of civilians shot
21 Dec 44	Stavelot	8 PW shot
31 Dec 44	Lutebois	At least one civilian shot
No date given	Trois Ponts	11 PW and ten civilians shot
10 or 13 Jan 45	Petit Thier	1 PW shot

All these violations were attributed to *Kampfgruppe Peiper*, and it should be noted that none of the other formations of Sixth Panzer Army had their names directly connected with other Ardennes war crimes trials. The truth of the matter was that the Baugnez Crossroads incident had completely blotted the minds of American officialdom and general public alike. The other incidents were unearthed during the pre-trial investigation, but no one seems to have asked the question as to why, if Dietrich had issued an Army order that prisoners could be shot in certain circumstances, that it was only one *Kampfgruppe* which took advantage of this. With four supposedly hardened SS Panzer Divisions under his command, one would have expected other incidents involving other units to have come to light.

Be that as it may, within a few days of the opening of the trial the United States Press, having heard the general case for the prosecution, had already returned their verdict. 'These seventy-four will get their punishment . . . because the conscience of humanity has not quite been stilled', as one newspaper put it.[21] In Dietrich's case the evidence used against him was his own admission of 22 March 1946 and those of Kraemer, Peiper and Gruhle. Dietrich, however, withdrew his admission that he had stated that prisoners could be shot, although admittedly, part of the Sixth Panzer operation order did contain the following:

'Action by armed civilians must be anticipated. These civilians in general belong to the movement known as the Resistance Movement. It is likely that roads will be mined and charges placed on railways and bridges. Headquarters, telephone lines and convoys etc must be guarded . . . Resistance by armed civilians must be broken.'[22]

Kraemer, too, withdrew his previous confession and stated that the operational order dated 8 December 1944 referred to above specifically stated that all loot and prisoners of war were to be collected quickly and that corps were to attach special escort units to forward detachments, who would use returning empty logistic transport to get the prisoners to the rear. Collection of prisoners was not to be taken on by forward units themselves, who were to send them back to collecting points. As for the Malmédy massacre, he stated that one of his staff officers had heard about it on the radio from Calais on 20 or 21 December and that a radio message had been sent out reminding units that the Army Commander prohibited all actions and conduct in violation of the laws of war. The *Leibstandarte* had reported on 26 December that no prisoners had been shot in its sector, although it must be pointed out that, as Peiper himself said, radio communications between him and Divisional HQ over the period were, at best, poor. The Chief of Staff of LXVII Corps, who appeared as a witness for the defence, stated that he had received an order from Kraemer specifically stating that the mistreatment of prisoners of war was forbidden. Dietrich Ziemssen, who was chief operations officer of the *Leibstandarte* at the time and who also was a defence witness, confirmed this, as did Hubert Meyer, Chief Operations Officer of the *Hitlerjugend*. Rudolf Lehmann, in his capacity as Chief of Staff of I SS Panzer Corps, also supported Kraemer's statement about prisoner collecting points. Georg Maier, who was on the staff of Sixth Panzer Army at the time, Ziemssen, Lehmann and Kuhlmann, who commanded the *Hitlerjugend*'s Panzer regiment, also affirmed that Dietrich's special order of the day had not contained anything about a wave of terror or any suggestion that no humane inhibitions were to be shown. While Dietrich had said in prejudicial statements that he had been reflecting Hitler's words at the Bad Nauheim conference on 12 December 1944 in his order of the day, Priess, who was present at the conference, said that Hitler had never mentioned anything of this nature, nor did he speak of prisoners of war, and neither did Dietrich's order of the day, which he regarded merely as propaganda. He did, however, accept that the operation order did mention the possibility of armed civilians being encountered. He also said that the logistic order, which had been signed by Kraemer, did refer to the method of getting prisoners of war to the rear. He also, however, stated that under German principles, a corps commander was not responsible for the behaviour of his troops and that the highest ranking officer who was held to be so was the divisional commander. One cannot help, however, but suspect that he declared this as a means of trying to save his own skin.

The fact that so many officers asserted that the question of what to do with prisoners had appeared in the logistic order does, however, conflict with a point made by the prosecution at the trial. Apparently, when Dietrich held his formal orders group on 14 December, one person present asked about prisoners, thinking that Dietrich had missed this point out. Dietrich is supposed to have replied, and he did not deny it at the trial: 'Prisoners, you know what to do with them.'[23] Dietrich himself said that he implied that the Laws of War were to be respected, although he could have also been referring to the fact that this topic was covered in the logistic order. Jacques Nobécourt, however, interviewed a Wehrmacht colonel who had been present at this conference, albeit the interview took place in the mid-1950s. This colonel stated that:

'Addressed to the generals and senior officers of the Waffen SS and in the atmosphere of the time, a phrase of this nature can mean only one thing: get rid of the prisoners. And that is the way that it was interpreted.
In fact the Americans were at fault in condemning to death only those who committed the crimes and not Sepp Dietrich. He was the man really responsible for the Malmédy massacre and the way in which I SS Panzer, the *Leibstandarte* Adolf Hitler, shot down civilians throughout their advance, particularly at Stavelot. The least that can be said is that the commanders were letting their men run riot.'

Thus, there is a conflict of evidence and the prosecution were unable to produce primary documentary evidence that Dietrich had specifically said or implied that prisoners could be shot. On the other hand, it could be argued that such evidence was destroyed at the time for fear that it would be incriminating, bearing in mind that it was clear to all but the most fanatical Nazi that the war was by then lost.

The key figure in the trial was undoubtedly Joachim Peiper. He, too, rescinded his extrajudicial statements, and repeated what the others had said about prisoner collecting points and that armed civilian resistance was to be expected. Preiss had held a conference on 15 December 1944, which Peiper attended and at which Dietrich's order of the day was read out, but it was merely an appeal to German soldiers, with nothing on prisoners of war or civilians. Skorzeny was present and the outline of Operation *Greif*, with its object of spreading panic and confusion within the American lines, was explained. Nothing was verbally raised on prisoners of war, and Peiper's own operation order was concerned merely with tactical matters. This seems to have been supported by his adjutant Gruhle. Others said that the *Kampfgruppe* HQ held two meetings at the command post – a hunting lodge in Blankenheim Forest – on 15 December and the subject of prisoners of war and civilians was not mentioned. This seems surprising, bearing in mind Peiper's mission. One would have thought that, bearing in mind the vital time factor with regard to the Meuse bridges, there would have been some emphasis on not allowing the momentum of the advance to be slowed down by becoming involved with prisoner handling.

Nevertheless, that at least some of the incidents took place there is no doubt. There were the frozen corpses discovered by the Americans at the Baugnez cross-roads, none of them with any weapons found by them. A further eight bodies were found behind the Hotel du Moulin at Ligneuville and from their postures there was little doubt but that they had been executed. Furthermore, the bodies of twenty-three Belgian civilians – men, women and children –

were discovered outside a house in Stavelot. There were, too, the witnesses. Survivors of the Baugnez cross-roads massacre, including Lt Lary, were there to testify in court, and Belgian civilian witnesses to some of the incidents had also been located. In other cases, though, the prosecution's case looked distinctly weak. La Gleize was the most prominent example of this. The defence was able to produce both McCown (now a lieutenant colonel) and a Belgian curé, both of whom were positive that no killings of American prisoners had taken place there.

Most of the junior ranks of *Kampfgruppe Peiper* who stood accused of these atrocities had said in their extrajudicial sworn statements that they had shot prisoners on the orders of their superior officers. Some, significantly, did not take the stand during the trial, while others stuck to their extrajudicial statements, but yet others denied that they had been at the scene of the alleged atrocities at the time at which they took place, or had witnessed them. Many of the defendants, however, testified that they had been subjected to beatings, hoodings and mock executions during the pre-trial investigation, which, apart from the beatings, was not denied by the prosecution, and it was this that had caused them to make false statements. Typical of these was the case of former *Obersturmführer* Franz Sievers of the 1st SS Panzer Engineer Battalion, who would receive the death sentence for his part in the killings at Baugnez cross-roads.

'The accused testified that after solitary confinement for three months, he was interrogated on 25 February 1946 at Schwabisch Hall for the first time. He was asked his name and upon replying "Sievers", he received a blow in the mouth. Then he was pushed into a cell with his face toward the wall where he received a blow in his right hand. Shortly afterwards a hood was torn off his face. Two interrogating officers were standing in the cell. The accused was told to bare the upper part of his body. When he took off his shirt, they said: "You pig, you smell of perspiration. You haven't washed lately. Pick up your arms." The accused stated he had not had an opportunity to bathe in the last twelve weeks. He only received two or three litres of water daily for washing. The accused was pushed against the wall by Mr Thon who said that he was the public prosecutor. The accused was told that he had shot at prisoners of war with a bazooka. The accused further testified that Mr Thon told him he would bring a vial or a rope so that the accused could finish his life. The accused responded that it was not necessary as he did not have any prisoners of war on his conscience. When Lieutenant Perl wanted to give him some tobacco for a cigarette, Mr Thon jumped up immediately and said: "That guy's not going to get any tobacco. He will have to confess first." Then he was confronted with several men of his company. The first one that was led in was Sprenger [Gunter Sprenger was in Sievers' Company and was later also sentenced to death], who was put under oath in the regular manner and then asked if he knew the accused. The accused was then put into a machine room. Lieutenant Perl showed him some men working there. He said they were all from the Adolf Hitler Division and now had a good life because they had confessed. On the way back, Lieutenant Perl said: "Sprenger shot upon your order and he will only get six to eight months and then he'll be free again, and you acted under orders of Peiper and carried out the order. What could happen to you? You are just a little *Obersturmführer*. We don't even want you. We dont even want Peiper. We want Sepp Dietrich and we'll have a trial for him about which the world will gaze with wonder." The accused was moved by that and made his first statement which was immediately torn up by Lieutenant Perl because he was not satisfied with the contents. The accused then wrote another statement which was dictated by him [Perl]. He was then taken to the famous death cell by Lieutenant Perl. In the afternoon, the accused was again called out for interrogation. He still did not know of any order [to shoot prisoners]. He finally became tired of this treatment and wrote out another statement. The accused frequently protested and once got up and said that he would not have any more dictated to him. Lieutenant Perl kicked him and told him to sit down and write or he would be beaten. The accused asked Lieutenant Perl for permission to relieve himself, but this was refused. The accused was again interrogated on 11 March 1946. He was told to change his statement and, on his refusal, was threatened with hanging. The accused was compelled to stand in the hall for four hours with a hood on his head. The interrogating officer came quite often and asked his name. When the accused did not answer he was hit in the stomach.'[24]

Needless to say, in court both Perl and Thon denied striking the prisoner. Another defendant, when asked why he had made a self-incriminating statement said in court that, having undergone treatment like this, 'I was in a spiritual and mental state such that nothing seemed to matter to me.'[25]

Colonel Everett seized upon the fact that these extrajudiciary statements, which formed the main cornerstone of the prosecution's case, were inadmissible because they had been obtained through trickery and coercion, and went further. Since the accused were prisoners of war, then the Geneva Convention applied and they were entitled to be tried by the same courts and under the same procedure as in the case of members of the armed forces of the occupying power. It would seem here that the members of the court were guided by Wheaton's *International Law*, which stated:

'If men are taken prisoners in the act of committing, or who had committed, violation of international law, they are not properly entitled to the privileges and treatment accorded to honorable prisoners of war.'[26]

This, though, could only be proved at their trial and hence could only apply once they had been found guilty. Thus, it could be argued that removing the prisoner of war status from the defendants prior to the trial was an illegal act. But, as part of the preparations for war crimes trials, a United States Joint Chiefs of Staff directive issued in the summer of 1945 had empowered the Commanding General United States Force's European Theater (USFET) with the setting up of courts separate from those trying offences against the occupation and that they should adopt 'fair, simple and expeditious procedures designed to accomplish substantial justice without technicality'.[27] The outline of procedure to be followed by such courts was laid down by the USFET Judge Advocate in November 1945 and, among other rules it laid down, was that:

'To admit in evidence a confession of the accused, it need not be shown such confession was voluntarily made and the Court may exclude it as worthless or admit it and give it such weight as in its opinion it may deserve after considering the facts and circumstances of the execution.'[28]

But while the rules of evidence, as recognised in American and British municipal law trials, were not applicable, and, indeed, the question of involuntary confessions does not seem to have been catered for in the Judge Advocate USFET's rules of procedure, American justice did recognise that:

'. . . while artifice and deception will not in themselves render a confession involuntary, if there are combined with the deception any inducements which excite hope of benefit from the making of the confession or fear of consequences if he does not make such a confession, the confession is involuntary.'

It was, however, up to the court to decide whether such inducements had been made, which would thus render the confession involuntary and hence inadmissible.[29] As for extrajudicial statements against co-accused, Everett pleaded that in British and American municipal criminal law courts these were inadmissible, but the prosecution pointed out that in this case the defendants were not 'honorable' prisoners of war, and hence this rule did not apply. This was upheld by the court.[30]

It would seem, therefore, that the rules of procedure were being adapted as the court saw fit and the members were fully aware of the pressure in the United States at large to find the defendants guilty. It was thus not surprising that all except one, who was discharged on 11 July, were found guilty, and they were sentenced on 16 July. No less than forty-three were sentenced to death by hanging and the remainder to varying terms of imprisonment, from life to ten years. Dietrich himself was sent down for life, Kraemer for ten years, Priess for twenty years and Peiper received the death sentence. That they recognised the efforts made by Everett on their behalf was reflected in the fact that Kraemer wept openly during his summing up on 11 July and Dietrich shook him by the hand and thanked him afterwards.[31]

On 17 July, the day after the end of the trial, Dietrich and the other defendants arrived at the fortress of Landsberg. How much the poetic justice of this struck the new arrivals, if at all, in view of the fact that this was where Hitler had written *Mein Kampf*, while imprisoned there after his 1924 Munich trial, cannot be gauged. Perhaps, more to the point, it appeared to many that Landsberg would be their last home on earth. Yet, they did have one ally on their side. Willis Everett was convinced that there had been a miscarriage of justice. The Malmédy affair had by no means come to an end.

CHAPTER 11

War Criminal and After 1946-66

On arrival in Landsberg, those who had been sentenced to death were issued with red track suit jackets which they had to wear all the time, thus never allowing them to forget that they were condemned men. Indeed, Wolf-Dieter Dietrich remembers this aspect of Landsberg far more than he does his father, when he, his mother and brothers were allowed to begin periodic visits at the beginning of 1948.[1] To begin with, apart from a daily exercise period, the prisoners were confined to their cells and were held almost incommunicado. Ursula and the children had not been able to get back to Karlsruhe and were living at Unterjoch, east of Sonthofen and on the Austrian border, and it was this that Dietrich gave as his home address. He was now officially designated a War Criminal Prisoner and had the prison number of 160. Landsberg itself enjoyed the official US title of War Criminal Prison No 1.

The findings of the court at Dachau had to be confirmed. In the meantime, during the latter part of July and the next few weeks, several pleas of clemency were lodged by friends and relatives of the Malmédy prisoners. Dietrich himself had none on his behalf, but this may well have been because he did not want anyone to intercede on his account, especially his family, preferring to fight his own battles. It is of interest to note, however, that two letters were received by the US authorities in the last part of July protesting that Dietrich should have been sentenced to death. One was from an Egbert Bruckner and the other from 'A German Cosmopolitan'.[3] The wheels of US justice, faced with an increasing flood of war crimes trials, were, however, grinding slowly, and it was not until 28 December 1946 that Willis Everett formally filed a petition for review of the case. By this time, the review itself was automatically underway and had been entrusted to Maxmilian Kössler of the US Judge Advocate General's Office.

Yet, as early as January 1947, the US Press was beginning to wake up to the fact that there had been irregularities, although they had ignored them at the time of the trial. For instance, *The New York Herald Tribune* of 22 January 1947 carried a piece on accounts of pre-trial brutalities inflicted on the defendants. By February 1947, however, Kössler had only reviewed fifteen out of the seventy-three cases, recommending that the guilty verdicts stand for twelve, but that the other three be quashed on the grounds of insufficient evidence. His work was now taken over by Lieutenant Colonel C E Straight, the Deputy Judge Advocate for War Crimes, who rejected what Kössler had already done and began again. Not until 20 October 1947 did he complete his work.

The general drift of Straight's recommendations was that the procedures had been correct, although he clearly was not too sure in his own mind about the validity of the pre-trial confessions, that is whether they were extracted under undue duress, but he sided with the evidence of those, such as Perl and Thon, who had carried out the pre-trial investigations. He did, however, acknowledge that many of the defendants were young, of limited mentality and were acting under orders. Mainly on these grounds, the death sentences were reduced to 25. Of the eighteen whom he now recommended should be spared, seven were to receive life sentences, ten should be given lesser sentences and one, Fritz Eckmann, a tank radio operator in 1st SS Panzer Battalion, who had been accused of taking part in the shootings at both the Baugnez crossroads and La Gleize, be quashed entirely, on the grounds that there was insufficient evidence that he was present on either occasion. As for the life sentences, he recommended that only five out of the twenty-two be upheld, including that of Sepp Dietrich. 'The accused held a high position in the German Reich and the Waffen SS. He was an essential moving force in applying the plans for the application of terrorism for the counteroffensive.'[4] The remainder of the life sentence should be reduced to ten or fifteen years, Straight recommended.

In the meantime, Willis Everett, now a civilian attorney once more and practising in Atlanta, Georgia, had already applied in early 1947 for the execution of any approved death sentences to be stayed until he had had the opportunity to apply to the Supreme Court of the United States for a writ of habeas corpus. He was assured by the Deputy Commander US European Command, on 27 March 1947, and again on 30 January 1948 that no confirmed death sentences would be carried out for sixty days in order to give him the time to do this. In view, however, of the number of petitions up before the Supreme Court of the United States, the Commander-in-Chief in Germany ordered an indefinite stay of execution of all death sentences on 29 January 1948. Against this background, the work of Straight was reviewed by a board chaired by Colonel Howard F Bresee. In its report, dated 8 February 1948, the panel concluded that there was 'much evidence' of improper pre-trial investigations, especially in terms of mock trials and concocted confessions, as well as improper procedural rulings by the Dachau court. It recommended that twenty-nine of the defendants, including Dietrich, should be immediately released.[5]

Straight's report had also been sent to Colonel J L Harbaugh Jr, the Judge Advocate at Headquarters HQ European Command, and he took a somewhat different view. Commenting on the pre-trial confessions, he wrote:

'in none of these 21 cases [where the defence had claimed such evidence as inadmissible] is there any direct testimony that the confessions involved were induced by promise of reward or fear of punishment . . . In some incidents there is no question but that the confessions are true. . . . Assuming, but not conceding, that such inducements were present in connection with confessions here involved, there is no requirement in war crimes trials that such confessions be rejected in their entirety. The correct rule in war crimes trials is that a confession may be received in evidence, without any foundation of voluntariness, subject to being attacked and discredited by the defense because of the circumstances under which it was obtained.[6]

He recommended the release of only twelve men on the grounds of insufficiency of evidence. Twelve of the death sentences should be upheld, including that of Peiper, fourteen sentences of life imprisonment should be confirmed, including that of Dietrich, and the remainder should serve varying lesser terms of reduced length. While the Bresee Board had recommended disapproval of the verdicts on Dietrich, Kraemer and Priess, Harbaugh commented on the orders issued by Sixth Panzer Army and the conflict between the extrajudiciary statements and the testimonies given at the trial, making the point that it was the duty of the court 'to consider the record as a whole'.

'It does not necessarily follow that because Peiper's troops were told they were to fight ruthlessly, so as to create a wave of terror, and to shoot prisoners of war when the combat conditions required it, that such instructions emanated from the army commander. Such instructions *could* have originated with Peiper. But they *could* have originated with Dietrich and his chief of staff, Kraemer; and the probabilities are that at least that part with reference to fighting without humane inhibitions and creating a wave of terror and fright originated with Dietrich. In fact he says that his Order was so directed. The Court certainly was justified to believe this despite the testimony from the other witnesses that the Order contained nothing of the kind. And assuming that his order made no mention of shooting prisoners of war, a direction to troops to fight without humane inhibitions is at least an invitation to fight without giving quarter (which, as a general instruction is illegal), if not an excitation to kill prisoners. As officers and commanders of experience, Dietrich, Kraemer and Preiss should have anticipated that such instructions to troops would be taken by them as license to commit deeds made unlawful by the rules of war. In my opinion the evidence is sufficient to support the convictions of these three accused.'

This was in direct contrast to findings of the Bresee Board, which considered that such an order was hardly a 'violation of the laws and usages of war' and was more aimed at instilling an offensive spirit in the troops in order to break the enemy's will.[7] Nevertheless, General Lucius D Clay, the US Commander-in-Chief in Europe, accepted Harbaugh's recommendations without reservation and, on 20 March 1948, thirteen Malmédy defendants left Landsberg as free men and twelve continued to wear the red track suit top.

No evidence exists as to how Dietrich took the news that his sentence had been confirmed, but one can imagine disappointment at least, but also determination not to allow it to lower his morale too much. By March 1947, work had been found to keep the prisoners at Landsberg occupied and Dietrich was assigned to an outside work detail, as leader of what the prison authorities called the Dietrich gang. At the beginning of 1948, Ursula, who was still at Unterjoch with the children, wrote to the prison governor and requested that she be allowed to see him, especially since his mother had just died and she wanted to break the news to him personally. Up until this time, the prisoners had not been allowed visits by anyone other than lawyers. Although they were allowed to receive mail (signing a statement to the effect that they accepted the right of the authorities to censor it), they were only permitted to send out two letters per week. With the sentences now confirmed, visits by relations were agreed, each visitor being allowed one visit of two hours once a month. To be able to see one another again must have been welcome to both, but to have to speak to one another through a wire grill and with the distinct possibility that Dietrich might remain in prison for the rest of his life made these meetings painful as well. For his sons, on the occasions on which they accompanied their mother, their father remained a remote figure. Given that they had seen so little of Sepp during their short lives, this was understandable.

Dietrich's conduct in prison at this time was generally good and there is only one entry on his prison crime sheet at this time – impertinence on 17 January 1948, for which he was reprimanded. During the summer of 1948, though, his health began to give some cause for concern. He increasingly suffered from pains in the legs if he walked any distance. Towards the end of August 1948, he was admitted to the prison hospital, where the problem was diagnosed as claudification and the beginnings of Buerger's Disease, which is a circulatory problem. This was attributed to the frostbite that he had suffered during the winter of 1941-42. Although treatment brought about an improvement, it was something that would continue to bother him.

Meanwhile, the Malmédy trial controversy was by no means dead. There was rising agitation on both sides of the Atlantic over the conduct of the war crimes trials and over Malmédy in particular. This brought together strange bedfellows, with pacifists and civil libertarians joining with pro-Nazis and anti-Semites in condemnation. Thus, in Germany, Dr Rudolf Aschenauer, a former Nazi Party member and defending counsel for the notorious Otto Ohlendorf, commander of the infamous Einsatzgruppe D which murdered some ninety thousand people in the Ukraine during 1941-42 and was hanged in June 1951, became the main spokesman for the Malmédy prisoners. On the other hand, Dr Johannes Neuhäusler, the Auxiliary Bishop of Munich, who had spent four years as an inmate of Dachau Concentration Camp, also believed that the prisoners had been treated unjustly. He based his doubts on information given to him by the priest who had administered to the prisoners and, on 25 March 1948, sent a letter to the US Congress expressing his concern. [8]

General Lucius D Clay was becoming concerned for another reason. In a Top Secret signal to Under Secretary for the Army William H Draper Jr of 24 May 1948, he noted that, as a result of various legal delays, there were now five hundred war criminals with the death sentence hanging over them. If the Supreme Court ruled that the sentences should be upheld, then:

> '. . . I find it difficult to adjust my own mental processes to requiring what looks like to be almost a mass execution of more than five hundred persons. I believe that it also gives an appearance of cruelty to the United States even though in my mind there is no question that the crimes committed fully justify the death sentence. Moreover, more than three years have elapsed since these crimes were committed. I am somewhat inclined to consider the commutation of these death sentences to life imprisonment in substantial measure.'[9]

He went on to press for the setting up of a clemency board in order to relieve him of the responsibility resting merely on his shoulders, although a few days later (31 May) he corrected the figure of death sentence prisoners held to 150. [9] On 9 June he pressured Draper even further:

> 'I would like to remove the indefinite stay in execution of military war criminals convicted by the military government courts at Dachau and to proceed with the execution of sentences unless the clemency board is set up in the immediate future.' [10]

It may be that Everett had sensed that some pressure was being applied to remove the indefinite stays, for, on 14 May, he had entered pleas of habeas corpus before the Supreme Court, but, after dividing 4-4, his application for leave to file was turned down. All was not lost, however, since on 23 July 1948, Secretary of the Army Kenneth C Royall set up a three man commission to review the death sentences from the Dachau trials in line with Clay's request. It so happened that one of the members, Judge LeRoy van Roden was known personally to Everett as they had spent three months together in the same hotel in Frankfurt. Everett now began to try to exert influence on van Roden through letters to the latter's wife. [11] The Royall Commission considered sixty-seven cases in under two months and accepted that the twelve remaining Malmedy death sentences should stand, although it did express reservations over 'tricks and ruses', especially the mock trials. [12] It leaked out to the media, however, that van Roden had accepted all Everett's accusations over the conduct of the pre-trial investigation and the trial itself. During the second week in October there were a number of comments in the US Press. *The New York Times* asserted that: 'A decent respect for the opinion of others demands that no final action be taken . . . until a complete and satisfying explanation is given.' [13] The *Chicago Tribune* went even further, stating that 'never has American justice sunk to the degradation depicted by Judge E L van Roden'. [14] What had caused this *volte face*?

By the autumn of 1948 the Cold War had arrived and the Soviet Union was perceived in Western eyes to be casting a long shadow over Western Europe. It was the Berlin Blockade especially, which was imposed by the Soviets on 24 June 1948, and increasing restrictions on travel between the Soviet and other Allied Zones of Occupation, which had brought this about. With the huge Allied wartime armies run down, and mere 'constabularies' rather than operationally ready combat forces available to defend West Germany, in the face of what was increasingly seen as a massive Soviet military threat, more and more people were beginning to realise that West Germany itself might well have to contribute to the defence of Free Europe. This was, of course, what many Germans themselves had been saying from 1945 onwards. What this did was to evoke a general feeling that West Germany could no longer be considered as a conquered nation under occupation, and this change of heart was to be reflected in the establishment of the Federal German Republic in 1949, although it would not achieve status as a fully independent state until 1955.

Meanwhile, the Royall Commission continued to sit and submitted its final report on 14 February 1949. By now its attention had been very much focused on the pre-trial treatment of prisoners. It concluded that there had been mock trials and physical force 'in the heat of the moment', rather than premeditated, that there had been threats to punish prisoners' relatives, especially by removing their ration cards, and that '. . . the conditions obtaining at the prison and the methods employed in the interrogations had a definite psychological effect on the defendants and resulted in their being more amenable to giving statements'. Yet, the Commission did no more than recommend that their conclusions be considered in any future reviews of the Malmédy cases. [15] The Royall Commission report was now passed to General Clay so that he could now come to a decision over the death sentences.

The affair now took a new turn when Senator William Langer, a Republican from North Dakota, informed Clay that he was intending to introduce a Senate resolution calling for an investigation of US military justice in Europe. General Clay, who reflected the general view of the Army that the executions should go ahead, now requested cancellation of the stays of execution from Assistant Secretary of the Army Tracy Voorhees. A few days later, when asked to comment on a report in The *New York Times*[16] that torture had been used to extract a statement from a witness in the Malmédy trial, Clay commented:

> 'It is quite clear that, just as SS troops who massacred our soldiers were organized to maintain silence, that they have since been organized to paint a greatly distorted picture. Unfortunately, in the heat of the aftermath of war, we did use measures to obtain evidence that we would not have employed later when initial heat was expended. However, there are no grounds whatsoever for expanding these mistaken measures with a distorted picture of unbelievable cruelty that cannot be explained except from the testimony of the suspects, vigorously denied by various members of the prosecution.'[17]

There were many Americans who still shared General Clay's views, including the unnamed senator who declared in 1949 that 'there is nothing that any of us can recall in recorded history that approaches the unwarranted type of mass slaughter that occurred at Malmédy'.[18]

By now General Clay had begun to review the death sentences himself and concluded that there was sufficient evidence against those concerned to convict six of them without taking any pre-trial statements obtained under possible duress into account.[19] These six sentences were confirmed, but the stay of execution remained, pending further instructions from the Department of the Army. However, increasing pressure from senators, especially one Senator Joseph McCarthy of Wisconsin and a member of the Senate Investigations Subcommittee, caused Royall on 29 March 1949 to set up a Senate subcommittee to investigate the Malmédy allegations. McCarthy himself was not a member of the sub-committee, but was invited to participate as a gesture to the Senate Investigations Subcommittee. The proceedings opened on 18 April and would initially be dominated by McCarthy. Those who had participated in the trial and pre-trial investigation were questioned, and McCarthy made much of the fact that, although still technically prisoners of war during the pre-trial investigation, the Malmédy defendants had not been treated according to the Geneva Convention. Colonel Rosenfeld, the legal adviser to the Dachau court, appeared as a man whose objectivity was much in doubt. This was reflected in the court's refusal to allow the defence on occasion to challenge the credibility of prosecution witnesses, but especially Rosenfeld's view of Hal McCown, a key defence witness. He told the Subcommittee that he simply did not believe McCown's evidence – 'I have no faith – and I am glad to say at this time I didn't have one bit of faith in the testimony as given by the then Major McCown.'[20] Those involved in the interrogations all denied that they had used torture to extract confessions. It was, however, William R Perl for whom McCarthy reserved his greatest venom, and, indeed, against whom the majority of accusations had been levelled. He established that Perl had been an active Zionist, who before the war had, while a lawyer in Vienna, assisted the emigration of Jews to Palestine. He himself had then emigrated to the United States. Perl consistently denied that physical brutalities had taken place and was equally consistently accused of perjury by McCarthy. McCarthy now demanded the use of a lie detector, but this was vetoed by the sub-committee. As a result, on 20 May 1949, McCarthy stormed out of the hearings and accused the Sub-committee of a 'whitewash'. It was not only 'impugning the fair name of the millions of men and women who served with valor and distinction in the armed forces' but also 'sabotaging our efforts under the European Recovery Act'. The United States Army was guilty of using 'Gestapo and OGPU tactics' and 'the United States can never protest the use of these methods by totalitarian countries'.[21] And so McCarthy left the Malmédy stage, but not the American political arena. From 1950-54 he would acquire an infamous reputation as the leader of the anti-Communist witchhunt in the States and his name would become part of the English language as a result.

Undeterred, the sub-committee continued with its investigations, moving to Germany to interview witnesses there. The evidence of some witnesses that they had been subjected to brutalities was considered doubtful, but others did impress the sub-committee. The final stage was to interview the fifty-nine remaining Malmédy prisoners at Landsberg and this was done during the early part of September 1949. Forty-eight of them, including Dietrich, claimed to have suffered physical brutalities, of whom eleven claimed that they still bore the physical evidence in the form of scars and missing teeth. Ten incidents of trauma, possibly caused by beatings, were found but none were incapacitating. It was thus concluded, albeit three and a half years after the injuries were supposed to have been inflicted, that evidence of maltreatment was relatively minimal. The sub-committee produced its report on 13 October 1949. The use of physical maltreatment was entirely rejected and, while evidence of trickery and threats was accepted, little criticism was made of the way the pre-trial investigation had been carried out, especially since those under investigation had been 'hardened, experienced members of the SS who had been through many campaigns and were used to worse procedure'. [22]

The continuing public attention paid to the Malmédy prisoners and the fact that the death sentences were being gradually whittled down, gave them all cause for hope. Dietrich himself, having spent three months in the prison hospital in the autumn of 1948, was found unfit for outside work and was transferred to the potato kitchen, where he worked for a month, his rating being 'Excellent'. Just before Christmas 1948, he was moved again, to the bookbinding shop and would work here until his eventual release. Early in 1949, Ursula and the boys managed to get back to Karlsruhe, where they lived with her parents. Unlike many of the families of the Landsberg prisoners, there were no serious financial problems at this time. While Dietrich himself lost his savings when the Reichsmark lost its legality, the Moninger brewery was still operating and hence her parents were able to support her.

During the latter part of 1949 and throughout the next two years there was a continuous flow of protest over the fact that six of the Malmédy prisoners were still under sentence of death and that others still faced long terms of imprisonment. The establishment of the German Basic Law, which gave Germans jurisdiction over themselves, in May 1949, encouraged such comment from Germans themselves. Doctor Aschenauer was especially vocal, writing a stream of pamphlets, which were translated into English and distributed in America by the Washington-based National Council for the Prevention of War. More sinister perhaps, was a pamphlet produced in Buenos Aires in 1950, which was reproduced from the monthly cultural review *El Sendero*. Entitled *Das Martyrium der schwarzen Kapuzen* (The Martyrdom of the Black Cowls), [23] it asserted that not all the American soldiers at the Baugnez crossroads had, in fact, surrendered, but that some had taken to the woods and opened fire. It said that the world press had only begun writing about German atrocities since the Nuremberg trials, and that the trials themselves were 'supposed to be the foundation of a new world order and for that one needed evidence. An entire people was to be sacrificed as a deterring example for all other peoples.' Obviously, this article was the work of those Nazis who had been able to escape to South America before being picked up by the Allies in the immediate aftermath of the war.

Other demands for clemency came in the form of affidavits sworn by men who had known Dietrich well and could testify to his character. Rudolf Lehmann recalled an incident in Italy in October 1943 when he was the Chief of Staff of the *Leibstandarte*. An officer of the Division, *Obersturmbannführer* (although Lehmann actually called him *Oberstleutnant*) Stoltz informed him that he had heard from the local German consul that an *SD-Kommando* was holding a large number of Jews prisoner in a hotel on Lake Maggiore and that some of them had already been murdered.

'As Stoltz was my closest co-worker [he was also on the Divisional Staff], we discussed extensively what steps to take. It was not possible to inform the superior command authority (Army Group Rommel). It was only possible, if at all, to contact them via wireless. But we knew that *Obergruppenführer* Dietrich, to whom we were in no way subordinated, was in Merano to organise the staff of his new General's Command. That's why I gave him a ring and reported the situation to him. He, knowing well that this was not within his authority, immediately ordered a staff officer to go there, together with some military police, to liberate the Jews and to arrest the SD leader in charge and bring him back to the *Wehrmachtkommandatur* in Milan. I immediately gave this order to Stoltz who reported execution of the order that very evening via wireless . . . I have to emphasise that *Obergruppenführer* Dietrich never had any command authority over the SD or any other service relationship with the SD. We nevertheless contacted him because we knew that he was the only man who not only found such crimes repulsive but also the man who tried to prevent these crimes, if he knew about them, regardless of the eventual consequences to himself.'[24]

Another who took similar action was Heinz Guderian. He stated that he had known Dietrich before the war and that Dietrich had served under him in the 1940 campaign in the West.

'Because of the impression I gained in peace and in wartime I can give the following judgement on him:
In character, he was a simple, straightforward, rough soldier, with a lot of heart for his soldiers. An extremely good comrade who stood up as much as he could for his subordinates, irrespective of the consequence for himself.'

He went on to relate how Dietrich reacted to Guderian's dismissal at the end of 1941 and then discussed the *Leibstandarte*:

'Dietrich insisted on manly discipline [*Mannszucht*]. No excesses committed by members of units under his command are known to me.
Dietrich had good relations with the Army generals. He considered himself as entirely a friend of the Army. In this, he was entirely different to Himmler with whom he had bigger and bigger differences the longer the war lasted.
During my numerous inspections of Waffen-SS units, I always had the best impressions of the manly discipline in these units, which I always felt was related to a very good comradeship.

He had good words to say about Kraemer and Peiper, whom he praised as having not only 'good military capabilities', but 'great idealism, a heart for the soldiers and understanding for the difficult situation of the civilian population'. Peiper was not only brave, but 'chivalrous' as well. Finally, he had some pertinent words to say about the trial at Dachau.

'On the 17 June 46, I was brought to Dachau as witness of the defence to give evidence in favour of the three above mentioned officers [Dietrich, Kraemer, Peiper] in the trial against the LAH.
After questions on my personal record and after having taken the oath, I realised that I was hindered by the objections of the prosecution in answering the first question of the defence. The reason for this illegal behaviour by the prosecution was: "We are dealing here with a trial because of shootings of American soldiers. Therefore the prosecution cannot allow any witnesses for the defence. This witness has been called by the defence. Therefore, I appeal that he had not heard and that he is dismissed." The court did not need any discussion on this point.
The members quickly looked at each other and decided in favour of the prosecutor. I was led out of the courtroom without being allowed to say a single word. The proceedings in Dachau against members of the LAH was illegal. The treatment of the soldiers of this formation, who

had been designated as witnesses was improper; they were mistreated by the US non-commissioned officer on guard simply because they greeted me. Only after my protest was this stopped.'[25]

This was strong evidence of judicial mismanagement and it is unlikely that Guderian would have taken this step if he had not felt so strongly about the treatment of the Malmédy men.

However, there was still a stay of execution on the remaining six Malmédy 'red jackets', but a further review was launched in the autumn of 1950 which embraced prison sentences as well. The introduction of the Basic Law for Germany had meant an end to military government and the handling of war crimes in the US European Command was now handled by the European Command War Crimes Modification Board, which worked closely with the Judge Advocate General's Department. Willis Everett was continuing to agitate for the release of all and was beginning to be regarded as almost a national hero by some sectors of the German population. At the same time, the outbreak of the Korean War had resulted in another increase in tension in Europe and once again the eyes of the Western Allies were turning to the West Germans as a means of strengthening Western defences. One popular German view of this was reflected by the Hamburg weekly *Die Strasse* (The Street), which ran a series of articles entitled *Gerechtigkeit fur die Rotjacken* (Justice for the Red Jackets) in early 1951. One response to this from a reader was:

'If Eisenhower wants German soldiers, he should first respond as a soldier and human being to the Landsberg case, for Peiper and his men are our comrades. If the noose should be put around their necks, hate would ever be sown, and words "grass grows over battlefields but never over gallows' would become the watchword for those whom the Western Powers wants as their hirelings.'[26]

That the United States authorities were clearly sensitive to German public opinion became clear when the Commander-in-Chief US European Command, General Thomas T Handy, announced on 31 January 1951 that the remaining six death sentences for Malmédy, including that on Peiper, had been commuted to life imprisonment. It was a great moment for the inmates of Landsberg, although it brought no reduction to Dietrich's sentence, and Peiper was moved to write to Everett:

'We have received a great victory and next to God it is you [from] whom our blessings flow. In all the long and dark years, you have been the beacon flame for the forlorn souls of the Malmédy boys, the voice and the conscience of the good America, and yours is the present success against all the well known overwhelming odds. May I therefore, Colonel, express the everlasting gratitude of the red-jacket team (retired) as well as of all the families concerned.'[27]

Reaction in the United States to this decision was mixed, with motions from 'Posts' of the Veterans of Foreign Wars bitterly condemning the move and even the *New York Times* considering it a 'compromise between justice and expediency'.[28] In Germany, though, many leading figures of the new state expressed disappointment that the review had not gone far enough. This was, directly or indirectly, heeded by the United States authorities. On 10 August

1951, General Handy commuted Sepp Dietrich's sentence to one of twenty-five years. With remission and taking the beginning of his term of imprisonment as the date of his original capture, 9 May 1945, it meant that he had every prospect of becoming a free man on 19 February 1962. Many others, too, received reductions in their sentences and hopes were now rising that the Malmédy prisoners would, in the not too distant future, leave the confines of Landsberg.

Dietrich soon noticed that the reductions in sentence were also accompanied by a relaxation in some of the prison rules. For a start, he was allowed visitors outside his immediate family and lawyer. Thus when Wilhelm Keilhaus, who had first come in proper contact with Dietrich in 1934 when he commanded the Signals Platoon of the *Leibstandarte*, wrote to the Director of Landsberg requesting permission to visit Sepp on the grounds that he was an old friend, permission was given immediately.[29] The ration of one visit per month was also made a little less rigid. There was also a slight relaxing of discipline. Sepp Dietrich had been found guilty of a second offence, after that of impertinence in June 1948, of failing to get out of his bed at the 0600 hours gong on 9 December 1949 and received another reprimand. On 4 May 1951 he was found guilty of boxing during working hours in the bookbinding shop with Georg Fleps, the man who was supposed to have fired the first shot in the Baugnez crossroads massacre, and reprimanded once more. Finally, some six weeks later, on 15 June, he was late for the 1300 hours head count, for which he was regraded from first to second conduct grade for a period of fifteen days, but suspended dependent on good behaviour. It is interesting to note that, while it was agreed that he arrived in time, he should have been there five minutes before and that he was normally the first man to be present – military discipline dies hard! It was, however, to be the last petty charge that he would face at Landsberg, although, as we shall see, there was to be one other and much more serious offence committed by him.

Yet, although his optimism about the future was now increasing, there was a small dark cloud just looming over the horizon. One of the powers that the May 1949 Basic Law had handed over to the West German authorities ws the right to try their own nationals for crimes against the state, which included war crimes. At the beginning of April 1951 the Director of Landsberg received a summons to be passed to Dietrich from the *Landgericht Berlin*.[30] What it was for is not clear, but the response from the Director was that only the Provost Marshal, European Command (EUCOM), could give permission for Dietrich to be transferred to their custody, but that the Berlin legal authorities were at liberty to interrogate Dietrich at Landsberg. It was a warning to Dietrich that, although he would be eventually released from Landsberg, he would not necessarily remain a free man.

The agitation for the release of the remaining Malmédy prisoners was still present, however. In 1952, Dietrich Ziemssen, chief operations officer of the

Leibstandarte in the Ardennes campaign and a defence witness at the trial, published his pamphlet *The Malmédy Trial*. This reviewed the whole case from the beginning, and concluded:

> 'It is indifferent whether 73 or 41 men are kept in confinement. It is indifferent whether a man is confined for his life or for 25 years. The decisive fact is that German soldiers as prisoners of war were forced by phsyical and psychological pressure to make wrong confessions; that they, after having been deprived of the legal protection of the prisoner of war status and prevented from any regular defense, were sentenced in a show trial by a non competent tribunal, and that they never got oral or written reasons for such sentences.'

He then quoted a speech made by the US High Commissioner for Germany, John J McCloy, had made in December 1951 at Stuttgart, in which he said:

> This is not a time to be cynical and sceptic. It is a time for positive decisions and deeds; if you keep to the high ideas and ideals of your great poets and thinkers, then the future of the German Federal Republic and finally of a re-united Germany within a large, wealthy and peaceful European community will be assured'.

To Ziemssen such goals could only be reached if injustices such as the continuing imprisonment of the Malmédy men were put right:[31] Dr Aschenauer, of course, was still very active and maintained a steady correspondence with the Landsberg prisoners, including Sepp Dietrich. At the beginning of June 1953, Aschenauer requested a medical report on Dietrich from the prison authorities and this was duly sent. It noted that the problem with Sepp's legs had 'got worse continuously' and that he could not walk more than 150 metres without severe pains in his right calf. (Dietrich had been supplied with special orthopaedic shoes in July the previous year, because of flat and splayed feet, but these clearly were not helping much.) In conclusion, the report said: 'The frostbites during World War II and the damage suffered *during captivity* [Author's italics] must be considered as the probable causes of this affliction.'[32] It may have been this that brought about what was, at the very least, a serious indiscretion on Dietrich's part.

At the beginning of August 1953, it was discovered that some stencils had been smuggled out from Landsberg and that Dietrich was the perpetrator, using a German civilian employed at the prison. It would appear that the stencils contained a message to the German Government to the effect that it was not doing enough for the Malmédy prisoners and should apply pressure on the United States prior to the German elections, which were to take place the following month. It seems to have caused the United States authorities in Germany much embarrassment and the Director of Landsberg was ordered to conduct a discreet rather than a formal inquiry and not to inform the participants in the act that such an inquiry was taking place. The 'quiet' investigation achieved nothing, but in mid-September the Director was authorised to make more open enquiries. The Director therefore indirectly let it become known to Dietrich that he had been discovered and that the stencils had not reached their destination. A week later, he was summoned in front of the Director to explain himself. He had he said, against his better judgement, given in to pressure from the Malmédy 'group' to commit such an act. He fully realised that he had violated prison regulations and that he had been very foolish. The Director, who was now Colonel E C Moore Jr, considered that Dietrich had had sufficient punishment in the mental anguish he had suffered, especially since he was applying for parole, and decided to take no further action.[33]

The American authorities had laid down a ruling that a war criminal prisoner could be considered for parole after serving a third of his sentence. For Dietrich this meant that he was eligible to be considered from September 1953. He submitted his application on 14 November. Apart from giving details of his life – he put down his previous occupation as 'professional soldier' – he also had to give the names of three character witnesses. These were Rudolf Lehmann, who was now a businessman in Heidelberg, a lawyer from Stuttgart, Dr Heinrich Simon, and General Hans Speidel. The last-named was now the chief military delegate with the German Delegation to the Conference for the Organisation of the European Defence Union in Paris, and in his reply to Dietrich's request that he be a character witness Speidel wrote that he had never become 'tired of working for a just solution of the Landsberg problem'.

> 'I have no objections to being cited in your request for a parole release as a character witness. If the Parole Board will ask me to make a statement regarding your reputation, I will call their special attention to your character qualities as a military leader and human being, which I have experienced during the years of 1943 to 1944, because I can never forget the efforts made by you everywhere in a most severe situation.'[34]

Dietrich also had to make a summary of his offence and stated that it was on the grounds of his having issued an Order of the Day just prior to the Ardennes offensive. He felt that he should amplify this statement and wrote a letter to Colonel Moore. He said that he had never condoned violations of the laws of war and had been unable to act at the time because he did not have any information. 'You may rest assured that a "Malmédy Trial" would never have been necessary if I would have known all the particulars at that time.' Nevertheless, he accepted that as an army commander he carried 'great responsibility'. 'If any crimes have been committed by my subordinates, there is no doubt that I, as the superior officer, carry a certain responsibility, and after having realised that, I am able to conceive my conviction in a certain way.' He appreciated that, in view of his former position, his parole might cause difficulties, but assured Colonel Moore that he 'was always a soldier and as such non-political. I was nothing but an "old warrior" who was esteemed by the German youth and did not have any political ambitions.' He had never been an enemy of the West and believed that its unification into a defence union against the East was 'the matter of the hour'. He would willingly co-operate in this if asked to do so by the 'competent authorities', but all he really wanted to do was care for his family in 'quietness and peace', especially since his father-in-law had been killed in a car crash just a few days previously.[35] He also had to give details in his application of his future employment and where he was going to live. The firm of Hartchrom GmbH of Karlsruhe had agreed to take Dietrich on as a salesman at a salary of DM259-350 per month and this meant that he could live at home.

The prison authorities noted that he was a keen student of military history and spent much time studying it, but also tried to keep himself fit with 'exercises and calisthenics for older personnel'. Colonel Moore considered him 'sincere' and stated that Dietrich had assured him that, if paroled, he would not join any organisation, 'even a bowling club'. He recognised that:

'The past political activities of this man have been such that only a complete "about face" would make him a good citizen. The Prison Administration is firmly convinced that such an "about face" HAS [sic] occurred, and that this man now realizes how wrong he was in his political belief. He has excellent character qualities, and it is felt can quickly adjust himself to civilian community life, and will become an excellent citizen.'

With references like these, it seemed that there would be a good chance of parole being granted.

Since 1952 the parole machinery had been modified. The new Mixed Parole and Clemency Board was now composed of three German members and a representative from each of the United States, Great Britain and France. It was, however, not empowered to consider the question of guilt, but merely parole and reductions in sentence. The final decision still remained with the appropriate Allied Commander-in-Chief. The Board considered Dietrich's application for almost six months and only on 14 May 1954 did the US Commander-in-Chief, General Hoge, turn it down. Although Dietrich was immediately informed, he was not given any reason for it. It is very possible that the stencil affair had had something to do with it and there were perhaps doubts that Dietrich fully appreciated his guilt. Also, as can be inferred from his subsequent parole applications, it would seem that allowing him to live and work at home in Karlsruhe was perhaps making life too easy. Above all was probably the feeling that the political climate, both in the USA and the Federal Republic of Germany, was not yet right.

Be that as it may, Dietrich immediately submitted another application. He retained the same three character witnesses. In the 'Summary of Offense' section he wrote that the contents of the Order of the Day were that 'every single soldier and officer has to do his utter duty and has to be brave, but this "Order of the Day" did not contain by any means any violation of the martial law as for instance an order to shoot prisoners of war'. He now proposed to work for a Hans Müller, with whom he would live, in Rastatt-Baden, some twenty kilometres south of Karlsruhe. Colonel Moore's own observations were even more glowing than previously:

'This 61 years old inmate is well adjusted to community life. He is cooperative, cheerful and in my opinion has the best moral and outlook [sic] of anyone in this institution. When told that his application for parole had been disapproved his reaction was commendable. He said he was sure the matter had been given due and just consideration and if that was the decision, he was not going to complain, because he thought that the matter had been given plenty of thought by the Board and others. He showed no bitterness whatsoever over the decision and his cheerfulness and morale have not dropped in the least. He made the statement that he wanted to apply again as soon as he could because his desire was to be able to be with his family and especially his children again as he felt that they were at an age where they needed their father and that his desire was to be where he could see his children and try to make up for some of the things that he had not been able to do for them.

This man continues to have the best outlook and morale of anyone in the institution and I strongly recommend that he be considered favorably for parole.'

This time Dietrich decided to write a covering letter to Colonel Snodgrass of the Judge Advocate's Office and whom he seems to have met on a number of occasions at Landsberg. He assured him that, while the rejection of his first application had been a disappointment, he felt no bitterness and considered that 'the gambles of war and those of Parole are the same'. He assured him, though, that the views which he had expressed in his letter to Colonel Moore which accompanied his first application had not changed. [37]

This time it was eight months before a pronouncement was made. On 17 January 1955 General Hoge rejected the application. Once again, Dietrich immediately applied again. This time he proposed to live in a furnished room in Heidelberg and to work for the Building Society *Wurstenhoth* in Ludwigsburg as an agent. Since it is some distance from Heidelberg to Ludwigsburg one presumes that he would be based in the latter for his work. Colonel Moore wrote:

'This inmate took the denial of his second application in his stride but expressed great disappointment. He stated substantially as follows: He could not understand why it took 8 months for action, and that action then being a denial. He said that he was at a loss to understand this because of what he had heard of American justice and fair-play, this did not tie in as this situation did not seem to follow the right pattern. He stated, he had had many offers from outsiders for assistance in securing his parole but had refused all of them, because he did not want the Board or any higher headquarters to receive the impression that there was any pressure being brought on them on his behalf. He stated, he was going to continue to refuse outside help of any kind because he felt that he would receive proper consideration through the proper channels. He further stated, that inasmuch as he did not know why his second application for parole was denied, that the only thing, he felt, he could do was to resubmit the same application that he had forwarded before. He stated, he wanted to apply immediately because he was eligible, and he felt that he might get earlier consideration, and that his one desire was to be free in order to be with his children again as this has been his main hope all along to be with his family once more.' [38]

The parole board, however, had reservations about his parole plan, probably because they considered that there was not sufficient supervision over Dietrich's daily life. Eugen Engelhardt, who had offered him the post with the Building Society, now proposed that he should come and work as a clerk in the commercial and advertising agency firm *Ernst Grieshaber*, which was owned and run by him and his wife. It was in Ludwigsburg and Dietrich could live with them. This was approved by the parole officers at the US High Commission, who also proposed that Dietrich should have two parole officers, as opposed to the normal one. Engelhardt was to be one, while Doctor Adolf Schwartzkopf, the Moninger family's physician, who had been the original sponsor, should be the other. The reason for this was to 'extend every possible means for the subject's reconciliation with his family'. [39] An examination of Dietrich's visit and mail registers in Landsberg reveals that Ursula, who up until then had visited very regularly, did not come to Landsberg again after 29 January 1954 and that there was a sharp decline in the correspondence between the two in 1954 as compared with earlier years. It may therefore be that Ursula had lost hope of him being paroled and had decided that she and the boys must live more independently of him.

In spite of the efforts of Colonel Moore and the parole officers, the United States authorities remained unconvinced. A Judge Adjutant General's report of May 1955 considered Dietrich '. . . an unscrupulous and aggressive opportunist . . . Character of Dietrich not changed during incarceration . . . tried to smuggle out political articles against the German Federal Republic just before the 1953 elections . . . third parole application should be rejected.'[40] Thus on 23 May 1955 it was formally turned down. In this case, the Commander-in-Chief United States Army Europe was General Anthony C McAuliffe, the man who had defended Bastogne in December 1944, but whether his personal feelings came into play cannot be established. Four other Malmédy prisoners were, however, granted parole at this time.

There is no doubt that the Director of Landsberg, Colonel Moore, did have much sympathy with the plight of the inmates and what he did on Dietrich's behalf is but one example. This was acknowledged by the prisoners. On the occasion of Moore's 56th birthday, 3 May 1955, Dietrich made a speech on behalf of all the inmates. He spoke of their deep appreciation of Moore's understanding of their problems, and went onto say that 'none of us has ever acknowledged the legal situation and the resulting consequences under which we have been kept here since the end of the war. But, on the other hand '. . . we don't expect you to act against orders from above.'[41] Dietrich then presented him with a copy of a Spikweg painting of the early 19th century. In August, however, Moore's term of office came to an end and the occasion was marked by another Dietrich speech.

'. . . we know that it is not your fault that we are still here – after such an unbelievably long period of imprisonment – but that you did all you could to get us out of here. . .
. . . you have not only treated us correctly, which should be self-evident of course, but you have always tried to understand us, our problems and worries and those of our families and it is not an exaggeration to say that you have helped us whenever you could. Of course, this was also a very intelligent policy from the general point of view of the American Army, as it was the best way to try and balance the bitterness which we feel because of our more than 10 years unfair and unjust imprisonment; and furthermore, your more than fair personal attitude towards us has made it impossible for us to make any trouble here, which we would have perhaps otherwise have done, but then this would have been unfair to you.'[42]

As a leaving present from the prisoners, Moore received a wooden cigar box. What, however, is significant about Dietrich's speech was the fact that the prisoners would have seriously contemplated making trouble if the Director had been less humane in his approach. In the continuing dilemma over the Landsberg prisoners, especially the Malmédy men, it is very likely that Moore was carefully chosen for the post just to minimise the possibility of trouble inside the prison which would have inevitably added to the overall problem and caused increased embarrassment for both the American and German authorities.

Dietrich, himself waited until July 1955 before applying for parole once more. It may well have been that he wanted to gauge which way the wind was blowing now that the Federal German Republic had obtained full sovereignty and, indeed, become a full member of the NATO alliance. This gave her the right to raise her own armed forces once more, and Wolf-Dieter Dietrich, who was in the age bracket for conscription for the *Bundeswehr*, recalls going before a selection board and being warmly welcomed, with enquiries as to his father's well-being. Wolf-Dieter's reply was that he had no wish to be a member of the *Bundeswehr* until his father had been released. He was never conscripted and neither were his two brothers.[43] Sepp Dietrich submitted his fourth parole application on 18 July. Three months later came the news that it had been accepted and, on 22 October 1955, he turned his back on Landsberg for what he hoped would be the last time. He left behind him just three of the Malmédy men, but the last of these, Joachim Peiper would be released just before Christmas the following year.

It was purposely a quiet departure, but when the news got out there were protests from various American veterans' organisations. The press, however, noted it, but with little comment. Thus the London *Times* merely contented itself with reminding its readers that Dietrich was credited with killing Röhm during the Night of the Long Knives after Röhm had refused to commit suicide.[44]

The conditions of Sepp Dietrich's parole were strict, as they were for all war criminals. For a start, there was no question of him being allowed home, even for the briefest of visits. Instead, he had to proceed by the 'most direct route' to Ludwigsburg and report immediately to Eugen Engelhardt, who was to send off a report to the US Parole Officer within forty-eight hours of Dietrich's release from prison. Dietrich was not allowed to leave the *Land* Baden-Württemberg without written permission of the US Parole Officer and every two weeks had to submit a written report to the latter. Nor surprisingly, he was not allowed to indulge in any form of political activity, nor could he issue any written or oral public statement of a personal, historical or military nature without prior approval. He was to keep away from bad company, which included his co-defendants at Dachau and, indeed, anyone convicted of war crimes. He would, however, be allowed to visit his family in Karlsruhe at weekends and public holidays, provided he took the most direct travel route.[45]

For Sepp Dietrich now began a long struggle to become a proper part of his family, which with the war and his imprisonment, he had never been. Wolf-Dieter Dietrich remembers that with each weekend visit the barriers were gradually broken down. Yet, he never spoke to his family about what he had gone through during the past ten years, although they could all sense his bitterness. While he was very interested in his sons, he never tried to dictate to them how they should live their lives. Certainly, he never attempted actively to encourage them to become soldiers, although he did say on one occasion that if they joined the *Bundeswehr* they should aim to become officers of high rank. While the Moninger brewery probably ensured that the family had no financial problems, Sepp himself had little money, apart from the salary which Eugen Engelhardt paid him, which was some DM400 per month. As a member of the Waffen-SS he was not entitled to a state war pension, unlike his Wehrmacht counterparts and civil servants, although many former SS men managed to get round this. Thus the widow of Reinhard Heydrich received DM1000 per month on the grounds that her husband's death, which had been the work of Czech patriots in Prague in 1942, had been the 'direct result of war' and not a political act.[46] Indeed, this was a major reason why in 1954 the *Hilfsorganisation auf Gegenseitigkeit der Waffen SS* (Waffen SS Self-Help Organisation) or HIAG, as it is better known, was founded. Obviously, under the terms of his parole, Dietrich could not have anything to do with it.

Meanwhile, the Federal German Government was continuing to pursue war crimes, although rather than being 'crimes against peace' and crimes against humanity, as the Allies had viewed them, they were seen as crimes in violation of existing statutes against murder and manslaughter. They covered not only the war but the period of the Third Reich, from its inception. Early in 1956, the Munich authorities began a detailed investigation into the Night of the Long Knives and, in August, arrested Sepp Dietrich and Michael Lippert for their part in it. They were released on bail and would have to wait ten months before the case was heard. Their lawyer was Dr Alfred Seidl, who had defended Rudolf Hess at Nuremberg. Dietrich himself had been using Dr Seidl's legal advice while he was in Landsberg, and it is certain that he was a relation to his first wife, probably a brother. Indeed, Dietrich also occasionally wrote to Betti while in Landsberg and, at one point the mail register gives the same address for both. Seidl himself is still alive and practising in Munich, but efforts by the author to make contact with him in order to confirm this failed.

Dietrich and Lippert were both charged with manslaughter. In Dietrich's case the charge related to the list of six SA men which had been given to him by Hitler, and for Lippert it was Röhm. The trial opened in Munich on 6 May 1957 and attracted much attention since there had always been widespread curiosity over exactly what had taken place on 29-30 June 1934 and this was the opportunity to find out. The story of what did happen, as much as it can be pieced together, has already been recounted in Chapter Three. Suffice it to say that Dietrich did not deny having carried out Hitler's order, while Lippert asserted that he had stayed outside the door of Röhm's cell and had never entered it. Only Eicke went inside. It was noticeable, however, that Dietrich referred to Hitler as '*der Führer*' and defended the Waffen SS. 'If you study their careers in and after the war you will have to agree that they were a respectable, clean lot', he told the court.[47] On 10 May, came the summing-up and Dr Weiss, the prosecutor demanded a sentence of twenty-seven months for

Dietrich and two years for Lippert. Both represented a 'pitiless, police-state system', but that Dietrich 'will always remain a puzzle . . . but Dietrich was given the task because he was the loyal follower of Hitler'. Lippert was much the more intelligent of the two.[48] On Monday 13 May, the two defendants were invited to make personal statements. Dietrich declined, while Lippert pleaded that he was a patriot. The next day, the President of the Court, Dr Graf, found both guilty and gave each an eighteen month sentence. He viewed Dietrich as a 'simple man', but whose wartime achievements showed that he had sufficient intelligence to recognise that the killings were illegal. On the other hand he had 'shown the more insight and, in carrying out the deed, the evil of his own action came to his conscience and he showed it by staying in the background'. Furthermore, the President had also taken into consideration the fact that Dietrich's 'bravery and comradely bearing are generally recognised'. Lippert, in contrast, he considered as 'filled with a dangerous and unrepentant fanaticism'.[49]

Dietrich did not begin to serve his sentence until 7 August 1958, presumably because of appeals but, when he did so, it was once more at Landsberg. It is difficult to imagine what must have gone through his mind to find himself back in the same prison, then as a prisoner of his wartime enemies, but now as a prisoner of his own country. Like the old soldier that he was, though, it was just one more burden to be borne and he probably gritted his teeth as he had done so often in his life. This time, though, his body was to let him down. The circulatory problems with his legs became worse and matters were aggravated by the onset of a serious heart condition. This resulted in his premature release on 2 February 1959. Now, at last, especially since his parole terms had now been dropped, he could spend time with his family under the same roof.

The family settled in Ludwigsburg, acquiring the house next door to that of Eugen Engelhardt in Hohenzollernstrasse. For the few years remaining to him, Sepp Dietrich, besides his family, devoted himself to HIAG and hunting. Indeed, it was through their common interest in the last-named that Wolf-Dieter says that he really got to know his father, although they never actually hunted together. Indeed, Sepp's medical problems precluded him from indulging himself in the sport as much as he would have liked. With HIAG it was a different matter. To the former members of the Waffen-SS Dietrich was the hero that he always had been. One German newspaper, reporting a gathering of some sixteen thousand HIAG members at Hamelin in August 1959, noted that Dietrich's arrival on the platform was greeted with 'enthusiastic applause lasting several minutes'.[50] Indeed, as the right wing monthly *Deutsche Soldatenzeitung* (German Soldiers' Newspaper) described him, Dietrich was regarded as a 'commander respected by all of us – a soldier who never acted other than in the interest of his Fatherland'.[51] Yet, there were those both inside the Federal Republic and without, who looked with concern at what seemed to be an increasing aura of respectability being accorded to Hitler's men. It was this which was a main theme of John Dornberg's *Schizophrenic Germany*, which was published in 1961. It was also one of the centrepieces of the German Democratic Republic's ceaseless propaganda against its capitalist other half. Typical of this was a publication entitled *War and Nazi Criminals in West Germany*, which provided a 'list of SS, SD and Gestapo murderers who penetrate the state, police and economic apparatus of West Germany and the special territory of West Berlin or who occupy respectable positions in public life'. Dietrich's name was listed, with the fact that he was active in HIAG and that his troops had 'committed crimes against humanity in the Soviet Union, Italy and France', as well as Malmédy.[52]

It is unlikely that this criticism bothered Dietrich much. John Toland, the distinguished American historian, recalls meeting Sepp at a HIAG picnic at this time and was impressed by the stoicism with which he had accepted his fate.[53] He was content to be with his family and former comrades and, apart from his HIAG activities, stayed well clear of politics. When his end came, it was quiet. On 21 April 1966 he died of a massive heart attack in his bed.

CHAPTER 12

In Perspective

Sepp Dietrich's funeral took place at Ludwigsburg and was attended by some six thousand people, mainly former Waffen-SS comrades. His coffin was covered with the flag of the Iron Cross and resting on it were a helmet and sword. Six Knights of the Iron Cross bore it to the graveside and the many wreaths were carried by former members of the *Leibstandarte*. The funeral oration was given by General Willi Bittrich, who, bearing in mind that Sepp always hated 'to make a lot of words', kept it very short. Indeed, 'We cannot express our thoughts and feelings at the farewell of the soldier Sepp Dietrich in words. Only our hearts can speak!'.[1] After further speeches, those present ended the proceedings by spontaneously singing the song of the Waffen-SS.

What upset his former comrades most were the obituaries in some sections of the West German press which sneered at Dietrich's lowly origins and asserted that, as such, he was unfitted for the high rank which he achieved. An editorial in *Die Freiwillige* (The Volunteer), the house journal of HIAG, saw the implication that 'it was disgraceful to rise from a travelling journeyman to Colonel General and leader of the 6th SS Panzer Army. Did not Freidrich Ebert as well rise from journeyman saddler and innkeeper in Bremen to be the first *Reichspresident* of the Weimar Republic?'.[2] Yet, there were few of his men who did not doubt that he was promoted beyond his capabilities. Max Wünsche admits that he did not always agree with what Dietrich ordered, although 'one can and could not deny that he had a healthy commonsense and an eye for the essential things'.[3] According to John Toland, who discussed Dietrich at length with Peiper, the latter considered that he had limitations as a commander, but performed satisfactorily provided he had a good chief of staff, which he certainly had in Kraemer.[4] We have seen, too, several other comments of this kind and it seems fairly certain that Dietrich was well aware of his own shortfalls.

Dietrich's strength lay in his appreciation of what motivated soldiers, especially when the going was hard. The secret was that he was utterly dependable and his troops knew that he would never let them down if he could possibly help it. Max Wünsche likens him to 'a lump of Bavarian rock which has yet to be hewn', but that 'he was also a person who had a heart for his men, who went through thick and thin for them. But he did not ask more of them than he was prepared to do himself.'[5] As we have seen, he was not a man given to making flamboyant speeches of exhortation, but his instinct for being at a point of crisis in person was enough to give his soldiers the inspiration that they needed. While he was commanding the *Leibstandarte* he was able to implant his personality deeply on every part of it. Indeed, one can almost say that Sepp Dietrich *was* the *Leibstandarte*. Once, however, he was elevated to the command of a corps and then an army he could no longer enjoy such direct contact with his soldiers. This he undoubtedly considered frustrating and probably found it hard to accept that the place of a corps and army commander was at his headquarters during a battle and not with the leading battalion. He was a man of action rather than a thinker and a planner, as he would have been the first to admit.

While the political hierarchy of the SS consistently tried to exacerbate the differences between the *Waffen-SS* and the *Wehrmacht*, the *Waffen*-SS generals themselves, especially Hausser, Steiner, Bittrich, and Dietrich, considered themselves as soldiers foremost. This was especially so of Sepp Dietrich who, from very early on in his life, wanted to be a professional soldier. There is no evidence, apart from his singular outburst on Rommel to Milton Shulman and his attacks on the likes of Keitel and Jodl to his American interrogators, that he voiced his dislike for the *Wehrmacht* field commanders, the majority of whom he clearly admired. They themselves clearly found it more difficult to reciprocate. Dietrich's earthy manner was not what they were used to and there was always the lingering suspicion that whatever they said to Dietrich, would be immediately reported back to Hitler. An illustration of this was when von Manstein visited the headquarters of the *Leibstandarte* in the early spring of 1943. Rudolf Lehmann recalls that von Manstein initially made it very clear that he wanted to avoid Dietrich, preferring his staff to brief him. Von Manstein then made to depart, but Dietrich asked him to come into his office for a drink. As usual, it was cognac and, once it had been served, Rudolf Lehmann, who was present, states that Dietrich said:

> ' ''Herr *Generalfeldmarschall*, I have the impression that you think I have a special line to the *Führerhauptquartier*. I can formally report to you that this is not the case. I lead my division like any of my neighbouring commanders, without evading official channels.'' When mentioning the *Führerhauptoquartier*, Sepp Dietrich did not express himself formally but said literally: ''. . . a special line to that one'', while he was pointing to his upper lip. The GFM stood up and replied: ''*Obergruppenführer* Dietrich, that was a good word at the right time. I have to beg your pardon.'' '[6]

Yet, it does seem that Dietrich did have such a direct line of communication over the time of the July 1944 bomb plot, although this may well have been to Himmler's rather than Hitler's headquarters. Furthermore, there is no doubt that some *Wehrmacht* generals did take advantage of the close contacts that Dietrich enjoyed with Hitler. All this, of course, belies what many German generals told their interrogators immediately after the war, but one cannot help feeling that much of this was in an effort to save their own skins. By distancing themselves from the *Waffen*-SS and claiming that they were professional soldiers merely carrying out orders, as opposed to ideological men-at-arms, they hoped to create a favourable impression, which would gain them sympathy.

Much evidence has been given in this book that Dietrich himself was not an ideologically committed Nazi. True, he owed the high position which he eventually reached almost entirely to Hitler, who had pulled him up from obscurity. Yet, Dietrich's involvement with Hitler must be seen in the context of the confusion and disillusionment that was Germany in the years after 1918. Anarchy and brutality were inevitable as the German people struggled to swallow the bitter pill of defeat and to salvage something from the wreckage created by Versailles. Having always been used to strong government, many could not accept that what they perceived as the watery democratic approach of the Weimar Republic was the right way forward. Internal conflict within a state inevitably drives people to extremes, and this was what happened in Germany's case. For those who feared the spectre of Russian-dominated Communism, Hitler's creed began to offer an increasingly hopeful alternative. The discipline, which was an inherent part of his policy, was something that appealed to the German character, and Fascism seemed to be the best way to make Germany great once more. Where their perceptions were flawed was over the nature of the state that Hitler created once he had gained power. It became an absolute dictatorship which would brook no opposition and brutality became endemic. Nothing can lessen the guilt of either party or nation for the instigation of 'The Final Solution' or the existence and nature of the concentration camps. As a man of limited intelligence, who had finally decided to hitch his wagon to Hitler's star, Sepp Dietrich was prepared to give his *Führer* complete personal loyalty. However, that did not mean that he was prepared to do the same for Hitler's subordinates. He soon realised the nature of Himmler's warped mentality and did everything possible to avoid getting bound to him. This, however, brought him into conflict with Hausser. To Dietrich, it was inevitable that they would have the same differences, given Hausser was a general staff officer of the old school, while Dietrich had been merely a warrant officer in the old army, however both agreed that the *Leibstandarte* should not become an ideological battleground and that it was first and foremost a military unit. Given, too, the growing evidence of corruption and skulduggery among Hitler's underlings, as they wrestled with one another for even greater power, Dietrich became more and more inward looking, concentrating merely on the *Leibstandarte* and keeping well out of politics.

Yet, the popular view of Sepp Dietrich, to use William Shirer's words, is as 'one of the most brutal men of the Third Reich'.[7] True his manner and the reputation gained when he was responsible for Hitler's security, prior to the formation of the *Leibstandarte*, support this. It could also be argued that the Night of the Long Knives also reinforces that view. On the other hand, as far as Dietrich was concerned, he was carrying out a direct order from Hitler in a highly charged situation. The evidence available shows that what occurred was a source of deep shock and concern to him. Even then, though, as the court in Munich in 1957 accepted, he did have second thoughts when actually confronting those whom he had to execute and the evidence of 'Putzi' Hanfstaengl indicates that he was afterwards very shaken.

Shirer's comment, however, is probably as much directed towards the atrocities committed by the *Waffen*-SS troops under Dietrich's command during the years 1939-1945. In this context, there is no doubt that unit discipline within the *Leibstandarte* during the campaigns in Poland, the Low Countries and France was not all that apologists would have us believe. The incidents of looting in Poland and Holland were many and, as well as a lack of fire control, as evidenced in the wounding of General Student in Rotterdam, are signs of bad discipline. The shooting of the British prisoners at Wormhoudt in May 1940 is a more serious indicator. Significantly, it is the one atrocity charge levelled against *Leibstandarte* which Rudolf Lehmann does not mention in his definitive history. To others in Russia and Italy he is at great pains to refute, and those in the Ardennes are outside the trilogy, which finishes at the end of 1943. While it is obvious that Dietrich had nothing to do with the actual murders of the Royal Warwicks and others, since he was stuck in his ditch, it would have been very surprising if knowledge of it had not come to his ears afterwards, that is unless Mohnke imposed the oath of secrecy at battalion level. Yet, there is no evidence that Dietrich every initiated any form of inquiry or disciplined Mohnke and one can only presume that, if he did know about it, he decided to keep quiet since, if the news got out, it would sully the name of the *Leibstandarte*, to which he was so devoted. Nevertheless, his failure to act made him an accessory after the fact. Interestingly, Hoepner's XVI Corps headquarters did demand an enquiry into the parallel massacre of British prisoners carried out by the *Totenkopf* at Le Paradis, but Himmler's headquarters did nothing about it. Indeed, the officer responsible, Fritz Knochlein, finished the war as a regimental commander and holder of the Knight's Cross, before finally being tried and hanged by the British.

In the 1941 campaign in the Balkans and Greece the *Leibstandarte* had matured and there are no recorded incidents of ill discipline, let alone atrocities. Indeed, the treatment of prisoners, Greek and British, seems to have been a model of chivalry. Russia, on the other hand, was a very different matter, especially given the fanaticism with which both sides fought. However, the two specific incidents of brutality on the part of Dietrich's men are difficult to substantiate. We have already seen the confusion of historians brought about by Erich Kern's description of Soviet prisoners being shot as a result of atrocities on German troops, especially the six *Leibstandarte* corpses found in Taganrog. As for Kharkov, the incident at the hospital is equally difficult to prove either way. For a start, apart from one brief mention of it by the Soviet Prosecutor at Nuremberg, in the context that evidence on it had been submitted to the court,[8] the Soviets took no further steps to see that the alleged perpetrators were brought to justice until 1967. Then they submitted evidence to the Federal German Government, and this was largely based on the findings of the investigatory commission of September 1943. In response the judicial authorities in Nuremberg carried out a lengthy inquiry, examining no less than 688 witnesses, all but thirteen of whom were former members of the *Leibstandarte*. Only four of them professed to having ever heard of Soviet prisoners having been shot and the general view was that the *Leibstandarte* would never have been permitted to shoot defenceless prisoners. What could be established, though, was that the hospital itself was within the area of the attack made by 1st SS Panzer Grenadier Regiment and that the main Soviet defensive belt was just north of the hospital. It is thus very likely that it became embroiled in the battle and, given that street fighting is often confused and merciless, it is quite possible that *Leibstandarte* soldiers may have believed that they were being fired upon from the hospital and decided to eradicate all possible opposition inside it. On the other hand, it could have been a fabrication done for propaganda purposes. In any event, the court found that there was insufficient evidence for individual culprits to be identified and no further action was taken.[9] On the other side of the coin, however, Lehmann quotes an eyewitness of the disinterring for identification purposes of the bodies of the *Leibstandarte* who had been killed during the original withdrawal from Kharkov:

'Here we saw a picture I had never seen before and would never see again in my life: all of the men were undressed, and heavily mutilated. A lot of them, who had gone missing at the time, were slain, stabbed to death, had cut off limbs and eyes put out. Thus it was difficult to identify them. . . From this moment, we were paranoid about being taken prisoner by the Russians.'[10]

That the war on the Eastern Front was brutalising there is no doubt and one cannot but help repeat Max Wünsche's comment that no one who had not fought on it could have any conception what it was like. Those who wish to moralise on it are on weak ground if they have no personal experience of it. The brutality on both sides was horrific. Both Wehrmacht and the SS had much to answer for, particularly after the outbreak of partisan warfare. That the Russians behaved as they did, was in no small part due to the savagery of the treatment meted out by the Germans to many thousands of peasants and villagers.

The 1944 campaigns in the West were, however, a different matter. Here it was expected that both sides would observe the rules of war. Yet atrocities did occur. Panzer Meyer was found guilty, as commander of the 25th SS Panzer Grenadier Regiment of the *Hitlerjugend*, of the massacre of forty-five Canadian prisoners in Normandy on 8 June 1944, although, as has already been stated, Sepp Dietrich asserted that he did try and conduct an inquiry at the time. This now brings us to the most emotive area of all, that of the Ardennes. What is clear from examining the judicial procedures surrounding the trial was that, as far as the Americans were concerned, it was not just Peiper and his men, but all Waffen-SS who fought in the Ardennes who were on trial and were guilty from the start. As has been said before, no one can deny that atrocities took place in the Ardennes. However, given the circumstances of *Kampfgruppe* Peiper's mission, which became one of deep penetration and was carried out amidst increasing confusion, both because of Peiper's lack of communication with divisional headquarters and because his men had cut deep into the American lines, there was inevitably a great deal of nervousness and a tendency to fire first and ask questions afterwards. Thus, some at least of the atrocities were hardly premeditiated, and indeed can be put under the label of 'accidents of war'. Others, though, especially the murder of Belgian civilians, even given Dietrich's warning over the Resistance, were inexcusable. It must, however, be pointed out that the Americans, too, were guilty of atrocities in the Ardennes. In the aftermath of Malmédy there were numerous incidents, as Jean Paul Pallud in his in-depth study *The Battle of the Bulge; Then and Now*[11] reveals. 328th US Infantry Regiment, which was part of 26th Infantry Division, in its order for 21 December 1944, specified that 'No SS troops or paratroopers will be taken prisoner but will be shot on sight' and Pallud goes on to detail a number of incidents when this order was actually put into effect by US units.[12] Revenge, however, is not considered as an extenuating circumstance in the Geneva Convention and hence the Americans were just as guilty as their enemy of atrocities. The only difference was that they were the eventual victors. Unfortunately, in the singular circumstances of combat, where it is so often a matter of whose finger is first to squeeze the trigger and emotions are stretched to their ultimate, the Laws of War are often broken.

Notwithstanding this, there is the matter of whether Dietrich himself ever gave any order, written or verbal, that in certain circumstances the shooting of prisoners was allowed. It would have been surprising, given the desperate situation at the time, if Dietrich had not exhorted his men to fight ruthlessly and, as Colonel Bresee pointed out in his review of the Malmédy case, this was a perfectly reasonable order. Likewise, there was nothing illegal about warning his men of Resistance activity. Indeed, the treatment of armed civilians not wearing a recognisable uniform is not subject to the Geneva Convention. As for prisoner handling, it is worth pointing out that it was common German practice to issue the administrative order separately from the operational order, as is still the NATO procedure today, and that prisoners would be covered by the former. Kraemer's assertion that he ordered collecting points for prisoners to be set up and that leading tactical elements were not to concern themselves with them is also logical and makes sound military sense. The prosecution could produce no primary written evidence that Dietrich had given any order that prisoners were to be shot in certain circumstances and could only point to the extrajudicial confessions, which were later retracted, as evidence. At best, therefore, the case is non proven and it is hard not to conclude that the Americans were determined to bring Dietrich to book, not for what he or his troops might have done, but merely because of who he was. For a man who saw himself as solely a professional soldier and not a Nazi fanatic, it does not seem to be in character that he would have actively countenanced such behaviour in his troops. For many reasons, as have been shown, the Malmédy trial was a miscarriage of justice, but it was so because the intense pressure of American public opinion would accept no other result than guilty verdicts for all the defendants.

During Dietrich's ten years in prison there is no doubt that he conducted himself with dignity and resilience, as he did at and after the 1957 Munich trial. The prison authorities at Landsberg, especially Colonel Moore, praised him for his honesty and openness, qualities which his *Waffen*-SS comrades also recognised. Yet, there is one niggle of doubt over this and that is why Dietrich should have been so cagey about aspects of his early life? Why did he for so long have it believed that he had originally been a cavalryman rather than artilleryman? Why was he so contradictory about his dates of service in the *Landespolizei* and the jobs he took after it? Why did he pretend to have been a regular soldier from 1911 onwards? There is no clearcut explanation to this, especially since his record of service during the First World War was nothing to be ashamed of. One can only surmise that he felt keenly that it was a disgrace to have been invalided out after only a month's service and that the cavalry had a greater social cachet than the field artillery. As for the post-war period, no documentary evidence has been found that he was in fact a member of the Oberland and that which does exist is merely that of Hans Weber, a fellow Oberlander, and the fact that Dietrich held the Silesian Eagle. Nevertheless, it would have been in character for him to have fought in Upper Silesia. For Dietrich to have left the Munich Police in 1923 would have been logical if he had taken part in the November Beer Hall putsch, and it was this date which he put in his SS Personal forms. Yet, it was not until 1927 that he actually left the police and, bearing in mind the post-putsch purge, it is unlikely that Dietrich would have been allowed to serve on if he had taken an active part as an Oberlander in the events of 8-9 November 1923. It is therefore very possible that he was not involved, but that the assertion that he did was a 'window dressing' exercise by the Nazi propaganda machine in order to give him, in his capacity as one of Hitler's inner circle the right type of 'respectability'. In spite of these doubts, there was clearly much in Dietrich's character that appealed to his soldiers and officers and also to those who came to know him in later years. That he was a very brave man is certain, and this was not just physical bravery, but also moral bravery, especially when it came to men's interests versus the hierarchy of the Third Reich. Even given his rough exterior, he was essentially a very warm man underneath. John Toland, who met him in his last years, formed a very favourable impression of him and wanted to reverse the picture that he had earlier painted in his *Battle: The Story of the Bulge* as a 'burly, rather uncouth chap with a taste for alcohol'.[13] Indeed, the popular image of him was largely shaped by Allied wartime and immediate post-war propaganda.

In truth, Sepp Dietrich was a child of his time, whose career personified the lives of many Germans who lived in the first part of the 20th century. Indeed, he was present on stage, or just off in the wings, for many of the momentous events that are the history of Germany in these troubled times. That he had outstanding natural leadership qualities there is no doubt. He also achieved some remarkable successes as a general, given that he lacked the training and education normally enjoyed by commanders of his seniority. Yet, in many ways he was just an ordinary man, who saw himself as nothing more than a simple soldier faithful to the ideals of duty, honour and Fatherland. In following these precepts he at times made choices, or avoided making them, with consequences that on other grounds must be regarded as morally reprehensible. Unfortunately, though, he was probably not intelligent enough always to perceive where his actions would lead. There were many Germans like him.

It can also be argued that he was a man propelled to the forefront of German history by forces not under his control and was not master of his own destiny. Nevertheless, as a powerful member of the Third Reich, who had Hitler's ear, he cannot be absolved of all responsibility for what happened during the years 1918-1945. The extent of that responsibility must itself depend upon how much one believes the maxim that men must bear the burden of the consequences of their actions, whatever the circumstances which surround them. Notwithstanding this, those veterans of the *Waffen*-SS who served under him will continue to revere him for as long as they live. To the rest of us Sepp Dietrich should be judged as a man caught up in the evil of his times who none the less and according to his own lights normally behaved with honour and devoted dedication to a mistaken cause.

APPENDIX 1

Text of the Surrender Terms agreed by Sepp Dietrich and Greek General Tsolakoglou on 20 April 1941

III Army Corps [Greek]
Chief of General Staff

Protocol

On the armistice concluded between us and the Germans

The signing Generals of the brave German and Greek Armies, Dietrich and Tsolakoglou have met today on 20 April 1941 in Votonassi as representatives of their armies and have agreed the following:

1. Hostilities between Greece and Germany will cease today, at 18 hrs. A couple of hours later, the hostilities between Greece and Italy will cease, through the mediation of the German Commander-in-Chief.

2. The German Army will be granted passage from (one word is missing in the original Greek text) until Monday 21 April in order to place itself between the Italian and Greek forces, thus facilitating the bringing about of the following agreements:

    (a) The Greek Army is obliged to withdraw behind the prewar Greek-Albanian border within 10 days.

    (b) The armies in Epirus and Macedonia will be demobilised. The soldiers are to hand over their weapons at collecting points especially designated by the leadership and then they go home.

    (c) As a matter of honour, officers are to keep their equipment and weapons and are not considered as prisoners. The army will be newly organised and the officers will be subject to orders according to Greek law.

    (d) The Greek Army will be responsible for its own catering.

Signatures

Commander-in-Chief of the Greek Army in the Epirus and Peloponnese	Commander of the Leibstandarte SS Adolf Hitler
C. Tsolakoglou Lieutenant General	Dietrich General

(Copy in German obtained from Paul Zimmermann via Hubert Meyer. A slightly different and longer version is given in Rudolf Lehmann *Die Leibstandarte* Vol I pp 462-463.)

APPENDIX 2

Waffen-SS Divisions

1st SS Panzer Division	Leibstandarte Adolf Hitler	Germans
2nd SS Panzer Division	Das Reich	Germans
3rd SS Panzer Division	Totenkopf	Germans
4th SS Police Panzer Grenadier Division		Germans
5th SS Panzer Division	Wiking	Germans
6th SS Mountain Division	Nord	Germans
7th SS Mountain Division	Prinz Eugen	Ethnic Germans
8th SS Cavalry Division	Florian Geyer	Germans/Ethnic Germans
9th SS Panzer Division	Hohenstaufen	Germans
10th SS Panzer Division	Frundsberg	Germans
11th SS Panzer Grenadier Division	Nordland	Germans/Scandinavians
12th SS Panzer Division	Hitlerjugend	Germans
13th SS Mountain Division	Handschar	Yugoslavs
14th SS Grenadier Division	Galizische No 1	Ukrainians
15th SS Grenadier Division	Lettische No 1	Latvians/Germans
16th SS Panzer Grenadier Division	Reichsfuhrer-SS	Germans/Ethnic Germans
17th SS Panzer Grenadier Division	Götz von Berlichingen	Germans/Ethnic Germans
18th SS Panzer Grenadier Division	Horst Wessel	Germans/Ethnic Germans
19th SS Grenadier Division	Lettische No 2	Latvians

HG—H

20th SS Grenadier Division	Estnische No 1	Estonians
21st SS Mountain Division	Albanische No 1 – Skanderberg	Albanians
22nd SS Cavalry Division	Maria Theresa	Germans/Ethnic Germans
23rd SS Panzer Division	Kama	Yugoslavs
23rd SS Panzer Division	Nederland	Dutch
24th SS Mountain Division	Karstjäger	Italians/Ethnic Germans
25th SS Grenadier Division	Hunyadi No 1	Hungarians
26th SS Grenadier Division	Hunyadi No 2	Hungarians
27th SS Grenadier Division	Langemarck	Flemish/Belgians
28th SS Grenadier Division	Wallonie	Walloons/Belgians
29th SS Grenadier Division	Russische No 1	Russians
29th SS Grenadier Division	Italische No 1	Italians
30th SS Grenadier Division	Russische No 2	Russians
31st SS Grenadier Division		Germans
32nd SS Panzer Division	Böhmen-Mahren	Germans/Ethnic Germans
33rd SS Grenadier Division	January 30	Germans
34th SS Grenadier Division	Charlemagne	French
35th SS Grenadier Division	Landstorm Nederland	Dutch
36th SS Police Grenadier Division		Germans
37th SS Grenadier Division	Dirlewanger	Germans
38th SS Cavalry Division	Lutzow	Ethnic Germans
39th SS Panzer Grenadier Division	Nibelungen	SS cadets

APPENDIX 3

Waffen-SS Ranks with US and British equivalents

Waffen SS	Britain	U.S.A.
SS Oberst-Gruppenführer und Generaloberst der Waffen SS*	Field-Marshal	General of Army (5 stars)
	General	General (4 stars)
SS Obergruppenführer und General der Waffen SS**	Lieutenant-General	Lieutenant-General (3 stars)
SS Gruppenführer und Generalleutnant der Waffen SS**		
	Major-General	Major-General (2 stars)
SS Brigadeführer und Generalmajor der Waffen SS**		Brigadier-General (1 star)
SS Oberführer	Brigadier	
SS Standartenführer	Lieutenant-Colonel	Lieutenant-Colonel
SS Sturmbannführer	Major	Major
SS Haupsturmführer	Captain	Captain
SS Obersturmführer	Lieutenant	First Lieutenant
SS Untersturmführer	Second-Lieutenant	Second-Lieutenant
SS Sturmscharführer	Warrant Officer 1st Class (RSM)	Sergeant-Major
SS Hauptscharführer	Warrant Officer 2nd Class (CSM etc.)	1st and Master Sergeant
SS Oberscharführer	Quartermaster-Sergeant (RQMS/CQMS etc.)	Technical-Sergeant
SS Scharführer	Staff-Sergeant	Staff-Sergeant
SS Unterscharführer	Sergeant	Sergeant
SS Rottenführer	Corporal	Corporal
SS Sturmann	Lance-Corporal	Acting Corporal
SS Oberschütze		Private 1st Class
SS Mann,*** SS Schütze, SS Panzerschütze etc.	Private, Rifleman, etc.	Private etc.

* Rank introduced on 7th April 1942.
** Waffen SS rank introduced in late 1940.
*** Discontinued during the war.
No precise equivalents can be given in every case, especially with those of General rank.

Source Notes

Full bibliographical details are only given where the work is not mentioned in the bibliography.

CHAPTER 1

1. For example, MacDonald, Charles B *The Battle of the Bulge* p160 and Weingartner, James J *Sepp Dietrich, Heinrich Himmler and the Leibstandarte SS Adolf Hitler 1933-1938* Central European History Vol 1 (1968) No 3 p265.
2. Medical Report, No 1 War Criminal Prison, Landsberg, dated 27 August 1948 (Dietrich's Parole File, US National Archives, Washington DC, Record Group 338).
3. Baedeker, Karl *Southern Germany including Württemberg and Bavaria* (Baedeker, Leipzig, 1895) pp33-34, p199.
4. There is much conflict among sources over details of Dietrich's early life. I have used an amalgam of Degener, H A L *Wer ist's*, Shroeder, Christa *Er war mein Chef* p327 n103, Krätschmer, E-G *Die Ritterkreuzträger der Waffen-SS* p13, Dietrich's SS Personal File (Document Center, Berlin), Parole Application dated 14 November 1953 (Parole File), US Seventh Army Interrogation Report SAIC/43 dated 11 June 1945 (US National Archives, Washington DC, Record Group 238) and information from Dip.-Ing Anton Joachimsthaler based on personal data gathered by No 5 Criminal Court, *Landesgericht* Munich on 4 July 1956.
5. See, for instance, SS Personal File op cit, in which Dietrich states that he was in the 1st Uhlans, which some writers have taken to mean that he was in the Prussian Army, and SAIC/43 op cit.
6. SS Personal File op cit and Parole Application dated 14 November 1953 op cit.
7. *Kurze Aufstellung meiner militärischen Laufbahn* dated 29 June 1951. Copy obtained from Paul Zimmermann via Hubert Meyer.
8. Letter Dr Heyl, *Bayerisches Hauptstaatsarchiv*, 23 April 1985.
9. Schroeder op cit. Anton Joachimsthaler, who compiled the biographical note on Dietrich, used Sepp's mobilization papers for details of his life at this time.
10. Shirach, Baldur von *Ich glaubte an Hitler* p309.
11. I have based my information on letter Dr Heyl of 23 April 1985 op cit, Munich Court deposition dated 4 July 1956 op cit and US War Crimes Office File 100-365-1 (US National Archives, Washington DC, Record Group 153).
12. Snyder, Louis L *Encyclopaedia of the Third Reich*.
13. Medical Reports dated 23 July 1946 and 20 October 1949, Dietrich Parole File op cit.
14. Ibid and Munich court deposition dated 4 July 1956 op cit, which states that this was Dietrich's only wound.
15. SS Personal File op cit.
16. I am most grateful to Dip.-Ing Franz Kosar for information on this gun.
17. Information on the formation and organisation of Stormtroops and infantry gun batteries is taken from Gruss, Helmuth *Sturmbataillone im Weltkriege*, Franke, Hermann *Handbuch der neuzeitlichen Wehrwissenschaften* pp682-685, Lupfer, Timothy L *The Dynamics of Doctrine: The Changes in German Tactical Doctrine during the First World War* and various Military Intelligence Branch, British War Office publications during 1916-1918 on the German Army.
18. *In Stahlgewitten: Ein Kriegstagebuch* (Berlin, 1926) p265.
19. Letters Dr Heyl, *Bayerisches Hauptstaatsarchiv*, 23 April and 18 June 1985.
20. Quoted, Fuller, Maj Gen J F C *Memoirs of an Unconventional Soldier* (Nicolson & Watson, London, 1936) p81.
21. I am indebted to a series of articles on the A7V by Max Hundleby and Rainer Strasheim in *Tankette*, journal of the AFV Miniature Association, for much of my information on the origins of the German tank force.

22. *Bayerischen Kriegministeriums* Nr 98 995 A dated 2 May 1918.
23. Description of this action is largely drawn from Volckheim, Maj Ernst *Die deutschen Kampfwagen im Weltkriege* pp52-62, Jones, Rarey & Icks *The Fighting Tanks since 1916* pp100-102 and information, especially on Dietrich's part, from Rainer Strasheim. The date of Dietrich's award was given by Dr Heyl.
24. Krätschmer op cit pp 16, 26. He also claims that Dietrich took part in the first German tank action on 21 March 1918, but this cannot be so.
25. The War Diary of *Abteilung* 13 gives no details and what information has been gleaned is from Edmonds, Brig Cen Sir James and Maxwell-Hyslop, Lt Col *History of the Great War: Military Operations France and Belgium 1918* Vol 5 (HMSO, 1947) pp457, 460, and Volckheim, Maj Ernst *Die deutsche Panzerwaffe* in *Die deutsche Wehrmacht 1914-1939* (Mittler, Berlin, 1939) p306.
26. *Abteilung* 13 War Diary, *Bayerisches Hauptstaatsarchiv.*

CHAPTER 2

1. Waite, Robert G L *Vanguard of Nazism: The Free Corps in Postwar Germany 1918-1923* p42.
2. Watt, Richard M *The Kings Depart* p247.
3. Abel, Theodore *Why Hitler came to Power: An answer based on the life Stories of Six Hundred of his Followers* pp25-26.
4. Krätschmer op cit p16.
5. Letter from Dr Heyl dated 29 April 1986. There are 25 volumes on *Wehrregiment* 1 held in the *Bayerisches Hauptstaatsarchiv.*
6. I am indebted to Anton Joachimsthaler for photocopies of these.
7. Letters Dr Heyl dated 23 April and 18 June 1985.
8. Schroeder op cit p327 n103.
9. Efforts to track down Dietrich's *Landespolizei* personal file proved fruitless. The Police handed over the files for policemen who served in the 1920s to the *Bayerisches Hauptstaatsarchiv* in the early 1970s, but Dietrich's was not among them. One can only conclude that it was destroyed, but when and why are impossible to establish.
10. SAIC/43 op cit.
11. Carr, William *A History of Germany 1815-1945* p302.
12. Hansard, House of Commons Debates, 1921, Fifth Session, 13 May 1921 columns 2382-2385.
13. SS Personal File and SAIC/43 op cit for example.
14. Thuron, Hans-Jörgen *Freikorps und Bund Oberland* pp78-79.
15. *The Outlaws* pp 217-218.
16. Krätschmer op cit p16.
17. Letter to the author, August 1986. Weber served in the Freikorps Oberland and is its unofficial historian.
18. Thuron op cit p108.
19. Bundesarchiv, Koblez R 43 1/2707 (Freikorps Oberland)
20. Waite op cit pp231-232.
21. Ibid p230.
22. SAIC/43 op cit.
23. Pridham, Geoffrey *Hitler's Rise to Power: The Nazi Movement in Bavaria 1923-33* p9.
24. Weingartner, James J *Hitler's Guard: The Story of the Liebstandarte Adolf Hitler 1933-1945* p3.
25. Some Oberland rolls for 8/9 November 1923 do exist, but Dietrich's name is not shown. NSDAP *Hauptarchiv* (Hoover Institute Microfilm Collection) Institute of Contemporary History and Weiner Library, London, Ref 35/704.
26. Thuron op cit p179.
27. The most detailed account is Gordon, Harold J Jr *Hitler and the Beer Hall Putsch.*
28. SAIC/43 op cit.
29. Parole Application, November 1953 op cit and Krätschmer op cit for example.

CHAPTER 3

1. Pridham op cit p41.
2. Ibid p78.
3. Cameron, Norman and Stevens, R H ed *Hitler's Table Talk 1941-44: His Private Conversations* 3 January 1942, p167.

4. SAIC/43 op cit. Dietrich told his US interrogators that he worked in the Austria Tobacco Company 1923-1929, with Christian Weber and his garage 1929-1931 and only then joined Eber Verlag, but this is contrary to other sources. See, for example, Note 5 below.
5. Horkenbach, Cuno ed *Das Deutsche Reich von 1918 bis heute* (1930 edition) p654.
6. Weingartner *Hitler's Guard* op cit p4.
7. *Illustrieter Beobachter* Vol V No 45 (8 November 1930) pp790-791.
8. Wagener, Otto *Hitler: Memoirs of a Confidant* p183.
9. Lockner, Louis P trans & ed *The Goebbels Diaries 1941-43* p288.
10. Krätschmer op cit.
11. Mollo, Andrew *To the Death's Head True: The Story of the SS* p17.
12. Wagener op cit pp239-242.
13. Ludecke, Kurt G W *I Knew Hitler: The Story of a Nazi who Escaped the Blood Purge* p468.
14. Delmer, Sefton *Trail Sinister: An Autobiography Vol I* pp147-152.
15. NSDAP *Hauptarchiv* op cit 29/549.
16. Cameron and Stevens op cit p197.
17. Munich registration forms op cit and Hoffmann, Peter *Hitler's Personal Security* p175.
18. NSDAP *Hauptarchiv* op cit 29/556.
19. Ibid 29/557-559.
20. Delmer op cit p187.

CHAPTER 4

1. US Seventh Army Interrogation Report SAIC/11 dated 11 June 1945 (US National Archives, Washington DC, Record Group 153).
2. Mollo op cit p18.
3. *Himmler: Evil Genius of the Third Reich* p37.
4. Interview with Wolf-Dieter Dietrich, 25 September 1986.
5. Dietrich to NDSAP Liaison Staff, 12 October 1933 from Weingartner *Sepp Dietrich, Heinrich Himmler. . . .* op cit p271.
6. Lehmann, Rudolf *Die Liebstandarte* Vol 1 p34 and Weingartner *Sepp Dietrich, Heinrich Himmler . . .* op cit p273.
7. Lucas, James and Cooper, Matthew *Hitler's Elite: Liebstandarte SS* pp35-36.
8. Lehmann op cit p35.
9. Ibid p47.
10. Weingartner *Sepp Dietrich, Heinrich Himmler . . .* op cit p283.
11. Weingartner *Hitler's Guard* op cit p26.
12. Dietrich Munich Registration Documents op cit and Hoffmann op cit p175.
13. Degener, H A L ed: *Wer ist's!*, Dietrich's SS Personal File op cit and Munich Registration Documents op cit.
14. Wistrich, Robert *Who's Who in Nazi Germany* p7.
15. US Office of Strategic Studies Research and Analysis Branch, Dietrich Biographical Report dated 16 September 1944 (US National Archives, Washington DC, Record Group 153, File 100-365-1).
16. SAIC/11 op cit.
17. For a contemporary account of this emphasis, see Müller, Albert *Germany's War Machine* (Dent, London, 1936).
18. Baynes, Norman H *The Speeches of Adolf Hitler, 1922-39* Vol 1 (Oxford University Press, 1942) pp865-866.
19. Seaton, Albert *The German Army 1933-45* pp45-46.
20. Shirer, William *The Rise and Fall of the Third Reich* p217.
21. SS Personal File op cit.
22. Delmer op cit pp224-225.
23. Weingartner *Hitler's Guard* op cit p12 states that the practice alert was ordered on the 23rd for the 25th and that it was also on the 25th that Deitrich visited the War Ministry. I have, however, preferred to follow Lehmann op cit pp50-51.
24. Lehmann op cit p51.
25. Many accounts state that it was Otto Dietrich, Hitler's Press Chief, who accompanied him. These probably stem from Shirer op cit p221.
26. *The Times* (London) 7 May 1957.

27. Ibid.
28. Hanfstaengl, Ernst *Hitler: The Missing Years* p252.
29. Weingartner *Hitler's Guard* op cit p17. This visitor also noted the glow in his men's eyes.
30. Hoffmann op cit p162.
31. Letter Max Wünsche (then Hitler's SS Adjutant) to Himmler, 31 August 1940. Original in the possession of Ian Sayer.
32. Wingartner *Hitler's Guard* op cit pp20-21.
33. Lucas and Cooper op cit p19. Unfortunately they confuse the Saarland with Hitler's occupation of the Rhineland the following year, an operation which was carried out by the Army alone.
34. Lehmann op cit p74.
35. Weingartner *Sepp Dietrich, Heinrich Himmler*. . . . op cit p281 fn63.
36. I am indebted to Andrew Mollo for a copy of the relevant page of the catalogue listing the contents of Dietrich's pocket book in detail.
37. Interview, 25 September 1986.
38. SS Personal File op cit.
39. Letter to the author, 8 May 1986.
40. Lehmann op cit p102.
41. Höhne, Heinz *The Order of the Death's Head: The Story of Hitler's SS* p448.
42. Weingartner, *Hitler's Guard* op cit p22.
43. Höhne op cit p448.
44. Heiber, Helmut ed *Reichsfuhrer!* . . . *Briefe an und von Himmler* p51.
45. Himmler to Dietrich 25 July 1938, Ibid p56 and SS Personal File op cit.
46. Himmler to Dietrich 27 August 1938, Ibid p59.
47. Hausser to Himmler 10 May 1938 and report by Wolff of same date, SS Personal File op cit.
48. Tloke, Hildegard von ed *Heeres adjutant bei Hitler 1938-1943: Aufzeichnunge des Majores Engel* pp19-20.
49. Guderian, Heinz *Panzer Leader* p50.

CHAPTER 5

1. Statement of military services, Landsberg 29 June 1951, op cit.
2. Höhne op cit p439.
3. *Ritterkreuzträger der Waffen-SS* op cit pp10-11.
4. Weingartner *Hitler's Guard* op cit p35.
5. Lehmann op cit p209.
6. SAIC/43 op cit.
7. Ibid.
8. *The von Hassell Diaries 1938-1944* p177.
9. Sydnor, Charles W Jr *Soldiers of Destruction: The SS Death's Head Division, 1933-1945* p39.
10. Taylor, Fred ed *The Goebbels Diaries 1939-1941* p32, 27 October 1939.
11. Ibid p46, 11 November 1939.
12. Lehmann op cit p214.
13. Weingartner *Hitler's Guard* op cit p38.
14. Lehmann op cit p239.
15. Guderian op cit p117.
16. Weingartner *Hitler's Guard* op cit p43.
17. Letter to the author, 19 February 1986.
18. Guderian op cit p118.
19. Aitken, Leslie *Massacre on the Road to Dunkirk: Wormhoudt 1940* pp63-64.
20. 2nd Royal Warwicks' War Diary, Public Record Office (PRO), Kew, London WO 167/839.
21. Lehmann op cit p261.
22. Lucas and Cooper op cit p150. They do not, however, make any mention of the massacre and neither, somewhat surprisingly, does Weingartner, who gives the impression of an easy day's fighting. He also states that Dietrich's predicament in the ditch occurred on 26 May.
23. Cunliffe, Marcus *History of the Royal Warwickshire Regiment 1919-1955* (William Clowes, London, 1956) pp59-60.
24. Lehmann op cit p267.
25. SAIC/43 op cit.
26. Lehmann op cit p308.

27. Ibid p315.
28. For a detailed account of Eicke's behaviour see Snydor op cit Ch 5.
29. *Goebbels Diaries 1939-1941* op cit p158.
30. Lehmann op cit p323.
31. ibid p379.
32. Meyer, Kurt *Grenadiere* p64.
33. Lehmann op cit. p398.
34. Letter 19 February 1986 op cit.
35. Weingartner *Hitler's Guard* op cit p55.
36. *Goebbels Diaries 1939-1941* op cit p275, 21 May 1941.
37. Unpublished Mss p 69. Kindly lent to the author by Sir George Kennard Bt.
38. Weingartner *Hitler's Guard* op cit p56.
39. Warlimont, Walter *Inside Hitler's Headquarters 1939-1945* p372.
40. Letter 19 February 1986 op cit.
41. SAIC/43 op cit.

CHAPTER 6

1. Weingartner *Hitler's Guard* op cit pp 56-57.
2. Lucas and Cooper op cit p84.
3. Ibid p86.
4. Ibid p88.
5. Lehmann *Die Liebstandarte* Vol 2 p96.
6. *Der Grosse Rausch* (Thomas Verlag, Zurich, 1948) and *Dance of Death* (Collins, London, 1951).
7. Lehmann Vol 2 op cit p115.
8. *Dance of Death* op cit pp 55-61.
9. *The SS: Alibi of a Nation* pp170-171.
10. *The Waffen SS: Hitler's Elite Guard at War 1939-1945* p133.
11. *Order of the Death's Head* op cit p469.
12. Lehmann Vol 2 op cit pp115-116.
13. Letter 19 February 1986 op cit.
14. Bartov, Omar *The Eastern Front 1941-45: German Troops and the Barbarisation of Warfare* (St Anthony's, Oxford/Macmillan, London, 1986).
15. Lucas and Cooper op cit p92.
16. Weingartner *Hitler's Guard* op cit pp61-62.
17. Lehmann Vol 2 op cit pp214-216 gives a detailed breakdown of the strength of each company as at 31 October 1941.
18. Seaton, Albert *The Russo-German War 1941-45* p148.
19. Lehmann Vol 2 op cit p236.
20. Lucas and Cooper op cit p95.
21. Lehmann Vol 2 op cit p243.
22. Medical Report dated 29 June 1953. Parole File op cit.
23. Weingartner *Hitler's Guard* op cit p66.
24. Lehmann Vol 2 op cit p259.
25. *The Memoirs of Field Marshal Keitel* p161.
26. SAIC/43 op cit.
27. Full text is quoted by Lehmann Vol 2 op cit pp276-277.
28. Ibid p278.
29. Cameron, Norman and Stevens, R H ed: *Hitler's Table Talk 1941-44: His Private Conversations* pp177-182. Dietrich stayed 4-6 January 1942.
30. Ibid p178.
31. 2 January 1942.
32. 8 January 1942.
33. Von Hassell op cit 24 January 1942, p214.
34. Lockner, P trans & ed: *The Goebbels Diaries 1942-3* 25 January 1942, p12.
35. Ibid 27 January 1942, p18.
36. Guderian op cit p272.
37. Letter Burger to Himmler, 22 January 1942. Höhne op cit p441.

38. SS Personal File op cit.
39. *Inside the Third Reich* p190.
40. Lehmann Vol 2 op cit p338.
41. Ibid pp292-294.
42. *Der Freiwillige* 6/1980 pp25-26.
43. *Führer-Hauptquartier* Memorandum by Julius Schraub dated 8 May 1942. *Bundesarchiv*, Koblenz R43 II/958a.
44. *Bundesarchiv*, Koblenz Catalogue of Documents pp1555-1561.
45. See, for example Brett-Smith, Richard *Hitler's Generals* p155.
46. Lehmann Vol 2 op cit p317.
47. First Canadian Army Interrogation Report, Theodor Wisch, Public Record Office, Kew, London WO 205/1021. Research into the British Free Corps reveals that the Londoner was probably Thomas Hellor, a one-time solicitor's clerk from Chiswick, who served with both the *Liebstandarte* and *Das Reich*, and the lorry driver was Paul Manton, who had been captured in France in 1940. I am indebted to Bruce Quarrie for this information.
48. Heiber op cit p170.
49. Himmler to Oberg, 5 January 1943, Himmler to Dietrich, 4 February 1943, Ibid pp178-179.
50. Krausnik et al *Anatomy of the SS State* pp344-345.
51. SAIC/43 op cit.
52. Ibid.
53. *Hitler's War of Russia – Vol 2: Scorched Earth* pp217-220.
54. Interview Otto Kumm, 1 March 1986.
55. Lockner op cit, 9 March 1943.
56. Ibid, 17 March 1943.
57. SS Personal File op cit.
58. Lehmann *Die Liebstandarte* Vol 3 p222.
59. *Soviet Government Statements on Nazi Atrocities* pp106-107.
60. *The People's Verdict: A full Report of the Proceedings at the Krasnodar and Kharkov German Atrocity Trials* pp57-59, 121-122.
61. Unreferenced report in WOWIR series, but possibly WOWIR No 7. Author's archive.
62. MI14(d)/Apprec/116/44 dated 19 April 1944, PRO WO 208/3130.
63. WP(44)330 dated 16 June 1944, PRO WO 32/10790.
64. OSS Biographical Report dated 16 September 1944 op cit.
65. Lockner op cit, 20 April 1943.
66. Most accounts state that Dietrich did not leave the *Liebstandarte* until 27 July 1943, the official date of the formation of I SS Panzer Corps and after *Citadel*. I have preferred to follow Lehmann Vol 3 op cit p224.
67. Lehmann Vol 3 op cit pp224-225.
68. Letter dated 30 August 1943, SS Personal File op cit.
69. Hoffmann, Peter *The History of German Resistance 1933-1945* p299.
70. Lehmann Vol 3 op cit p295.
71. Irving, David *The Trail of the Fox* p272.
72. *Hitler's War 1942-1945* p299.
73. Liddell Hart B H ed: *The Rommel Papers* p444.
74. Lehmann Vol 3 p322.
75. *The Rise and Fall of the Third Reich* p1005.
76. Lehmann Vol 3 op cit p312.
77. Collier, Richard *Duce!: The Rise and Fall of Mussolini* (Fontana Paperback edition, London, 1972) pp304, 308.
78. Lockner op cit, 9 November 1943.
79. SAIC/43 op cit.
80. Lockner op cit, 9 November 1943. Goebbels definitely appears to have had an 'off' day!
81. Warlimont op cit p541. Discussion Hitler, Jodl, Zeitzler, 27/28 December 1943.

CHAPTER 7

1. Kraemer, Gen-Maj *I SS Panzer Corps in the West* p10 (MS C-024, Imperial War Museum, London AL 2727/1-2).

2. Ibid p13.
3. First Canadian Army Interrogation Report Kurt Meyer, PRO WO 205/1021 and Shulman, Milton *Defeat in the West* p105.
4. Ibid and First Canadian Army Special Interrogation Report on *Oberstgruppenführer* Josef 'Sepp' Dietrich, PRO WO 205/1021.
5. Kraemer op cit p18.
6. PRO WO 205/1021 op cit.
7. Young, Desmond *Rommel* pp205-206 and Liddell Hart *The Rommel Papers* op cit pp474-478.
8. Lucas and Cooper op cit p155.
9. Kraemer op cit p41.
10. Speer op cit p354.
11. Wilmot, Chester *The Struggle for Europe* p349.
12. Ruge, Freidrich *Rommel in Normandy* diary entry 21 June 1944.
13. First Army Special Interrogation Report on Dietrich op cit.
14. Kraemer op cit p51.
15. Carell, Paul *Invasion: They're Coming* pp215-216.
16. First Canadian Army Special Interrogation Report General Heinrich Eberbach, PRO WO 208/3167 and Weingartner *Hitler's Guard* op cit p106.
17. Speidel, Lt Gen Hans *We Defended Normandy* p125.
18. Meyer op cit p272.
19. Irving *Trail of the Fox* op cit pp376-380.
20. First Canadian Army Special Interrogation Report – Dietrich op cit.
21. Bishop, Geoffrey S C *The Battle: A Tank Officer Remembers* p46 (published privately).
22. Canadian Special Interrogation Report – Dietrich op cit.
23. Dietrich's role in the events of 20 July 1944 is based on Schramm, Wilhelm von *Conspiracy Among the Generals* (he was an official German war correspondent in Normandy and close to both von Rundstedt and Rommel) and Hoffmann, *The History of the German Resistance* op cit p475.
24. Wegner, Bernd *Hitler's Politsiche Soldaten: Die Waffen SS* p184.
25. Kumm Interview 1 March 1986 op cit.
26. Gersdorff, Rudolf-Christoph Freiherr von *Soldat im Untergang* pp164-165.
27. *Der Angriff* 24 July 1944.
28. Speidel op cit p135.
29. Ruge op cit, diary entry 22 July 1944.
30. *Trail of the Fox* op cit p380.
31. Von Schramm op cit p146.
32. Shulman op cit pp146-147. As a major on the Intelligence Staff of First Canadian Army, Shulman carried out interrogations of the key German commanders in Normandy cited in this chapter in September 1945.
33. Canadian Special Interrogation Report – Dietrich op cit.
34. *An Interview with Genmaj (W-SS) Fritz Kraemer: Counterattack on Avranches* November 1945 (US Department of the Army Historical Division, ETHINT 24 – US National Archives, Record Group 338).
35. Canadian Special Interrogation Report – Meyer op cit.
36. Shulman op cit p151.
37. Weingartner *Hitler's Guard* op cit p112.
38. Hastings, Max *Overlord: D-Day and the Battle for Normandy 1944* p174.
39. Wilmot op cit p464.
40. Shulman op cit p150.
41. Canadian Special Interrogation Report – Dietrich op cit.
42. Full text is given in Shulman op cit pp153-154.
43. SAIC/43 op cit.
44. Wilmot op cit p484.
45. Von Gersdorff op cit p161.
46. Canadian Special Interrogation Report – Eberbach op cit.
47. Von Gersdorff op cit p163.
48. SAIC/43 op cit.

CHAPTER 8

1. Bormann, Martin *The Bormann Letters* p112.

2. Young op cit p231.
3. Lehmann Vol 1 op cit p17 quotes Speidel to this effect.
4. *An Interview with Obstgrf "Sepp" Dietrich: Sixth Panzer Army in the Ardennes* 8-9 August 1945 (US Department of the Army History Branch ETHINT 15, US National Archives Record Group 338).
5. Weingartner *Hitler's Guard* op cit p120.
6. ETHINT 15 op cit.
7. Kraemer, Generalmajor (Waffen-SS) *Commitment of Sixth Panzer Army in the Ardennes 1944-1945* (MS A-924, October 1945, US National Archives Record Group 338)
8. Bormann op cit p145. Letter to Magda Bormann dated 31 October 1944.
9. Degrelle, Léon *Campaign in Russia: The Waffen-SS on the Eastern Front* p261.
10. SS Personal File op cit.
11. Interview Wolf-Dieter Dietrich 25 September 1986.
12. Detwiler, Donald S ed *World War II Military Studies* Vol 3 Interview with Guderian, 16 August 1945 (ETHINT 39).
13. Kraemer MS A-924 op cit and *An Interview with Genmaj (W-SS) Fritz Kraemer* 14-15 August 1945 (US Department of the Army Historical Branch ETHINT 21, US National Archives Record Group 338).
14. Detwiler op cit *An Interview with Genobst Alfred Jodl* 26 July 1945 (ETHINT 50).
15. ETHINT 15 op cit.
16. Canadian Special Interrogation Report – Dietrich op cit.
17. SAIC/43 op cit.
18. Nobécourt, Jacques *Hitler's Last Gamble: The Battle of the Bulge* p182.
19. MacDonald op cit p87.
20. Detwiler op cit *An Interview with ObstLt Von der Heydte: German Paratroops in the Ardennes*, 31 October 1945 (ETHINT 75).
21. Nobécourt op cit p182.
22. Ibid p191.
23. Richardson, William C and Freidin, Seymour ed *Fatal Decisions* p232, Manteuffel, Hasso von *The Ardennes*.
24. *An Interview with Obstgrf "Sepp" Dietrich: Sixth Pz Army Planning for the Ardennes Offensive* 10 July 1945 (US Department of the Army Historical Branch ETHINT 16, US National Archives Record Group 338).
25. *An Interview with Obst (W-SS) Joachim Peiper* 7 September 1945 (US Department of the Army Historical Branch ETHINT 10, US National Archives Record Group 338).
26. Kraemer MS A-924 op cit and ETHINT 21 op cit.
27. ETHINT 21 op cit.
28. Detwiler op cit *An Interview with Genlt (W-SS) Walter Staudinger: Sixth Pz Artillery in the Ardennes Offensive* 11 August 1945 (ETHINT 62).
29. Nobécourt op cit p138.
30. Ibid *An Interview with Gen Pz Hasso Von Manteuffel* 21 June 1945 (ETHINT 45).
31. Kraemer MS A-924 op cit.
32. ETHINT 10 op cit.
33. ETHINT 15 op cit.
34. Kraemer MS A-924 op cit.
35. ETHINT 10 op cit.
36. Weingartner, James J *Crossroads of Death: The Story of the Malmédy Massacre and Trial* p65.
37. Smith, Bradley F *The Road to Nuremberg* p116.
38. *Massacre at Malmédy* pp137-138.
39. Skorzeny, Otto *Special Mission* (Futura, London, 1958) p177.
40. SAIC/43 op cit.
41. ETHINT 15 op cit.
42. Kraemer MS A-924 op cit.
43. Degrelle op cit pp264, 267.
44. Detwiler op cit *An Interview with Genobst Alfred Jodl* 31 July 1945 (ETHINT 51).
45. ETHINT 15 op cit.
46. Ibid.
47. Speer op cit p418.
48. Detwiler ETHINT 51 op cit.

49. Detwiler ETHINT 50 op cit.
50. Detwiler op cit *An Interview with FM Gerd von Rundstedt* 3 August 1945 (ETHINT 47).
51. *Panzer Battles* p408.
52. *Fatal Decisions* op cit p238.
53. ETHINT 15 op cit.
54. North, John *N.-W. Europe 1944-5: The Achievement of 21st Army Group* p30 (HMSO, London, 1953).
55. ETHINT 10 op cit.

CHAPTER 9

1. Bormann op cit p172. Letter dated 5 February 1945.
2. Ibid p176. Letter dated 7 February 1945.
3. Information from Wolf-Dieter Dietrich.
4. Trevor-Roper, Hugh ed: *The Goebbels Diaries: The Last Days* p23, 2 March 1945.
5. SAIC/43 op cit.
6. Trevor-Roper op cit p124, 13 March 1945.
7. SAIC/43 op cit.
8. Trevor-Roper op cit p198, 21 March 1945.
9. Weingartner *Hitler's Guard* op cit p136.
10. Brett-Smith op cit p157.
11. Trevor-Roper op cit p245, 27 March 1945.
12. Irving, David *Hitler's War 1942-1945* p785.
13. Trevor-Roper op cit p252, 27 March 1945.
14. Maier, Georg *Drama zwilfen Budapest und Wien* p345.
15. Trevor-Roper op cit p253, 27 March 1945.
16. Brett-Smith op cit p157.
17. Reitlinger op cit p370 fn2.
18. PRO WO 205/1021 op cit.
19. Maier op cit p347.
20. Interview 1 March 1986 op cit.
21. Maier op cit p453, Wolf-Dieter Dietrich and Andrew Mollo, who first became aware of this when he was lucky enough to be allowed to see one of Dietrich's uniforms housed in the Red Army Museum in Moscow.
22. Von Shirach op cit p313.
23. *Dance of Death* op cit p231.
24. SAIC/43 op cit.
25. Von Shirach op cit p309.
26. *The Times* (London) 3 April 1945.
27. SAIC/43 op cit.
28. Von Shirach op cit p315.
29. *New York Times* and other newspapers, 9 April 1945.
30. Mitcham, Samuel W Jr *Rommel's Last Battle: The Desert Fox in the Normandy Campaign* p90.
31. Interview, 1 March 1986 op cit.
32. Von Shirach op cit pp315-316.
33. Steinert, Marlis G *Capitulation 1945: The Story of the Dönitz Regime* (Constable, London, 1969) p180.
34. Details of Dietrich's movements during 8-9 May are from SAIC/43 op cit.
35. *The SS: Alibi of a Nation* op cit p371fn.
36. *Stars and Stripes* 14 May 1945.

CHAPTER 10

1. See for example *Stars and Stripes* 14 May 1945 and *The Times* (London) of the same date, which also spoke of Dietrich as one of Hitler's 'collaborators in the Munich *Putsch* of 1923' who had 'remained one of the chief executors of his policy until the end'.
2. Interview Wolf-Dieter Dietrich 25 September 1986.
3. SAIC/11 op cit.
4. Wolf-Dieter Dietrich interview op cit.
5. See for example *New York Times* and *Chicago Tribune*, both of 29 June 1945.

6. SAIC/43 op cit.
7. Interview 12 April 1986.
8. ETHINT 16 op cit.
9. ETHINT 15 op cit.
10. ETHINT 21 op cit.
11. PRO WO 205/1021 op cit.
12. Interview 12 April 1986.
13. *The London Cage* p94.
14. Weingartner *Crossroads of Death* op cit pp89-91.
15. MacDonald op cit p197.
16. Lengthy excerpts of the Peiper statement are given in Ziemssen, Dietrich *The Malmédy Trial* pp19-22, and others are in Whiting op cit pp201-207.
17. Extracts given in Whiting op cit pp193-198.
18. Interview 12 April 1986.
19. Weingartner *Crossroads of Death* op cit p250.
20. The exact dates of Dietrich's stays in the various POW camps are given in a document written in his own handwriting, a copy of which came from Paul Zimmermann via Hubert Meyer.
21. *St Louis Star Times* 22 May 1946.
22. Nobécourt op cit p125.
23. Ibid p126.
24. *United States v Valentin Bersin et al. Review and Recommendations* pp180-181, Deputy Judge Advocate's Office, 7708 War Crimes Group, US European Command dated 20 October 1947 (US National Archives, Record Group 260).
25. Ibid p197.
26. Vol 2, Seventh Edition p180 and Ibid p35.
27. *Review and Recommendations* op cit p31.
28. *Outline Procedure for Trial of Certain War Criminals by General and Intermediate Military Government Courts* dated 30 November 1945 pp4-5.
29. Ibid pp38-39.
30. Ibid pp40-41.
31. Weingartner *Crossroads* op cit p160.

CHAPTER 11

1. Interview 25 September 1986.
2. Dietrich's Parole File op cit from which much of the information on his time in Landsberg is taken.
3. *Review and Recommendations* dated 20 October 1947 op cit p70.
4. Ibid.
5. Weingartner *Crossroads* op cit p180 and Bower, Tom *Blind Eye to Murder* p273.
6. Memorandum Harbaugh to CinC USEUCOM dated 8 March 1948.
7. Weingartner *Crossroads* op cit pp180-181.
8. Ibid p186.
9. Smith, Jean Edward ed *The Papers of General Lucius D Clay* Vol 2 pp685-659, 661-662.
10. Ibid p671.
11. Weingartner *Crossroads* op cit p190.
12. Ibid p 191.
13. 10 October 1948.
14. 13 October 1948.
15. Weingartner *Crossroads* pp192-193.
16. 8 March 1948.
17. Clay to JAG *Clay Papers* Vol 2 op cit p1045.
18. Smith op cit p115.
19. *Clay Papers* Vol 2 op cit pp1043-1048, 1051-1052.
20. Weingartner *Crossroads* op cit pp226-227.
21. Ibid p221.
22. Ibid pp228-230.
23. *El Sendero* November 1949. Pamphlet published by Talleras Graficos "VERDAD", Buenos Aires.
24. Affidavit, Heidelberg, dated 11 July 1950. Copy from Paul Zimmermann via Hubert Meyer.

25. Affidavit dated 28 May 1950. Copy from Paul Zimmermann via Hubert Meyer.
26. *Die Strasse* 4 February 1951.
27. Letter 6 February 1951. Weingartner *Crossroads* op cit p237.
28. 2 February 1951.
29. Keilhaus to Colonel Howard C Curtis 1 December 1951 and reply dated 7 December 1951. Parole file op cit.
30. Director to *Geschafsstelle der Staatsanwaltschaft, Landgericht* Berlin 5 April 1951. Parole File op cit.
31. Ziemssen op cit pp42-44.
32. Letter Aschenauer to Prison Administration, Landsberg dated 7 June 1953 and Medical Report dated 29 June 1953 by Dr F Puhr, Prison Physician. Parole File op cit.
33. Director to Interim Mixed Parole and Clemency Board dated 30 January 1954. Parole File op cit.
34. Letter 4 November 1953. Parole File op cit.
35. Dietrich to Moore, 25 November 1953. Parole File op cit.
36. Parole Application dated 19 May 1954. Parole File op cit.
37. Letter Dietrich to Snodgrass, 30 May 1954. Parole File op cit.
38. Parole Application dated 22 January 1955. Parole File op cit.
39. Letter Capt Deforest A Barton, Assistant Parole Officer, US High Commission to Moore dated 9 March 1955. Parole File op cit.
40. Bower op cit p377.
41. Transcript from Paul Zimmermann via Hubert Meyer.
42. Transcript of speech dated 9 August 1955 from Paul Zimmermann via Hubert Meyer.
43. Interview, 25 September 1986.
44. 25 October 1955.
45. Order of Parole dated 19 October 1955. Parole File op cit.
46. Dornberg, John *Schizophrenic Germany* p43.
47. *The Times* (London) 7 May 1957.
48. Ibid, 11 May 1957.
49. Ibid, 15 May 1957.
50. *Welt der Arbeit* 14 August 1959.
51. October 1958.
52. National Council of the National Front of Democratic Germany (Dresden, 1965).
53. Letter to the author dated 26 May 1986.

CHAPTER 12

1. *Die Freiwillige* Issue 5/6 1966.
2. Ibid.
3. Letter to author, 19 February 1986.
4. Letter to author, 26 May 1986.
5. Letter 19 February 1986 op cit.
6. Lehmann Vol 3 op cit pp225-226.
7. *Rise and Fall of the Third Reich* p222fn.
8. *Trail of the Major War Criminals before the International Military Tribunal Nuremberg 14 November 1945 – 1 October 1946* Vol XXI (Nuremberg, 1948) pp327-328.
9. Lehmann Vol 3 op cit pp206-213.
10. Ibid p205.
11. Battle of Britain Prints International Ltd, London, 1984.
12. Ibid pp189-190.
13. Letter 26 May 1986 op cit and *Battle: The Story of the Bulge* (Random House, New York, 1959).

Bibliography

Soviet Government Statements on Nazi Atrocities (Hutchinson, London, 194?)

Abel, Theodore *Why Hitler came to Power: An Answer based on the Original Life Stories of Six Hundred of his Followers* (Prentice-Hall, NY, 1938)

Aitken, Leslie *Massacre on the Road to Dunkirk: Wormhoudt 1940* (Kimber, London, 1977)

Angolia, Lt Col John R *The Fuhrer and Fatherland: Military Awards of the Third Reich* (R James Bender Publishing, San Jose, Cal, 1974)

Baur, Hans *Hitler's Pilot* (Muller, London, 1958)

Bleuel, Hans Peter *Strength through Joy: Sex and Society in Nazi Germany* (Secker & Warburg, London, 1973)

Boldt, Gerhard *Hitler's Last Days: An Eyewitness Account* (Arthur Barker, London, 1973)

Bormann, Martin *The Bormann Letters: The Private Correspondence between Martin Bormann and his Wife from January 1943 to April 1945* (Weidenfeld & Nicolson, London, 1954)

Bower, Tom *Blind Eye to Murder: Britain, America and the Purging of Nazi Germany – Pledge Betrayed* (André Deutsch, London, 1981)

Brett-Smith, Richard *Hitler's Generals* (Osprey, London, 1976)

Bullock, Alan *Hitler: A Study in Tyranny* (Penguin Paperback, London, 1976)

Burden, Hamilton T *The Nuremburg Party Rallies: 1923-39* (Pall Mall Press, London, 1967)

Cameron, Norman & Stevens, R H *Hitler's Table Talk 1941-44: His Private Conversations* (Weidenfeld & Nicolson, London, 1973 edition)

Carell, Paul *Invasion, They're Coming* (Harrap, London, 1962)

Carell, Paul *Hitler's War on Russia* 2 vols (Corgi Paperback edition, London, 1971)

Carr, William *A History of Germany 1815-1945* (St Martin's Press, New York, 1969)

Cooper, Matthew *The German Army 1933-1945: Its Political and Military Failure* (Macdonald & Jane's, London, 1978)

Degener, H A L ed: *Wer ist's* (Berlin, 1935)

Degrelle, Léon *Campaign in Russia: The Waffen-SS on the Eastern Front* (Crecy Books, Bristol, 1985)

Delmer, Sefton *Trail Sinister: An Autobiography Vol I* (Secker & Warburg, London, 1961)

Detwiler, Donald S ed: *World War II German Military Studies* Vol 3 (Garland, New York/London, 1979)

Deutsch, Harold C *Hitler and His Generals: The Hidden Crisis January-June 1938* (University of Minnesota Press, 1974)

Diehl, James M *Paramilitary Politics in Weimar Germany* (Indiana University Press, 1977)

Dornberg, John *Schizophrenic Germany* (Macmillan, New York, 1961)

Erickson, John *The Road to Stalingrad* (Weidenfeld & Nicolson, London, 1975)

Bibliography

Erickson, John *The Road to Berlin* (Weidenfeld & Nicolson, London, 1983)

Fest, Joachim C *Hitler* (Weidenfeld & Nicolson, London, 1974)

Franke, Hermann Genmaj *Handbuch der neuzeitlichen Wehrwissenschaften* Vol 2 (Verlag von Walter de Gunter, Berlin/Leipzig, 1937)

Frischauer, Willi *Himmler: Evil Genius of the Third Reich* (Odhams, London, 1953)

Gersdorff, Rudolf-Christoph Freiherr von *Soldat im untergang* (Ullstein Verlag, Frankfurt/Vienna/Berlin, 1977)

Gordon, Harold J Jr *Hitler and the Beer Hall Putsch* (Princeton University Press, 1972)

Görlitz, Walter *The German General Staff: Its History and Structure 1657-1945* (Hollis & Carter, London, 1953)

Graber, C S *History of the SS* (Hale, London, 1978)

Grunberger, Richard *A Social History of the Third Reich* (Weidenfeld & Nicolson, London, 1971)

Grunberger, Richard *Red Rising in Bavaria* (Arthur Barker, London, 1973)

Gruss, Helmuth *Die Deutsche Sturmbataillone im Weltkriege* (Junker & Dunnhaupt, Berlin 1939)

Guderian, Heinz *Panzer Leader* (Michael Joseph, London, 1952)

Hanfstaengl, Ernst 'Putzi' *Hitler: The Missing Years* (Eyre & Spottiswoode, London, 1957)

Hassell, Ambassador Ulrich von *The von Hassell Diaries 1938-1944* (Hamish Hamilton, London, 1948)

Hastings, Max *Overlord: D-Day and the Battle for Normandy 1944* (Michael Joseph, London, 1984)

Hausser, Paul *Waffen SS im Einsatz* (Plesse Verlag, Göttingen, 1953)

Hausser, Paul *Soldaten wie andere auch* (Munin Verlag, Osnabrück, 1966)

Herber, Helmut ed *Reichsführer! . . . Briefe an und von Himmler* (Deutsch Verlaged-Anstalt, Stuttgart, 1968)

Hoffmann, Peter *Hitler's Personal Security* (Macmillan, London, 1979)

Hoffmann, Peter *The History of the German Resistance 1933-1945* (Macdonald & Jane's, London, 1977)

Höhne, Heinz *The Order of the Death's Head: The Story of Hitler's SS* (Secker & Warburg, London, 1969)

Horkenbach, Cuno ed Das Deutsche Reich von 1918 bis heute (*Verlag für Presse, Witschaft und Politik* GmbH, Berlin, 1930 edition)

Irving, David *The Trail of the Fox* (Weidenfeld & Nicolson, London, 1977)

Irving, David *Hitler's War* 2 vols (Papermac, Macmillan, London, 1983)

Jones, Maj Ralph E, Rarey, Capt George H, Icks, 1st Lt Robert J *The Fighting Tanks since 1916* (National Service Publishing Co, Washington DC, 1933)

Keitel, Wilhelm *The Memoirs of Field-Marshal Keitel* (Kimber, London, 1965)

Kern, Erich *Dance of Death* (Collins, London, 1951)

Koehl, Robert Louis *The Black Corps: The Structure and Power Struggles of the Nazi SS* (University of Wisconsin Press, 1983)

Krätschmer, E-G *Die Ritterkreuzträger der Waffen-SS* (*Verlag K W Schütz, Preussisch-Oldendorf*, 1982)

Krausnik, Helmut, Buchheim, Hans, Broszat, Martin, Jacobsen, Hans-Adolf *Anatomy of the SS State* (Collins, London, 1968)

Lang, Joehen von *Bormann: The Man who Manipulated Hitler* (Weidenfeld & Nicolson, London, 1979)

Lehmann, Rudolf *Die Leibstandart:* 3 vols (*Munin Verlag*, Osnabrück, 1977-1982)

Lewis, John R *Uncertain Judgement: A Bibliography of War Crimes* (ABC-Clio Inc, Santa Barbara, Cal/Oxford, 1979)

Liddell Hart, B H ed *The Rommel Papers* (Hamlyn Paperback edition, London, 1984)

Lockner, Louis P ed *The Goebbels Diaries 1942-3* (Hamish Hamilton, London, 1948)

Lord, Walter *The Miracle of Dunkirk* (Allen Lane, London, 1982)

Lucas, James & Cooper, Matthew *Hitler's Elite: Leibstandarte SS* (Macdonald & Jane's, London, 1975)

Ludecke, Kurt G W *I Knew Hitler: The Story of a Nazi who Escaped the Blood Purge* (Jarrolds, London, 1938)

Lupfer, Timothy L *Leavenworth Papers No 4 – The Dynamics of Doctrine: The Changes in German Tactical Doctrine during the First World War* (Combat Studies Institute, US Army Command and General Staff College, Fort Leavenworth, Kansas, 1981)

MacDonald, Charles B *The Battle of the Bulge* (Weidenfeld & Nicolson, London, 1984)

Macksey, Kenneth *Guderian: Panzer General* (Macdonald & Jane's, London, 1975)

Maier, Georg *Drama zwilfen Budapest und Wien* (Munin Verlag, Osnabrück, 1985)

Maier, Hedwig *Die "Zweite Revolution" – Der 30. Juni 1934* (*Viertjahrshifte für Zeitgeschichte* No 2, January 1953)

Manvell, Roger & Fraenkel, Heinrich *Heinrich Himmler* (Heinemann, London, 1965)

Mellenthin, Maj Gen F W von *Panzer Battles* (Futura Paperback edition, London, 1979)

Meyer, Kurt *Grenadiere* (*Schild Verlag*, Munich, 1957)

Mitcham, Samuel J Jr *Rommel's Last Battle: The Desert Fox and the Normandy Campaign* (Stein & Day, New York, 1983)

Mitchell, David *1919: Red Mirage* (Cape, London, 1970)

Mollo, Andrew *To the Death's Head True. The Story of the SS* (Thames/Methuen Paperback, London, 1982)

Nash, D B *Imperial German Army Handbook 1914-1918* (Ian Allan, Shepperton, 1980)

Nobécourt, Jacques *Hitler's Last Gamble: The Battle of the Bulge* (Schocken Books, New York, 1969)

Oertzen, F W von *Die deutsche Freikorps 1918-1923* (F Brudmann Verlag, Munich, 1936)

Pallud, Jean Paul *Battle of the Bulge: Then and Now* (Battle of Britain International Ltd, London, 1984)

Pridham, Geoffrey *Hitler's Rise to Power: The Nazi Movement in Bavaria, 1923-1933* (Hart-Davis, MacGibbon, London, 1973)

Reimann, Viktor *Joseph Goebbels: The Man Who Created Hitler* (Sphere Paperback edition, London, 1979)

Reitlinger, Gerald *The SS: Alibi of a Nation 1922-1945* (Arms & Armour, London, 1985)

Richardson, William & Freidin, Seymour ed *The Fatal Decisions* (Michael Joseph, London, 1956)

Ruge, Friedrich *Rommel in Normandy* (Macdonald & Jane's, London, 1979)

Salomon, Ernst von *The Outlaws* (Cape, London, 1931)

Schäfer, Lothar *The Development of the SS Combat Units: The Genesis of a National Socialist Wehrmacht?* (Unpublished extended essay submitted for an MA in War Studies to King's College, London, 1986)

Schirach, Baldur von *Ich glaubte an Hitler* (*Mosiakverlag*, Hamburg, 1967)

Schmidt-Pauli, Edgar von *Geschichte der Freikorps 1918-1924* (Robert Lutz/Otto Schramm, Stuttgart, 1936)

Schramm, Wilhelm von *Conspiracy among the Generals* (Allen & Unwin, London, 1956)

Schroeder, Christa *Er war mein Chef: Aus dem Nachlass der Sekretärin von Adolf Hitler* (Albert Langen/Georg Müller Verlag GmbH, Munich, 1985)

Scotland, Lt Col A P *The London Cage* (Evans Bros, London, 1957)

Seaton, Albert *The German Army 1933-45* (Weidenfeld & Nicolson, London, 1982)

Seaton, Albert *The Russo-German War 1941-45* (Praeger, New York, 1970)

Shirer, William *The Rise and Fall of the Third Reich* (Book Club Associates edition, London, 1971)

Shulman, Milton *Defeat in the West* (Mercury Books, London, 1963)

Smith, Bradley F *The Road to Nuremberg* (André Deutsch, London, 1981)

Smith, Jean Edward ed *The Papers of General Lucius D Clay, Germany 1945-1949* 2 vols (Indiana University Press, 1974)

Snyder, Louis L *Encyclopaedia of the Third Reich* (Hall, London, 1976)

Speer, Albert *The Slave State: Heinrich Himmler's Masterplan for SS Supremacy* (Weidenfeld & Nicolson, London, 1981)

Speer, Albert *Inside the Third Reich* (Weidenfeld & Nicolson, 1970)

Speidel, Lt Gen Hans *We Defended Normandy* (Herbert Jenkins, London, 1951)

Stein, George H *The Waffen-SS: Hitler's Elite Guard at War 1939-1945* (Cornell University Paperback edition, 1984)

Steiner, Felix *Die Freiwilligen: Idee und Opfergang* (*Plesse Verlag*, Göttingen, 1958)

Sydnor, Charles W Jr *Soldiers of Destruction: The SS Death's Head Division 1933-1945* (Princeton University Press, 1977)

Taylor, Fred ed *The Goebbels Diaries 1939-1941* (Hamish Hamilton, London, 1982)

Taylor, Telford *The March of Conquest* (Hulton, London, 1950)

Thuron, Hans-Jürgen *Freikorps und Bund Oberland* (Unpublished Inaugural Dissertation *der Philosophischen Fakultat der Friederich-Alexander-Universitat du Erlangen*, 1960)

Tloke, Hilgegard von ed *Heeres adjutant bei Hitler 1939-1943: Aufseichnunge des Verlags Anshalt*, Stuttgart, 1974)

Toland, John *Adolf Hitler* (Doubleday, New York, 1976)

Toland, John *The Last 100 Days* (Bantam Paperback Edition, London, 1967)

Trevor-Roper, Hugh ed *The Goebbels Diaries The Last Days* (Pan Paperback edition, London, 1979)

Volckheim, Lt Ernst *Die Deutschen Kampfwagen im Weltkrieg* (Verlag E G Mittler & Sohn, Berlin, 1923)

Volckheim, Maj Ernst *Deutschen Kampfwagen greifen an!* (Verlag E G Mittler & Sohn, Berlin, 1937)

Wagener, Otto *Hitler: Memoirs of a Confidant* (Yale University Press, 1985)

Waite, Robert G L *Vanguard of Nazism: The Free Corps Movement in Postwar Germany 1918-1923* (Harvard University Press, 1952)

Warlimont, Walter *Inside Hitler's Headquarters 1939-45* (Weidenfeld & Nicolson, London, 1964)

Watt, Richard M *The Kings Depart – The Tragedy of Germany: Versailles and the German Revolution* (Weidenfeld & Nicolson, London, 1969)

Wegner, Bernd *Hitler's Politische Soldaten: Die Waffen SS 1933-1945* (Schoningen Verlag, Paderborn, 1982)

Weingartner, James J *Hitler's Guard: The Story of the Leibstandarte Adolf Hitler 1933-1945* (Southern Illinois University Press, London, 1974)

Weingartner, James J *Crossroads of Death: The Story of the Malmédy Massacre and Trial* (University of California Press, 1979)

Weingartner, James J *Sepp Dietrich, Heinrich Himmler and the Leibstandarte SS Adolf Hitler, 1933-1938* (Central European History Vol 1 (1968) No 3)

Wetzell, Gen Georg ed: *Die Deutsche Wehrmacht 1914-1939* (E G Mittler Mittler & Sohn, Berlin, 1939)

Wheeler-Bennett, Sir John *The Nemesis of Power: The German Army in Politics 1918-1945* (Macmillan, London, 1961)

Whiting, Charles *Massacre at Malmédy* (Leo Cooper, London, 1971)

Wilmot, Chester *The Struggle for Europe* (Collins, London, 1952)

Windrow, Martin & Mason, Francis K *A Concise Dictionary of Military Biography* (Purnell, London, 1975)

Wistrich, Robert *Who's Who in Nazi Germany* (Weidenfeld & Nicolson, London, 1982)

Young, Desmond *Rommel* (Collins, London, 1950)

Ziemssen, Dietrich *The Malmédy Trial* (privately, Brackenheim, 1952)

Index

Index

Index